PATHWAYS TO POWER

Indians and the Politics of National Unity in Trinidad and Tobago

Selwyn Ryan

Institute of Social and Economic Research
The University of the West Indies
St. Augustine, Trinidad
Republic of Trinidad and Tobago

ISBN 976 618 027 X

Printed by:
Caribbean Paper and Printed Products 1993 Limited
60A Boundary Road Ext.
SAN JUAN

Contents

Contents - Continued

Contents - Continued

Contents - Concluded

Acknowledgements

For some time now, I had given thought to writing a political biography of Basdeo Panday whom I consider to be one of the more colourful and quixotic figures in Caribbean politics. It was nevertheless a project which was intended for the future and not for 1995-1996. I had in fact given thought to writing a history of the People's National Movement to mark the 40th anniversary of the founding of that party in 1956. The decision to write this particular book instead of the planned volume was prompted by the decision on the part of the then Prime Minister of Trinidad and Tobago, Mr. Patrick Manning, to call a general election in November 1995 instead of in November or December 1996. and by the outcome of that election.

When I began working on this manuscript, my initial intention was to deal only with the political events of 1995 and 1996, and the *fin de ancien régime* and the coming to power of the United National Congress, a party which had its centre of gravity in the Indo-Trinidadian community. As I wrote, however, I felt that there was need to locate those events in the social and political history of that community, and to identify some of the strategies which its members used over time to come to terms with the environment in which they found themselves upon arrival in Trinidad and Tobago in 1845 and subsequently. Thus the title of the book, *Pathways To Power.*

The subtitle of the book, *Indians and the Politics of National Unity* reflects the fact that the need for political unity was one of the themes consistently articulated in the politics of Trinidad and Tobago by political élites of all ethnic identities throughout the 20th century and not one that emerged in 1986 or

1995 as some would have us believe. There were of course other themes as well. There were, for example, voices which stridently argued for communal and even separatist solutions to the political problems of Trinidad and Tobago. *Apanjhatism* at times seemed more attractive to some élites than arrangements which sought to be ethnically inclusive. So too was cosmopolitanism. Communalism and cosmopolitanism were in fact always in dynamic tension, and Indo-Trinidadians were not the only ones guilty of political parochialism. One of the aims of this book is to explore this phenomenon generally, but more particularly as it expressed itself in the Indo-Trinidadian community. The book must be regarded as a companion volume to *Race and Nationalism in Trinidad and Tobago* which focussed largely on the nationalist preoccupations of the Afro-Trinidadian community.

In the writing and preparation of this volume, thanks are due to many persons. Foremost among them is Mr. Roy McCree who edited the manuscript and who advised on content whenever he felt such advice was needed. I owe a debt of gratitude to Mr. McCree for the diligence, care and expertise with which he undertook this responsibility. I also owe a debt of gratitude to Dr. Hamid Ghany, Dr. John La Guerre and Dr. Taimoon Stewart all of whom were kind enough to read and evaluate those chapters of the book which were sent to them for comment.

Sincere thanks are also due to Mrs. Gloria Lawrence who typed and formatted the manuscript with her usual patience and care. I also wish to thank Miss Marva Amos and Mrs. Carol Grant-Francique, members of ISER's secretarial staff, for the assistance which they provided as this study went through its various drafts. Thanks are likewise due to Miss Bernadette Carrington and Miss Patricia Sampson for the valuable clerical and administrative support which they gave to the project.

Finally, I wish to thank Gerry Besson for the creative way in which he captured the essence of the book in his clever cover design.

Selwyn Ryan
July 1996

Abbreviations

AATT - Airport Authority of Trinidad and Tobago
ACDC - Action Committee of Democratic Citizens
ADB - Agricultural Development Bank
ATSEFWTU- All Trinidad Sugar Estate and Factory Workers Trade Union
BWIA - British West Indian Air Ways
CES - Centre for Ethnic Studies
COSSABO- Conference of Shop Stewards and Branch Officers
CPTU - Council of Progressive Trade Unions
CSHAA- Centre for the Study of Harassment of African Americans
CSO - Central Statistical Office
DAC - Democratic Action Congress
DLP - Democratic Labour Party
EBC - Elections and Boundaries Commission
ICFTU - Island Wide Cane Farmers Trade Union
ICN - International Communications Network
INA - Indian National Association
IRA - Industrial Relations Act
LAP - Liberation Action Party
LASCO - Lake Asphalt Company of Trinidad and Tobago
MATT - Media Association of Trinidad and Tobago
NAMOTI - National Movement for the True Independence of Trinidad andTobago
NAR - National Alliance for Reconstruction
NATUC- National Trade Union Council
NCB - National Commercial Bank
NCC - National Carnival Commission
NFM - National Flour Mills
NGC - National Gas Company
NIC - National Indian Council

NJAC -	National Joint Action Committee
NLM -	National Liberation Movement
NP -	National Petroleum
NUFF -	National Union of Freedom Fighters
OWTU -	Oil Fields Workers Trade Union
PDP -	People's Democratic Party
PETROTRIN-	Petroleum Company of Trinidad and Tobago
PLIPDECO-	Point Lisas Industrial Port Development Company
POPPG -	Party of Politically Progressive Groups
PSA -	Public Services Association
PTSC -	Public Transport Services Corporation
SARA -	St. Augustine Research Associates
SBDC -	Small Business Development Company
SDLP -	Social Democratic Labour Party
SDMS -	Sanatan Dharma Maha Sabha
TCL -	Trinidad Cement Limited
TFM -	Trinidad Flour Mills
THA -	Tobago House of Assembly
TICFA -	Trinidad Island Wide Cane Farmers Association
TIDCO -	Tourism Industrial Development Company
TLP -	Trinidad Labour Party
TTEC -	Trinidad and Tobago Electricity Commission
TTMC -	Trinidad and Tobago Methanol Company
TTT -	Trinidad and Tobago Television
TWA -	Trinidad Workingmen's Association
UDLP -	United Democratic Labour Party
UDS -	Union of Democratic Students
UFP -	United Freedom Party
ULP -	United Labour Party
UNIP -	United National Independence Party
URO -	United Revolutionary Organization
WASA -	Water and Sewerage Authority
WINP -	West Indian Independent Party
WIUSBOI-	West Indian United Spiritual Baptist Sacred Order Incorporated
WWSP -	Women Working for Social Progress

Introduction

From the Canefield to the Twin Towers

On May 30th 1845, a development took place which was to shape and influence the history of Trinidad and Tobago in many fundamental ways. On that day, the *Jahag, Fath al Razak,* (Victory of Allah the Provider) docked outside the harbour at South Quay, Port of Spain with human cargo that was quite different to that which had been landed at those facilities during the slavery era. The ship, which had departed from the Hoogly River near Calcutta 103 days earlier, had on board 225 persons who had been recruited in India. They were to replace Africans who had abandoned the sugar plantations following the abolition of slavery and apprenticeship in 1838. The Indians were enthusiastically welcomed by the white planters who were desperately looking for sources of cheap labour to maintain the viability and profitability of their sugar estates. The African population, which had been depicted by the plantocracy as being lazy and unwilling to work, resented the insertion of the Indians into what they considered to be their economic and social space, especially since they believed that the presence of the newcomers on the job market would serve to depress the premium wages which they were able to command in the cash economy that developed in the post-apprenticeship period (Ryan 1972:21; Ryan and Barclay 1992:3-4; Green 1976:163-228).

One recalls that the Indians who came on the *Fath al Razak* were contracted indentured servants and not enslaved persons.

Unlike the Africans who were captured and sold into slavery with no expectation that they would ever be allowed to return to their native land, the Indians were workers with a contract which made provision for them to return to India at State expense after 5 years. In the early years, they were allowed to enter into verbal one month contracts or a written one year agreement if they so wished. In those early years, they were also free to move from estate to estate.[1]

The favourable treatment of the Indians was driven by the fact that the planters wanted to appease those who were opposed to this "cooly body trade" which abolitionists viewed as a new and disguised form of the slavery which had only recently been terminated. The trade, which actually began in 1838 with immigration to British Guiana, had in fact been suspended because of protests from abolitionists in Britain and from lobbyists in India. The terms and conditions which defined the indenture relationship became harsher as the programme became more established and planters sought ways to keep the Indians in a condition of "perpetual servitude." Many Indians however chose the route of emigration to Trinidad and elsewhere because of famine and the harsh social and economic conditions which obtained in their homeland. Many were also tricked, kidnapped or in other ways coerced into emigration by unscrupulous recruiters (Ramesar 1994: 11-1; Klass 1961: 8-10).

The circumstances under which the Indians first came to Trinidad helped to determine the manner in which they responded to the society. Their first concern was of course physical survival. Physical survival was difficult and presented a continuous challenge, since the planters were primarily concerned with squeezing whatever effort they could extract from their hired work force, especially in crop time, when one literally worked from dawn to dusk Comins (1893:214-218) noted that the indentureds often worked "for twelve, fourteen, sixteen hours" at a stretch. The planters in fact wanted slavery without slaves by that name. As Samaroo (1995:11) notes, "many of the planters could not bring themselves to treat these Asiatics any differently than they had so recently treated their African predecessors." While the indentureds and their descendants "survived," and in the process made a major contribution to the economic survival of the sugar economy, many were afflicted by hunger and stricken by diseases of various kinds — malaria, diarrhea, hookworm, chiggers, malnutrition, dysentery, typhoid, tuberculosis, yaws, alcohol addiction, beri-beri — which were either debilitating or which caused prolonged illness or premature death. Vitamin deficiency was a major cause of illness. Life on and around the plantations was continuously punctuated by funerals which could have been avoided had proper medical attention and living facilities been available. Life in the barracks was primitive and privacy was non-existent. Dr. Vincent Tothill (1939) an English doctor who practiced in South Trinidad, described the barracks in the following way:

> The last barracks I saw were in 1937. They were filthy, verminous, full of rats, leaking and very dark. No water was laid on. The people really were no better off than the rats who lived with them. These are not isolated cases, and up to 1937 they were the rule rather than the exception. And how can people possibly live and support a family on two shillings a day? The answer is that they do it. Yes, but at a cost which human beings have no right to be called upon to pay.

Dr. Winston Mahabir (1987:68) expressed amazement that the debilitating conditions in the uncaring world of indenture failed to kill the soul or impair the genes of Indians.

Survival was rendered easier for the Indians than it was for Africans by reason of the fact that Indians in the diaspora were not formally deprived of the use of the cultural baggage which they brought with them to the Caribbean, as was the case with the Africans. Despite the hostility of the Europeans and the Africans to their religion, language, dress, music and other social and cultural forms which were deemed pagan, heathen and idolatrous, and the various attempts which were made to coerce them into abandoning these in favour of western forms, the Indians in general, and the

Hindus in particular, continued to invoke and worship their various gods and practice other elements of their culture. They sang, beat their drums, danced individually and collectively and in other ways clung tenaciously to their ancestral inheritance, aided by the few religious men who also made the journey and who helped them, however imperfectly, to understand the Gita, the Ramayana and the Qur'an, and who also helped them to celebrate birth, death and other rites of passage and the festivals in their religious calendar. As Klass (1961:24-25) notes:

> ... Although they shared a common culture, they derived from different villages scattered over northern India. The first settlers were not kinsmen or village-mates coming back together after a long separation; they were strangers to one another who shared only a common memory of membership in roughly similar kin groups and communities. For such men to form a community, some consensus had to be achieved as to what constituted appropriate behaviour for given relationships within given institutions.[2]

The fact that they were able to fall back on the social and cultural capital embedded in their religion, language, music and culinary traditions proved to be a critical resource in the struggle which they waged surreptitiously, and often openly, with the Eurocentric and Christian forces which sought to establish religious and cultural dominance over them. It gave them the power and the will to resist even while seeming to acquiesce. As Professor Bhattacharya (1995: 16) observed:

> ... the Indian man, in a way in spite of the rigors of forced migrations and demeaning surroundings, was internally a happy man who believed in his mud polished yard, his mud hut, his personal family and his inner divinity ... in spite of the bloody history of the Caribbean, the Indian man's little humble flag continued to flutter atop Bamboo lengths which he so worshipped with devoted dedication.[3]

If culture and religion helped to facilitate physical survival, reconstitution of community, and cultural resistance to European dominance, it also facilitated and encouraged those who sought to achieve mobility by becoming economic entrepreneurs. Studies done at the Institute of Social and Economic Research, The University of the West Indies (Ryan and Stewart 1995; Ramsaran 1993) have argued that the religious values embedded in both Hinduism and Islam played a critical role, *in the context of the Caribbean,* in fostering the attitudes of thrift, willingness to work hard, and to postpone the gratification of wants which allowed savings and investment to occur. The attachment of Indians to the land *(Maha Bharat)* also had a religious dimension to it. As Winston Dookeran (1995:215) observed, "the Indian's fervent desire to acquire land ... had both cultural and economic origins. On the cultural aspect, Eastern religion attached a mysticism and high esteem to powers of the land." This love for the land helped to foster an interest in food cultivation which not only helped the Indian peasant to survive in time of need, but also encouraged the acquisition of large tracts of land and a willingness to invest in agro-business. Ownership of land also provided many with a platform which was later used to move into other expanding areas of the economy. Some of the lands which were acquired proved to be oil bearing, and the sale or lease of these to the oil industry in the early years of the 20th century made millionaires of several Indian families.

There were however reasons other than religion and the thirst for land that led Indians to chose the economic pathway to power. For one thing, circumstances and arrangements of indenture encouraged a disposition among Indians to accumulate a nest egg with which to return to the land from which they came. Several studies (Ramesar 1994; Ramsaran 1993) have documented the fact that substantial sums of money were saved from the meagerest of incomes which were either repatriated in advance of return, deposited in Government and other saving institutions, or hoarded in various places pending the day of return. Much wealth was also stored in the form of jewelry. As Brereton notes:

> The Victorian virtue of thrift seemed almost like a vice. The Indians were single-minded in saving their miserable

wages and putting off present comforts for future goals. They hoarded money; they lent at scandalous rates of interest. All this contrasted with the lower class negro, famous for his love of spending money on clothes, drink, or feting. (Brereton 1972:22)

Indians have however reacted negatively to this attempt to stereotype them as miserly *paisa* counting machines. In their view, accumulation of wealth through savings derived from wages earned in the agricultural sector and through self-employment was the only route available to them for social advancement since access to the bureaucracy and the professions were not readily available to them. Most of them were outside the educational mainstream, illiterate in English, and therefore not considered employable in certain high status sectors of the society. Social marginalisation thus forced them to concentrate on other pathways to power where access and mobility were not inhibited by the gatekeepers of the establishment. Blocked mobility thus forced them to focus on the niches that were being opened up on and around the plantations. Over time, many became cartermen, coachmen, sellers of grass, milk, coals, fish, fruit, vegetables, rice, coconuts, jewelry, ethnic foods, clothing, and of course alcohol. Before long, they would grasp other expanding opportunities to transform themselves from itinerant hustlers into owners of substantial retail and wholesale establishments and manufacturers and owners of a variety of transportation services. As Charles Mitchell, a Protector of the Immigrants noted as early as 1888:

Nearly the whole of the retail shops in the island are in the hands of coolies except those in the town which are held by Portuguese and Chinese; but all over the island, nearly all the retail shops and public houses are in the hands of coolies.... If you go along the Eastern Road, with the exception perhaps of a Chinaman here and there, you will find nearly all the retail dealers, except the shops in Arima which are branches of larger houses in town, all belong to coolies. In fact, they form nearly the whole of the shopkeeping population of the island (cited in Ramesar 1993:87; cf. also Annexe 1).

Comins (1893:16) made the same observation:

> ... the Indians are the principal shopkeepers in the Colony: in fact it looks very much as if they are going in the course of years to take entire possession of this beautiful island, through the principal forest of which they are boring in every direction and turning what was dense jungle into a highly cultivated garden... (cited in Ramsaran 1993:9).

From: J.H. Collens Guide to Trinidad (1886)

Physically, the Coolie is well shaped, with regular features, wiry, though not over muscular, and possessing considerable powers of endurance. He is frugal and saving to a fault, living on the plainest and coarsest of diet, often denying himself sufficient even of this fare to gratify his love of hoarding. The Coolies, though mostly labourers and small shopkeepers, yet managed to deposit in the government Savings Bank the sum of £44,774 during the year 1885. But even this by no means fully represents the wealth of this section of the population. Many of them look upon banks with the greatest suspicion, and prefer to conceal their hard-earned gains in hollow trees or in holes in the ground, keeping at times the secret of their hiding place so closely, that it is often buried with its owner. Now and then, an oriental will withdraw all or a great part of his deposit from the Treasury without in the least requiring it, but simply to satisfy his uneasy mind that it is safe. In spite of this, however, they place much more confidence in the 'Queen's Bank' as they term it, than in any other. In their simple manner they reason — 'He good da Queen's side, spose any man go tief um money, God sabby help um, — Queen *must gi* um.' Every year, some take their departure for the land of their birth with the view of enjoying their savings among their relatives, but frequently finding no trace of either family or friends, or perhaps being coldly received, they re-emigrate to Trinidad, and start a little shop, or buy a patch of land. In 1885 upwards of six hundred returned to India, taking with them the sum of £11,000 in bills and specie, besides gold and silver ornaments to the value of another £1,000. Fancy the wife of an English peasant having a dozen silver bangles, or a beautiful and valuable necklace of gold coins! The thing is incongruous, and as difficult to imagine, as it is unlikely, and yet it is a common occurrence with these people. As a friend of mine smartly puts it in an unpublished essay, 'Coolies have three gods, *L*, *S* and *D*, which they worship in a variety of forms. One method they have of amassing wealth is by usury; 10 per cent *for a month*, or in reality 120 per cent per annum is the moderate rate of interest asked where the security is faulty.'

In 1885, there arrived from India 2,162 immigrants, of whom 104 had originally emigrated to this or other sugar-producing colonies, saved a little money, gone back to their own country, and had now once more returned to the West. Six of these even paid their own passage money! As another instance of their thrift, I may mention that in 1853 a coolie named Moolchan was indentured as a labourer on the St. Madeleine Estate; in 1878 he died a respectable and respected merchant of Port of Spain, leaving effects to the value of $60,000. This is no exceptional case. I know at this moment, two Coolies who, commencing some years ago as indenture labourers, are now worth fully double the sum just named. Within the last decade, and for two or three years in succession, the principal events in the annual races were taken by horses belonging to two well-to-do Indians.

The fact that the Indian community was concentrated in villages and in certain counties which had a considerable degree of "institutional completeness" also helped to provide the "closure" needed to allow their businesses to survive, grow, and later expand to other geographical locations. Before long, they had displaced the Portuguese, the Chinese and the Africans in the area of retail trade as well as pose a significant challenge to European dominance in the major urban centres. Closure in itself may however not have been the critical variable. What was perhaps more important was the fact that unlike what obtained with respect to African businesses, Hindus patronized each other. So too did the Muslims. There also emerged an informal network which facilitated the growth and viability of many business ventures which might not have survived without these hidden helping hands (Ryan and Stewart 1995; Ryan and La Guerre 1992:272-273).[4]

Education also served as one of the principal pathways to power. During much of the 19th century and the first half of the 20th century, education was not the most frequently travelled road to social and economic empowerment as it was for the African population. For much of the 19th century, Indians in fact stayed away from the schools which the state and the Christian churches had established. They felt that they were sojourners and that there was no need to send their offspring to the existing pubic schools. Many felt it made better economic sense to have their children earn the supplemental income which they needed both for use and for saving.

Indians also kept their children away from school in order to avoid race mixing, religious conversion, ritual pollution or the cultural contamination which they feared would result from exposure to Western traditions and values which were alien to their way of life. Many also found that they were really not welcome in the schools either by teachers, parents or other students, many of whom humiliated them and disparaged the customs that defined them. These and several other factors served to keep young Indians outside the established school system. Some did patronize the special primary and the secondary schools which were established for them by the Canadian Presbyterian missionaries, the Anglicans and the Catholics. Most of these — and the majority were Hindus as opposed to Muslims — were forced to take the route of conversion in order to escape from the canefields and gain access to the opportunities for mobility provided by these agencies in the teaching profession. One by-product of this reluctance to attend such schools as were available was the low level of literacy which prevailed among Indians. According to the 1921 Census, over 80 per cent of the Indian population were illiterate.

The primary goal of missionaries like Rev. Morton was of course "soul saving." The provision of education was a secondary concern. Converts were in the main more anxious to access the education that was being offered. Conversion on the appearance of it was the price to be paid. Given this, many of the early converts did not abandon their ancestral cultures but maintained furtive and at times open links with it. They kept both Christian and Hindu icons in their homes. They belonged to both the world of the ethnic and the world of the cosmopolitan, darting uncomfortably between one and the other, as circumstances warranted (Neehall 1992:8; Jha 1974:14). While cultural persistence was more in evidence among those who remained on or near the plantation, it also prevailed among many who moved into the urban centres (Klass 1961:137-144).

The products of these mission schools would be among the first to go to Universities in Canada and to become professionals in law and medicine. In the process, many became or appeared to become cosmopolitans and assimilationists rather than communalists, at least in terms of how they identified themselves in public. Ismith Khan's portrayal of the upwardly mobile Indian reveals the extent to which that generation was torn between the urge to bury or ignore their roots and the bickering and divisions of their primal society and the frustration they experienced when they failed to gain acceptance within the cosmopolitan world which they sought to inhabit (Khan 1987:54).

Various studies have dealt with the struggle which the Hindu and Muslim communities waged to secure state support for the construction, maintenance and servicing of their own schools in response to a growing rise in ethnic consciousness in the thirties, and the various ways in which these efforts were frustrated by the plantocracy, the colonial authorities and the creole Christian establishment which wished to preserve their own dominance (Mohammed 1995:43; Ryan 1971). There was strong opposition to the efforts of the Hindu Maha Sabha's efforts to build primary schools to accommodate Hindu children. The argument was that denominational schools were divisive and should be phased out to make room for secularized state schools (Ryan 1972:123). There was also a political dimension to this determination to phase out denominational schools.

As Winston Mahabir (1987:75), who was a member of the first PNM Cabinet, remarked:

> ...the linkage of a major political party to a Hindu religious body which had been a prime mover in the education movement caused a multiple alarm reaction across the country. The alarm was racial, religious, political, social, economic. Indians, largely of non-Christian background, were visualized as capable of attaining political power. Some renowned racialists were heard to say "these Indians came to Trinidad with jobs assured and the promise of land,usurping the rights of the Negroes as they emerged from slavery. Now they're educating themselves fast, fast and organizing themselves politically fast, fast. They are much too fast. We must contain them.

From 1950 onwards, however, a massive thrust was made by the Arya Samajists, the Maha Sabha, the Kabir Panth Association, the Tackueeyatul Islamic Association and the Anjuman Sunnat-ul-Jamaat to build schools which were funded partly by the State and partly by donations from their respective communities. The establishment of these schools, many of which were built within or close to the heartlands of the Indian community, led to a dramatic expansion of the number of school places available to Indians at both the primary and secondary levels. Many of the products of these schools are now to be found in the professions, in salaried jobs in the public and private sectors, in politics, and indeed in almost every walk of life. As Mohammed (1995:95) notes:

> ...the entry of the Hindu and Muslim bodies into the field of education in Trinidad has ensured the survival and continuation of their religious and cultural beliefs and traditions. Assimilation into the national curriculum has created entry for Indians into the professions and positions of leadership in the wide society. These schools have provided an avenue for social mobility that would hardly have existed if education was solely confined to the Christian denominational Boards.

Many Hindus however feel that not enough was done to establish Hindu and Muslim secondary schools, and they accuse the PNM of discriminating against these bodies by allocating the bulk of the available resources to state and Christian owned schools. Complaints were also heard that the PNM controlled state discriminated against Hindus by not allowing Hindi to be taught as a subject for the CXC level. As one Hindu complained:

> The absence of Hindu secondary schools throughout Trinidad is indeed responsible for the lack of development associated with the Hindu community. Whenever principals of secondary schools hold their meetings, religious bodies make contributions to determine educational policies. No input comes from the Hindu organizations, a significant group of citizens in the society. The denominational schools are highlighted when football, cricket and other sporting activities are taking place. The schools again occupy prominent positions in society when the awards of scholarships are announced on the basis of academic excellence at the GCE A Level examinations. The allocations of the 20 per cent places to Board Schools goes a long way in society to promote the practice of religion. The presence of Hindu secondary schools would certainly enhance the status, dignity and pride of the Hindu citizens of this country. (Lackan 1996:15)

Another pathway to power chosen, somewhat fitfully and belatedly by the Indians, was the public service. Indians entered the public service in significant numbers quite late. The reasons for this were varied. Given their delayed entry into the public school system, there were not many qualified to enter the service. Many did not apply. Those who did generally found that they were less successful than persons of European, mixed or African descent since the job market was segmented and the public service seen as the preserve of creole elements. This may well have served to deter potential applicants. The cultural (and culinary) environment of the public service or sections thereof also discouraged Indians from applying. This would certainly have been true in the Police Service. It is also true to say that many Indians did not consider employment in the public service to be as attractive as was the case with creole elements in the society for whom salaried employment in the public sector meant the conferral of status and security. Whatever the reasons, and they are many, Indians were not to be found in the pubic service in large numbers until the mid-seventies.

This subject has been dealt with at length in Chapter 12, and there is no need to treat it here at any length. Positions in the bureaucracy are however now regarded as a valuable economic and political resource, and Indians are competing very successfully for places within it at all levels. Indeed, even though Indians do not now dominate the upper levels of the Central Public Service, this will certainly be the case before the turn of the century. The only areas in which dominance is unlikely to occur in the near future is in the Security Services, especially the Armed Services, the Police Service and the Prison Service, which are all likely to remain preserves of the Afro-Trinidadian community for some time to come.

The professions also constituted an important pathway to power, and our study has shown the extent to which Indo-Trinidadians have emerged as major stake holders in professions such as law, medicine, teaching, accounting, banking, pharmacy, dentistry and information technology. In these professions, they either enjoy dominance or have come close to doing so. Competition is keen in several other areas, and given what is taking place in the education system and in the Afro-Trinidadian family system (Jules 1992), it would not be long before dominance becomes generalized. When this coming dominance in the bureaucracy and the professions is combined with dominance in the economy and in the political system as well, what one is in fact witnessing is a fundamental shift in the ethnic basis of power in Trinidad and Tobago, the creation of a new hegemony.

Another pathway where the right of passage is now being robustly contested is in the area of culture. Indo-Trinidadians have always complained that creole society was contemptuous and dismissive of their cultural contributions and that the latter behave as though the Caribbean Sea was an Afro-creole waterway and that the Indo-Caribbean cultural presence had no authenticity, validity or legitimacy. To a considerable degree they are correct in that view. The mixed and Afro-Trinidadian population were and continue to be demonstrably unwilling to share symbolic space with Indo-Trinidadians not only because they regard these as scarce, but because they deemed cultural dominance to be their legitimate and prescriptive right by reason of their earlier historical presence in the territory and the greater proximity of their culture and patterns of behaviour to the superordinate colonial culture by which public norms are referenced. Gordon Lewis notes that Afro-Caribbean scholars (and one might add Afro-Caribbean people generally) regard the region as the preserve of the African diaspora, forgetting that there is also an Asian and European diaspora in the region as well (cited in Premdas 1995:54).

The Afro-creole population argues that its cultural capital has been created in the Caribbean out of Caribbean experience whereas that of the Indians was imported. As Earl Lovelace contended:

> The Indians ... were tied to their culture because in this new land where they were strangers, it gave them a sense of being. They had their pundits and divali and hosay and their weddings and teeluck and had no reason to want to change them. Their religion gave them a hold on self in a situation where without it they would have been purely economic animals, and quite naturally they held to it. There has been, so far, nothing dignified to put in its place. Whether those old forms are going to endure in the midst of modernity and with the fact of their increasing political power, which should demand a greater national concern instead of a sectional one, is a question now being debated. (Lovelace 1988:340)

Indo-Trinidadians are however no longer prepared to be marginalised culturally, and have challenged the notion that the steelband, calypso, carnival and even Christmas and Easter (which many of them have accepted as part of their own calendar of events to be celebrated) constitute the national culture of Trinidad and Tobago. Some Hindus have made equivalent claims for the use of the harmonium as the instrument of choice in their school. Indians generally also claim that the festivals of Eid, Divali, Siw Ratri, Phagwa, Hoosay, Kartik Nahan, Matikor and enactments of the Ramayana (Ramleela) have equal claims to be considered as valid inputs into the "stew" that constitutes Trinidad and Tobago culture.[5] These they argue have been indigenized and creolized as have idioms derived from Africa. They also note that Trinidad is home to many immigrants from the Southern Caribbean who came to the island long after their ancestors came from India in 1845. Who, then, is the authentic Trinidadian?

Claims are also increasingly being made for greater use of Indian religious and other symbolic inputs in national official functions in which Christianity continues to enjoy primacy. There is also contestation over the use of Christian symbolism in the country's highest national honour, the Trinity Cross (cf. Annexe 8). The demand is that the symbol should be made ethnically neutral. Contestation is also evident in the area of religious holidays which, for historical reasons, have tended to favour Catholics. The latter have five such holidays as opposed to two which relate to Indians, Eid and Divali. Broadly speaking, Indians have charged that European and Afro-creole nationalists have appropriated the symbolic capital which they derived from their link with Christianity and European culture to authenticate and legitimize their political dominance and its institutional expressions, and the access which this gave to economic capital.

The struggle of the Indians for a legitimate place in the Caribbean sun also took the form of sustained protests against a "creole" legal system which discriminated against their joint family system and their patterns of marriage. As Haracksingh (1995:8-9) noted, the inheritance of property was rendered difficult because of the non-recognition of "under the bamboo" Indian marriages:

> The offspring of such marriages were in law illegitimate and did not succeed on intestacy to the family property. Even in indenture, some of the meager savings of immigrant labourers had gone to the Crown on the ground that there were no heirs in the colony, and that it was virtually impossible, because of the transliteration of names, to trace relatives in India. Indeed, the naming system which Western law seemed to demand — a forename (sometimes unfortuituously described in official documents as "Christian" name) and a surname — sometimes created more complications. This state of affairs could hardly have convinced sons and daughters of the justness of the legal system. The particular situation with respect to marriage spawned a vigorous campaign for the recognition of marriages performed according to Hindu and Islamic custom which had the effect of remedying the situation somewhat.

Similar problems arose because of the non-recognition of Indian customs relating to the joint family. The systems in use in Trinidad and Tobago, joint tenancy and tenancy in common, were not appropriate for dealing with the kinds of arrangements which were practiced within Indian families, and many an offspring, widow, or dependent discovered to their mortification that arrangements which they assumed were in place to ensure that they got their due share of family property were not in fact legal, and could not be enforced in a court of law. Family feuds over property thus became a norm as unscrupulous individuals sought to cheat others out of their inheritance. Efforts were made to by-pass or supplement the English legal system by a parallel alternative in the form of the *panchayat* (Klass 1961:173). This worked in some cases in the early years, but eventually had to give way to a system in which adjudication was legally binding as opposed to being merely customarily so.

The activities of the protestors have borne fruit and there are now no legal arrangements which uniquely discriminate against Indo-Trinidadians, though there continue to be irritants which relate to the law of blasphemy and to trusts and deeds of covenant to Hindu places of worship some of which are structured differently from Christian congregational churches.[6] Muslims opposed to the charging of interest also experience difficulty with some details of the law as it relates to mortgages, for example. Hindu and Muslim marriages are however now fully recognized by the law and accredited Pundits and Imams have the same authority to perform such marriages as do Christian priests. The law banning the sale of alcohol on Sunday, a Christian day of worship, has also been abolished by the UNC government. One can also now swear on the Gita and the Qua'ran and not merely on the Bible as had earlier been the case. As Dr. Winston Mahabir (1987:73) remarked with satisfaction, "there is no longer any form of legal discrimination against Indians in this country.... It was not always thus."

In the area of music, Indians were of the view that their music (other than that provided by the tassa drum, and perhaps the *tabla* and *dholak*) was neglected and even suppressed by media owners and managers who deemed it unfit for mainstream exposure and who therefore relegated it to special time slots reserved for "ethnic" music. Indians argue that their music, whether classic, (raaga) folk, or inspirational, should be incorporated into the mainstream and played throughout the day as are the various forms of western music. Over the years they fought to establish that music and visual programmes that relate to their cultural experience should not have to be enjoyed at special times or on special days. There was also the general complaint that the established media and the advertising companies had a class bias and catered mainly to the urban creole population, and were therefore blindsided to the fact that close to half the population were rural and Indian, and swayed to other genetically programmed rhythms, or had an interest in cultural offerings of Indian provenience (Ryan 1994b).

Rather than wait on the established media to come around to their point of view, Indians relied heavily on short wave radio, cassettes and video tapes to access music and movies from Suriname, Guyana and India. They also took advantage of the opening up of the media in the eighties and established radio stations which virtually play only Indian music. The first station, which was established in 1994, became so popular that some families boasted that they never changed their dials to any other stations. Advertising revenues earned by that station prompted two others, including one owned by the state, to follow suit. These stations play music from Indian films as well as the hybridized music called chutney. Many in fact regard the popularity of chutney among non-Indians as evidence that Indians have finally arrived. As the Political leader of the UNC, Basdeo Panday puts it:

> The level at which chutney music has entered the Carnival celebration this year (1995) is indeed symbolic of the times in which we now live — the time of awakening and of coming together of our people as never happened before. There is a new energy flowing in the country, and we should do well to capture this in Carnival and the music market ... (*Guardian,* January 22, 1996)

Chutney may be "rising" along with Indian social, economic and political power, but purists, both of Indian music and calypso music, are unhappy about this development. Classical sitar player Mungal Patassar (1995:84) observed that:

> Chutney is a bastardized form of Indian music and has its flaws. It is limited to very few tunes, the lyrics are the words of bhajans or religious songs and the singers themselves are helpless in the area of creating new tunes.... Modern day thinking is that Trinidad Indian music is moving ahead. People are led into a false sense of comfort that Chutney is an advanced form of Indian music. We should be careful in stating this assessment. Chutney is definitely an easy music in which to revel, but it should never be seen as representative of the whole of Indian music.

Patassar, however, seems to miss the point, viz., that "chutney soca" represents a symbolically acceptable bridge between Indian and African musical idioms. It is acceptable precisely because it is douglarized. Like Patassar, some Afro-Trinidadians have also expressed resentment that chutney is now competing with soca and calypso during and after Carnival, and some have been heard to complain that Carnival is now being overrun by the Indian presence. As one said to me, "what is Carnival coming to?"

Roseanne Kanhai (1995:23-24) has observed that chutney is a vehicle for the empowerment of Indian women. Chutney, which combines religious and secular singing with sexually overt dancing, represents an attempt on the part of Indian women to liberate themselves from the male dominated Hindu social order. As she writes:

> It is undeniable that a liberation movement is taking place. No longer can the stereotype of the docile, sexually passive *Bhowjee* hold sway. These *Bhowjees* have been able to take what is valuable to them from the calypso/carnival culture. The locations of chutney may resemble the calypso tent but, these women stay within their communities, performing for predominantly Indian audiences. As these *Bhowjees* expand their Matikor space, drawing creative energy from their familiar surroundings, it is clear that they will not be repressed. Collectively, they are demanding the right to celebrate their female bodies in a way that denies neither their Indian heritage nor their claim to elements of Afro-centric cultural expression available to them.

All of the mechanisms and strategies identified above (and others as well) form part of the unrelenting struggle waged by the Indian population to achieve full incorporation in Trinidad and Tobago society. They supplemented and gave strength to the quest for political empowerment discussed in the succeeding chapters.[7]

Indians have always resented the fact that the wider society felt that the post of Prime Minister was not one that they should be allowed to hold. And they were correct in this belief. Non-Indians both feared and distrusted Indians as dominant political actors. It was said that Hindu value systems put a high premium on group mobility, loyalty and reciprocity (*praja*) to kith and kin, both real and fictive, as well as to caste allegiances. Hindus, it was said, had a world view that differed from that of Christians and Afro-Saxons and could not therefore be trusted to be "fair" when allocating public resources any more than they were when hiring help in firms which they own. If they were "fair" to others at the expense of doing their duty to their own kin, they would be deemed "*nimakarams* (ingrates).[8] The view that Indians were "ethically challenged" was captured by the saying "never trust a coolie," which was widely held during the colonial period and which continues to be regarded as conventional wisdom.

Distrust was reinforced by the concern of Afro-Trinidadians that if Indo-Trinidadians gained control of the state, they would use the political capital that would accrue from such control to augment the considerable economic power which they already possessed to the disadvantage of others. This issue is treated more fully in Chapter 12. Suffice it to say that the very fact that every effort was made to keep them out of the citadels of political power enhanced and drove their anxiety to capture it. The fact that they had over the years held every other important nationally significant state office viz., that of President, Chief Justice, the Speaker (3 times), the President of the Senate, the Ombudsman, several senior cabinet posts, Deputy Political Leader, was not compensation enough for their exclusion from what was considered to be the ultimate prize, the prize that would signal to all and sundry that they had finally arrived. As Sham Mohammed, a former Minister in the PNM Government (1981-1986) put it:

> The substantive post is if you are Prime Minister or if the party puts you as Political Leader. Those LID stints [acting as Prime Minister] are not what I am talking about. You could have 15 ministers in the Cabinet of Indian descent; that does not answer my question at all (*Guardian,* March 15, 1992).

In a lecture given at The University of the West Indies on March 1, 1994, I argued that Indo-Trinidadians would eventually win the political power which they sought within 10 to 15 years (*Express,* March 1, 1994). My basic argument then was that Indian dominance in the middle levels of the bureaucracy and in the professions was already evident. I also argued that political parties which represented the Indo-Trinidadian community would win more seats — perhaps 20 — in the near future because of shifts that were taking place in the urban-rural balance of the population. It was noted that there was a movement of Indo-Trinidadians out of the rural areas into the East-West Corridor where many constituencies were located. My estimate, based on surveys done in my capacity as a pollster, was that the population of the Corridor was now 25 per cent Indian. Given this, it was possible that some of these constituencies which were only narrowly won by the PNM in the past because of the ethnic balance therein, could be won by the UNC or its equivalent. I had in mind constituencies such as Tunapuna, Barataria, San Juan, and St. Joseph.

That opinion was challenged by many, including political scientist Dr. John La Guerre, then Head of the Department of Government and Mr. Trevor Sudama, a Member of Parliament on the Opposition bench. La Guerre argued that census data showed that the direction of the demographic shift was from urban to rural (*Express,* March 7, 1994). While the data in fact shows that the population of Port of Spain and San Fernando was shrinking, the movement was to the suburbs in the West and East and not to the rural areas. Indeed, the growth of housing developments all along the East West Corridor raised questions as to what precisely was urban and what was rural in a society such as Trinidad where the characteristics of communities literally changed overnight. Census data provide no meaningful help in characterizing which areas are urban or rural. In fact, both the urban and the rural populations are shrinking to make way for a new type of community, one which is physically close to what were once rural areas but which now have many of the characteristics of urban housing areas. Many of these are to be found in the Corridor.

Mr. Sudama raised some of the queries articulated by Dr. La Guerre, but added a few others which he claimed were derived from data that I myself had either generated or had referred to in other published comments. In his view, my prognosis "flies in the face of the statistical evidence available and the acknowledged electoral tendencies of the major racially and ethnically defined groups in the society." He noted that even though Indians were said to be the largest ethnic group in the society by the 1990 Census, when the mixed community was factored into the equation, the prospect of an Indo-Trinidadian electoral majority vanished. The mixed element, he noted, invariably voted with the Afro-Trinidadians.

Sudama also argued that the Indo-Trinidadians were less homogenous politically than were Afro-Trinidadians, and that those in the urban and sub-urban areas were more likely to support parties led by Afro-Trinidadians. The MP for Oropouche also made the following assertions:

- Afro-Trinidadians have displayed over the years a far higher degree of racial and ethnic consciousness and solidarity than Indo-Trinidadians. The political and bureaucratic leadership by the Afro-Trinidadian middle class has been confident, uncompromising and unaccommodating.

- Access to state resources and state patronage at the disposal of an African-dominated party such as the PNM for such a long period of time have conferred an enormous electoral advantage on the latter. Such a situation will militate against an

Indian-dominated party [being able] to dispense patronage on achieving power.

- For electoral purposes, the non-Indian or "creole" population was more strategically dominant in the urban and semi-urban areas which carried greater political significance (*Sunday Express,* April 3, 1995).

In addition, Sudama noted that I myself had observed that the fertility rate among Indians was declining faster than all other groups. Moreover, rates of outward migration for Indians appeared to be higher for Indians than for non-Indians. Given all of these demographic indices, it was Sudama's view that my 'pontifications' "hung only on the threadbare and loose argument that the pattern of internal migration of the Indo-Trinidadians showed that there was a movement from the rural to the urban and pre-urban areas." The conclusion also assumed that the electoral boundaries would be left as they were.

Sudama, like others, was of the view that the projections made constituted "undiluted propaganda," and suggested that I was perhaps seeking to alarm the Afro-creole population and in so doing, encourage them to re-affirm PNM dominance. Sudama also complained that I had put the question of power sharing on the agenda in the context of the emergence of the new Indo-Trinidadian hegemon, but did not do so during the era of PNM dominance, or during the tenure of the People's National Congress in Guyana. "In the meantime and for the next ten to fifteen years, the African hegemony has earned the right to rule unencumbered by any notion of power-sharing.... Power sharing thus becomes a convenient issue depending on the interests to be served and the agendas to be pursued" (ibid.). Mr. Sudama was however incorrect in terms of these latter assertions. Following Arthur Lewis (1965), and my own experiences living in Africa, I had long become a convert to the need for power sharing arrangements in Third World societies. As I wrote in one of my columns (*Sunday Express*, December 8, 1991):

> Caribbean states such as Guyana, Suriname, and Trinidad and Tobago ought in fact to put in place some sort of power sharing formula that falls short of a formal coalition or a national government. The formula should be attempted even if one party wins sufficient seats to form a government on its own. One is thinking here of changes in the mechanisms of policy making and not in the formal or constitutional framework. We are now fully aware that winning electoral coalition produced by high-tech public relations campaigns with their emphasis on the negative features of rival parties or candidates do not necessarily produce effective governing political coalitions.
>
> These campaigns not only stigmatize the parties. They also delegitimize the political system. The experience of the NAR between 1986 and 1990 confirms that there is a fundamental difference between electoral "stagecraft" and "statecraft" ...it may yet be that circumstances would force us to experiment with power sharing formulas despite what the PNM and NAR might prefer.

Much of what Mr. Sudama said concerning the demographic data was correct. Mr. Sudama however focussed on the "arithmetic" of the issue and not its "chemistry." What he seemingly (perhaps deliberately) chose to ignore was the change in the consciousness of the Indo-Trinidadian population which became increasingly manifest in the nineties following the collapse of the NAR which was driving them to consider bloc voting in a last ditch effort to remove the PNM. SARA surveys had made this clear. Mr. Sudama also failed to indicate that I had publicly indicated that I did not expect the power shift to take place in 1996. Given this, it is not evident how the allegation that I had a disguised agenda could be substantiated.

One of the basic arguments of this book is that that power shift which one anticipated would occur in the first decade of the

21st century has been fast forwarded and is now a virtual reality. The UNC leadership has been trying to secure a soft-landing by talking about power sharing and national unity. This has helped to disguise the fact that there has been a paradigm shift in the politics of the country. The incessant talk about national unity is in fact a tactical imperative to defuse and abort any attempt on the part of displaced élites to contest the process frontally or unconstitutionally. Learning perhaps from the experience of Guyana, the new power holders are anxious to avoid triumphalism, and have gone to great lengths to signal to other communities that they have nothing to fear and that nothing fundamental has been changed. In reality, however, a revolution or at least a basic re-engineering of the society is in the process of becoming manifest. The attempt to use honeyed rhetoric to conceal the process has however not been very effective since what the UNC leaders say in public is not what they and their supporters do "under the bamboo." The rhetoric that emerges from their social selves and their shadow selves are often in tension and the non-Indian element in the society knows it. King Creole is however dead, even if not yet entombed. One waits to see what is raised in"his" place. Would it be a *jahajibhai* or a *dougla* republic?

This book is not intended as a comprehensive social or political history of the Indians in Trinidad and Tobago in the 150 years that have elapsed between their arrival in 1845 and the coming to power of the United National Congress on November 7th, 1995. What it seeks to do is to identify some of the many political and social paths that were taken by the survivors and descendants of that crossing as they sought to come to terms with the challenges of their new environment, the various strategies which they used over time, both intentionally and otherwise, to empower themselves, whether individually or collectively, and the reactions which those strategies provoked.

The essays were written over several years. Most of them deal with the efforts on the part of political parties dominated by Indo-Trinidadian élites to use national unity strategies to gain an effective share of political power, including the capturing of the prized post of Prime Minister. Some of the issues have been dealt with in my earlier publications, some of which are now out of print. The book draws heavily on *Race and Nationalism in Trinidad and Tobago* (1972) and *Revolution and Reaction: Parties and Politics in Trinidad and Tobago 1971-1981* (1989).

The book reproduces 18 of my *Sunday Express* columns which directly address the issue of Indians in politics in the nineties. These are included as annexes which are to be read as companion pieces to the chapters to which they relate. Also included was the speech made by Basdeo Panday in October 1988 at the rally which marked the formal launch of the United National Congress. We include it not only because it serves as an important milestone in the struggle of Indo-Trinidadians for a meaningful place in the political sun, but also because it provides an important backdrop against which Mr. Panday's performance in the office could be evaluated.

The cut off date for the chronological narrative was June 1996, the month in which Local Government elections were held. As in any contemporary history project, there is always the likelihood that subsequent events or the availability of new data might serve to render one's analyses and conclusions obsolete. The book should thus be seen as a work in progress.

Selwyn Ryan
July 1996

End Notes

[1]Kusha Haracksingh (1995:3) has observed that there were many problems relating to the contracts that were negotiated between the indentureds and agents of the sugar planters. As Haracksingh notes, "the indenture contract was a special creature. The parties to it were not bound together by a course of dealings of the kind on which village and caste networks were sustained; the principal making the offer was a sugar planter thousands of miles across the seas. His offer was communicated by agents or recruiters who were generally so eager to secure a complement of workers that they routinely misrepresented the position of their principals. In the later years of the indenture system, when returning migrants had exposed the emptiness of the promises which had been held out, the recruiters were often able to approach the villages only at their peril. It seems certain that many contracts had been induced by fraud, but even where that was not the case, the parties often were not of the same mind as is usually required to ground a valid contract. The rendering in the Indian languages of the English terms was not always exact and at the end of the day, there was a substantial gulf between what the Indians thought they had agreed to and what in fact they were to experience on the plantations."

[2]Selwyn Cudjoe has made the point that for much of the 19th century, one of the critical problems which Indians faced was to construct a language in which they could understand each other. Since some spoke Hindi, Bhojpuri, Tamil, Bengali and several other radically different languages, they had to learn patois and English in order to communicate. Many (and their descendants as well) never got the syntax of the colonial language correctly. According to Reverend Gamble, the Tamils did better than the Bengalis. While Indians continued to struggle with English, many continued to resist proselytization although some did do so in order to increase their social and economic mobility. For many, there was continuous pressure to migrate between the oriental

value systems which they and their ancestors brought with them and those which were being propagated by the various Christian groups who sought to struggle for their minds. As Cudjoe, drawing on other commentators puts it:

> It should not be presumed that as the East Indians invented their new world, that they lacked an indigenous store of historical wisdom. Indeed, they brought with them a rich store of epics, fables, folktales, and so on, which they adapted to their new situation. In doing so, they also brought an Eastern vision to bear upon the Western world. J.H. Collens describes this encounter, tinged though it is with his Eurocentric biases:
>
> "The philosophy of our coolies in this colony is substantially that which their forefathers (well, not quite) adopted some 2,500 years ago in the philosophic age; their theology, or rather mythology, is that of the Puranas of much more modern date. It must be acknowledged that the Puranas are a mass of contradiction, extravagance, and idolatry, though couched in highly poetical language. It is, nevertheless, astonishing how familiar the Trinidadian coolies are with them; even amongst the humble labourers who till our field, there is a considerable knowledge of them, and you may often in the evening, work being done, see and hear a group of coolies crouching down in a semicircle, chanting whole stanzas of the epic poems *Ramayan,* etc."
>
> Clearly, the East Indian adapted his way of looking at the world to fit his new situation. Even the most classic work of the East Indian experience in the New World, V.S. Naipaul's *A House for Mr. Biswas,* concerns, among other things, the conflict between these two visions of the world and is structured very much after the celebrated story of the *Ramayana.* Indeed, *A House for Mr. Biswas* is very much a re-telling of the *Ramayana,* adapted to reflect the contemporary situation of the East Indian in Trinidad and Tobago (cited in Mahabir 1985:16-17)).

[3]Roseanne Kanhai (1995:9-10) has observed that the Indian woman, the *Bhowjee,* was not as "happy" a person as was the Indian male. She was doubly indentured and alienated. She

suffered physically on the plantation as well as in the home where she became a victim of physical and sexual abuse at the hands of her rum drinking consort. As she writes:

> Suffocated in her hut, anticipating the terror of male violence, *Bhowjee's* voice is muffled into silent prayer. Male violence is common to women of all societies; the Indo-Caribbean community is no exception. Indeed the history of Indian presence in the Caribbean seems to be a chronicle of abusive male control within the community.

Most were forced to remain silent "lest it bring shame to the community and/or threaten the family unit."

[4]As I wrote elsewhere (Ryan and La Guerre 1992:273):

> Many firms are run as family enterprises and the children of employees often regard and refer to the owner of the business with respect. Employees who have worked in a business for a long time invariably approach the owner to give their son, daughter, relative or other kinsman a job. Generally, consideration would be given to the request. The only factor that might prevent the kinsman of an employee from being favourably considered would be whether the particular job required particular skills or qualifications which the individual clearly did not possess. Many Indian entrepreneurs also believe that if they employed members of their own kin or ethnic group, they would command greater loyalty from such employees. Further, there is a perception among some Indo-Trinidadian entrepreneurs that by employing their own, some measure of distributive justice is ensured. They claim that the State is controlled by the Afro-Trinidadian community and that over time, that group has used the State Sector and Public service to employ Afro-Trinidadians and raise their income level and status. As such, they feel it is their duty to employ persons whose social and occupational mobility they consider to have been blocked to effect a measure of balance in the labour market. Ironically, many Afro-Trinidadians justify the hegemony which they once enjoyed in the Public Sector in terms of their under-representation in the private sector

where whites, Indians and Chinese were seen to be concentrated.

[5]According to Kanhai:

> ... Matikoor reflects the collective resistance of Indians during the indentureship period when creativity could only find expression in secret performances within the confines of the plantation. Bhowjees got the opportunity to adorn themselves, with jewelry and saris and to rub *sendoor* in each others hair. (Kanhai:1995:22)

[6]Many Hindus have temples on their own properties. Whereas deeds of covenants to congregational churches are claimable against taxes, this would not be allowed in terms of gifts to such temples.

[7]The British Government appointed a Committee (the Sanderson Committee) to review the indentureship system in 1909. The East Indian National Association protested the Colonial Office's decision not to allow a representative of the Indians to visit Britain to testify before it when it was willing to pay for two anti-immigration spokesmen, the Hon. C.P. David and Alfred Richards, to do so. Their protests met with a favourable response and barrister George Fitzpatrick was chosen to speak on their behalf. Fitzpatrick complained that Indians were unfairly treated and had no voice in the colony's Legislative Council. Fitzpatrick was chosen to represent Indians on the Legislative Council in 1911, 6 years before the indenture system was terminated.

[8]As Klass argues:

> "Fair play" is part of Anglo-Saxon life, at home and in the off-shoot cultures, and it turns up both in *habeas corpus* and sports-handicapping, formal institutions, and in seemingly unpatterned daily dealings of man and man. By the same token, caste turns up here as "nation." (Klass 1967: xvii)

> Every East Indian is a member of a far flung circle of kinsmen. This kindred, as a whole, is exogamous and committed to a principle of mutual support and assistance.... An individual's first allegiance is to his family, and second to his kin group (ibid., 232, 239). The East Indian... conceives of himself as a member of a large social group occupying a position as one unit within the social structure of Trinidad. As the status of the entire East Indian group advances, so does his own status. "We going up!" the impoverished cane-labourer says proudly, referring to other East Indians in politics and business. (ibid., 245).... The East Indians of Trinidad — in terms of their view of their own position within the total society, and their attitudes toward the main group — might be termed a "caste." (ibid., 246)

Some Hindus would question this analysis arguing that Hindu Shastras (holy texts) proclaim that "the world is my family — *Vasudaiva Kutumbakam*." The historical context in which this statement was made suggests that the "world" referred to was an "Indian" world. It could therefore not be used to support ecumenism or universalism as is currently being attempted.

Chapter 1

Indian Responses to Nationalist Politics in Trinidad and Tobago: 1917-1956

The participation of Indians in the political process in Trinidad and Tobago in the post-indenture era was marked by two contrasting orientations, the one cosmopolitan, the other communal. The first was preoccupied with achieving full social and political citizenship in the adopted homeland. As part of that goal, aspiring elements sought to obtain access to or membership in what were considered "mainstream" organisations, both in civil society and in state institutions. The second approach sought to create ethnically specific organisations to cater not only to the religious needs of Indians, but to their economic, social, and political ambitions as well. This orientation often sprang from a perception that established elements in the society were not anxious to concede their demands for full incorporation and that every effort was in fact being made to exclude them from such institutions. The tendency towards a communalistic orientation and the creation of ethnically specific organisations were however not entirely a function of rejection by the host society. There were elements who saw such an orientation as both desirable and necessary.

One of the arguments of this study is that both tendencies have been at work in the society in both the post- and pre-indenture era, and have often been entertained and articulated by the very same individuals or groups many of whom, *faut de mieux*, became "hybrids." At times, Indian élites have been strong advocates of the desirability of creating national transethnic organisations and related ideologies. At other times, the *apanjhat* and *jahajibhaiya* orientation prevailed over the thrust towards cosmopolitanism or what some uncharitably would call "cosmetic Indianism."[1] Invariably, the time and the context determined which orientation was given prominence.

In the latter years of the 19th Century and throughout the early decade of the 20th, dozens of journals and newspapers were formed to cater to the specific needs and aspirations of the Indian community. Among them were the *The Minerva Review, The Observer, The Statesman, The East Indian Weekly, The East Indian Herald, The Indian, The Sentinel and The Koh-i-noor.* Several Indian only organisations were also established. Among them were the East Indian National Association, The Indian Club, The East Indian Destitute League, The East Indian Night Shelter, The United Indian Welfare Committee, The Home for Destitute Indians, The Indian Association, The Indian National Council, The India Club, The Indian Democratic League, The East Indian National Congress and the Young Indian Party. There were even attempts to establish an Indian Chamber of Commerce to give expression to the commercial aspirations of Indians in Trinidad and Tobago.

These were but a few of the better known organisations which were created by Indians in the era prior to the Second World War. But, as the authors of the biography of H.P. Singh observe:

> ... throughout the colony, in almost every district, there existed some kind of organized Indian group devoted to welfare, social, cultural and religious activities. The dominant principle of organisation was race. Indian, and

> even religious groups viewed themselves as being Indian first.... Indians were the most organised community in Trinidad. This type of Indian organisational activity did not transfer to political organisation or the founding of an Indian political party. But before 1946 it would have been impossible to do so, and by 1947-48, a decline in Indian organisations set in. Most of the Indian organisations disappeared.
>
> In India, Indian nationalism was a response to foreign domination .... In Trinidad, the nature of Indian nationalism was different. The experience of leaving India, the long journey to the Caribbean, the experience of living and working in a foreign environment which at times was hostile to the Indian presence, bonded all Indians together and created a strong sense of Indianness, and in time, resulted in the founding of Indian religious and secular organisations, the high phase of this organisational activity reaching its peak in 1945 (Persad and Maharaj 1993: xxvii).

One of the events that illustrated the problems of choice faced by the Indian community in the years immediately following the ending of the indenture system was the visit of a Colonial Office investigatory commission under the chairmanship of the Hon. E.F.L. Wood, M.P. in 1921. The appointment of the commission had been triggered by the rash of strikes and politically motivated demonstrations which had erupted in the colony following the return of soldiers who had served in the imperial armed forces in World War I.

The visit of Major Wood helped to crystallize the attitudes of Indians towards their involvement in the political process in Trinidad and Tobago. The ending of indentured immigration in 1917 forced Indians to make some attempt to come to terms with the society which they had chosen to adopt. Two groups testified before Major Wood, the East Indian National Congress and a delegation from the established communal élite. The East Indian National Congress, which claimed to represent the younger and more "progressive" elements in the community, agreed to constitutional changes that would democratize politics in the colony, but insisted that such changes must be on the basis of communal representation. They claimed that they would be swamped under a system of open electoral politics. They also insisted that the Indian community should be considered a single political unit. As they told Major Wood: "Religious differences in the East Indian population did not create any political issue between the Christian [Indian], Hindu and Mohammedan, and could not fairly be adduced as a reason for refusing [Indians] separate representation as a race (Ryan 1972:30)." The Congress also opposed any educational or literacy test on the ground that all taxpayers had a stake in the society and should therefore be allowed to vote without discrimination. If a literacy test were to be imposed, however, they insisted that one in their own languages be regarded as adequate.

The second Indian group opposed change altogether. They felt that the system of nomination by the Governor to the Legislative Council was the one in which Indians would be guaranteed representation in proportion to their numbers and influence. They claimed that the Indian community had been denied the benefits of education and could not maximize the possibilities of the democratic political method. The fact that they were illiterate in English and spoke not one but five Indian languages was also seen as an obstacle to effective political combination. As Major Wood himself agreed, "The East Indians, the backbone of the agricultural industry ... are the "underdogs" politically when compared to the Negroes, owing to the superior educational advantages of the latter" (ibid.).

A third group, the Young Indian Party, which at the time of Wood's visit was not yet fully organized, but which was to become vocal as the decade advanced, rejected the positions taken by their elders.[2] The Party opposed both communal representation and the nominated system on the grounds that Indians had no unique interest to protect. While a few members of the party agreed that Indian culture and identity were worth preserving, the majority did not regard as "unfortunate" the tendency of a growing number of Indians to adopt Western modes of dress and behaviour and to become "creolized."[3] They believed that the established Indian leadership was mistaken in its attempt to ritualize "the dead past" and in its unwillingness to identify with the other have-not groups in the society. Essentially the Indian radicals sought to mobilize the Indian masses for what they viewed as a class struggle which cut across racial and creedal lines.[4] This point of view however never became dominant within the Indian community, which looked askance at this detraditionalized element.

The constitutional advances which followed upon Major Wood's visit were extremely modest. The new arrangements provided for the election of 7 members of the Legislative Council, but the right to vote was confined to those who had substantial property or incomes. Only 21,794 persons were registered to vote in the first general elections of 1925. The election witnessed the emergence of Captain Arthur Andrew Cipriani and the Trinidad Labour Party as the dominant democratic political force in the country. The cleavages within the Indian community between the cosmopolitans and the communalists which surfaced during Major Wood's visit were again in evidence during the Cipriani years. Radical Indians, some of whom were members of the Young Indian Party, chose to associate themselves with Cipriani and the TLP. This link in fact prompted Dr. Eric Williams to claim that "with these Indian colleagues, Cipriani brought into the working-class movement a substantial section of the Indian working class, giving to the Trinidad movement for self-government an inter-racial solidarity which augured well for the future" (Ryan 1972:30).

The evidence however indicates that this radical element was very much a minority within the Indian community generally and more particularly within the Hindu community. The bulk of the Indian population, working-class or otherwise, did not identify with the nationalist movement. The rural Indian in particular was not yet able, or in fact willing, to identify with abstract institutions like "council" or "party"; nor did such symbols as "national self-determination" and "socialism" mean much to him. He thought mainly in terms of persons who could understand his language and his problems, and who would safeguard and promote his ethnic interests. For him, it was still very much a case of *apanjhat* — Indian for Indian. This is not to say that the Indians did not admire Cipriani for the stands he took on their behalf, and for his struggle to improve the working conditions of the masses; but they were decidedly aloof to his fight for self-government and federation (ibid.).

Cipriani died in 1945. Long before that, however, leadership of the proletarian elements in the society had passed to Tubal Uriah Buzz Butler, one of the many immigrants who had come from Grenada to work in the oil industry. Butler's appeal was strongest among the African descended element in the oil belt and parts of the urban areas of Port of Spain and San Fernando. But as was the case with Cipriani and the TLP, some Indian professionals and sugar workers openly associated with the Butler movement. The conditions of life and work in the sugar industry were far worse than those in the oil industry, as bad as those were, and it was hardly surprising that when industrial unrest broke out in 1937, many Indians heeded Butler's calls to strike. The Forster Commission, which visited Trinidad and Tobago to investigate the causes of the unrest in 1937, noted that

> Employers engaged in the sugar industry appear to have displayed a lack of regard for the well-being of their labour. ... In no direction is this lack of regard more apparent than in the deplorable conditions in which a large number of the labourers and their families are housed. ... The consequent undercurrent of discontent could not fail to find expression among a large section of the work-people when the out-break of the disturbances on 19th June awakened in them a more or less conscious sense of common interest in the removal of common disabilities. (Ryan 1972:52)

Spokesman of the planters claimed that the Indians were coerced by African militants to join the strike activity. Indians were said to be "perfectly happy in their conditions." The Governor disagreed, arguing that the seeming passivity of the Indian was a function of lethargy which was induced by disease and hunger, a lethargy "broken only on festive occasions or in times of disorder" (ibid., 52).

It was not always a case of Indians opting to join or not to join "creole" led political or trade union organisations. In one noteworthy case, African oil workers invited an Indian professional, Andrian Cola Rienzi, ne' Krishna Deonarine, to be the leader of the first union to be founded in the oil industry, the Oilfield Workers Trade Union. Faced with the need to select a new leader because of the imprisonment of Butler by the colonial authorities, the workers did not hesitate to ask Rienzi to lead them and to negotiate on their behalf. Calder Marshall, a British journalist who was in Trinidad at the time, observed that "had there been two men who could help them equally, one a Negro and the other an East Indian, the Negro would have been chosen. But here, the issue was clear cut. There was only one man and he was of a different race. The race question became insignificant" (Marshall 1939: 232-233).

The struggle for constitutional reform in the period after the second world war provided yet another theatre in which the Indian community would find itself having to decide whether it would join those forces that were seeking to wrest self-government from the colonial authority or whether it would support that authority against the reform movement led by creole militants. The choices that the community took were shaped to a considerable degree by the positions which elements in that reform movement took during the debates on the burning issue of adult suffrage which was on the agenda in 1941-1944.

The majority Report of the Franchise Committee traumatised the Indian community. The majority recommended that in order to be qualified to vote, one had to understand spoken English. What was worth noting was that three leading members of the radical movement, Albert Gomes, Quintin O'Connor and

Ralph Mentor endorsed that particular recommendation. Rienzi spoke for the bulk of the Indian community when he remarked that

> To insist that a voter should understand the English language when spoken would lead to the irresistible conclusion that this qualification has been introduced to deprive a large proportion of the Indian community of the right to vote. ... This is quite naturally resented as an unfair discrimination against an important section of the population which has made a valuable contribution to the prosperity of the Colony. (cited in Ryan 1972:69)

Rienzi noted that English was not required of Indians when they went to war. Moreover, Indians owned extensive properties and should not be denied the instruments with which to safeguard their interests. The Indian community, led by Rienzi and officials of the India Club, mounted a powerful opposition to the provision, and in the end it had to be withdrawn. The Secretary of State for the Colonies instructed the Governor to use the official vote to overrule the majority decision on the literacy question and made it abundantly clear that he wished to have suffrage placed on the widest possible basis. The acute group-consciousness and seeming cohesiveness of the Indian community in relation to other elements in the society in the postwar years, received a great deal of its driving force from this event, perhaps just as much as it did from the independence movement in India itself.

It should be noted, however, that Rienzi was not expressing the sentiments of the whole Indian community when he came out in support of universal suffrage. Other Indians vigorously opposed it as being inimical to the best interests of their community. As one declared:

> The mass of East Indians in the colony are definitely opposed to adjust suffrage for another fifty years because an election by adult suffrage would endanger the aims and aspirations of the Indian masses. (Blanshard 1947: 227)[5]

The dominant reaction was fear and apprehension that they would be over run by an intolerant African majority. Because of this fear, and perhaps for no other reason, a majority of the Indians in Trinidad and Tobago functioned as a counter-revolutionary political force, the aim of which was to delay as long as possible the transfer of power to native elements. With the growing feeling of nationalism that developed among African elements in the postwar era, this opposition to political change was to become even more vehement.

Nineteen forty-five was an important year in the political history of the Indian diaspora in Trinidad and Tobago. In that year, Indians celebrated their victory in the struggle for universal suffrage without the screening device of a literacy test. That year also marked the 100th year of the arrival of Indians in Trinidad and Tobago. Indians felt that they had not merely survived the crossing of the dreaded "black water", but had done much to improve their economic and social well being and that of their adopted home as well. In their view, there was much to celebrate. The outpouring of "Indianness" which marked the centenary gave rise to anguished debates as to where the Indian community stood in relation to Trinidad and Tobago. Which country was home: India or Trinidad and Tobago?

Many non-Indian elements saw these celebratory activities and the extent to which Indians in Trinidad identified with events in India and things Indian as evidence of communalism, disloyalty to Trinidad and Tobago, and of a desire to create a "Little India" in the Caribbean. Some Indians were concerned about "creole" hostility to their activities and suggested that Indians should de-emphasise political activity and concentrate instead on the educational, health and social needs of the community. As one Indian had put it in 1944:

> Politically, Indians, as good Trinidadians, will have to march hand in hand with other elements which realise their power and their value to Trinidad. But along general welfare lines, Indians will have to help themselves with the hope

> that the Government will offer whatever facilities it can in order to bring the Indian masses abreast of the other progressive elements in the colony. (Persad and Singh 1993: xxix)

There was concern that any show of political aggressiveness on the part of Indians would invite reaction and be counter productive. By 1945, the mood was however becoming less defensive. Indian spokesmen told those who questioned their loyalty to Trinidad and Tobago that a love for India and things Indian did not cancel out a love for Trinidad and Tobago. Perhaps the clearest statement on this point was made by H.P. Singh, who, writing in 1947, had the following to say:

> The Indians of this Colony have more than once declared their position in local and West Indian politics. They are firmly in favour of self-government for Trinidad and Tobago and of the ultimate federation by mutual consent of the scattered British Colonies of the Caribbean. Their first loyalty is to the country where they live, do business, raise their families and have social and other ties. If self-preservation is the first law in the life, then it would be unnatural if this were not so.
>
> But the Indians in this colony have come from an ancient land which has now awakened to seek its rightful place among the great nations of the world, and it would be equally unnatural were they not drawn by bonds of affection and pride to the land of their origin. If others find that they are not so fortunate, then the fault surely is not ours!
>
> It is either a very simple or a very malicious mind that cannot understand that Trinidad Indians must be fundamentally loyal to this country if only because of their unchallenged economic power and stability here. This did not come by making empty speeches or writing ponderous and illogical articles in the newspaper; it came as the result of tears and sweat, of years of wresting with the wilderness, of unremitting toll. Inherent qualities of industry and thrift made it possible. And we will not be denied the fruits of

> our labour by partial publicists and demagogues. The Indian community will smile good-naturedly at pin-pricking, but it will not tolerate a vindictive assault. We serve notice to all that in this land which is very much our own we shall be as loyal as anyone, as strong as anyone and as jealous of our interests as anyone. (Persad and Maharaj 1993: xix)

The post-second world war period witnessed the founding of the West Indian Independence Party (WINP), the Trades Union Council and Socialist Party, The Federated Workers Trade Union and the United Front. All of these parties, to a greater or lesser degree, sought to bring together workers and "little men" of all ethnicities under the banner of socialism. They were however led or dominated by "creole" elements (in this context non-Indians generally) who assumed that the values which they espoused were "national" and universal and that men of progressive inclinations should have no difficulty endorsing them. These movements became beached largely because they did not take into account the fact that the Indian population was driven less by a desire for political change leading to political independence and more by fears as to what political progress, as seen by the creole élites, would mean for them. Albert Gomes, a leading politician of that era, lamented the fact that instead of serving to bring together the little people of all ethnicities, the 1946 election served to harden the cleavages in the society. As he observed:

> We have not yet reached the stage where political impulse is guided by cognate considerations. As a people, we have not yet crystallised into that hard mould of objective opinion which guarantees stable development to a country. The pattern of our population in terms of loyalty to fundamental patriotic motifs is confused and chaotic. ... Unless we can produce in the next five years a fusion of the disparate and extraneous loyalties that now bedevil us, then the progress of Trinidad as a cohesive organism is a mere fantastic notion of the idealists in our midst. Our position, as revealed by the election, is not a happy one. (Ryan 1972: 77)

The leaders of the United Front were spectacular in their failure to understand the social psychology of the people whom they sought to mobilise. The Front represented itself to the public as a genuine multiracial unit consisting not only of the WINP, the Federated Workers Trade Union, and the Negro Welfare, Cultural and Social Association, but the Indian National Council as well. Its team included one Chinese creole, two European creoles, one Syrian creole, two Indians, and three Afro-Trinidadians, all of whom insisted that their politics were based on class rather than on the ethnic factor. Despite its efforts to project a multiracial appeal, the Front became identified with Afro-Trinidadian progressivism, and was completely shut out in constituencies that were predominantly Indian.

Ranjit Kumar, an Indian engineer who chose to settle in Trinidad and who emerged as one of the principal spokesmen of the Indians in post-war Trinidad, was blunt in his view of what lay at the root of the reaction of the Indian community to appeals for unity. Kumar believed that an Afro-dominated majority party would not deal fairly with the Indian community, which he felt was not yet sophisticated enough to take full advantage of a transfer of political power. As he declared:

> In Trinidad, we have a minority problem, and it is the duty of the majority to gain the confidence of the minorities by showing them that in any proposal for self-government, the minorities would have equal rights. I am afraid that in this colony, the majority community has not yet done that. It has made no effort to try and instill confidence in the hearts of the minorities. In fact, there have been leaders whose actions and utterances have given minorities suspicion of the very opposite. (Ryan 1972: 82)

Kumar struck closer to the core of the problem when he suggested that the colony's constitutional system should be structured in such a way as to allow non-elected members to hold a balance of power between the two ethnic groups. When there was unity among the elected members, they should prevail. But on issues which threatened to divide the community, there was need for the restraining hand of the Crown and its nominees. As he pointedly declared:

> I do not think we should invite the possibilities of a political party which might gain a slight majority at an election, controlling the whole colony and entirely over-riding the interests of the other portion that might find itself with a small minority.... We have to make provision to see that Government is not controlled by a dictator and his party (ibid.82).

Kumar's efforts to impede the granting of responsible government were buttressed by action outside the Legislature. During the 1940s, Hindu pundits and lay persons went up and down the country warning their flock that they would be politically and culturally swamped by the African descended majority if self-government was granted. Thousands flocked to the temples to hear the movement for self-government opposed as the work of creole demagogues who, in pursuit of power, were willing to trample on minority groups.

The People's National Movement, which emerged in 1955 under the leadership of Dr. Williams, recognised the weakness in the political style of the movements which preceded it. What Trinidad needed most of all, Dr. Williams argued, was a genuine multiracial party:

> Earlier attempts had been made to create a party that would cut across the vertical and horizontal interests of the society. Their weakness stemmed in part from the failure of those who led them to inspire the necessary confidence in the genuineness of their multiracial idealism. Cipriani, Solomon, Butler, Hamel-Smith, and others never offered the minorities any constitutional safeguards with which they could defend themselves in time of need. (Ryan: 72:112)

Williams felt that if these constitutional safeguards were conceded, people of varying ethnic backgrounds would feel free to join a mass trans-ethnic nationalist party. Williams put the blame for the failure of the attempts at multiracial unity on the political class in Trinidad and not on the Colonial Office as many radicals were wont to do. As he said later on, "the last apology or excuse for colonization will have been removed when Caribbean democracy can prove that minority rights are quite safe in its hands" (ibid.).

In the People's Charter, the PNM's mission statement, the following was said on the question of race and class in Trinidad and Tobago:

> We are not an ordinary party in the narrow sense of the word. We are rather a rally, a convention of all and for all, a mobilisation of all the forces in the community, cutting across race, class and colour, with emphasis on united action by all the people in the common cause. (Ryan 1972: 120)

Despite its recognition of the need to build bridges to the Indian community, the PNM for a variety of reasons was unable to do so in any significant way during the 1956-1986 period when it held continuous power. To be sure, it did place Indians on its election tickets and did appoint Muslims to positions in the Cabinet. Indians of all religious persuasions were also appointed to offices of a national character. Indians in general and Hindus in particular nevertheless felt that they were peripheralised in the political and bureaucratic system and that their cultural offerings were never valorised in the manner which they believed it deserved. In their view, the PNM's vision of Trinidad and Tobago society was one in which an hegemonic unitary creole culture would absorb that of other groups which were deemed to be less autochthonous and therefore not entitled to full incorporation in the pureed mix that was being held aloft as essentially Trinidadian or Caribbean.

The Indian community was deeply divided in its responses to the PNM. As with Cipriani and Butler, a minority, consisting mainly of Vedic, Christian and Muslim elements cast their lot with the PNM instead of with the Hindu dominated People's Democratic Party (PDP) and in 1958 with the Democratic Labour Party (DLP).

This element was persuaded that Dr. Eric Williams and the People's National Movement offered a more progressive option for Trinidad and Tobago and the Caribbean and that the PDP and the DLP were reactionary communal organisations. The fact that the latter were dominated by Hindu elements was also a consideration. The bulk of the Indian community however opposed the PNM, feeling, not without justification, that that party had its centre of gravity in the African community. Many agreed with H.P. Singh that a "vote for the PNM was a vote against the Indian community" (Persad and Maharaj 1993: xiv).

Those Indian élites who for one reason or another either joined the PNM or bought into the PNM's vision of the society, were seen to be somewhat less Indian than those who remained more fully wedded to the traditions of their ancestors. What the latter wanted was a society which offered them and the culture to which they subscribed full social incorporation and a political system in which they were equal stake holders rather than subalterns who had to genuflect to the hegemonistic creole political élite (cf. Annexe 2).

THE DANGERS FACING TRINIDAD & TOBAGO AND THE CARIBBEAN - DR. ERIC WILLIAMS (1958)

From: *Race and Nationalism in Trinidad and Tobago* (Ryan 1972)

Williams disclosed that during the campaign, a letter addressed to My Dear Brother Indian had been circulated throughout the countryside. The letter accused Williams of 'favouring his own kind in the cabinet', and of selecting 'a few Indians merely to mislead other Indians into supporting his movement in order to have a majority.' It concluded, 'If, my dear brother, you have realise these occurrences, and the shaky position in which our Indian people are placed, woe unto our Indian nation in the next ten years. Williams saw this appeal to the Indian 'nation' as an insult to the people of the West Indies. 'The Indian nation is in India', he snapped, 'it is the India of socialism, of Afro-Asian unity, the India of Bandung.' Indians in Trinidad, far from being genuine Indians, were a 'recalcitrant and hostile minority masquerading as the Indian nation, and prostituting the name of India for its selfish, reactionary political ends.' The growing tendency towards racial chauvinism, towards the exploitation of race as the basis of political power, was the great danger facing Trinidad and the West Indies.

Leading members of the Party insist that the only purpose [of the Speech] was to bring the racial issue out in the open so that the country might face it in a mature fashion. But it was clear that behind the glitter of cold statistics there were also hidden propaganda appeals to the [Black] population, both in Trinidad and the West Indies. Williams betrayed his purpose openly when he declared:

> We sympathize deeply with those misguided unfortunates who, having ears to hear, heard not, having eyes to see, saw not, who were complacent, for whom everything was in the bag, who had the DLP covered, who were too tired or busy to vote, who wanted a car to take them to the polling station around the corner. ... They will understand hereafter that he or she who stays home and does not come out to vote PNM, in effect votes DLP. They have learnt their lesson. Today they regret it bitterly, and they are already swearing that it must never happen again.

It was a clever attempt to rouse the [Black] population from their apathy and lethargy. They were fighting among themselves and treating the vote irresponsibly while the Indian community was mobilizing all its energies to capture power. Sympathy for the Movement was not enough. 'It is only the actual votes that matter in the long run! Nothing else!'

MASSA DAY DONE (1961)

From: *Race and Nationalism in Trinidad and Tobago* (Ryan 1972)

Indian proletarians and cane-farmers were reminded that they too were the victims of the 'massa' system.' 'Sahib day done,' he told them. Williams informed the Indians that he had concerned himself with the history of their degradation as much as he had with that of the Negroes. 'I know the history of every one of you here better than anyone else in Trinidad,' he boasted. 'I have made that my business, and knowing that history, I know the road we have to go. The only alternative to that road is the road we have come from, the road of the planters and the road of the merchants in Port of Spain

.... Free education was for Indians too, he reminded them: 'We don't have any segregation in the PNM. You have to understand that this is a social revolution at work in Trinidad and Tobago that knows no colour, that knows no race, that distinguishes only between the depressed and the disinterested, and those who have always had too much. The election issues are social not racial. Race has only confused and complicated the issue. We can't work miracles, but our goal is racial integration.

Williams was trying to appeal to the Indians over the heads of their leaders, who he said had done nothing in the pre-1956 period to help the people's economic plight, but had merely ridden on their backs into power. They, the sons of the sahibs, had now joined the plantocracy to keep the masses where they were. The PNM's aim was to forge a revolutionary front of the 'have-nots' against the 'haves.'

Williams considered it strategically necessary to win at least one seat in the Indian strongholds. It was the evidence which he needed to show that his Movement could cut through the inherited prejudices of the colonial past. In 1961, however, he was not too sanguine about the possibilities; nevertheless he felt sure that, if not in 1961, certainly in the near future, 'DLP fathers would produce PNM sons' once the revolution had begun to have its full impact.

End Notes

[1]Ramesh Maharaj (1992: 38) used the term in a lecture given in Toronto in 1992. To quote Maharaj, "some of these PNM Indians must therefore be regarded as cosmetic Indians who serve merely to give the PNM the superficial appearance of being a national government while it is committed to polarization of the races." This characterisation was uncharitable and fails to recognize that Indians were subjected to a great deal of cross-pressure and found themselves pulled in many directions as they sought to come to terms with the society. The cosmopolitan of yesterday often re-emerged as the radical communalist, someone who, in the interest of winning political power, felt he had to change his style and become a spokesman of his "people." The leader of the PDP/DLP, Bhadase Sagan Maraj, for example, began his political career as a nationalist who opposed the creation of the Indian Nationalist Association, an organization which some, including the Indian High Commissioner, was seeking to create in 1952-1953 in order to bring together all of the leading Indian organisations into one overarching federal body. Maraj had warned of the "dangers" of creating such an association. He feared that the creation of an organization with so many Indian political aspirants at its helm would generate fears in the non-Indian community and make it more difficult for him and the Sanatan Dharma Maha Sabha (SDMS) to obtain the help which was then being sought for its ambitious school building programme (Persad and Maharaj 1993: xxxvi). By 1957, Bhadase felt confident enough to challenge the creole establishment and to make a bid for a stake in the country's political establishment.

[2]As the *East Indian Weekly* noted (April 27, 1929), "It was a case of the particularity of age against the audacity of youth."

[3]"The process of nationalization is undermining the people, and unless something is done to check its progress, the race will be a standing disgrace to the Indian nation." (*East Indian Weekly,* August 11, 1928).

[4]The editor of the *East Indian Weekly,* C.B. Mathura, announced on March 7, 1928 that the policy of the paper "will be to represent the views of the masses and classes irrespective of colour or creed." The *Weekly* consistently supported the TWA and Cipriani, and sought to encourage a pro-Federation attitude on the part of its readers..

[5]Paul Blanshard commented on the problem as follows: "East Indian jealousy of coloured leadership is still an important factor in Trinidad labour and politics, and the two groups tend to form their own instruments of power. This national racial division explains why a small British official group at the top of Trinidad society was able to hold control of the colony for so long without any semblance of democratic institutions. Protest movements have tended to be either Negro and Mulatto, or East Indian, with the East Indian movements showing consistent weakness. One reason for this weakness is a sharp political division within the East Indian community itself." (Blanshard 1947:83)

Chapter 2

The Elections of 1961: The Contestation for State Power

The 1961 election witnessed a near fatal confrontation between Afro-Trinidadian nationalism and Indo-Trinidadian reaction to that phenomenon. The pivotal issue on the agenda of that election was the question of which of the descendants of the plantation experience would take Trinidad and Tobago into independence. It was a bitterly fought election, one in which Trinidad and Tobago almost became consumed by ethnically driven civil war.

One of the main weaknesses of the Democratic Labour Party, the principal opposition to the PNM, was that it was almost always riven by factionalism and rivalry over leadership. The party's basic need was for a leader who would command the type of loyalty and respect which PNM followers had for Dr. Williams. But it was also clear that the DLP was not attracting the younger and more progressive people in the community, the professionals, the white collar workers, and people who for one reason or another were alienated from the PNM and were looking for a home. To attract these people, the DLP would have to project a new image. There was need for a party which had a challenging programme, one that was thinking seriously about the possibility of forming an alternative government,a party that was ready to get down to the time-consuming task of organizing a mass following.

The seeming imminence of a general election during 1959 and 1960 had given special urgency to the need for a new DLP leader. All efforts to form a third political force which would be truly "non-racial" or "all-racial" having failed, it was agreed that the only real hope for a viable, competitive two-party system in Trinidad lay in a reformed DLP. Many Hindus were convinced that Dr. Rudrunath Capildeo, the son of a prominent Hindu pundit who at the time was a mathematics lecturer at London University, was the man to do it. It was expected that he would do what Maraj could not do, viz., attract the white creoles and Afro-creoles who were disenchanted with the PNM to the DLP. It was also assumed that he would lead the DLP out of its stubborn opposition to the People's Nationalist Movement. With the parties agreeing on the fundamentals of the national community, they could then compete on political rather than on racial issues.

After some hesitation, Capildeo accepted the leadership. But the transfer of leadership generated a bitter power struggle that almost wrecked the DLP. While Indians generally seemed willing to accept Capildeo, DLP chieftains were divided among themselves as to whether he was the right man for the job. Some felt that he had been away from the country for too long and was not sufficiently aware of the pitfalls of Trinidad politics. Others did not want to see the party's founder, Bhadase Sagan Maraj, pushed out if it meant a recurrence of the crisis of 1958-1959 when a similar leadership dispute caused Maraj to walk out of the party with the bulk of its Hindu membership. It is evident too that some party professionals were anxious to retain Maraj because he was a proven vote winner and easier to manipulate. With Capildeo as the new leader, there were too many uncertainties about candidacies, policy and authority in the party.

A combination of circumstances nevertheless forced a reluctant Maraj to hand over the leadership. The transfer, which was effected amidst a show of unity and loyalty at a convention held in March 1960, seemed to augur well for the future. But the crisis which many insiders had predicted was not long in coming. Capildeo's attempts to redefine party policy landed him in difficulty with those who had supported his candidacy as well as those who had opposed it. The disagreement was extremely fierce and affected both the parliamentary party and the party in the country. The conflict, in fact, centred on the relationship of the party in the country to the party in the Legislature, a problem which the DLP had never been able to settle. The DLP could not even decide whom it wanted as its parliamentary leader.

The confusion alienated the "French Creole" element which had joined it in 1958 in the hope of forging a national coalition to defeat the PNM. The "French Creole" group made an abortive attempt to dislodge Capildeo on the grounds that he had proven inadequate to the task of reforming the party. Capildeo retaliated by dismissing the entire executive. The convention, he argued, had given him the sole authority to reorganize the party. The DLP leader was visibly shaken by the fiery baptism which he had received from the DLP notables.

The crisis took a serious toll on the health of Capildeo, who had to seek extended medical attention in England without having done much to rejuvenate the Party. He managed to return to Trinidad in May 1961 to lead the DLP into the 1961 elections, but he was still a sick man who felt it necessary to receive psychiatric help from an English spiritual healer.

By the end of 1960 the leadership issue was thus thrown wide open all over again, with Maraj (who was recovering his health) trying to regain control. He based his claim for the leadership on what he felt was the spineless capitulation of Capildeo to the PNM and the Colonial Office on the boundaries commission. Maraj at one point was openly making plans to form a new party to smash the DLP, which was rapidly collapsing from within, while the PNM appeared on the verge of obtaining complete one-party dominance. The PNM had also done its share to harden the split by selecting two dissident opposition council members to participate in the conference on Chaguaramas. The whole show became "curiouser and curiouser" when the Capildeo faction began accusing Maraj of having sold out to the PNM. Maraj counter-charged that false rumours were being spread about him because he was a threat to the leadership. But, he warned, I am still the only man to beat Eric Wiliams and his Party. I did it twice in the past two years.

Maraj was however successfully contained, and the DLP deputy Political Leader, Ashford Sinanan, began what turned out to be a highly competent job of building up the party's electoral machine. A fairly successful attempt was made to establish a women's auxiliary and a network of co-ordinated party groups in each of the polling districts to serve as the vanguard of the vote-getting effort. The drive to register Indian voters also provided useful activity around which the groups could be mobilized. The urgency of the electoral struggle stimulated a mass rally of minorities behind the Capildeo-Sinanan "reform" faction of the DLP. Substantial numbers of prominent English, French, Syrian, and Chinese creoles decided to come off the fence to join the "crusade of respectable people" against the PNM. Several established families publicly identified with the party, and the handpicked executive was crowded with businessmen from the Chamber of Commerce.

The DLP was enthusiastic about the response to its appeal for a "crusade" to stop the march of the PNM into a "Castro-ite version of totalitarian dictatorship." Members were especially delighted that Sir Gerald Wight, a white creole "patrician", chose to return to politics under the DLP banner. This was perhaps one of the most significant events of the entire campaign, an event that helped to shape its entire tone. It was a significant coup for the DLP. Wight's decision to enlist helped to legitimize the party, and brought many of his type — "the massas" as Williams promptly dubbed them — out in the open.

Despite these feverish efforts to reorganize the party, no attempt was made to give it any permanent or autonomous foundation. There was always something temporary about the whole operation. The chronic unwillingness to create a firm and lasting base was in part due to the fact that DLP leaders did not want to be strait-jacketed. It was much easier to select executive members and candidates when one had no recalcitrant party groups or conventions to contend with. The DLP preferred to remain as it was conceived, a collection of notables rather than a democratically structured mass party. But this is not entirely adequate as an explanation of the organizational weaknesses of the party. Unimaginative leadership, lack of revolutionary zeal, and a general feeling that the party could always count on the automatic loyalty of the Hindu masses also inhibited the urge towards organizational effort. It is worth noting that, in general, the persons who wished to give the party genuine organization and coherence came from non-Indian groups whose main concern was not mass democracy but control of the volatile Hindu faction. DLP intra-party conflict was almost always at the élite level.

It should be observed that this alliance of the Hindus and the upper and upper-middle classes, at the expense of Maraj, caused grave misgivings among some orthodox Hindus who felt that the "Chief" had been cruelly used by the old POPPG faction. There were also complaints that the new DLP executive was too heavily weighted against Indians. Of the twenty-nine members, only nine were Indians, and they were mainly from the parliamentary arm of the party. Of the remaining twenty, nine were of European stock, five were Afro-Trinidadians, four were of Chinese stock, and two were Syrians — all men of high professional or business standing in the community. Of the nine members of the inner "cabinet" of the executive, only two were Indians. The remaining seven included four Afro-Trinidadians, two Europeans and one Chinese. Of the thirty candidates chosen to contest the election, only eleven were Indians. The élite was clearly a mixed bag. No less than 63 per cent of the party's candidates were non-Indian, and among Indians, Moslems did as well as Hindus. While it is true that all the Hindu candidates were given safe rural constituencies, two such constituencies were given to Afro-Trinidadians and another to a Moslem. The DLP thus felt quite justified in its boast that it was "a miniature United Nations, a rally of all creeds, races, and walks of life." It had leaned over backwards to prove to all that it was not a mere Hindu faction.

It was clear to the DLP leadership that the party could not defeat the PNM without the help of non-Indian elements. The party needed the financial backing of the European business community as much as it needed the voting support of Moslems, anti-PNM Afro-Trinidadians, and others who were uncommitted. Dr. Capildeo made it quite clear to the Hindus that alone they could win only thirteen seats. They needed Afro-Trinidadian votes, especially those in the two Tobago seats, and it was mainly for this reason that the party endorsed the proposal that Tobago be given independent status in the proposed West Indian Federation. The major premise that guided the reorganization of the party and the selection of notables was that it would take nothing short of a grand coalition of all "out" groups to overthrow the PNM. DLP faithfuls talked glibly of the new formation as a 'way of life', something that would last beyond the noise of election battle, but few were misled. It was a fragile house of cards, a rally of convenience, which almost disintegrated before election day.

For a while, the DLP was quite undecided as to whether or not it should contest the election. Party officials complained that not only were they not consulted by the government about the decision to use voting machines as an alternative to the tried and tested ballot box, but they were not even given adequate opportunity to examine them. The veil of secrecy which surrounded the machines made the DLP quite suspicious that the PNM was tampering with them in their place of storage. Members could not understand why they were not allowed to import one privately so that they could satisfy themselves that it was tamper-proof. So desperate had Capildeo become, in fact, that he issued a clarion call for "thousand of his followers to come forward on election day and smash up a thousand voting machines." He assured his followers that if the PNM won the election, only a revolution could dislodge them in the future.

But it was over the question of PNM "hooliganism" and the partisanship of the police that the temper of the DLP really exploded. The DLP complained that their "people" had become the principal targets of Afro-Trinidadian vandalism. Items on the catalogue of woes related by the DLP press included the stoning of mosques and temples, the looting of Indian homes and retail establishments, the pulling down of DLP streamers, the breaking-up of DLP election meetings, police brutality, and the use of insulting expressions, for example, "We don't want no roti government", and "Coolie must feed nigger."

The DLP organ was replete with bold headlines: 'Dark Times Ahead', 'Floods of Strife', 'The PNM, the Police, and Violence', 'Rule By Force', 'Sleep No More', 'Towards a Crisis', 'Congolese-Type National Guard.' There is no doubt that the Indians felt themselves a persecuted minority. They were convinced that the PNM élite was not really making more than a token effort to contain their followers. Dr. Williams' invitation to his followers to "march where the hell you like" was seen as an open invitation to attack the Indian community. In their view, Woodford Square had become a shrine of hate where minorities were offered up for sacrifice. So tense had the situation become that Indians were ready to believe that a programme of inoculation in the countryside was the beginning of mass genocide. Wild but groundless rumours began circulating that six hundred Indian children had died following the inoculations. There were also similar reports that Indians planned to retaliate by attacking police stations and schools in Port of Spain.

In the last two months before the elections, DLP politicians were becoming increasingly desperate and seemed ready to plunge the community into open strife, which now seemed the only redressive measure at hand. On October 8, Capildeo told his constituents:

> The day we are ready, we will take over this country and not a thing will stop us... If [the Governor] is so misguided as to tell us no, we are going to Macleod, and if he is stupid enough to tell us no, then we will come back and take over. It is as simple as that. (*Guardian,* October 8, 1961)

On October 10, the statements became even more extreme.

> The only remedy to PNM persecution is to adopt the South American method of bloodshed and riot, revolution or civil disobedience, until you grind Government operations to a full stop, and then you get possession. (*Guardian,* October 10, 1991)[1]

The racial bloodbath which many were beginning to fear seemed more imminent on Sunday October 15; one of the largest crowds to assemble for a political meeting began dispersing in alarm when they heard Capildeo tell his supporters:

> ...arm yourselves with weapons in order to take over this country.... get ready to march on Whitehall; get ready now. Get ready to march on Government House... that is what I am asking you to do. (*Guardian,* October 16, 1961)

The meeting, which was held on Queen's Park Savannah, not far from the Governor's residence, was viewed by the DLP as a test case to determine whether they would be allowed to conduct their meetings in peace. They claimed that they had deliberately avoided Woodford Square for the serene atmosphere of the greens in front of the Governor General's home. Reports vary about how much heckling there was, but Capildeo felt it was more than enough. If the police and the government could not or would not restrain the crowd, whose behaviour in his view was nothing short of hooliganism aided and abetted by the law, there was no alternative but to turn crowd against crowd:

> Wherever PNM holds a meeting, break it up; wherever PNM holds a meeting, destroy them. Do not give them a chance. Those are my instructions to you today. Wherever Dr. Williams goes, run him out of town; wherever Dr. Solomon goes, run him out of town. From now on, the chips are down, and I expect you to stand with us, and free this country from this type of hooliganism once and for all. I am asking you to arm yourselves with a weapon in order to take over this country. I have stood as much of this nonsense as I can stand. (*Tape of Proceedings*)[2]

Trinidad seemed poised on the brink of racial war; security forces were immediately alerted. The *Guardian,* (October 16, 1961) which appealed for an "armistice" between the two "warring" groups, warned the leader of the DLP that it would not support him or anyone else who threatened the flouting of the law. "Force", declared the *Guardian,* "was alien to our tradition.... An Opposition is expected to conduct itself with the restraint of an alternative Government" if it expects to enjoy public confidence.

The PNM was quite convinced that the aim of the DLP leadership was to incite violence as a method of forcing the Colonial Office to intervene and postpone the elections. But the government itself was taking no chances. Minister of Home Affairs, Dr. Patrick Solomon, who was given the sobriquet "Minister of War", warned Dr. Capildeo that "anyone who adores the guillotine must be equally ready to caress its cold steel" (*Guardian,* September 16, 1961). When Capildeo showed no willingness to recant, but in fact reprimanded his followers for their cowardice and irresolution, Solomon again warned: "If Capildeo incites violence, I will slap him in gaol so fast... and he would not get out again. Nobody will be able to bail him out.... No tupenny ha-penny dictator [is] going to walk through this country and tell people to take up arms." Belatedly remembering that there was "due process of law," Solomon added, "I would take him before the Judge, and the Judge would impose the necessary sentence" (ibid., November 23, 1961).

As a precautionary measure, a state of emergency was declared in a number of areas where fatal violence had occurred.[3]

The office of the DLP political leader was also raided for evidence of sedition. The DLP protested that emergencies were not declared in areas where violence directed at them had also erupted. They also complained that during the search for hidden arms, Indian women were indecently frisked by Negro policemen. The precautionary measures served to harden the hostilities that embittered both sides, but they did have the effect of shocking the community out of its complacent feeling that "it could never happen here." It was to the credit of both parties that they chose to hesitate at the brink. Had Capildeo been preventively detained, his "martyrdom" would most certainly have been the signal for racial war. But Capildeo had clearly proven to be the DLP's greatest liability during the campaign, provoked though he most certainly was.

Both the PNM and the DLP were confident of electoral victory. Both parties were sure that they would win a minimum of ten seats and a fair share of those where the two major ethnic groups were relatively evenly balance. Though the PNM 'ran scared', it nevertheless felt certain that it would win twenty of the thirty seats. The DLP, fooled by the large crowds which followed its meetings, perhaps out of curiosity and the expectation of excitement, widely anticipated that it would win twenty-three to twenty-five seats. That the party won only ten seats came as a shock to many. One DLP candidate, Lionel Seukeran, on the morrow of the election, declared:

> Surprise more than disappointment agitates me at the result of this election. All of us believed we had an excellent chance to form the Government. We worked ceaselessly as a team to achieve this aim. Now, in retrospect, I can visualize that we were not as well organized as we thought. Perhaps too, we made tactless mistakes and underrated our opponents. (*Guardian,* October 6, 1961)

Other members of the DLP were not as graceful. They were frankly puzzled by the showing which the PNM made in presumably Indian strongholds. The political leader of the DLP declared, "We did not fight an election. We simply went through the motions of a monstrous farce. We were given certain seats by the PNM and we wrestled two from them - Pointe a Pierre and Fyzabad." Far from providing a method which would ensure free elections as far as human ingenuity could guarantee, as Williams had claimed, "the PNM has found a way to win elections without popular support" (*The Statesman,* December 1961).

The PNM was jubilant over its victory and the fact that by winning 58 per cent of the popular vote it could no longer be accused of being a minority government. The party was also enthusiastic about the wide distribution of its support. It had won two of the three rural constituencies in the eastern counties of the island, and ran very well in the third. It had also won the two St. Patrick constituencies that had given birth to the revolutionary nationalist movement in the 1930s and which, until then, had remained relatively faithful to Butler. Butler himself was decisively defeated, gaining only 617 votes or roughly 6 per cent of the votes in his constituency. Both Tobago constituencies, predictably, went to the PNM. Victory in Port of Spain North was especially satisfying to the party, though the white and near-white upper and middle classes of that constituency had again rejected the PNM. In the three sugar seats of Caroni, the PNM ran fairly well, gaining an average of 33 per cent of the votes, with a 40 per cent share in Caroni East which it had been accused of gerrymandering.

It can be argued that, had the DLP not suffered as much in the past from leadership crises, and had Capildeo not frightened the population to such an extent by his call to arms, the results might very well have been different in terms of popular votes, if not in seats. There are people who believe the DLP could have won the election had Capildeo proven equal to the expectations which many held in 1960. The thesis of this study — that ethnicity has always been more relevant than cognitive evaluations in voting behaviour in Trinidad and Tobago — leads me to reject this contention. The figures are quite eloquent in their support of this assumption: the DLP won only in those areas where the total Indian population exceeded 50 per cent.

The DLP was however convinced that the election results were fraudulent, and that the voting machines had been manipulated to produce the desired percentages. It felt that the PNM's margin of victory was too nearly identical with its pre-election predictions to be accidental. The DLP claimed too that there was an evident pattern in the way in which the machines malfunctioned. Most of the mechanical breakdowns and delays allegedly occurred in areas which were heavily Indian. Officials were late or else were unfamiliar with the apparatus, and nothing had been done to ensure that polling booths were properly equipped with the proper electrical outlets. This was regarded as part of a deliberate attempt to slow down the voting procedure so as to reduce the DLP's popular vote and, if possible, to deprive late-arriving rural field workers of the franchise. It was also noted that there were frequent discrepancies between the figures recorded on the machines and those proclaimed by officials.

The DLP, in fact, claimed that it had won twenty two seats, many of them in the northern part of the island. It was especially sure that it had won the Barataria constituency where the Indian population is large. The party claimed that it had run very well in the sections of the constituency where Afro-Trinidadians were concentrated but had been surprisingly defeated where Indians predominated. It was so convinced that it had been defrauded at the polls and that the results did not represent the true position of the country that it decided to boycott the Legislature and seek redress in the courts. As Capildeo told his followers, "The DLP will not offer themselves as any prisoners tied to the triumphant chariots of the PNM" (*Guardian,* December 14, 1961).

Capildeo however rejected the claim of some DLP extremists that they should resign their seats and petition the British Government for partition. Capildeo was sensible enough to know that partition would never be conceded, even if it were a desirable solution to the problem; neither would he resign: "If we resigned, the PNM would get the usual stooges to come forward to fight the vacant seats. We have no intention of resigning to allow them to do what they like. We will seek to put into effect the DLP Manifesto as far as possible within the limitations imposed by the House. We will not let the PNM have everything to itself in a one-party State" (*Guardian,* December 14, 1961).

The DLP was still hoping to invite British intervention. As the party organ warned, now the constitutional struggle was coming to a close, foreign policy would be used to create crises: "Democracy will be struck on the head with a heavy hammer while the grass under our feet will be cut by a sickle. Let the Colonial Office play Pontius Pilate" (*The Statesman,* December 22, 1961). But the Colonial Office was not disposed to listen to the entreaties of the DLP. As far as the Colonial Secretary was concerned, Trinidad was internally self-governing, and he had no intention of telling it how to run its affairs. His main hope was that the PNM would agree to remain with the rest of the southern Caribbean in a new federal unit. The Colonial Office had long concluded that the DLP was not a genuine alternative to the PNM government and that it had nothing to fear from the PNM.

Forming the Government

In staffing the ministries and the Senate, the PNM tried as far as possible to give expression to its multi-racial philosophy. Of the twelve cabinet places, two went to Moslems, two to persons of European stock, and eight to Afro-Trinidadians, including one female. There were however no Hindus among the PNM legislative team, and for the second time, the Hindus remained unrepresented in the government. This deficiency was somewhat compensated for in the Senate by the appointment of a Hindu party member. One senate place each was given to Syrian and Chinese creoles. The remaining nine senate places which the government had at its disposal went to Afro-Trinidadians and mixed elements. Seven of these were predominantly Afro-Trinidadian; one trade unionist was included among them. The Governor's senate appointees (i.e., the independents) redressed the ethnic balance somewhat. There were three white creole businessmen, one trade unionist, one solicitor, one musical director, and one Hindu businessman. Three of the Government's appointees were Afro-Trinidadian. The DLP refused to make any nominations. Given that together they constituted roughly 37 per cent of the population, they felt they deserved far more than the token two places they received. This they claimed was a shocking denial of the vaunted multiracialism of the PNM regime. Demands for "Parity or Partition" were already being heard in certain places.

THE STRUGGLE OVER THE CONSTITUTION

Between the end of 1961 and August 1962, an epic battle was waged between the PNM and the DLP on the nature of the constitution that Trinidad and Tobago was to have in the era of independence. Because of haste and more than a touch of arrogance, the PNM did not consult with the DLP before drafting the constitution. But while the PNM blundered in not doing so, it is to be wondered whether any co-operation was possible in the climate that prevailed after the 1961 election.

At the opening of The Independence Conference which was held at the Marlborough House in London on May 29, 1962, the last of those frustrating pilgrimages to London, the leader of the DLP stated succinctly but emphatically what his delegation was after:

> We want a judiciary which is independent, we want provisions which really guarantee effectively the rights and freedoms which ought to exist in a democratic society: we want parliament democratically constituted. We want a procedure for the amendment of the Constitution which effectively protects us from the arbitrary exercises of the power to amend. We want the various commissions so constituted as to ensure that they function effectively and impartially. (*Guardian,* May 29, 1961)

He was also insistent that new elections must be held before Independence to determine which of the parties would be the immediate beneficiaries of the transfer of power. This, he observed, was a vital precondition of harmony, unity, and confidence.

The demands of the Indian National Association (INA), led by H.P. Singh, went even further. The INA wanted "parity or partition"; they did not believe that the DLP, committed as it was to other ethnic groups, was in a position to make an effective case for the Indian population. As the President of INA stated:

> The Indian community must spear-head the demand for proportionate representation for all the ethnic groups in the councils of the nation. If, perchance the 'obscurantist' minorities are not interested in protecting themselves in this way against PNM racialism, then we the Indians, must demand parity with the Afro-Trinidadians in government, in the Civil Service, in the Police and every aspect of government. If they are thirty seats in the House, we insist on having fifteen. If there are twelve Ministers, we demand six. We demand that 50 per cent of the jobs in the Civil Service be given Indians and 50 per cent of the men in the Police Force be of our community, as well as 50 per cent of the officers. (Singh 1962: 9-10)

Singh believed that these stark alternatives could be avoided only if the "dishonest machinery for election" was eliminated. The Trinidad Partition League also supported this claim in a cable to the Colonial Secretary.

None of the principals, including the DLP, endorsed the demands of what was considered an extremist minority of the Indian community. The Colonial Secretary, Mr. Maudling, rejected partition quite firmly. As he advised:

> The last vestiges of external control, for better or worse, are about to be removed, and a heavy responsibility therefore lies upon those attending... to ensure that the new Constitution they are devising will be one under which the peoples of a former dependency can emerge and govern themselves as a single nation. (*Guardian,* May 24, 1962)

Since both the PNM and the DLP were in agreement that partition or proportional representation was undesirable and, in the case of partition, meaningless, no consideration was given to such proposals in the negotiations.

The proceedings of the conference were unduly long and frustrating. Neither side was anxious to concede, even though Maudling had made it clear that differences would have to be narrowed before Independence was granted. The Maha Sabha wanted the conference abandoned completely until new elections could be held. Those elections, moreover, would have to be held after an independent boundaries commission consisting of representatives from either the United Kingdom or the United Nations, had redrafted the constituencies. Reintroduction of the ballot box was also demanded. Dr. Capildeo admitted that both methods were open to fraud, but he felt that abuse of the machines could be more "total" (cf. Annexe 10).

Williams angrily rejected these demands. The appointment of such a commission would be harmful to the reputation of the country. Moreover, he believed the country could not afford the luxurious delays that these proposals would involve. He estimated that Independence would be delayed for at least four months. The DLP felt new elections were a small price to pay for social peace. Williams feared, however, that rather than promote harmony, new elections would only serve to rend even further the tattered fabric of the society.

On the question of entrenchment, the DLP demanded a three-quarter majority in both Houses, and an entrenched right of appeal to the Privy Council on all issues relating to the interpretations of the constitution. Dr. Capildeo declared that he had no faith in the integrity of Dr. Williams, and could not accept his pledges or those of his party. Williams had "torn up" the federal constitution and the old Trinidad constitution, and there was nothing to stop him from "tearing up" the new constitution and making Trinidad a republic, as Nkrumah had done in Ghana. The

DLP also wanted some sort of firm guarantee that the civil service, the police force, and the national guard would be more representative of the ethnic physiognomy of the community. Capildeo complained that at present, "one section of the community was armed against the other."

Deadlock in London only served to aggravate tensions in Trinidad. According to the President of the INA, extremists in the Indian community were already arming themselves in preparation for any emergency which might arise in case of an unfair imposition. It was the INA, its President later asserted, which brought home to the Colonial Office the gravity of the crisis in Trinidad. The DLP organ in fact accused the *Guardian* of deliberately suppressing news of violence in the territory in the hope of strengthening Williams' hand. "Dr. Williams", *The Statesman* declared, "could not afford to let the Colonial Office know that Trinidad was sitting on a volcano of racial hate... a volcano which may violently blow up at any moment." The PNM was warned that racialism would develop into a Frankenstein which it would not be able to control; the PNM "have whipped racialism to such a pitch that it now threatens to become an inferno consuming everything. The schism between Afro-Trinidadians and other minorities, East Indians in particular, has become a yawning unbridgeable chasm... The white heat of anger is spreading" (*Statesman,* May 25, 1962).

The Marlborough House Compromise

Whether at the instance of reports from Trinidad, or intuition that Trinidad might indeed witness a bloodbath, the PNM delegation finally agreed to compromise. The conference seemed on the verge of complete collapse when Williams decided that he would make a statement which he hoped would meet some of the objections of the DLP.[4] The concessions were:

> Special entrenchment of an increased number of provisions by a three-fourths majority of the

members of the lower house and a two-thirds majority of the members of the upper house. These included clauses relating to the composition of Parliament, the amendment clause of the constitution, annual meetings of parliament, dissolution of Parliament, general elections, the boundary and elections commissions, provisions for review of constituency boundaries, the Supreme Court, and tenure of judges, the right of appeal to the Privy Council, freedom of speech in Parliament, and the Independence Act of 1962.

- An independent boundaries commission which would delineate new constituencies which would vary by no more than a margin of 20 per cent.

- An elections commission which would be responsible for the conduct of elections and the registration of voters. The commission was also to be responsible for ensuring the accuracy and competence of voting machines and for seeing that these were fully tested and sealed in the presence of representatives of political parties. The commission was to be completely free of any direction or control from the executive or any other authority.

- The widening of the right of appeal to the Privy Council in matters other than constitutional rights.

- Limitation to six months of the period during which a proclamation of a state of emergency could remain in force without being extended by Parliament.

- Strengthening of the provisions for the independence of the auditor general.

- Entrenching of the provision that Trinidad remain a constitutional monarchy.

- Entrenching of provisions relating to the independence of the judiciary from partisan political pressure.

- Consultation with the Leader of the Opposition on important appointments, including the chairmanship of the elections and boundaries commissions, and on all the important national issues.

This last concession was not promised as a part of a constitutional requirement. A promise was also given that a bipartisan committee of national integration would be appointed to examine the methods by which the community could be more satisfactorily integrated.

Somewhat surprisingly, Williams argued that he had made no concessions. Even the 75 per cent provision, which he agreed was a "stiff measure of entrenchment," he did not view as a concession. He noted that he would have nothing to do with a police state, and had no objections to any safeguards which would strengthen the independence of the judiciary. The DLP, for its part, accepted those promises and agreed to drop its demand for pre-Independence elections and for the constitutionalizing of the principle of consultation. It also agreed to the use of voting machines on the understanding that every machine would be fully examined before use and sealed in the presence of representatives of the political parties. Williams, who was extremely anxious to attend the Prime Minister's Conference in September which would deal with the question of Britain's role in the Common Market and Commonwealth, declared that he was not surprised that DLP negotiators agreed to his proposals, and that there was a meeting of minds on the essential outstanding questions. This was a rather curious statement, especially since Williams disclosed that "one or two of the Colonial Secretary's proposals were a little hard to take, but we agreed to them." It has never been made clear just what these proposals were.

In his post-conference broadcast to the people of Trinidad, Williams declared, "we on the Government side approached the Conference from the point of view that... if there was any particular safeguard that we could introduce for the benefit of the community as a whole, no matter what the origin of the proposal, we gave it the most serious consideration." This was an obvious attempt to conceal defeat, but a useful one in the circumstances. Williams quite rightly sought to convince the people of Trinidad and elsewhere that agreement was achieved on a "happy note."

> The Conference involved this question of inspiring confidence in the community and removing tensions. So, at the end of the Conference, as the leader of the delegation, I made a clear statement indicating that we of the Government Party intended to extend an invitation to the Opposition to discuss all issues on our return to Trinidad which might retard or could retard the promotion and development of national unity. (*Guardian,* June 9, 1962)

It is worth noting that DLP spokesmen were quite convinced that Capildeo had triumphed over Williams. As one Member of Legislative Council exclaimed, "You [Dr. Capildeo] outfoxed Williams and he knows it. They are happy and so are we!" Another, also a member of the DLP delegation, observed:

> The Constitution... contains all the safeguards that it is possible to build into a constitution. If this Constitution fails to achieve the objective of safeguarding the democratic rights of the people, it will not be the fault of the Constitution, but of the men who have failed to exercise the eternal vigilance without which no constitution, however cleverly drafted, can prevail. (*Statesman,* June 19, 1962)

The London press also seemed to feel that the Opposition had achieved most of its main aims. The *Trinidad Guardian,* however, observed in a rather puzzling headline that "Williams' Team Wins All, Opposition Gets Nothing."

Dr. Capildeo was not as happy as some of his followers, but he was honest enough to admit that the DLP was as much to blame for its defeats as was the PNM. As he reflected:

> The DLP could have achieved a great deal more, but had to struggle against the history of its own leadership, with its internecine conflicts; but their defeat [especially on the elections issue] was also due to the fact that the assiduous propaganda of its opponents, that the country had no genuine alternative to the present Government, had been swallowed by the Colonial Office. (August 12, 1962)

Capildeo also argued that the PNM did not want to "knock out" the opposition completely; it preferred to retain the mirage of a democratic two-party system while at the same time enjoying functional one-party control. He also ascribed his party's reverses to the communications media and to the fact that the upper classes had turned their backs on the DLP regardless of how they felt about the PNM:

> Whatever purpose the ... Constitution exercise may have served, it revealed one unpalatable fact, that the loudest well-to-do critics of the Government, and those who criticized from what they fondly-believed were well entrenched positions, did not want the DLP to form the Government.... The sources of public information were also arrayed and marshalled against us. This is a grave defect in the body politic of Trinidad, and, in my opinion, constitutes a far greater danger, in that it creates the atmosphere conducive to a one-party state, and so encourages such results even if the direction of political leaders were otherwise oriented. (ibid., August 24, 1962)

He also disclosed that he, like Williams, was driven to compromise because of fear of the consequences for Trinidad, both internally and in terms of its reputation abroad, if racial war should break out. At the start of the... Conference, the decision confronting the leaders of the DLP was whether they should plunge the country into chaos with civil commotion and strife, or try to explore whatever reasonable avenues may be presented to us as the Conference developed.... It is easy to let slip the dogs of war; it is impossible to return to the positions before they were unleashed (T*rinidad Guardian,* August 19, 1962).

Trinidadians were immensely relieved that what had begun on so ominous a note had at last been brought to a happy conclusion. Generally speaking, a majority of the population were pleased with the settlement. They were also proud that their leaders had been able to rise to levels of statesmanship of which they had already begun to despair. If there were persons who had reservations about Independence, they were quite mute in the months of July and August 1962, when the umbilical cord that had bound Trinidad and Tobago to the British Empire for 165 years was finally cut.

End Notes

[1]Capildeo was well aware that this was an idle threat and that Caroni, a predominantly Indian county, was perhaps the only area where he could make a successful "stand." As he told a prayer meeting in Caroni on April 17, 1960, "We shall not rest until final victory is achieved... even if Caroni alone is left. The fight will be carried on and we will make people outside feel the force of our arms, the strength of our intellect and the breadth and vision of our character." (Ryan 1972: 268)

[2]For a pro-Capildeo version of this incident and the speech in question cf. *Lotus and the Dagger: The Capildeo Speeches,* ed. Samaroo Siewah 1994: 97-107. The DLP defence is that the provocation was extreme and that the Police refused to protect their meeting and their rights to political expression. The call to "arm yourselves" was said to be conditional. Capildeo always insisted that he had threatened violence against machines and never against persons. But we find him declaring in one speech in San Fernando that "today I have come, but I have come not to bring peace, but to bring a sword. We have brought peace long enough and they cannot understand." In another speech, he said as follows: "I thought I was leading men, not women. I thought you had red blood in your veins. You don't have. Which of you would slap Dr. Williams in his face? ... Not one of you" (Capildeo at Streatham Lodge, November 19, 1961). Capildeo explained later that his threats of violence were meant to dramatize the plight of the opposition and force the community and the media to listen to it. He bitterly complained that the communications media were opposed to the DLP, and that the government had also refused to grant them time on the radio network to state their case. A content analysis of the *Guardian* during the period reveals a clear PNM bias. The daily played down many of the reports of hooliganism

which are a rather normal part of tropical elections, but which reached rather alarming propositions in 1961. The new *Guardian* ownership, it appeared, had abandoned the oppositionist policy of its predecessors for television rights.

[3]It appears that in certain areas traditional gang rivalries had become politicized. The main purpose of the emergency, in addition to whatever arms nests might have been uncovered, was to give confidence to the terror-stricken population of the area. The government also requested the Federal government to release the Trinidad contingent of the West Indian Army, a request which was refused, much to the anger and dismay of the Trinidad government. The Federal government took the position, a correct one, that the Army was a federal unit, and as such no island had the right to request specific elements of it. It is in the context of this crisis that PNM demands for a national guard began to be heard.

[4]Williams had first planned to have the Colonial Secretary serve as a liaison between himself and Capildeo, but later decided to inform the opposition leader personally that he planned to make some new proposals. Capildeo made his reply contingent upon the content of the proposals. According to his version of the event, "Dr. Williams came to me and said, I intend to make a statement that we shall co-operate, that we shall meet and that we shall discuss our differences. I replied, that statement is very good to make under any circumstances. Go ahead and make it by all means. If you make that statement, I would underline it." (*Statesman,* August 21, 1962).

Chapter 3

Indians, "Black Power" and the Elections of 1971

A great deal of academic controversy surrounds the question of how Indo-Trinidadians reacted to the dramatic confrontation between radical and not so radical blacks, the ruling black political élite and the white economic power structure in 1970. Most accounts indicate that Indo-Trinidadians, like most other minority groups, were hostile to "Black Power" in all its hegemonic manifestations, were terrified of the implications of a possible seizure of power, whether by the National Joint Action Committee (NJAC) and the Black Power militants led by Geddes Granger *et al,* or by the army even though one of its leading radicals was a young Sandhurst trained Indian, Raffique Shah. Various accounts of this encounter between Indo- and Afro-Trinidadians are to be found in *Black Power Revisited* (Ryan and Stewart 1994), and *East Indians and Black Power in the Caribbean* (Gosine 1986).

Typical of the conventional view is the one by Dr. John La Guerre (Ryan and Stewart 1994:273) who writes as follows:

> For the African organizations and activists, the world that they knew was an urban world in which the antagonisms and resentments were expressed in terms of black versus white. The Indians and their problems were not ignored; they were assumed to be integrated into the overall programme. It hardly occurred to them that they were dealing with a distinctive people with differing perspectives and a different set of priorities. In formulating their own

> agendas, the African radicals forgot that they were dealing with a plural society. For radicals such as Williams, it was enough to announce that he was fighting the cause of the 'black man'. Part of the problem too, was the fact that most of the models of analysis and protest were drawn from abroad, particularly the United Kingdom and the United States. In these societies, Indians were not until recently a substantial presence. For this reason there was little to prepare the radical activists for the peculiar problems posed by the Indian presence in societies such as Guyana and Trinidad.

Dr. Ken Parmasad, who was then an activist on the St. Augustine Campus of The University of the West Indies, and a member of the Society for the Preservation of Indian Culture (SPIC) has a different view. He feels that the Black Power Movement was welcomed by many Indians in that it helped to embolden those who also wished to go back to their ancestral roots. It legitimized and validated their search for ancestral roots. To quote Parmasad:

> All along Indians had been resisting a black label. For many, to describe the island as black was to deny their existence. They saw in Black Power a movement back to African "roots" and culture, and welcomed it, because previously, to go back to one's roots was seen as "anti-Trinidadian." At the same time, Indians were not prepared to commit cultural suicide. At least they would not have to be drawn into the "melting pot" of nationalism, which was perceived to be dominated by African culture. So several SPIC members openly supported the Black Power movement (Parmasad 1995).

Parmasad also insists that there was a class dimension to the struggle and argues that radical Indians identified with the struggle against white and imperialist aggression the world over. All Indians were not hostile to the Movement, he insists. The real enemies were the holders of power in the political system at the time, the ruling élite which still wields power. Writing before November 1995, he claims that Indians still exist in the same political relationship with the society — on the margin.

Parmasad is not entirely incorrect in what he says about the attitude of some younger campus-based Indians like himself. The evidence however suggests that most Indians were fearful of the "Black Power" movement, and for the first time, saw the PNM as the guarantors of their security — as did the whites. La Guerre is closer to the truth than is Parmasad.

The 1971 election which followed the dramatic Black Power events of 1970, which came close to toppling the PNM was full of political surprises, the most dramatic being that the PNM won all thirty-six seats in a poll that was the lowest in the nation's history. One of the most significant political events of the election was the fact that the coalition which had been formed in December 1970 between the Action Committee of Democratic Citizens and the Democratic Labour Party to contest the election (ACDC-DLP) withdrew from the contest. The group had spent a great deal of money advertising its programme, and appeared to many to be gearing itself for a close and bitter contest. Three days before nomination day and two weeks before election day, the coalition's leader, ANR Robinson, who had resigned from the PNM, declared to a stunned nation that he would neither contest the elections nor support any party or candidate who did. Some of his party colleagues who were on the rostrum with him, and who had in their speeches talked about going to the polls were dumbfounded. Vernon Jamadar, the leader of the DLP, complained bitterly and angrily about Robinson's autocratic behaviour.

There are a number of possible explanations for Robinson's decision. He himself justified his behaviour in terms of principle. He argued that a successful election boycott would indicate clearly that the existing political system was no longer legitimate, and that the ensuing crisis would generate new social demands for a redefinition of Trinidad's political economy. Anything short of a fundamental reappraisal of the political and economic system would constitute a "mockery." Some of Robinson's critics, on the other hand, felt that an equally powerful explanation was his awareness that the alliance could not win the election and that he himself might not be re-elected. Robinson might indeed have calculated that he stood a better chance of victory at a subsequent election, and that it was not prudent for him to acquire the stigma of being a "loser." Like most opposition leaders, he did not relish being on the opposition benches, especially since he had himself enjoyed power for fourteen years. He would have Williams' "crown" or nothing at all. Robinson must also have been aware that if the alliance was not victorious, Jamadar would have a stronger claim to leadership since Indians would dominate the opposition benches.

DLP leaders were certain, however, that they would retain the twelve seats which they held previously, and felt that there was a good chance that the ACDC could win the extra seats needed to defeat the PNM. They were constantly puzzled by Robinson's campaign strategy of concentrating on "sure" DLP constituencies and there was speculation that having failed to break up the PNM, he was hell-bent on smashing the DLP. Others even believed that there was a racially motivated plot between Robinson and the PNM to destroy the DLP! As the Democratic Liberation Party's organ, the *Bomb,* put it:

> There were several unsavoury features about the campaign... [one being] the plot between Williams and Robinson to bamboozle Jamadar and company and deprive the Opposition from serving in Parliament... Every move made by Robinson since he quit the PNM and became leader of the DLP nailed him as the man sent to block the Opposition from going to Parliament.

The DLP leadership did not accept the collusion thesis, but they strongly believe that Robinson's aim was to "emasculate" the DLP as an organization. As the Party declared after the election:

> Mr. A.N.R. Robinson broke with the PNM and formed the ACDC. After a few private discussions with Mr. Robinson and members of his team, the DLP cabinet appointed a negotiating team lead by Dr. Elton Richardson to discuss a merger with the ACDC. Early in the talks it appeared that

> the ACDC wanted a unitary Party in which youth and new faces would be the dominating characteristic. With patience we explained that our Party, the DLP had roots deeply embedded in a slowly changing world and that partnership and equality was our concept of unity. After some difficulties, agreement was reached. The agreement and its supplementary decisions weighed heavily in favour of the ACDC. They insisted on control of the treasury, organization and the leadership.
>
> We conceded in the interest of unity and the deep felt need to answer the PNM challenge. Despite our over generous concessions, we were assured that 'partnership and equality', which were the cornerstones of our agreement will be scrupulously respected. This has proven not to be so. Despite pious pronouncements, it is now clear to everyone that the objective of the ACDC and its leadership was the emasculation of the DLP, the capture of its support and the discreditation of its leadership. Mr. Robinson appears convinced that all politicians and political parties except the ACDC are irrelevant and should be disbanded totally. (*Trinidad Guardian,* June 19, 1971)

But it is also clear that Jamadar was hoping to use Robinson not only to unseat Williams, but also to maintain leadership of the DLP in the face of challenges from Bhadase Maraj (whose electoral threat to contest whatever constituency he chose, he took very seriously). Although there was strong pressure on Jamadar by Indian communalists to desist from the merger which could lead to the creation of another Afro-Trinidadian prime minister, Jamadar felt that this was the best opportunity ever presented to the Indians to break out of the role of opposition into which history and the racial structure of the society had confined them. Robinson likewise needed a popular base in the rural areas if he was to unseat the PNM, and thought he found this in the DLP. But he was fully aware that unless the DLP appeared in a new guise, urban blacks would not give the merger their support.

It is difficult to disentangle the facts from the myths surrounding the crisis of the ACDC-DLP, but it is known that the strategy committee of the coalition was badly split over the issue of whether to contest the election or not. A vote taken to determine the policy to be adopted indicated that a narrow majority was in favour of doing so. Robinson, who was in the minority, was not only concerned about the possibility of losing the election, but was also under strong pressure from radicals to co-operate with the no-vote campaign. Robinson's strategy (perhaps it was sheer indecision) was to recommend that the decision ought not to be made public until the people had been consulted. A voters' rally was called on May 9, 1971 and Robinson, after engaging in a dialogue with the crowd, felt that he had been given a mandate to boycott the "mock" election. The crowd, he felt, had confirmed what his own political conscience had pre-disposed him to do.

Robinson's colleagues in the merger accused him of treachery, undemocratic behaviour, and political cowardice. A crowd at a party rally was not the electorate, they argued. It was also felt that Robinson had cleverly manipulated a section of the crowd into opting for the no-vote strategy without giving those who disagreed a fair opportunity to be heard. The executive of the strategy committee believed that the decision ought to have been taken collegially and not by Robinson alone.

Those who felt that the election should be contested (and they included elements of the ACDC) opted to continue without Robinson. It was argued that staying out of the election was an irresponsible tactic, given the political climate in the country. The preservation of the system of conventional politics had to take priority over the legitimate demands for electoral reform:

> A decision not to vote means defeat for the constitutional system of government and an unsettling period in which the constitutional and the unconventional forces will sooner or later have to resolve which of the two will handle the running of the country, and whether constitutional progress will be replaced by another system of government. (*Trinidad Guardian,* May 11, 1971)

But despite the fact that some elements in the business community were bank-rolling the coalition, the demoralization caused by Robinson's decision proved too difficult to overcome, especially since he had control of the purse strings. Jamadar was not certain that he could defeat Maraj, and attendance at rallies had made it clear that no major breach could be made in PNM strongholds. In spite of its previously expressed concern with constitutional propriety, the DLP decided to join the boycott campaign.

Radical groups were elated by the collapse of the merger. The PNM, which was certain it would be returned, was dismayed, and invited the DLP to change places with the jackasses in the canefields. The *Guardian,* (May 11, 1961) although agreeing with the validity of some of the demands of the opposition, spoke for moderate elements when it declared that "boycotting the election would open the door for the extremist and totalitarian elements to exploit the situation — indulge in violence, confuse the masses and disrupt the social and economic progress of the country. This would be an ideal situation for those who wish to obstruct the political and economic progress of Trinidad and Tobago."

Only two parties challenged the PNM electorally. The more important was Bhadase Maraj's Democratic Liberation Party, which offered no manifesto or programme. The Party sponsored twenty candidates, many of whom were political has-beens from the pre-Independence era. The African National Congress, of which few people knew very much, presented seven candidates. The PNM was unopposed in eight constituencies. The election campaign was marked by sporadic incidents of violence, including the throwing of home made bombs into the headquarters of the ruling party and into the homes of the Commander in Chief of the Defence Forces and a PNM minister. Attempts were also made to assassinate the Commander in Chief of the Coast Guard and the chief state prosecutor in one of the courts martial. Both were seriously injured.

The Democratic Liberation Party made little impact on the electorate and was supported by only 14,921 voters or 4.22

per cent of those registered. The Party did poorly even in areas which were heavily populated by Indians. It gained the support of no more than 4.88 per cent of the votes cast in areas previously held by the Labour Party, a performance that may well have brought to an end the political careers of Bhadase Maraj and persons like Lionel Seukeran, Surujpat Mathura, Stephen Maharaj, and other old political notables of the Indian community. Much to everyone's surprise, Maraj himself lost to a virtually unknown Afro-Trinidadian in an area which was over 90 per cent Hindu. For Maraj, the president of the powerful Hindu Maha Sabha, the defeat in a Hindu stronghold was so galling that he threatened to retire from public life. As he complained, "The people are not interested in me politically, union-wise, religiously or in any other form. It is clear they wanted a dictatorship and a one-party state" (*Moko,* May 28, 1971). Maraj however clung tenaciously to the leadership of the Sugar Workers' Union and was re-elected in June 1971 to the presidency of the Maha Sabha for the nineteenth consecutive term. Maraj died shortly after in October 1971.

The same pattern held for other DLP areas, even though PNM support actually declined in nine of these constituencies. Although PNM supporters claim that the capture of DLP seats represented a triumph for their Party, a more likely explanation is that the hard-core of PNM supporters who came out to vote were actively assisted by the Democratic Labour Party which was less concerned about a PNM victory than about the prospect that the Democratic Liberation Party would become the official opposition. Despite the fact that the Labour Party endorsed the no-vote campaign, they surreptitiously campaigned for the PNM in Maraj's constituency.

It is worth noting that despite their late conversion to the principle of boycotting the election, the Labour Party was very effective in keeping its supporters away from the polls. The highest incidence of non-voting was in the DLP areas, a fact which urban-based opponents of Williams conveniently ignored when they characterized the results of the polls in these areas as a vote of no confidence in Williams and an endorsement of their own programme. The fact that in seven DLP constituencies as much as 70 per cent of the electorate stayed away was more a gesture of deference to the DLP leadership than it was a vote of non-confidence in Williams and conventional politics. As Hiralal Bajnath notes, "The entire voting pattern was reversed in... DLP areas, that is, the percentages of voters almost equated themselves as non-voters in 1971. The magnitude of non-voters in the traditional opposition areas was chiefly responsible for the record low poll" (*Express,* June 8, 1971).

Chapter 4

Mixing Oil and Sugar: From the DLP to the ULF

As was the case in elections before the arrival of the People's National Movement in 1956, the General Elections of 1976 were characterized by a great deal of political fragmentation. Twelve parties entered the fray, four more than had done so in 1956 when eight parties contested. The public was however not misled, and only 5 parties were taken seriously as contenders for power. These were the People's National Movement, the United Labour Front, Tapia, the Democratic Action Congress and the Democratic Labour Party. "Parties" such as the West Indian National Party, the Liberation Action Party, the United Freedom Party and the Young People's National Party which fielded only one candidate had no sociological standing in the community, and were never taken seriously by the electorate. The National Joint Action Committee which had spearheaded the 1970 "black power" revolution opted out of the election. It claimed that the present level of corruption and repression in the society was such as to make free and fair elections impossible. As far as NJAC was concerned, Trinidad and Tobago was perpetually under an undeclared state of emergency.

West Indian National Party

The West Indian National party was led by Mr. Ashford Sinanan, a former member of Parliament. Sinanan, whose career in Trinidad politics went back to the mid-1930s when he emerged as a supporter of the Butler Labour Movement, re-entered the political fray at the instigation of a clique of businessmen who seemed convinced that he was an acceptable alternative to the PNM. The party was in essence an attempt to recreate the Party of Political Progress Groups (POPPG) which had brought together the white creole element and the upwardly mobile black professionals in the society in the 1950s. The Liberal Party, which appeared in 1966, was yet another version of this coalition. The party was however doomed to impotence from the very beginning, since most of the members of these groups had come to regard the PNM as a better guarantor of their long term interests. Even though most were not enthusiastic about the ruling party, they were nevertheless aware of its importance in securing their place in the system and its stability.

One widespread rumour which hurt the WINP was that it was created by Dr. Williams with the aim of splitting Indian votes. The rumour was based on the fact that Sinanan had supported the PNM in 1966 and was later sent to India as Trinidad and Tobago's first High Commissioner. It was widely believed that Sinanan had been suborned by the Government which kept him in Delhi and London at great public expense in order to abort his planned return to Trinidad. Many sugar workers also remembered that Sinanan was once a director of Caroni Limited. As one complained "as for Ashford Sinanan, the sugar workers don't want him at all. We don't trust him. He was a director of Caroni Limited, a big Indian leader, and we couldn't even get an extra day's work." The WINP did poorly in the election, receiving only 0.42 per cent of the popular vote. Mr. Sinanan also lost his deposit.

The Liberation Action Party

The Liberation Action Party (LAP) which, like the other mini-parties, did little more than create comic relief during the election, was a group which split off from the WINP for reasons which had more to do with personality conflict than ideological issues. The party spent a great deal of money ($160,000 according to its leader, Dr. Ivan Perot) to project itself and its leader, but its impact was extremely marginal. Dr. Perot's major claim on the public's attention was that he was "younger and better looking" than Dr. Williams. The party lost a great deal of credibility when it took a decision to dissolve and merge with the radical United Labour Front which it described as "the only organization with the principles, the personnel and the strength to initiate a progressive programme of change for Trinidad and Tobago," only to reverse the decision three weeks later. It appears that the latter decision was prompted by the failure of the party's leaders to gain entry to the top Councils of the ULF which did not even bother to process the applications of the LAP officials. LAP's performance in the election was worse than the WINP. It received only 0.28 per cent of the popular vote. Its leader also lost his deposit.

The Democratic Labour Party

Of the significant opposition parties, the Democratic Labour Party (DLP) was the oldest. It emerged in 1958, and up to 1971 was the official opposition party. It did not however contest the 1971 election, choosing to support the boycott. Following the disengagement from the Action Committee of Dedicated Citizens with which it was allied in 1971, the party experienced intense factional rivalry which it was not able to resolve despite several efforts. The basic issue at stage was who should lead the party. Both Mr. Vernon Jamadar and Mr. Alloy Lequay, who had been elected political leader at a party convention in December 1972, claimed that they controlled the mass following which the party was assumed to have among the Indian population. The Jamadar faction, which described itself as "democratic socialist", claimed that the convention was null and void. The matter was eventually referred to the High Court which ruled in favour of the Lequay faction and ordered Jamadar to pay costs. The Lequay faction subsequently sought to broaden its base by merging with what was left of the old Liberal Party, the African National Congress and the United Progressive party, a breakaway from the PNM. The new grouping, which was formed in December 1973, was renamed the United Democratic Labour Party (UDLP). Following a controversy about which faction was entitled to use the traditional party symbol, the torch, a fight which Jamadar lost, the latter named his movement the Social Democratic Labour Party.

An attempt was made to reunite the factions at a convention which was held in January 1975, but this ended rowdily as backers of both leaders sought to dominate the proceedings. Lequay, who had organized the meeting, swore that that was his last attempt to work with Jamadar. To quote Lequay, "we have had many internal problems in the past, but it was the first occasion in which mob-rule dominated." The split persisted right up to the election. So bitter was the relationship, that both men fought each other in the constituency of Siparia in the attempt to settle the score. Both lost badly, and in the process helped to destroy the DLP once and for all. The UDLP received 2.98 per cent of the popular vote and the SDLP 1.88 per cent. Both Jamadar and Lequay lost their deposits.

One of the issues which the UDLP had to resolve was the leadership problem since it was considered an electoral liability to have a predominantly Hindu party led by a "Chinese." Lequay had himself admitted that race was going to be an important factor in the election, but he felt that the Indian community regarded him as an Indian rather than as an "outsider who is encroaching." This attempt by Lequay to become accepted as an "associate" Indian did not however succeed, and the leadership of the UDLP was subsequently taken over by Simbhoonath Capildeo, an old political warrior who was organizationally linked to the Maha Sabha, then the main religious organization of the Hindus. But unlike in the election of 1956, the Maha Sabha proved to be a weak reed on which to lean. As one Hindu noted, "the old Maha Sabha will have little influence on voting preferences. These days, the political complexion of the existing executive is so varied that its members would find it impossible to agree on any one political party to back."

Tapia

The Tapia House Movement under the intellectual leadership of Lloyd Best, advertised itself as a non-tribal alternative to all the existing political parties in Trinidad and Tobago. It was to be thinking man's unconventional political organization. Tapia's objection to "black power" and nationalization during the 1976 election campaign was not of recent vintage. Its views harked back to the position which it had adopted in the early days of the New World Group which had declared that its "radicalism was at no point to be identified with any of the going political doctrines, be it socialism, liberalism, communism or radicalism or what have you. Rather we want our radicalism to be interpreted as nothing more nor less than the sustained application of thought to the matters that concern us deeply" (*Tapia,* September 2, 1973).

Tapia argued that salvationist doctrines such as black power or socialism were bound to produce "doctor prophets" and a spirit of dependence and expectation among the people. The real world being what it is, one had to play for change, rather than prescribe infallibly; one had to be flexible and take advantage of the next chance rather than manipulate truth in the interest of apparent consistency:

> The infallibility of the Prophet moreover has the most serious implications. By the principles of the prevailing mythology he can never be wrong. Since in real life men do make mistakes, the view of reality must then be constantly adjusted to meet the needs of the mystique. The manipulation of men implies the manipulation of truth. The practice of Prophecy breeds Orwellian double-think. It becomes increasingly difficult to apprehend reality, and finally the people are confirmed in an endless nightmare in which they are led blind from despair. In their delusion they keep up the wail of the messiah; but in fact they are in Babylon for good. (ibid.)

On the issue of class which featured so prominently in the election, Tapia had argued that the concept had no relevance for the Caribbean. It was an inappropriate concept which derived from European society which was quite different from the plantation societies of the Caribbean:

> There is no "bourgeoisie" here because we have had no "bourg." Nor have we had feudalism or any dynamic class of national capitalists so there need not be any "socialists" or "communists." What is the meaning of "middle class?" In almost every family we can find represented the full spectrum from professional through artisan through labourer. Tapia rejects all these imported categories and we seek to understand what is going on here in terms of Caribbean definitions. When we do that, we see all kinds of very rich possibilities for national integration and economic transformation. And we make all kinds of fresh interpretations. (ibid.)

The socialists however accused Tapia of being nothing more than a capitalist party which was simply promising to do more efficiently what the PNM had been trying unsuccessfully to do for the past twenty years. The socialists believed that

> The contradictions which had Williams and his regime reeling from crisis to crisis signalled that the time was ripe to smash capitalism — not to resuscitate it by creating a local capitalist class. Best and his colleagues had provided a brilliant, indeed Marxist, analysis of what was wrong with the West Indian economy, but rather than prescribe the obvious cure of thorough going socialization of the mans of production and the elimination of the profit system, he had launched a strategy aimed at claiming the worst fears of foreign companies by preaching "localization" and by directly appealing to the avaricious energies of both the established business interests and the aspiring petty entrepreneurs among the Africans and Indians. (ibid.)

On the question as to whether there were "classes" in Caribbean society, one might agree with Best that for a variety of reasons, the social distance between upper, middle and lower classes might be narrow. The size of the community may have helped to produce informal casual relationships across status lines. But as Ivor Oxaal reminded Lloyd Best:

> The tendency to practice a degree of fluidity with respect to the maintenance of social distance should not, however, be allowed to obscure the central fact of structural inequalities which, although mitigated by various personal bonds, formed the backbone of the Trinidad social system. Quite apart from the white elite, large disparities in income, power and lifestyles characterized the multi-ethnic but also hierarchical status order of the neo-colonial society.... An uncritical acceptance of the postulate of a unique Caribbean reality could obviously lend itself to a type of special pleading on behalf of a rising elite in need of a new form of ideological mystification to legitimate the continuing social inequalities generated by a reformed, West Indian national capitalism. (ibid.)

The Tapia group was never able to silence the doubt of the public that they were an idealistic and impractical bunch of intellectuals who had no feel for the practice of politics. The public conceded that the party was made up of bright and well-intentioned people, but as the findings of an opinion survey conducted by the author showed, less than 1 per cent of the sample believed that Tapia was the party best equipped to solve the problems faced by the country. Only 8 per cent picked Lloyd Best as the man they would like to see as the next Prime Minister while 6 per cent said they would like to see him lead the opposition. Five per cent of those who said they intended to vote planned to vote for Tapia, while only 3 per cent of the sample expected them to win. As Tapia leader, Lloyd Best conceded, "Tapia was picked to 'place' in the political stakes by most groups, but not to 'win'."

The Democratic Action Congress

Like Tapia and all other parties, the Manifesto of the Democratic Action Congress (DAC) contained a catalogue of afflictions from which the country was said to be suffering. DAC's "short list" contained twenty one items ranging from repressive legislation (The Sedition Act, Summary Offenses Amendment Act, Firearms Act and the Industrial Relations Act) to unemployment, underemployment, double digit inflation, inefficiency in the public services, flagrant and widespread corruption from top to bottom involving the Head of Government, who it was noted had "publicly denounced Cabinet Ministers with whom he continues to sit in Cabinet." DAC accused the PNM of "causing a general breakdown in morale and a psychology of degradation."

DAC's plan for the economy was based on the principle of restructuring the capitalist system in order to make it more efficient, rational and participative. Outside of the oil sector, DAC's concern was to create a strong nationally owned sector of indigenous manufacturing and service industries. DAC was critical of the "screwdriver" or assembly type industries which have been the pillar of the PNM'S industrialization effort, at least up to 1975. To quote the DAC Manifesto, "in most instances, neither the simple technology nor the limited resources brought in have been worth the cost, and the impact of monopoly promotion activities on the cost of lost of living in Trinidad and Tobago has been nothing short of disastrous for the people" (DAC Manifesto 1976: 9).

Like every other party, including the governing party, DAC was critical of the way in which the state enterprises were organized and run, and promised to re-organize them within a new legal structure requiring public accountability, diffusion of management to include public interest, worker and consumer representatives. DAC also pledged to ensure that persons of competence and integrity were appointed to the boards of these organizations and to free them from petty political harassment. DAC was also critical of the Government's policy in the oil industry which it described as being disorganized.

Since DAC had considered the 1971 elections to be "mock elections" and therefore illegal, it also promised to repeal all legislation which had been enacted since then and to re-negotiate all contracts which had been signed by the PNM. Like all other parties, DAC also campaigned on the theme that it was time for a change. Without change, "people in power no longer feel a sense of responsibility to the people who put them in power. They begin to think that power is an inheritance and theirs by right of birth...

and use the instruments of the state to prop up their own authority. [They] cease to listen... to be sensitive... and feel that [their] position is a legacy and not a trust" (*Express,* April 19, 1976).

The DAC, which had been calling for elections since 1971, was expected to give the ruling party a good fight. No one however expected the party to displace the PNM. The party however considered itself to be the only serious threat to the ruling party and made it clear that it was contesting the election in the hope of forming the government and not the opposition. Having regard to its experiences with the DLP in 1971, the party said that it would collaborate with other parties but would not merge with any. As Mr. Virgil Pestana, the Party's Public Relations Officer noted, "we have always stated that DAC is not prepared to give up its identity, and it is not going to merge with any other party. We have bitter memories of the attempt to merge with the Democratic Labour Party. But DAC is certainly prepared to work with any progressive movement or party for the benefit of Trinidad and Tobago. An alliance may become a merger later on, but initially what we see is certain opposition parties combining their strengths as a tactical move in particular geographic areas" (ibid.).

Although most observers considered DAC to be a middle class party which was simply promising to be far more efficient than PNM had been, DAC considered itself to be a "revolutionary party." One of the leaders of the party, Dr. Martin Sampath, said it would be wrong to consider DAC as middle class. "You must look at us as people who came up from the grass roots. We may have succeeded in various professions, but we all came from humble beginnings. The leaders of DAC are about as middle class as Fidel Castro." There was certainly nothing "revolutionary" in the party's manifesto or in the utterings of it spokesmen who were clearly seeking to win over the middle and lower middle class following which the PNM controlled. Mr. Virgil Pestana's description of the party as being "middle left" was nearer to the truth than Sampath's opinion that it was a revolutionary party (*Express,* November 11, 1973).

The party did at one time have a fair amount of supporters among the Indian population, some of which it had retained following the collapse of the merger with the DLP. Most were followers and supporters of those Indian professionals who were associated with it. More than half of the 40,000 members of which the party boasted of having in April 1976 were Indian. But as we shall see, most of them would bolt to the ULF as the election day approached. Tapia accused the DAC of being on the right of the PNM and of being "a bunch of opportunistic Jaycee types and cocktail party technocrats" (*Guardian,* January 7, 1975).

The United Labour Front

Although the general public did not become aware of the development until the very eve of the election, the formation which had come to replace the DLP was the United Labour Front, a coalition consisting of four of the major radical trade unions in the country. These were the Oilfields Workers Trade Union, the All Trinidad Sugar Estates and Factories Workers Trade Union, the Transport and Industrial Workers Union and the Islandwide Canefarmers Trade Union. The Front, which was formed in February 1975, declared its intention to form a political party in January 1976. Up to that time, there was some uncertainty as to whether it would take the political plunge. Part of this uncertainty was due to the fact that previous attempts on the part of radical trade unionists to enter the arena of parliamentary politics had not been very successful. The fate of the Workers and Farmers Party which was badly decimated in the 1966 election was only the last, though perhaps the most dramatic indication of the apparent unwillingness on the part of workers to vote unionists into political office. The public appeared to be quite skeptical about unionists who sought to combine the role of professional politician and professional labour leader, and the ULF began by insisting that it was not interested in getting into politics which it feared would divide the workers along ethnic lines and weaken the class struggle.

At the height of his struggle to gain control of the All Trinidad Sugar Estates and Factory Workers Trade Union in 1972, Basdeo Panday, who was then a Senator, insisted that he was not interested in politics "now or ever" since "work within the union and among the thousands of sugar workers is of a very serious nature. I do not have time for politics. It is one thing to get involved politically to secure benefits for the workers and quite another to function as a professional politician." OWTU Leader, George Weekes, also noted that he too was not interested in becoming a parliamentarian and would resist anyone who tried to encourage him to contest the election.

As late as February 2, 1976, Basdeo Panday and Raffique Shah were still ambivalent about their involvement in politics. Mr. Panday noted that the Front, which altogether controlled over 36,000 workers, was not bent on threatening other political parties. While both he and Shah could win seats easily, he felt that that would not be to their advantage since they "would not command a majority in the House." Panday however quite clearly left himself an opening by indicating that it would be "up to the workers" to decide whether or not the Front would take the electoral plunge.

On the Birth of the ULF - the Long-sought Merger of Oil and Sugar Workers
Basdeo Panday

I can attribute this to the fact that the three leaders: Brother Weekes, Brother Shah and I represent the three major religions and the two major ethnic groups. By this I mean that getting together with Weekes cemented the races, for he is of African and we are of East Indian descent. Before this, the emergence of Brother Shah, a Muslim, unified the cane farmers and sugar workers. For they had never been blessed with a Hindu and a Muslim leader at the same time.

Butler and the other fellows had failed because they failed to realized that this cannot be a one-man show. And that is where we succeeded, the three of us — one Christian, one Hindu and the other Muslim. People of African and Indian descent united. You see, the workers in the sugar and oil industries can now identify with us; their aspirations are ours. No longer could the wedge of racism be driven between us, nor that of religion, both of which had been easy targets before (From *Crisis 1976: 196*).

According to Mr. Panday the following conversation ensued between himself and Mr. Errol Mahabir, then Minister of Industry and Commerce.

"Panday, boy, I would like to see you."

"Well, you cyar come by my house and I ent coming by yours."

Eventually a neutral house was agreed upon. "The first thing, Errol told me was: 'Boy, the old man (Dr. Williams) say you win. Call Caroni tomorrow and they will agree to see you.'

"I went to see Caroni's Managing Director and I was advised that because of the legal difficulties which might be presented by Rampartap and his boys, I should form another Union. I refused knowing that if I were to form another Union, a long legal tangle as to which really was the representative Union would ensue and in the process I might have lost the workers. In any case, I knew that the minute Caroni decided to see me, Rampartap Singh was dead."

Mr. Panday said that during that fateful meeting with Errol Mahabir, he had been told that the Prime Minister did not mind the sugar workers having an Indian leader who would carry on as an Indian leader.

We are happy to know,' Errol said, `that the Indians have found their own George Weekes.'

"The minute I hear this, I realised that what the Government wanted most was to keep oil and sugar apart. I decided to play a game, and, again it worked like a charm. I had known George Weekes for a number of years (they had both contested the 1966 Elections on a WFP ticket). So shortly after Caroni decided to see me, I called George and told him" "George I don't want to see you for a year. Don't call me. Don't talk to me. Pay no attention to what you read in the Press even if it sounds derogatory. I have known and loved you for years. Just trust me."

"You see I had known that if Williams thought for a single moment that I was going to align myself with Weekes, my throat would be cut before I could become entrenched. So I played to the Press. For example, when I was asked if I have been influenced by George Weekes, I replied that I was the political scientist (I had majored in political science while taking my economics degree) and that if there was any influence it had to be flowing the other way. George was laughing all the time.

"By the end of September 1974, I had won the struggle for guaranteed work and I felt I had the loyalty of the workers. Entrenched now, I went to George and told him that the time had come to continue the job we started in 1966. We had to unite the workers in such a way as to get rid of the racial antagonisms that prevailed. We proposed a rally in December 1974 but because of some internal problems in the OWTU we postponed it to February 18. At that meeting some 30,000 workers attended and we declared the United Labour Front to be born" (From *Crisis 1976: 286*).

Although the formal decision to become a party was only taken on March 28, 1976, it is clear that Panday and Shah from the very beginning had their eyes on parliament but were constrained from making this clear by the ideology which they espoused and which required that the masses should provide the mandate for such a step. According to Panday, however, it was the workers themselves who came to the conclusion that is was necessary for the ULF to seek to win political power. This decision came following what the ULF described as a "religious march" to Port of Spain which took place on March 18, 1975. Permission to hold the march was refused by the Commissioner of Police from whom permission had been sought. The march was savagely repressed and the event is now referred to as "Bloody Tuesday." According to Panday:

> That march brought home clearly to the consciousness of the workers and leaders that if you are struggling for industrial objectives that can always be frustrated if political power is in the hands of opponents of that struggle and if those opponents intend to use that political power to frustrate the struggle. What became clear in the minds of all workers was that the industrial struggle was not enough. In order to really crystallize the gains of industrial struggle, in order to make them permanent and lasting and not have them taken away again, it was necessary to transcend the industrial struggle into the political scene, and it was with this in mind that the unions began holding something called joint COSSABOS which are the initials for a Conference of Shop Stewards and Branch Officers. We developed a new institution where the shop stewards and branch officers could get together, and discussion took place for several months, and this idea began to emerge that the ULF should transform itself into a political machinery to carry out political struggles which appeared to the workers to be a *sine qua non* of industrial victory. That is how the ULF as a political party came into being. The workers met and resolved themselves into a political organization. (*Guardian,* April 18, 1976)[1]

That at least is the formal position. What Mr. Panday did not spell out is the process by which the leaders had skillfully orchestrated the issue until the representatives of the workers could come to no other conclusion. Panday himself, in an article in *The People,* said that when he became President of the All Trinidad Sugar Estates and Factories Workers Trade Union, he called George Weekes of the Oilfields Workers Union to tell him of the need to continue the work they had began in 1966 with the Workers and Farmers Party. Panday had also told the workers at a Longdenville rally on October 1, 1975 that though "we had no political ambitions, we were aware of the political consequences of our actions. We weren't born yesterday." Similarly, on the day of the mammoth rally at Skinner Park in February 1975 which drew over 30,000 workers, Panday had told the crowd that

> ... we must now consolidate and institutionalize the de facto power which we now have to get control of the State. I believe we ought to learn a lesson from the failure of the black power movement. That we have got to go beyond the stage of marching. In 1970 they reached a tremendous height of de facto power, but they did not know that to do with it. Had they been able to do something with it, our political history would have been different. ULF must not make that same mistake. I will like to see ULF consolidated into a political movement, but that must not be a decision from the top. It must follow from the wishes of the people. The days of sitting down in the Holiday Inn and declaring a political party are over. For any political movement to be successful, it must burst forth from the bowels of the people. (*Express,* February 23, 1976)[2]

Not all workers were convinced about the inevitability of this step. Most of the sugar workers who followed Panday had no doubt that the step was a correct one, for as Mr. Ramnarine Binda, a political activist in the sugar area noted, "history shows that sugar workers will support a union leader who gets them work and money." Binda noted that Panday had done a great deal to win substantial benefits for the sugar workers and quoted a Hindu proverb (Binda's version), "who put food in me belly, is God for he." Binda and many other Indians in the sugar belt felt convinced that "God sent Panday for us." To quote another:

> When people look at Panday, they see that he stood up with us and fought with us and even assisted us to bury our dead. He is the most truthful leader we ever had. The standard of the sugar worker was worse than dog in the country. Before, we used to cry a drum of tears; now everybody is happy. Sugar workers are now making $14 a day.... Panday has given us a reasonable wage.... The man who fed us is the man we are going to back. (*Express,* May 13, 1976)

Binda, like Panday, was however aware that what was historically true of the sugar workers was not true of the oil workers. The last trade unionist representing oil workers who was returned to Parliament was Adrian Cola Rienzi, and it is not clear whether it was the workers' vote which elected him since the franchise was limited.

On a number of occasions, oil workers clearly hinted that while they supported their President General as a trade unionist, they were not going to endorse his link with the ULF. Many of them, particularly the older ones, were supporters of the PNM which in their view was the only available alternative to the racial and ideological threat posed by the ULF. Weekes himself was well aware of this feeling and this in part explains his decision not to contest a seat. Rejection at the polls might well have undermined his hold on the Oilfields Workers Trade Union.

The most dramatic indication of the oil workers attitude was their failure to turn out in support of a work stoppage called by the United Peoples Front, an ad hoc alliance of opposition groups which was formed to protest certain features of the new constitution which the Government had published in a draft bill. Although denying a report that only 200 oil workers turned out, Panday agreed that "the response of the oil worker was not as crushing as that of the sugar worker." Whereas the sugar worker had found a new sense of dignity and were militant on all fronts, "the oil workers... have been struggling for a long time and they may have thought (it pointless) struggling against the constitution since it (was) going to be passed any way and it may be that they are sharpening their teeth so to speak for the political struggle" (*Guardian*, April 18, 1976).[3] It was a clever attempt to gloss over a problem which was of genuine concern to the ULF leadership and one which they sought to solve by forging an electoral alliance with the Democratic Action Congress.

The ULF however insisted that it was a genuine multi-racial "party of the working class" which would revolutionize politics in Trinidad and Tobago. To quote Panday, "the United Labour Front of unions in oil and sugar is the greatest success in Afro-Indian unity and the Government is afraid of it politically" (ibid.).[4] Panday agreed that race had been a dominant factor in the past but felt that the developments which had taken place in the country since 1966 had combined to indicate a lessening of racial tension. The first change was evident among Indians themselves. According to Panday:

> In the past, Indian sugar workers and their leaders had always defended their struggle in racial rather than in class terms and this view tended to permeate the entire Indian community. The class interest of the worker thus tended to conflict with his racial interest which achieved dominance. Contrary to what had happened in the past, the Sugar Workers Union under my leadership had preached to Indians that they had a class affinity with African workers who suffered as much as they did at the hands of an exploiting capitalism. (ibid.)[5]

Panday accused the capitalists, the press and PNM and DLP politicians of having sought in the past to thwart the emerging class consciousness among Indian and African workers and felt that the activities of the ULF had managed to heighten that class feeling. "What has happened in the ULF is not merely the getting together of four unions. It is the getting together of two peoples of the same class" (ibid.).[6] Panday also felt that given the no vote campaign in 1971, the country had not had a serious election campaign since 1966. "There has been a very long stretch and racial feelings have subsided. During this time, class consciousness had begun to develop... racial antagonism has fallen to an all time low and it will take a tremendous effort to drive it up to a peak in 1976. Panday also felt that the work which the ULF had done in the rural areas had served to undercut the DLP. To quote Panday:

> The Indian worker had certainly swung away from the DLP, and one of the major reasons for this is the fact that the DLP has always been an amorphous thing that went to sleep after an election. It had no other organization and only sprang to life at elections on purely racial lines and afterwards died again.
>
> Now it takes something to trigger the racial sentiment. It takes a Rudrudnath Capildeo, someone with that racial charismatic appeal who could go to the Indians and push them to a racial frenzy and bring the DLP to life. The DLP has always been brought to life by a charismatic leader at election time. If it was not Capildeo it was Bhadase Maraj. In the present situation there is no such charismatic leader to whip the Indians into a racial frenzy. (*Guardian,* April 18, 1976)

As we have indicated above, however, Panday was regarded by many rural Indians as the new charismatic leader, the new "baba." Panday did seek to de-emphasize this in his public positions, but he could not have been unaware of it. Part of the reason for this de-emphasis was not that it was considered inadvisable for the ULF to become too closely identified with any one leader for both racial and organizational reasons. Collegial leadership, Panday argued, not only drew attention to the organization and what it stood for, but also avoided conflicts over leadership. The racial dimension of the decision not to identify any one person as leader is however clear, even though everyone recognized that the major vote getters in the party were Messrs. Panday and Shah rather than George Weekes and Joe Young, both of whom quite sensibly chose to avoid the polls. To compensate for the fact that neither Weekes nor Young were in the line up, an attempt was made to project Allan Alexander, a barrister at law, whom it was hoped would attract the moderate black middle class vote. Alexander was preferred to Dr. James Millette, the General

Secretary of the Party, whose image as a communist was considered to be an electoral liability. Alexander however came over as a damp squid and was never seen by anyone as a leader of the black working class.

The Ideology of the ULF

Some aspects of the ideology of the ULF could already be inferred from what has been said before. The basic plank in the Front's programme was racial unity between the oppressed peoples of Indian and African ancestry. Central too was the view that trade unions must seek to develop a political arm to reinforce their struggles on the labour front thought it must be recognized that obtaining seats in Parliament was only a subsidiary concern of the Front.

The Front's programme also emphasized the question of public ownership of the commanding heights of the economy. The Front's manifesto pledged:

1. the nationalization of all multi-national corporations in the principal sectors of the economy, in particular oil, petro-chemicals, construction and insurance

2. the nationalization of the foreign banking system which today masquerades as a localized banking system by grace of PNM deception and fraud

3. the nationalization of all new enterprises in these sectors which may be established in advance of the take-over by a ULF Government

4. the nationalization of the import-export sector particularly in respect of food, drugs, building materials and other vital necessities, with the specific aim of reducing the cost of living,

eliminating the outflow of foreign exchange and curtailing the importation of unnecessary and luxury items.

5. the nationalization of the Pitch Lake. In all such nationalized undertakings special attention will be given to working out policies which would introduce and extend workers' participation in the control and management of such industries so that the new nationalized undertakings will serve the interests of the people at large and not only the interests of a bureaucratic, corrupt and self-interested elite as obtains at present in the so-called public sector enterprises (United Labour Front Election Manifesto 1976:8).

The Front also insisted that no foreigners should be allowed to own land and that steps must be taken to eliminate land speculation or the use of scarce agricultural land for housing developments.

The Front came out against expropriation, however. It argued that whenever it became necessary to acquire property which was owned by foreigners, full compensation was to be negotiated. The other items in the programme which was a hastily drafted hodge-podge of radical ideas included diversification of industry using the country's agricultural and petroleum base, and the rationalization of the banking system to make banks and other financial institutions more accessible to workers and farmers on the basis of established social and economic needs.

Unlike Tapia, which disputed the relevance of the concept of class in Trinidad politics, the ULF insisted that class was critical. In Trinidad, which was seen as a capitalist society, the capitalist class was that group (both foreign and local) which owned the factories, the banks, the large estates, the finance and insurance companies and the media. The state which owned some of the means of production, was also part of the capitalist class. The bureaucrats and politicians who managed state enterprises and who enjoyed the perquisites which went with their role were the principal spokesmen of the coalition. The working class were those who owned nothing except their personal property and who had nothing to sell but their labour. This group, which was estimated to be about 800,000, was the group — the oppressed — which the ULF claimed to speak for. In the Parliament of the past, there were two "multi-class" capitalist oriented parties which showed that they could do nothing but talk and make cosmetic changes. The ULF, which was "inevitable and which crystallized the natural alliance between peasants and workers," claimed that it stood instead for fundamental structural changes. "The implementation of such changes will involve the use of parliament, but above all it will involve the mobilization of the people" (First Statements of the Policy and Programme of The United Labour Front 1976:8-11).

Although the ULF was supposed to be a United Front of all radical groups, it contained the seeds of its eventual disintegration. There were many cleavages in the Party which the Manifesto barely papered over. The cleavages within the party were not only along racial lines but were ideological and personal as well. All three factors interacted with each other to make the party a very fragile thing. The ULF was never a homogenous organization, but a sort of political banyan tree, which at a particular point in time provided shelter for many of the ideologically incompatible elements which were involved in the protest movement of the late sixties and seventies. In addition to the radical trade unions, the ULF served as a holding company for micro-sectarian groups such as the United National Independence Party (UNIP) led by James Millette, the New Beginning Movement, the National Movement for the True Independence of Trinidad and Tobago (NAMOTI), the National Liberation Movement (NLM), Students for Change, the Union of Democratic Students (UDS), the United Revolutionary Organization (URO) and the National Union of Freedom Fighters (NUFF).

Significantly absent from the radical coalition was Geddes Granger's National Joint Action Committee (NJAC), which since 1970, had adopted a cultural nationalist posture (pro-Black, pro-African). NJAC felt that the ULF was too closely wedded to Marxism-Leninism, an ideology which it regarded as an expression of white "reality." ULF politics was also much too conventional for NJAC, given the latter's disdain for parties, elections and parliaments which were viewed as dead ends for the black masses. Absent from the coalition too was Lloyd Best's Tapia which considered the class rhetoric of the ULF too simplistic and crude for its sophisticated intellectual palate. Tapia's aim was to build a multi-class progressive coalition rather than a party of the working class which was the aim of the ULF. Tapia's hostility to the ULF was reciprocated by the ULF which considered it to be a reactionary party that was not very different from the PNM in terms of its ideology.

The sectarian groups which identified with the ULF did so for a variety of reasons and with varying degrees of organizational commitment. Others, like URO, which prided itself on its ideological purity, stood relatively aloof from the ULF, giving it only "critical" support. URO's avowed aim was to build a communist party and society in Trinidad and Tobago and found the ULF too ideologically flabby for its puritan taste. URO claimed that the ULF was capable only of leading the "democratic stage" of the revolution and not its socialist or communist phases.

Other groups such as NUFF, a former guerilla grouping that emerged in 1971, New Beginning and NAMOTI actively supported the ULF in the 1976 election campaign and two members of the last named group were election candidates (cf. Harvey 1974). One candidate was a member of NUFF. All three groups however retained their organizational autonomy, insisting that the ULF's involvement with parliamentary politics had serious limitations. To quote NUFF:

> The ULF must use the election platform to point out to the oppressed masses that the main task of the revolutionary people is to destroy the capitalist state machine. The ULF must point out that the very instruments that the capitalist use to oppress us can never be transformed to serve us... we must understand that the ULF is not, and cannot be a true revolutionary party of the working class. ULF was born out of trade union struggles and is therefore a workers' organization, which has transformed itself into a mass party that anyone can join, but it is impossible for such a party to lead the oppressed masses in the fight against American Imperialism.[7]

While the various sectarian groups all recognized the limitations of the ULF, there was no agreement on what had to be done tactically or strategically to advance the revolutionary movement in Trinidad and Tobago. Some groups like New Beginning de-emphasized party politics and stressed the need for people's assemblies. How this was to be done in any practical operational sense was not all too clear.

The dominant figure in the ULF, Mr. Basdeo Panday, came out strongly against those in the Party who were arguing that the party should declare itself to be unequivocally marxist or those who were advocating armed solutions. As he said as early as 1975:

> We must concentrate on the worker achieving political power by conventional means. It is for this reason, in my view, that the United Labour Front is a significant development in the struggle of the working people. Armed revolution in this country is not a feasible idea for two reasons. Firstly our people don't have a history of revolution, so that we are not trained and it's most likely to fail. We can see the futility there. Secondly, because of the racial composition and the suspicion that has been engendered among the two dominant races, armed revolution is likely to degenerate into a racial conflict. Can you imagine an Indian guerilla killing a Negro child? This is likely to happen because in such conflicts, many innocent people are likely to be killed. That then is the end of your revolution. (*Express,* February 1975)

Panday insisted that although the ULF was a radical working class party it must not become wedded to any obsolete "isms." As he said:

> To call the (ULF programme) this 'ism' or that 'ism' would be to create confusion in the minds of people because 'isms' have different meanings to different people. The specific mechanism to bring our polity into operation will be determined by the objective realities at any given time and this will change from time to time. We do not wish to import models which are suited to other countries but not suited to our own. We must develop indigenous institutions relevant to our society, our own consciousness and our state of economic growth. (*Express,* April 26, 1976)

Panday in fact denied that he was a socialist or that he himself used the word socialist to describe what he stood for. Panday stressed that his chief goal was not to destroy capitalism but to extend it to the workers. Workers capitalism would destroy the myth that the interests of workers and managers were irreconcilably opposed.

End Notes

[1]The details of the event and the circumstances which gave rise to it are treated fully in *Crisis,* Owen Baptiste (ed.) 1976, Inprint, Port of Spain. The ULF leaders insisted that the march was a religious march and argued thus in the Courts which took the correct view that it was essentially a political march which was given a religious flavour to overcome the Commissioner's objections. Five ULF leaders decided to go to jail rather than pay the fines which were imposed. It was a palpable attempt to secure martyrdom and political mileage. The strategy did not work, however, and the fines were subsequently paid by their unions.

[2]*Express,* February 23, 1976. The Rally in San Fernando was one of the largest seen in the country since 1970, and was called to back demands which 3 of the 4 unions were making for increased wages (OWTU) profit sharing arrangements in Caroni (ATSEFWTU) and in the case of the ICFTU, recognition from Caroni Ltd. which was supporting a pro-PNM union, Trinidad Island-wide Cane farmers Association. For discussion of the rally, cf. *Crisis* 1976: 10-12.

[3]Sixty members of the General Council of the OWTU had unanimously passed a resolution calling upon the OWTU membership and the working class in general to support the ULF (*Guardian,* August 24, 1976).

[4]Panday admitted that the attempt which he, George Weekes and CLR James made in 1966 to unite the races failed. "We tried to on class lines, but our error was in attempting to do this from the top.... Real political organization stems from the rising consciousness of the people... If a political party were to be

formed, it had to blow from the bowels of the people, so to speak" (*Express,* April 6, 1976).

[5]Panday had said he was convinced that class perspectives would predominate in the election:

> The African worker now realizes he has been betrayed by Dr. Williams and has become more conscious of his economic role and the conflict in his mind between racial affinity and economic reality has been lessened. The economic aspirations of the workers of African descent are now predominant. The situation is the same with the Indian workers — economic aspirations take precedence over racial and political ones. Hence, the two groups can now come together and vote on the basis of class and economic interest for a party that they know will best represent those in-terests. (*Express,* April 18, 1976)

[6]Whenever it appeared that successful attempts were being made to bring Indian and African workers together for militant, industrial and possibly political action, the response of the PNM was to declare a state of emergency. This happened both in 1965 when the ISA was introduced and in 1970 when the radical leadership was detained. For a discussion of these events cf. my *Race and Nationalism* 1972:459-70.

[7]For a discussion of the origins of NUFF, cf. David Millette's essay in Ryan and Stewart 1995: 625-660.

Chapter 5

Race, Class and the Elections of 1976

The 1976 General Elections were characterized by a great deal of confusion and uncertainty. There was uncertainty as to how many parties would contest, about who would run on which ticket, whether there would be mergers or alliances or even whether there would be any election at all. The opposition groups were also skeptical. Some of the members of the radical United Labour Front believed that if an election were held, and the PNM were to lose to the ULF, attempts would be made to abort the result. Many persons also felt that there was a distinct possibility that no party would emerge with a clear majority and that the President would have to play the role of kingmaker. There was a great deal of anxiety about this, since it was assumed that the President would be partial to the PNM in the event Parliament was deadlocked.

At one point, it even appeared likely that the Political Leader of the People's National Movement might have chosen to opt out of the fray altogether. There was also a great deal of uncertainty and speculation as to what role, if any, race would play in the election. The ULF and its supporters claimed that given the working class struggles which had taken place since 1971, and particularly in 1975, class perceptions would triumph over race, with others claiming the contrary. There was also some curiosity as to how the urban upwardly mobile Indians would react to the socialist ULF. Would they support it on racial grounds, abstain, or vote PNM as their counterparts were doing in Guyana.

Of interest too was the question of just what difference, if any, the 18-year old vote would make to party fortunes.

One of the big question marks in the campaign was the ULF itself which had not made any appreciable impact on the northern half of the island until very late in the campaign and then with disastrous consequences. The general public and even the rank and file members of the party were very much in the dark as to what the party stood for ideologically, whether or not it was even going to contest the elections, whether it would go it alone or in alliance with the DAC.

In the absence of firm knowledge, rumours spread that the ULF was communist and atheistic. Typical of those who expressed this point of view was Mr. Stephen Maharaj, a former comrade in arms of Messrs. Panday and Weekes in the defunct Workers and Farmers Party which had contested the 1966 elections. Maharaj described the Manifesto of the ULF as "unadulterated communism," and said that Panday and Shah were being used by the communists in the party. Maharaj believed that Panday and Shah could not possibly have written the Manifesto, a point of view which was correct. Maharaj also claimed that Panday shared his view that the ULF should link up with the DLP in an attempt to secure either an overall majority or at least a strong opposition, but that this strategy was vetoed by the communists. Maharaj was here giving voice to a point of view within the Indian community which held that Panday and Shah should lead the Indians rather than forge links with "Black Power" or Marxist elements in the ULF. Slogans suggesting that this was what the ULF leaders had done were painted on walls all over the countryside. Anti-ULF Indians argued that Indians were basically petty capitalists who worked hard to save and set up businesses. The same was true of some black workers. "It is these workers who own private property and send their children away to study various professions upon whom you will inflict your policy of complete nationalization' (*Trinidad Guardian,* August 29, 1976).

Maharaj, who insisted that he was still a "socialist," alleged that whereas the Workers and Farmers Party had recommended that sugar lands should be broken up and given to thousands of cane farmers, the ULF's Manifesto had spoken of total nationalization. The ex-MP accused Shah of betraying the cane farmers whom he represented by associating himself with such a programme. Maharaj's accusations were however incorrect since the Manifesto talked about "encouraging co-operatives among farmers who cultivate privately owned or tenanted lands, with a view, among other things, to enabling farmers, especially cane farmers and food crop farmers, to benefit from the economies of large scale production" (ULF Manifesto).

Maharaj's outburst posed a serious threat to the ULF's electoral strategy which was designed to project an image of labour radicalism which was well within the conventional framework of the western democratic mold. The ULF leaders were well aware that the population was allergic to anything that smacked of communism, and were therefore forced to disavow and deny Maharaj's allegations. The ULF, Panday and Weekes asserted, was not a communist party, but a "party of the working class preaching the doctrine of the working class." In Panday's view, Maharaj's attack was motivated more by his failure to secure a place on the ULF ticket than by the fact that his visit to the Soviet Union in 1975 had opened his eye to what communism "that pernicious doctrine," had meant in Russia. Maharaj had given the latter reason for his change of mind about communism.

Similar accusations were made by the DLP and the media. The SDLP leader, Vernon Jamadar, accused the ULF of being a pawn in the control of extremists, a charge which was also levelled by the influential weekly newspaper, the *Bomb* which carried a front page caricature of Panday and Shah being dangled on strings pulled by "black power" elements and marxists. Jamadar was of the view that the people in the sugar belt were too sensible to be fooled by Panday. To quote Jamadar:

> They are not going to allow Mr. Panday to bag them up and deliver them up to some of the extremist radicals who dominate ULF, and are totally alien to the sugar belt. I think the sugar belt is comprised of moderate, sensible people who want peace. They want prosperity. They want harmony. They want happiness. The kind of fire and brimstone preaching that many of the alien radical ULF people are using to win support is inconsistent with the character of the people in the sugar belt, and Mr. Panday, I am sure, is going to be very surprised after the elections. He is trying to deify himself. The sugar people do not need this. They have their historic deities, and Mr. Panday is not their idea of a modern day deity. (*Trinidad Guardian,* May 2, 1976)

The Guardian alleged, without evidence, that communist money was entering the country to finance the ULF, and warned that the country should not be allowed to fall into the hands of communists, however well intentioned they might be, since, once in power, communists usually proceed to abolish all rights. To quote the *Guardian* (August 29, 1976):

> Communists have never come to power anywhere as the government of a country by election. ... To invite them is to commit virtual suicide, since they would have lost the right to prosperity, the right to think, the right to protest and the right to appeal in one full swoop. ... We have not had citizens exiled because of their dissent; we have not had them clapped into prison for years without trial or tribunal. What we have is the freedom of people to write in the Press their most bitter complaints against Ministers and even the Prime Minister. We have not had people flung into insane asylums for doing this or set into chain gang. The communists say they aim at a classless society. This is an elusive dream.

Dr. Williams also waged a subtle campaign to denigrate socialism by telling his audiences about some of the experiences which he had had during his state visit to Cuba in 1975. He told audiences that the people of Trinidad and Tobago were freer and far better fed and housed than those in Cuba. Williams said that he himself was a pragmatist and not a socialist, and that he would not know what a socialist blue-print was, even if he were to see one. Unlike the ULF, the PNM was not planning to take away people's homes or their farms, but were instead planning to give people such things. As he told a rally, "the PNM does not intend to take away anybody's land; it does not intend to take away the cane farmers' land; as far as the PNM is concerned, the cane farmer is the man of the future in the sugar industry, and so long as the PNM is the government, the cane farmers are safe" (*Express,* April 26, 1976).

The ULF denied all allegations that its aim was to take away the personal property of the little man. To quote Shah: "We believe that a man has a right to property, even to the investment of capital. That however does not give him a right to exploit his fellow man who may be in a more unfortunate position" (*The Bomb,* June 18, 1976). There was in fact nothing in the statements of the major leaders of the ULF which suggested that it was an extreme marxist movement.

The ULF had to deal with yet another persistent charge namely, that it was the old DLP "writ large." The question of race and voting had come alive following the visit of an Indian cricket team to Trinidad. A majority of Indians appeared to support the Indian team against the West Indian cricketers and there were some ugly incidents between Africans and Indians whose behaviour was described as being unreasonable. One commentator using the pseudonym Robert Ingram, noted that what was being celebrated by some West Indians in an extravagant manner was India's triumph over the West indies (*Express,* April 18, 1976). The feeling on the part of some political commentators was that these incidents gave a clue to what would happen on election day.

Indian commentators denied that the behaviour of Indians was unreasonable. They saw it as a predictable response given the racial patterns of the society which defined Indians as second class. As one put it:

> To ask the Indians to ignore all of this and still be loyal of the country is to ask them to display a quality not possessed by humans at all. This society has alienated Indians. The very values that this society stands for are anathema to Indians. Things may have been different had the Indians and Africans come together at an earlier stage and the way of life of both races been allowed to develop to its fullest potential thereby forging a 'national identity'. But this development was stunted first by the British and now by those who took over from them.... Moreover, the current upsurge of 'blackness' and attempts to incorporate Indians in that concept can have only disastrous consequences. The first step is for non-Indians in this country to stop thinking of Indians as outsiders and interlopers. Secondly, the inequalities in all spheres of national life must be obliterated. It is significant to note that whereas some black radical groups are calling for African-Indian unity, they have neglected to articulate any cause that is peculiar to Indians. They cast their eyes as far as Rhodesia and South Africa and denounce vehemently the apartheid and oppression of their 'black brothers' there. But their eyes never fall on Caroni and they breathe not a word about the oppression of their 'Indian brothers' there. Basically, the situation in 1976 is the same as it was in 1956 as far as racial unity goes. What exists now is not racial unity but Indian acquiescence in Negro domination. Such a situation does not augur well for the future for there will come a time when the problem will not be able to fit anymore under the carpet. (*Guardian,* April 25, 1976)

Indians were particularly upset when Mr. James Bain, Chairman of the state-owned National Broadcasting Corporation openly warned the public against the danger of a conjuncture of Indian economic and political power. As Mr. Bain warned:

> The East Indians have increasingly acquired education and have been increasingly invading the fields of the Civil Service, the professions, and the Government. As their numbers must now reach parity with people of African descent, there is a real possibility that in the not too distant future they will get control of the Government. Should this time come when the East Indian section owns most of the property, business and wealth of the country as well as

> control of the Government, an imbalance could develop in our society that would cause undesirable stresses and strains that would not be good for the nation. It is an urgent necessity therefore, that all of us give serious thought to these matters, and like sensible people, make a conscious effort to avoid the undesirable consequences that could develop from such a possible situation. (*Guardian,* April 25, 1970)

Bain was giving voice to sentiments shared by many other non-Indian Trinidadians.

The ULF leadership was very concerned about its image in the country, and felt that the only way to escape the trap into which the history and the sociology of the community had for it was to enter into an alliance with the Democratic Action Congress. It was felt that the country was not yet ready to accept an Indian Prime Minister. It was this very consideration which had led Vernon Jamadar, the former leader of the DLP, to offer the leadership of the DLP first to Dr. James Millette and later to ANR Robinson and the ACDC. The problem was compounded for the ULF since it was tarred with the communist brush. It therefore needed an alliance with a party which would help it appeal to African and Indian middle class voters as well as the African working class whose "false consciousness" might have led them to continue supporting the PNM despite what they had gone through objectively since 1970.

Panday had for long been of the view that an alliance with ANR Robinson was necessary if a viable national opposition party were to be created. As he said in an interview in 1975:

> We have the sugar workers fully committed and stage one is over. Soon, if we are lucky, we will have cane-farmers in the bag plus a certain tenuous liaison with the oil and transport workers. Which could complete stage-two, make us more than a worker party, give us most of the sugar belt and a promising image of a more fully working-class base by delivering some of these stubborn oil workers! But that is a big if ... so we don't dare at this stage to anticipate stage-three; we dare not broach the question of founding

> a national opposition party. If Jamadar and Lequay were suddenly to patch up their quarrel, then we could end up out in the cold and be left just like George, a trades-union leadership, incapable of political support. Think what a laugh Williams and Errol Mahabir would have on poor Basdeo Panday. No boy, I must keep my options open.... What we can do is open a little window on the possibility of a party by tying down ANR Robinson so that the respectable, well-to-do elements may draw just a little closer and abandon forever any thought of meddling with Jamadar or Lequay. Yes, we must bring Robbie into the game....

Other anti-PNM forces in the country were also anxious for some form of unity between the opposition groups. It was felt that in the absence of such unity, the PNM would win by default. Indeed the PNM itself was aware of its own weakness. As one PNM Minister, Mr. Hector McLean told a Party group, "the only thing that was saving the PNM was the inefficiency, bankruptcy and foolishness of the opposition. Do not believe that we have this big, well-run organization. It is not that. The fact is the other side is too stupid. We are winning by default. it's like a game when the other side ain't turn up" (*Trinidad Guardian,* August 18, 1975). The view of Stephen Maharaj was typical of this persistent belief that a united opposition could beat the PNM. To quote Maharaj:

> The whole electorate is confused about whom to support in this election. The reason for this is because we have a group of selfish leaders, chiefly in the camp of the opposition who refuse to come together and fight the PNM on a common front.... The PNM is basically weak throughout the country and is holding on to power only through the lack of a real challenge from the coalition of opposition forces. Any unified front of two or more opposition parties could beat the PNM this time around. An alliance of Panday's United Labour Front and another party could do it. The ULF and the Democratic Action Congress, or the ULF and the Democratic Labour Party, could beat the PNM. The public is thirsting for some sort of alliance; you hear it expressed at every street corner and all over the place. It seems to me the majority of Trinidadians would certainly like to see a change of government and even if the opposition does not

> get together officially, it is possible that the opposition parties could get enough seats to be able to form some sort of coalition government. (*Express,* May 5, 1976)

The ULF coalition was however split on the matter of unity with the DAC. Persons like Jack Kelshall, George Weekes and Basdeo Panday supported the attempt at forming an alliance. Kelshall noted that it was true that the ULF was more progressive than the DAC, but the first objective should be to remove the PNM. "We should not under-estimate the enemy or over-estimate our strength" (*Express,* March 29, 1976). Most of the radical elements in the party, groups which had in fact only reluctantly agreed to give the electoral route to power a try, however expressed horror at the idea of an alliance with a party which was seen as being basically a capitalist party.

The DAC was also divided on the merger issue. The pro-capitalist wing of the party did not take kindly to the proposed linkage with a "socialist" party, and that wing controlled a great deal of the party's funds. Many of the Indian professionals in the party were also opposed because they had long been nursing seats which the ULF considered to be "naturally" theirs. The DAC Indians had in fact been named to some of these seats since 1973, and were naturally reluctant to give way. Some members of the party also feared that an alliance with an "Indian" party would alienate the black constituency on which the party was counting to give it control of Whitehall. Yet others felt the ULF should not enter politics but should instead function as the industrial arm of the DAC.

The proposed merger never did materialize since both parties believed they were stronger than they really were. The ULF claimed that while it wanted the alliance, the DAC leadership did not. "There were too many capitalists in the DAC" asserted Mr. Panday (*Express,* July 13, 1976). Panday also accused the DAC of being "in collusion with the PNM by deliberately taking the ULF for a ride and then dropping us as they did Vernon Jamadar and the members of the DLP" (ibid.). The allegation was that the

DAC wished to maintain the "traditional" pattern of racial voting in the country. It was not a credible allegation, and indicated the suspiciousness and bitterness which the collapse of the merger had left in its wake.

The evidence suggests that the DAC was principally responsible for the collapse of the merger. For one thing, the DAC had pre-empted the merger arrangements by announcing the names of twenty-four candidates to seats before any firm agreements had been made with the ULF. The DAC claimed that it had to get ready for the elections, and that it could not wait, but they were clearly trying to pre-empt the ULF. In the "final" offer which was made to the ULF in July 1976, the DAC agreed to stand down only in 10 of the 36 constituencies, four of which were northern constituencies in which Africans and mixed persons held the balance of power: Barataria, St. Anns, Port of Spain East and Port of Spain North. The ULF quite rightly considered this to be an "insulting and inequitable proposal."

It was clear that one of the key issues which inhibited agreement was that both parties wanted to establish hegemony over the other, so that in the event of victory, they would dominate the Government. The DAC in fact openly maintained that it was the "premier organization" in that it was the older of the two parties and the one which had spearheaded the no-vote campaign of 1971 and the struggle against PNM repression between 1971 and 1976. To quote the DAC:

> The DAC remains hopeful that the ULF will recognize the historic continuing and national responsibility of the DAC to be in a state of complete readiness for General Elections, bearing in mind that the DAC spearheaded the historic and victorious no vote campaign of 1971, has never since recognized the 28 per cent Parliament, has been in the forefront of the struggle for fundamental human rights freedoms and against repressive laws, has effectively agitated all the major domestic and international issues over the past six years, and has been unswerving in its demand for electoral reform and immediate General Elections (The

ULF-DAC Alliance: The Truth About Why The Talks Failed, n.d.:5).

The ULF, for its part, quite rightly insisted that the situation was a dynamic one, and that things had changed in its favour in the last few months. The ULF wished to contest 16 of the 18 seats which it felt sure of winning. The DAC insisted that it would concede only 10, and on this basis the talks collapsed. It is however a moot point as to whether a merger would have in fact made any difference in more than two or three constituencies such as Fyzabad, Princes Town or Nariva. The ULF, however, felt that unity would have resulted in victory. It may well be that the DAC was never in fact interested in a merger at all, but simply went through the exercise in order to catch the ULF in a state of electoral unpreparedness.

The campaign itself was a lively one, particularly in the two weeks preceding the poll when the square and street corners which had previously stood virtually empty while political speakers addressed pitiably small audiences, gradually began to come alive. As election fever gripped the nation, people shifted from one public meeting to another; one was often reminded of a week before carnival when crowds moved from one pan yard or "mas camp" to another to see what the various bands were bringing out. As the crowds began to swell and people at last began to pay attention to what the parties were saying, the confidence of the leaders and the heartiness of their rhetoric grew. Every party boasted that its crowd was bigger and more committed than the other. Buoyed by the tremendous response he was receiving up and down the country, Mr. Panday boasted that he would cremate his opponent, Mr. Simbhoonath Capildeo, on the banks of the Caroni. Dr. Williams, for his part, bragged about his past achievements, and invited those who did not like his party's policy to "emigrate to the Bronx and clean toilets!"

Unlike previous elections, little violence was in evidence, except perhaps in language. Numerous candidates swore at their rivals, sometimes leaving expletives undeleted to the delight of the crowds. Whatever heckling there was, was good natured and polite. Fanaticism, particularly racial and religious fanaticism, was largely absent, though both were used as weapons against the ULF.

The star of the campaign was undoubtedly Basdeo Panday, who appeared to many as a new charismatic leader. Night after night, he harangued his audience with the gospel of working class unity. "Brothers and Sisters," audiences were told, "the issue is not race but class." All the big Indian capitalists in the country were vilified, as were the Syrians, the Europeans, the multi-nationals and their defenders in the PNM and the various DLPs . Panday's speeches were brilliant and brought alive the struggle of the African slave and Indian indentured labourer over the centuries with such clarity and pathos that few remained unmoved.

The PNM's campaign was a strange one. The Prime Minister spent a great deal of time criticizing his ministers, and admitted that his government had made many critical errors. When comments were made about the unorthodox nature of his campaign, Williams replied that he saw nothing wrong with the Prime Minister saying that he was not satisfied with the way in which certain departments were run. "If I had said that I was satisfied, my throat would have been cut. I said I wasn't satisfied, and I'm working to improve it." Williams' strategy was to suggest that the inefficiency was not of his own making, but that if given a new mandate, he would consolidate such gains as had been made over the last twenty years while moving to eliminate those responsible for the poor performance of the Government. To make his point, Williams in fact refused to campaign for five ministers whom the party had re-nominated, and it was left to the party groups and the party bureaucracy to mobilize support behind them. On more than one occasion, Williams hinted that he would in future rely heavily on nominated members from the Senate to staff his Cabinet.

The election raised some very serious issues, the most significant being the question of who should own the means of production and distribution. On this issue, it was virtually the ULF against the rest. The ULF's position was clear and unequivocal. "Those who labour must hold the reins." The party preached the gospel of nationalism up and down the countryside, telling workers that most of their problems would be solved if the commanding heights of the economy were seized by the state. The problem of unemployment would also be solved in five years. The PNM was depicted as the party which defended the capitalists by introducing harsh and repressive legislation to prevent the workers from getting their just deserts from the capitalists, both local and foreign.

The PNM and the two DLPs for their part, waged a deadly counter offensive in the countryside, both open and surreptitiously, against what the PNM Manifesto described as the "ideological presumptions of our age." The DLP and the PNM claimed that a vote for the ULF meant a vote against religion, against God, against the private ownership of lands, houses, cars and everything else. The DLP in fact circulated a pamphlet which alleged that the ULF was atheist and communist. Heavy stress was laid on the issue of political freedoms by Dr. Williams who promised that the PNM under his leadership would never circumscribe anyone's right to worship freely or dissent. Williams conveniently forgot the post 1965 package of repressive laws which had among other things restricted the right to strike, assemble, to read literature of one's choice and to march and demonstrate for political purposes. On the question of nationalizing industry, Williams argued that Trinidad's population of 1 million was much too small a resource base from which to draw all the expertise which the country needed. Partnership with multinationals was the only meaningful alternative.

Tapia, one of the other two serious parties in the campaign, also joined the issue of foreign domination of the economy. Unlike ULF, Tapia stressed localization rather than nationalization, arguing that localization was for the population as distinct from the Government. Tapia's view was that nationalization was no longer a radical solution. Socialism was described as a "lifeless doctrine which did not require the individual to think or discriminate." The crowds which followed Tapia in the last weeks of the campaign grew larger and larger, and the party was optimistic that it would win a few seats. The same was true of the DAC, which, however, appeared as if it had peaked much too early.

Results

The election results came as a shock to most people who had expected a keener contest. The only thing which was not very surprising was the fact that the poll was a low one. Only 55.83 per cent of the 565,646 electors turned out to vote compared to 88.11 per cent in 1961 and 65.79 per cent in 1966, the last seriously contested national election. While it was generally expected that the PNM would triumph, few expected it to win so unequivocally. Few persons expected that the leaders of the two DLPs would lose their deposits or that Tapia and the DAC would do so poorly. Tapia, which had declared that it was "the country's last hope," was only able to attract 12,021 of the total of 315,809 votes cast, or 3.81 per cent. The party did not win a single seat and all but one of its 29 candidates lost their deposits, after failing to poll one-eighth of the total votes cast. Only five Tapia candidates obtained more than 10 per cent of the votes cast in their constituencies. One was Lloyd Best who lost both to the PNM and ULF candidates.

The defeat of Best in particular came as a surprise to many who felt that Tapia would at least have won in the constituency which had hosted the party since its founding. One of Tapia's weaknesses was its inability to reach the rural or even the urban masses. It was seen as a reformist party with a heavy intellectual and middle class bias, and as such never got off the ground. The party however drew strong support from the younger white creole community, from civil servants and the intelligentsia, but its support was too thinly spread to have any electoral impact.

Tapia's problem was in part due to the fact that it was not able to get its message across to the man on the street who in a sense refused to listen. Tapia's image as a party of impractical people functioned as a sort of screen between the masses and the party's communicators, particularly Best, who, try as he might, always managed to hover over the heads of his listeners. The party also suffered the fate of most "third force" movements. It got caught between the two great racial power blocs in the society, which, given all the uncertainties prevailing, relied on the primordial link of race to help it decide what to do in the voting booth.

The other party whose performance was puzzling was the DAC which won the two Tobago seats and the support of only 8.1 per cent of those who voted. The DAC lost every seat in Trinidad with only seven candidates saving their deposits. Apart from Tobago, the party performed creditably in only four constituencies — Nariva, Toco-Manzanilla, Arima and Fyzabad where it obtained between 15 and 17 per cent of the votes cast. Constituencies in which the party expected to do well such as Siparia were lost to the ULF. Like Tapia, the DAC also got caught between the racial power blocs. Much of DAC's support among Indians melted away as the ULF came on stream. It also failed to break the PNM's stronghold on the black vote, except in Tobago where race was not a major issue.

In gaining 10 seats and 26.85 per cent of the popular vote, the ULF did better than many expected, but not as well as it had hoped. The party élite in fact felt that it would have won 19 seats, enough to form a government. Some of its candidates wagered heavily on a successful outcome. The party won all the seats which the DLP had formerly controlled except Pointe-a-Pierre. The party had been a victim of a gerrymandering operation which had removed a number of polling stations in which Indians were predominant from that constituency to Couva South, while others from Tabaquite and Naparima North, which had black majorities, were included. The same type of exercise was carried out in Fyzabad which the PNM had narrowly won in 1966 but feared they might lose. Pro-PNM polling stations were taken from Siparia which the party conceded to the opposition and relocated in

Fyzabad which it felt it could carry. As it turned out, even the combined votes of the DAC and the ULF candidates were smaller than that of the PNM candidate, 4,656 to 4,877.

The ULF victories in the "Hindu Heartland" were impressive and came as no surprise. Only in Princes Town did the party win by a narrow margin — 290 votes. This was a seat which the PNM had counted on winning. The ULF ascribed its overall defeat in the election to irregularities. It claimed that polling was deliberately slowed down in areas where the party was expected to do well. Mr. Raffique Shah said that at least 1,000 of his supporters were turned back at the polls because of irregularities on the revised list. The irregularities were attributed either to "total inefficiency on the part of the officers or a well conceived plot to frustrate voters." Shah however said he was not making apologies for the performance of the ULF (*Express,* September 15, 1976).

It was also alleged that many prospective PNM voters whose names were not listed were permitted to vote. Both allegations were correct. Although it was not possible to disenfranchise "ULF" voters in ethnically mixed areas without at the same time also disenfranchising "PNM" voters, it does appear that there was greater administrative chaos in certain strong ULF constituencies. It is difficult to determine whether this was deliberate or whether it was due to the fact that the irregularities were part of a very sophisticated strategy to deprive the ULF of seats, particularly in St. Patrick. Panday felt that had there not been what he called "massive electoral fraud" the ULF would have won the election. He said:

> I believe that the government deliberately chose officers to man the polling stations who were PNM agents and deliberately slowed down the voting, and who permitted different procedures to apply to different people, depending upon their political views. I do think it was a conspiracy and a massive fraud. (*Express,* September 21, 1976)

The ULF called for the appointment of a Commission of Inquiry to probe the irregularities, but there was no official response. There is no disputing the fact that there was a great deal of inefficiency on the part of officials and that there were numerous irregularities, including "polling day registration." But one doubts whether these were on a scale which would have affected the overall results in terms of seats, though percentages might have been different.

The PNM expected to win, but given the widespread disenchantment with its performance and the sentiment for change, the party was surprised that it obtained as many as 24 seats and as much as 53.57 per cent of the popular votes. The margin of victory was expected to be narrower, particularly in those constituencies where the Prime Minister refused to campaign for those whom he deemed to be "millstones." It is clear however that pro-PNM voters came out in support of these five candidates knowing that the vote was effectively a vote for Dr. Williams and the PNM. The PNM bureaucracy claims that the five candidates won in spite of Dr. Williams. The Party machine in fact did an impressive job of getting voters to the polls, not only in the five constituencies, but in all, except perhaps Tobago.

Two factors seemed to have led to the victory scored by the PNM. One was the fragmentation of the opposition. Even though time-for-a-change sentiment was strong, there were no alternatives which were considered viable or legitimate enough to provide a vehicle for change. People looked at the PNM devil they knew and at the alternatives they were presented with and opted to remain loyal to the government, or rather to Dr. Williams, who miraculously managed to convince a large part of the electorate that he was less politically bankrupt than those who were seeking to inherit the mandate of heaven.

The other factor which made the resolution of cross pressure in favour of the PNM easier was the question of race. In the last two weeks before the election, the ULF, which had been building up momentum in Central and South Trinidad, made a number of successful forays into the North along the East-West Corridor. Large numbers of people came to these meetings out of curiosity. Many however came from Central Trinidad and the garden areas of the North to cheer and support Messrs. Panday and Shah, who though they preached the gospel of working class unity, were seen as communal heroes. If professional Indians were cross pressured, the same was not true of working class Indians for whom both the race and the message of the leaders were satisfactory. The workers understood better than the media that communism and atheism were bogeymen which were being projected to frighten them.

The very factors which made the ULF acceptable to Indians raised questions in the minds of non-Indians. The ULF's decision to make a last-minute drive into the North in general and Port of Spain in particular, in a display of strength, was counter-productive, as some ULF members had feared. It gave rise to massive concern on the part of the African and mixed population as to what a ULF victory could mean in terms of race as well as ideology. The election-eve ULF motorcades (complete with tassa drumming) and the various candlelight processions which had been held earlier displayed in a manner which had not been fully perceived before what the racial basis of the ULF was. There were a number of ugly incidents which frightened non-Indians. It was as if Atilla had appeared at the gates of Rome. The subtle warnings of PNM spokesmen about what would happen if the "PNM" (read African) vote were split suddenly began to take on meaning, and many who had earlier been disposed to flirt with an alternative, went into the voting booth and "dropped their X on the balisier."

In his assessment of the election, Lloyd Best assigned great weight to the race factor as an explanation of what happened. To quote Best:

> On election day, and certainly a few days before election day, there was a polarization in the country in which people settled for the old arrangements and all the figures make

> this very clear, whether you take the data by polling divisions within constituencies like my own where the Indian areas voted for ULF and the African areas voted for the PNM. This happened everywhere in the country and the pattern is very clear. The ULF won the traditional DLP seats and the PNM won the traditional PNM seats with some slight changes. And, of course, you have important cases like Point Fortin where a man like Allan Alexander, a former oil worker, a national figure, a man born in Point, a considerable man, but he was in the wrong party in the public mind and was rejected. This happened not because they were rejecting Alexander but oil workers in Point are not going to vote for Panday. (*Sunday Guardian,* September 19, 1976)

Best argued that race was the overriding principle of selection and as such led many to consider parties like Tapia and DAC as non-starters. The PNM and the ULF were seen as torch bearers of African and Indian sentiment respectively. In Tobago, however, race was not a variable, and Tobagonians were therefore able to look the issues square in the face. "To be a Tobagonian is to be a different race for either African or Indian, and that is why DAC got their seats in Tobago."

That race played such a crucial role in the election was seen to be due to the identity crisis which the electorate faced. The fact that there was so much charlatanry and confusion in terms of parties and issues led voters to fall back on what was certain - their racial identification. Best also blamed the media for the outcome in that they did little to help people make sense of what they saw or heard. The media starved the electorate of information up until the last minute and then deluged it with material which it was not able assimilate. "You got a medical problem which is that if you give people a small dose it cures them and if you give them overdose it kills them, and that is exactly what happened" (ibid.).

On the specific issue of the motorcade and its impact on voter behaviour, Best had the following to say:

> The motorcade was the immediate development that triggered the polarization. ... On Saturday morning when the ULF motorcade came through the East West Corridor, there were any number of confrontation situations between Indians and Africans. Unfortunately, the African population in the North resent the intrusion of all these people from Central and South Trinidad. You could see the passion in the eye, you could hear the exchange of expletive and unseemly comment. You could feel the tension thicken. The sun was hot, the traffic was tangled up, conditions were ideal for fanning the flames of hate, especially in such constituencies as Tunapuna and Arouca and St. Augustine, where East and West clash most dramatically, at the frontier between the sugar belt and the urban industrialized north. You could imagine how tempers were high, and those who had to gain from it immediately exploited it. Loud speakers were all over Tunapuna pointing out the perils and risks of voting one way or the other. The battle lines were drawn between the ULF and the PNM, and Tapia was out of it altogether. We were ruled out and we didn't have a chance. Our votes did not reflect our political strength, and this is why everybody is surprised that Tapia did so badly. And even if people say that Tapia is idealistic and therefore could not succeed, how do you explain what happened to Robinson and DAC, a brand of politics everybody claims to understand? (ibid.)[1]

Best admitted that Tapia was seen as an African party competing with the PNM. Given the polarization, and the risks involved, Africans preferred to vote for the PNM. With respect to the ULF, Best shared the widespread view that it was a new version of the DLP:

> To say that the ULF is not an Indian party is to tell anancy-story. The party arose out of the circumstances of central Trinidad, with sugar workers as the motive energy and Panday as the main tongue of the people's disadvantage. With the disarray in the DLP and Indian frustrations, the ULF was bound to grow in the shadow of the traditional Opposition, it was bound to be the Indian party in the eyes of everyone. It was bound to be seen as the Indian party so long as the PNM maintained a stranglehold on the government machine and therefore enjoyed a rallying point

> of patronage for its traditional African support. In this sense, the ULF is a valid Indian party.

Best's analyses were correct. Race and class combined in a peculiar way to produce the result, though it would be difficult to determine which variable was most important for each voter.

Dr. Williams however denied that race had the impact which it is alleged to have had. To quote Williams:

> I was rather surprised ... when I read that if it hadn't been for — what was it? — a particular motorcade, where, whatever it was, wherever it came from or where the hell it went to, if it hadn't been for that motorcade I wouldn't be here tonight.... I don't know where the devil you'd be, following the motorcade, wherever the hell it went to. There is no accounting for the views of these commentators. So at once I went and looked at the election results, statistics, and so on; and then I looked at the obvious thing. We are the only party, my dear friends. I keep telling you this, you know this as well as I. Let's say it once more. Some day it's going to get into the hard heads of those commentators. PNM is the only party in the Caribbean which has uniformly controlled the capital city of the country. We controlled it in 1976 as we controlled it on other occasions in our 20-year record. (*Sunday Guardian,* September 26, 1976)

For Williams to admit the salience or race would be, of course, to belittle the PNM's performance. One agrees that given the PNM's control over patronage for the past 20 years, it had harnessed a large body of hangers-on and would have won, motorcade or no motorcade. One also agrees that the party would have carried the capital city and towns which have been the principal beneficiaries of PNM largesse in terms of amenities, special works employment, and other types of social outputs. What the commentators (this author among them) were trying to explain is just why Tapia and DAC did so poorly. While it is clear that neither would have won any seats, their percentage of the popular vote might well have been higher in the absence of the polarization which took place.

In the case of the ULF's performance in the North, one must also recognize the organizational dimension of their defeat. Whereas the PNM was familiar with the campaign trail and with the imperatives of electioneering, the ULF candidates were not. Many were not familiar with their constituencies, had little by way of loud speaking equipment, transport or ready made cadres who knew what to do on election day. This was a general problem, but it was particularly true in the North where the trade union base, which sustained the party in Central and South Trinidad, was absent.

It is true that the ULF fired the imagination of many blacks, especially the younger ones, who worked hard for the party which they saw as being the only meaningful ideological alternative to the PNM. It is also true that many Indians, particularly in the urban areas and market centres voted PNM for ideological reasons. It is however difficult to determine whether Africans who voted for the PNM did so because they thought it was the party which appeared to be best equipped to protect or advance their interests, both material and spiritual, or whether racial considerations were more significant. The same applies to the ULF. Did those Indians who voted for the ULF do so mainly because Panday and Shah "put food in their bellies and money in their pockets," or did they vote the way they did because they saw the ULF as being an Indian party, and Panday as the logical successor to Bhadase Maraj and Dr. Rudranath Capildeo? In the case of the ULF, the materialist motive and the ethnic identification were so closely intertwined that it is difficult for anyone to say for certain what was uppermost in the mind of the Indian voter, especially when one takes into account the fact that he had alternatives in the WINP, SDLP, UFP and the DLP whose campaign laid heavy stress on race and religion.

The same holds with respect to the PNM voter whom we might divide into three types. The first were those whom we might describe as the hard core for whom PNM is a way of life rather than an electoral alternative. Then there were the potential deviants or floaters who eventually rejected Tapia, DAC and the ULF and went back to the PNM fold. There were also those who were voting PNM for the first time. With respect to the first group, it is clear that most see PNM as the party which represents Africans. While there are quite a few Indians who consider themselves to be PNM hardcore, the PNM core consists mainly of people of African descent who support the PNM whether they benefit materially from it or not, and regardless of the quality or ethnicity of the candidate whom the party puts up to carry its standard. Clearly, it did not require the visual threat presented by ULF motorcades throughout the country to get them to vote PNM, *though the motorcades appeared to have brought quite a few more to the polls.*

But what of the second and third groups? Were these people frightened by the ideological hue of the ULF, the racial composition of the motorcades and rallies or both? It is indeed very difficult to decide definitively, but it would appear that both factors terrified potential deviants and drove them back into the welcoming arms of the PNM. Many floaters who had intended to switch to Tapia or DAC or who were clearly confused and cross pressured in the weeks before endorsed the PNM as the best safeguard against the ULF. The dominant racial composition of the ULF meetings and motorcades, plus the ideological thrust of the party was a combination which many found completely unacceptable. Rather than "split" their vote by supporting DAC or Tapia, they voted PNM, albeit with heavy hearts. The ULF turned out to be the ace card in the PNM pack which allowed Dr. Williams to hang the jacks of Lloyd Best and ANR Robinson. Many who thought that it was time for a change or that twenty years were enough were clearly not anxious to have the kind of racial and ideological change which they assumed a ULF victory would represent. Many wanted a government which would be less corrupt and more efficient in its management of the country's affairs, but they simply were not willing to opt for the root-and-branch change which they associated with the ULF.

The ULF made a number of tactical mistakes which cost them support among certain groups which they felt was part of their "natural" constituency, i.e., the black urban working class.

The extremism of their rhetoric was clearly counter productive in that it allowed its opponents to tarnish it with the communist bogey and to suggest that a ULF victory would lead to the transformation of Trinidad along Cuban lines. Williams himself used the Cuban bogey quite devastatingly. One is reminded of Fidel Castro's remark when asked why he adopted a reformist stance while in the Sierra Maestra mountains and then changed so radically within months after winning power. To quote Castro:

> If we had stopped at the Pico Turquino when there were few of us and said 'We are Marxist Leninists, possibly we would not have been able to get down to the plain. Thus we called it something else, we did not broach this subject, we raised other questions that the people understood perfectly.'

The radicals of the ULF would no doubt dispute this. From their perspective it was regrettable that the ideological confrontation was not sharper, and they no doubt hoped to push the ULF further to the left into a collision with the PNM. But as the Communist parties of Italy, France and Portugal discovered, extremism does not always pay off in electoral politics.

The ULF also had other difficulties. Many of their youthful sympathizers (both African and Indian) were late converts to electoral politics and were therefore not registered to vote. The 18-year-old vote in fact seems to have been a negligible factor in the electoral outcome. The ULF also did not have the same type of advance information about final registration lists which the PNM was able to get from election officials. The crisis over the merger with the DAC also hurt the ULF which did not have sufficient time to get their message across to voters, especially in the North. Panday was of the view that these factors had greater explanatory power than the motorcade thesis which he believed did not explain very much. "The reason I say this is that where the ULF did not contest seats, the swing appeared to be similar. If the reaction was against the ULF, why should it have occurred where we did not contest at all" (*Express,* September 21, 1976).

The problem with this assertion is that it ignores the fact that the election was seen as a national election, and that there is no denying that many persons who had been ambivalent about the PNM or had not planned to vote at all concluded almost at the last minute that it was important to close ranks and stop the ULF. It may well be that if all those who turned out to the polls did in fact get an opportunity to cast their vote, the margins of the PNM victories would have been wider. Dr Williams was in fact right when he said that it was a pity that the PNM was not tested more in Port of Spain. "It would have been nice to see what would have happened if people could have had the opportunity to vote" (*Sunday Guardian,* September 26, 1976). The result would have indeed been more flattering to the PNM.

It is perhaps worth noting that spokesmen of both DLPs played down the race factor and chose to resort to euphemisms. Mr. Alloy Lequay saw the ULF victory as a triumph of emotionalism over logic. "There was a very emotional swing over to the ULF in the last few days. Nothing in terms of logic or reason could get over to the voters" (*Express,* September 21, 1976). SDLP leader Vernon Jamadar saw the results as "a fair reflection of the political mood of the country. Obviously the majority of the population voted for what they considered the stable, secure, middle-of-the-road programme of the PNM. Equally, the radical policies of the ULF fired the imagination of the sugar belt, and between these two completely swept aside the other political parties" (*Guardian,* September 15, 1976).

All that is indeed true, but what is not explained is just what the people understood perfectly lay at the basis of the emotionalism and just why the radical policies of the ULF failed to fire the African workers in the oil industry who had been highly politicized by the ULF for more than a year. No doubt it is such questions as these which led persons like Raffique Shah to say, with modesty, that the ULF succeeded only partially on the race issue. Others were however tempted to make more exaggerated claims. Panday, for example, argued that the victories of the two African candidates in the "largely Indian constituencies of

Oropouche and Caroni East showed that Indians were voting on ideological lines." This of course ignores the fact that the DLP had run Africans in 1961, and that two of them had been successful. The voters clearly understood that they were voting party rather than any individual.

Another attempt to explain away the racial factor came from UWI economist Winston Dookeran who argued that the elections had begun the breaking down of racial political loyalties. To quote Dookeran:

> In general, it would appear that the Indian 'working class' came out strongly in support of the ULF and since the group is numerically strong in the traditional DLP areas, it is natural that these areas would have gone to the ULF. It was a positive vote for working class politics and the dismal performance of the DLPs in these areas spells a beginning to the breakdown of racial politics. It is clear that the African working class did not come out in full support of the ULF; for if that were so, a constituency like Laventille would have gone to the ULF. (*Express,* September 21, 1976)

In his post-election speech, Mr. Panday claimed that if the DAC-ULF alliance had been formed, "the PNM would be in Opposition today." This is difficult to accept if the election figures are to be taken as a guide. In no constituency not won by the ULF did the combined vote of the ULF and the DAC exceed that of the PNM. Only in three cases, Nariva, where the PNM only gained 39.9 per cent of the votes, Fyzabad and Point-a-Pierre did the tallies approximate that of the PNM. It may well be that the alliance would have made a qualitative difference to the campaign which would have increased confidence in the opposition and neutralized the ethnic factor. The Alliance might well have fared better than the parties did separately, but there is also the possibility that the support which the Alliance might have attracted from one element was neutralized by the defection of those who felt threatened or offended by it. In any event, there is little to sustain the belief that the Alliance could have dislodged the PNM.

End Note

[1]The *Bomb* also agreed that the motorcade swung votes away from the smaller parties ("Why the Reds Failed," *Bomb,* September 17, 1976):

> It was the ULF which forced free-loving citizens of this country to band themselves under the PNM banner for another five years. There is absolutely no doubt that the entire political climate swung the PNM way in those tension-charged 48 hours before election time. Hundreds of people interviewed by the *Bomb* this week, said unashamedly that events during the past two weeks and on the Saturday of that rally, changed their minds considerably. Some who had intended to patronize parties like Lloyd Best's Tapia, ANR Robinson's DAC, and Simbhoonath Capildeo's DLP suddenly realized that their vote was a vital one. And it had to be used to ensure that the ULF did not win. The election tempo was that *the ULF must not win,* rather than *we want the PNM.* Basdeo Panday had played right into Eric Williams' hands.

Chapter 6

The Futility of Opposition Politics: The Disunited Labour Front

The performance of the Front at the polls was greeted with mixed reactions by Trinidadians. To those who believed in the two-party Westminster system, the emergence of the ULF as a parliamentary opposition was very welcome. The fact that the PNM had controlled thirty-four of the thirty-six seats during the 1971-1976 Parliament was generally regarded as being politically unhealthy, and it was hoped that the presence of an opposition would keep the ruling party on its toes and help improve the quality of government in the country. The hope and the assumption of this element was that the ULF would function as a traditional union-based labour party and behave as if it were potentially an alternative government within the context of the existing constitutional system.[1]

There were also those who regarded the emergence of the ULF as only the first stage in the development of a full-blooded Marxist-Leninist Party which would lead the island along the path of socialism. Those who were chagrined by the success of the Front were however concerned about this very possibility. The fear was that in time, Trinidad would follow Guyana and Jamaica along what they viewed as the "ruinous road to socialism."

On August 9, 1977, less than one year after the ULF MPs took their seats in Parliament, the Central Committee of the party voted by a margin of 16 to 1 (seven members were absent and one abstained) to remove Mr. Basdeo Panday from the Central Executive as well as from the position which he occupied as Leader of the Opposition in Parliament. Shortly after, six of the ten members of the parliamentary party advised the President of the Republic that they no longer had confidence in Panday, and that they wished to be led by Raffique Shah, the Party's chief parliamentary whip. The decision to remove Panday was a serious one for the members of the Central Committee to take since Panday was widely recognized as the Party's most popular figure and its principal vote getter. Although the Party had deliberately deferred the question of naming the Political Leader and had opted for the principle of collective leadership (in part to skirt the delicate question of race), Panday was widely regarded as the Party's Political Leader.

One of the ULF "Big Four," George Weekes, claimed that it was the media and not the people who canonized Panday and made him leader. Weekes in fact argued that this was done deliberately in order to project the ULF as an Indian party, a strategy which he claims cost the ULF victory in the 1976 elections. To quote Weekes:

> Had it not been for the manipulation of the press which purposely projected Mr. Panday as the Leader of the ULF when in fact we had agreed to collective leadership of the four Unions, I feel confident that we would have won the election against PNM. But because of this plan on the part of the media to project Mr. Panday as leader of the ULF and because of the suspicions with regard to his credibility, the association with the PNM through Errol Mahabir, we were not able to win the government. So that the support that we really enjoyed in the country was withheld because of the manipulation of the media. (*The Sun,* October 17, 1977)

This is an astonishing argument which has no foundation whatsoever, and one doubts that Weekes himself accepted it. But the fact that the statement was made indicated quite clearly that race was one of the central issues in the ULF crisis, a fact which the ULF leadership often denied. There was always an element within the ULF which did not want Panday to be leader for reasons having to do with their calculations as to whether Trinidad was ready for an Indian Prime Minister or not. This point of view was articulated at meetings of the Central Committee before and after the election. During the election campaign, an effort had in fact been made to present Allan Alexander, an Afro-Trinidadian Attorney at Law, as the Party's public standard bearer. Weekes accused the media of sabotaging this effort, but the fact of the matter is that Alexander had no popular following, and came over like a damp squid. Whereas Panday was the hero *extraordinaire* of the Indian sugar workers and peasants, Alexander had no support either among the middle class or the working class, the other constituency to which the ULF appealed.

Weekes also blamed Panday for the fact that the ULF did poorly outside the sugar belt. To quote Weekes:

> When we attempted to organize the party outside of what is called the base area, the sugar area, there were tremendous battles in the Central Committee to prevent this from becoming a reality, because Mr. Panday saw that should we organize the East/West corridor or should we go into areas outside of his own, then his position would not be as secure. He prefers to be a leader of a small area in what he calls his base, rather than organizing a national party. (ibid.)

It is an accusation which is not supported by the available evidence. The ULF was weak outside of the sugar belt for reasons which had little to do with Panday's equivocation and more to do with the fact that the party had no election machinery in the North or supporters who had a vote which they were prepared to go out and cast. The party's urban support came mainly from young lumpen elements who were not registered. Older blacks and the middle class either supported the PNM or abstained. Race was a crucial variable which affected their behaviour as was the ULF's ideological posture. The ULF also had no union base in the North comparable to that which they had in Central and South Trinidad.

The public reacted to the ULF split with a mixture of glee, frustration and cynicism. Those who feared the advance of socialism were overjoyed about the fact that the ULF had come to early grief. Those who saw the ULF as the best hope which the country had to build a multiracial working coalition threw up their hands in despair. Cynics pointed to the fact that Trinidad opposition parties always displayed a tendency towards fragmentation, and argued that what had happened was hardly surprising.

Some sections of the left regarded the crisis in the ULF as a good thing. Panday himself declared that what happened to the Party was "a blessing in disguise," and saw it as an opportunity not to be missed "to purge our Party of all traitors." Panday appeared to be relieved that he had gotten rid of those whom he claims "rode his back to get into Parliament" and whom he now described as "a bunch of communists." To him, the radical elements who had forced him out were nothing but power hungry extremists who had "hijacked the ULF from the people." Panday also charged, with good reason, that there was an element of racism in the behaviour of the militants whom he said believed that as an Indian, he could not appeal to the young black urban elements. Panday was clearly anticipating the development which took place, and had entertained the idea of forcing some of his enemies to resign from the Central Committee. He had also given thought to relieving Lennox Pierre, Allan Alexander and Joseph Young, three of the ULF six nominees to the Senate, from their positions, but had hesitated for fear that the decision would be regarded as an anti-African move. It is worth noting that before he was actually removed as leader of the Parliamentary Opposition, Panday did in fact ask the President to recall these very persons whom he had reason to believe were linking themselves with the extremist elements on the Committee.

Those who engineered the crisis claimed that the split represented a triumph of the politics of principle. They held that "the party was bigger than any of its leaders or members" and accused Panday of seeking to run the Party as a "one-man show." He was also said to be elevating the race issue above that of class and in general of violating the principles which should inform a serious working class party. As Weekes explained:

> The ULF is threatened by the decision, the courageous decision it took, a decision of principle recognizing the consequences that will flow from that decision. We feel that it is better to have a truly organized party of the working class in small numbers than to have a mass party that resembles a whale which cannot move with the type of mobility that is necessary.... We are planning for years to come and for the first time since the days of Uriah Butler there is a party of the working class in particular and the people in general. This will take time to organize, but in taking time we are certain we will have the best party, superior to that of any existing party. We are confident of that. (ibid.)[2]

The radical wing of the party was however not united on the question of what should be done to deal with the divisions in the Party. Two radical members of the Party who were out of the island when the decision was taken to remove Panday from the post of Parliamentary leader declined to support the decision taken by their colleagues and in fact resigned from the Committee. One of them, Dr. James Millette, who was General Secretary of the Party, complained that "the decision taken by men who were unwilling to address themselves to real problems, namely, the phenomenon of ultra-leftism in the Party and the existence of a Party within the Party, determined at all times to oppose itself to legitimate decisions of the party." Millette believed that the ultra-leftists had "inflicted a grievous wound on the party from which it may never recover." As such, he felt it necessary to "put as much political distance between himself and those who refused to face reality and who preferred to destroy the party rather than to deal with the troublemakers who have been attacking it." Millette's criticisms, and those of Richard Jacobs, the Secretary of the Organization Committee of the Party, were confusing to many people who assumed that they would have supported the radical faction of the ULF rather than the more ideological moderate Panday. Both had been close associates of Shah during his struggle to organize the canefarmers.

In expelling Mr. Panday, the members of the Central Committee accused him of

> Making statements contradicting and violating the Party's principled position on "Race"; Divergence from the Party's principled position of collective leadership... relating to the selection of candidates and appointment of aldermen to local government bodies, and the Party's agreed position on the Tobago issue; Tarnishing of the Party's image and serious embarrassment to the Party by his behaviour; Subverting the party with a view to entrenching himself as the absolute leader; Fomenting problems in the Party. (*Guardian,* August 11, 1977)

The spokesman of the Central Committee, Senator George Sammy, explained that the Committee had for long been exercised by the question of party discipline, the question of the party line, and in particular the question of the powers of leaders, especially if it related to the question of the relationships between the leadership in Parliament and the Central Committee. The Central Committee argued that public support for the Party was not support for any personality, but for the Party and its principles i.e., anti-imperialism, working class unity, multiracialism and "the construction of a New Democracy in which those who labour held the reins." The Committee felt that there had been a manifest divergence on the part of Panday from those fundamental positions.

The crisis in the ULF came to a head as it prepared to take part in the local government elections of April 1977. The candidates whom Panday backed led some of his colleagues to feel that he was scheming to take the party in a communal direction. It was also believed that Panday was planning to dispense with the left whom he now considered a liability and a constraint on his maneuverability. Senator Sammy complained that

> As one of the persons who had major responsibility for the selection of (Local Government) candidates, Comrade Panday in several instances passed over sugar worker activists in preference for people who had no history of working class commitment and struggle and even for people

> who had been antagonistic towards the ULF. With respect to the selection of Aldermen, Comrade Panday attempted to pass over tried and tested party supporters and working class activists in preference for known opportunists. In so far as there has been any conflict over 'leadership' in the Party, the question has not been who should be leader as it has been misrepresented, but rather the powers of the leaders, and in particular the powers of Comrade Panday as leader of the ULF opposition in the House of Representatives. The divergences on the part of Comrade Panday from the Party's principled position of collective leadership have been legion. (*Guardian,* August 11, 1977)

Mr. Panday was also accused of trying to dominate the Party, of ignoring the decision of the Central Committee as to what he should do or say in Parliament, of excessive drinking and "womanizing" in public and in general of "behaviour unbecoming that of a leader of the Party." The Central Committee said that it had tried to get Mr. Panday to come and discuss the issues "for the last six months," but he had consistently refused. "Fed up" and disgusted with Panday's charismatic pretensions, the Central Committee deposed him. They felt he had given them no choice.

There was a deep split within the Central Committee as to what was the proper step to take to resolve the crisis. Older members felt that it would be disastrous to expel Panday, and argued that everything should be done to coax him into behaving responsibly. The young radicals felt otherwise. By refusing to attend, probably on the assumption that he could not be expelled, Panday undermined the arguments of the moderates and left them with no choice. It also seems that Panday wished to provoke such an outcome in the belief that this would give him the freedom and the flexibility which he needed to operate politically. This view was also held by Dr. Ramesh Deosaran, who observed that "Panday, sensing his popular support, had laid out a political bait. They took the bait. They expelled. And now he had a cause that detracts from the substance of the specific charges against him" (*Express,* August 21, 1977).

According to Deosaran, Panday was at first reluctant to force a break with his colleagues:

> Panday himself feels the burden of millstones, be they ideologues or parasites, but anticipates that his visions of consolidating the forces against the PNM could well be lost in this purge. Perhaps paralysed by ambivalence, he waits, hoping for the compromise before the convention.... (ibid.)

Panday had given up any hope that such a compromise could be worked out and had decided to precipitate a break.

The extreme left of the ULF had apparently also come to the conclusion that Panday wanted them out of the Party so that he would act without the ideological restraints which association with them required. Panday was described as a revisionist, a racist, a capitalist, and an opportunist adventurer who was secretly in league with the PNM and the CIA for whom he was allegedly a "frontman." *Classline,* the organ of the Shah faction, claims that Panday was only the most recent of a long line of union and political leaders who had used rhetoric to bemuse and win over the working people, only to betray them to imperialism or divert them into areas that did not threaten its interests. His predecessors were Alfred Richards, Adrian Cola Rienzi, Rudranath Capildeo, Bhadase Sagan Maraj and Eric Williams. *Classline* argued that

> Panday's function was to once more destroy the unity of the working class, which day by day was growing stronger under the leadership of the ULF and which was posing a serious threat to the system of capitalism/imperialism. Panday is travelling the road of Bhadase Maraj who posed as the messiah of the oppressed Indian masses, but who was in fact himself one of their biggest and most vicious oppressors. What we must realize is that the opposition parties that we have had in the past were the other side of the coin to the PNM. They have kept the regime in power by collaborating with the PNM in pushing racial politics. Without Bhadase, Capildeo and Jamadar, Williams would not have survived. The fact that these parties are no different from the PNM came out clearly in the last general elections when the DLP's and the rest turned all their energies into

> attacking the ULF, because they recognized that working class politics was threatening to destroy race politics, and the destruction of race politics was the beginning of real unshakable unity of the working class which is the first step towards the destruction of Capitalism/Imperialism. The opposition parties and the PNM failed to destroy the ULF and the only recourse that the imperialists had was to turn to Panday to do their dirty work for them and to make a last desperate bid to destroy the unity of the working class (*Classline* 1 (2), October-November, 1977:5.).

Bukka Rennie of the New Beginning Movement argued much the same. In an extended analysis of a discussion paper entitled *Perspectives for a New Economic Order* which Panday had presented at a ULF ideological conclave at Mayaro in early 1977, Rennie criticized Panday's position on worker's control in Yugoslavia as "worker's capitalism" and Yugoslavian Socialism as nothing but the most modern form of state capitalism. According to Rennie, Panday had endorsed the Yugoslavia model and recommended it for Trinidad and Tobago. He also came out in support of a collaborationist strategy with the national bourgeoisie. Panday had argued that

> The ULF must seek a wide class alliance. It must woo and win the middle-class and the local bourgeoisie. Since, by definition, classes seek only their self interest, the programme of the ULF must be such as to allay the fears and (for the moment) satisfy the aspirations of these two classes. Any new economic order must cope with this problem. The flag around which we successfully mobilize these various classes is "economic nationalism" i.e. anti-nationalism.... The new economic order must cater for bourgeois greed and workers' protection against exploitation resulting from that greed. In the new economic order, the "commanding heights" of the economy will be state-controlled. Undertakings must contain institutions for meaningful workers' participation in the decision-making processes at every level. There are several areas of the economy that are presently in need of development. This will involve new business ventures and new investment e.g. agriculture and agro-industries. Where such ventures are being undertaken the enterprise will be owned on a tripartite

> basis: that is to say 1/3 share each by government, private capital and the workers in that undertaking. Control of the enterprise will be determined accordingly. (*New Beginning* October-November, 1977:2)

New Beginning Movement saw this as being nothing but a "souped up" version of the PNM, mixed economy ideology, and a logical extension of Panday's earlier proposal that the sugar industry should be owned by the workers and run by a board appointed by sugar workers. Panday was accused of confusing tactics with principles and goals. While electoral tactics may require a clouding of the position as to where the ULF stood, the party could not alter its commitment to the "establishment of the solid power of freely associated workers councils and assemblies." Panday was accused of calling on the ULF to compromise its working class nature, identity, and major principles for a supposed alliance with the local capitalist and middle class (ibid.). This constituted a betrayal of the guiding framework handed to the ULF leadership by the Conference of Shop Stewards and Branch Officers in 1975.

The New Beginning Movement theoretician agreed that alliances with "ascending middle classes" were worth considering at certain historical points when the national bourgeoisie was progressive and itself struggling for democratic rights. In the context of Trinidad and Tobago however, the bourgeoisie was in its declining phase, and was infringing on rights already won. The Industrial Relations Act, the Summary Offences Act, the Sedition Act, the ban on "subversive" literature, and other such repressive bits of legislation were examples of this tendency. There was therefore no benefit to be derived by any alliance with this class. The economic nationalism of the local capitalist class was not anti-imperialist, as Panday asserted, but another dimension of international capitalism. "The role of local capitalists and local middle classes are inseparable and indivisible with the role and tasks of imperialist expansion and generation. The one is an extension of the other, though this is not to say that there might not be non-antagonistic conflicts between them." Given this,

Rennie saw no fundamental difference between Panday or Tapia's Lloyd Best, both of whom were calling for a strategy of broad class collaboration. Panday did not even insist on pre-conditions, and as Rennie saw it, the only difference between Best and Panday was that one was calling from within the middle-class and the other Best, from without.

The New Beginning Movement saw Panday's tactics and his anxiety to wield absolute power in the ULF as part of a strategy which was designed to permit him to function in terms of the class with which he objectively identified. To do this he would of necessity be forced to rely on DLP elements and other traditional middle-class reformers who had been rejected by the ULF. Rennie also predicted that Panday would also in time find it necessary to work more closely with the PNM:

> Panday's historic role in this place and time, is to pin the working-class movement or sections of it solely and only to a nationalist perspective, to a nationalist framework, to a furtherance of the nationalist movement, ridding the working-class movement of its natural internationalist perspective and so pin the movement to the most modern development or manifestation of capital today i.e. state capitalism in which the nation state inter-meshes completely with nationalized capital as the supreme form. Today, what is progressive to the middle-class is backward to the working-class. Today, Panday's clique boasts of PNM support with pride and are even seeking ways and means of collaborating with Girwar, that notorious anti-working-class hero. We are pointing out all this not to simply vilify Panday, but to alert the minds of those on the other side of the split, the Central Committee, to begin a most critical examination of themselves. (ibid.)[3]

Panday rejected all the claims and allegations made by the radicals and those members of the Central Committee who voted to expel him. The latter were accused of not going through the proper procedures before expelling him. It was said that the proper body to deal with the issues was the disciplinary committee and not the Central Committee. Panday argued that removing a party leader was a very serious step, and as such a Party Congress was the only appropriate body to determine the issue. He blamed the radical left for the fact that no Congress had been held even though the Central Committee was mandated to call one before the end of 1976. The congress had in fact been postponed twice. Panday also reminded his former colleagues that the Central Committee had only provisional status and was therefore not legally empowered to do what it had done.

Panday was of the view that the crisis facing the ULF was in a sense inevitable given the fact that the Party had literally "exploded" on the political scene before it had had time to settle its course of action:

> The ULF was born out of industrial unrest which means that it comprised people of similar goals but with different methods of achieving these goals. It was inevitable that there would be purges as one side tried to have its way.

What had happened was that a group of "power seeking extremists" who had no popular standing had staged a pre-emptive coup out of panic and insecurity about their own continued status in the Party:

> No sooner was the Party born than there developed within the Central Committee a clique whose sole function appeared to be one of frustrating the Party and preventing its development. The Central Committee meet once and sometimes twice per week. Meetings would go on for some 6 to 7 hours until 2.00 a.m. The Committee could decide nothing as the entire meeting would be one of ideological argument and conflict.... For example, decisions on the organization of the Party could not be reached because of ideological conflict on the purpose and methods of organization. The clique argued that the Party should not rely on the electoral method of change but should organize to capture power by other unparliamentary methods. At this time I did not know of the existence of NAMOTI or the extent of its infiltration into the Central Committee. These ideological conflicts prevented not only organization of the party, but obstructed decisions to establish a Party

> newspaper, a Party headquarters with paid staff, and a clear party line and other matters of fundamental importance to the Party. I told the Central Committee in no uncertain terms that I was totally opposed to any ideology of extremism. I was opposed to the idea of violence as a means of capturing political power in the multi-racial context of Trinidad and Tobago. I threatened to fight this madness at the Party Congress and attempted to secure an undertaking that I will be permitted to put forward my views at the Congress if those views conflicted with those of the Central Committee. I was not prepared to permit them to use me as an instrument to ride the backs of our people into the sunset of destruction. For this I was called dictatorial and accused of not subjecting myself to the will of the Central Committee. (*Guardian,* August 15, 1977)

James Millette also agreed with Panday that the militants lacked a sense of what was historically possible:

> Men make history, but the history that men make must be judged by reference to the objective factors existing at the material time, and the response that men make in the face of those factors. (ibid.)

The need at the present time, in Millette's view, was to "consolidate" the movement nationally, and only thereafter to seek to proceed on what they would perhaps call the "theoretically correct line." The fear of Millette and others was that by seeking to pursue a correct line, the "upper left" had alienated the ULF from its mass base, confused the masses, reduced the creditability of the ULF and ensured the continued triumph of the PNM and imperialism.

Panday argued that Messrs. Shah, Weekes and the others had been naively seduced by the NAMOTI extremists, and warned that the former would in turn "be dealt with" by them when they believed that the time was opportune. The union boss defended his political strategy and claimed that the "armchair ideologists" who had dislodged him had no conception of how "our people feel and think":

> They mislead themselves into believing that the working-class care what is happening in China, Cuba and the Soviet Union or that our people are ready to accept, lock, stock and barrel these foreign systems. I am of the view that the consciousness of our people must be lifted to the point where they and they alone decide the method of ending exploitation. (*Express,* August 11, 1977)

Panday's strategy in the crisis was to refer constantly to the importance of the people and the rank and file, and to suggest that his rivals were acting irresponsibly and that they represented no one but themselves. Two versions of populism were vying for predominance.. The one emphasized what ought to be done for the people, the other limiting itself to the existing state of the people's consciousness. Panday's argument was that the people should settle the leadership issue. "The Party had been hijacked by NAMOTI. The struggle must now be for the rank and file to regain control and to expel the hijackers."

Although he regarded his removal from the leadership as being "definitely unconstitutional," Panday let it be known that he did not intend taking the matter to court. "No judge is going to determine leadership among the people. Only the people can decide this, and that is where I am going to take the matter" (*Express,* August 14, 1977). Panday in fact carried his populist strategy further by promising to resign his seat and face a by-election, and invited Shah and the others to do the same. Such by-elections would clear the air in the most democratic way.

In his early statements following the crisis, Panday sought to distinguish between Weekes and the other members of the Shah "clique." When he asked the President to remove the senators whom he had appointed, Panday had specifically excluded George Weekes, whom he professed to have a great deal of "love, respect and affection for." Weekes' continued presence was said to be important for Afro-Indian unity. Unlike the others who were described variously as traitors who had ridden his back into Parliament as "nimakarams" i.e., "ingrates" — who had eaten from his "bowl and had turned around and bored a hole in the receptacle," Weekes was seen as "someone who had been misled."[4]

Egged on by his supporters who had never really been happy with his senatorial appointments, Panday admitted that he had erred in "pushing political nonentities such as Weekes, Lennox Pierre and Allan Alexander down their throats" (*Guardian,* August 20, 1977). He however indicated that he did not regret his action since it had all been done in the interest of Afro-Indian unity. "If I had to do it all over again, I would do it because I cherish African-Indian unity." Panday's greatest regret was that the unity for oil and sugar which had been forged in 1975 had now been aborted. "Nineteen Seventy five was the first time that an Indian sugar leader embraced and worked with the African leader of the oil union in 40 years. That unity collapsed in August "because the extremist element had planned to take the party on the road to madness and armed revolution."

Panday repeated his off stated view that Trinidad and Tobago was not a racially homogenous society and that revolutionary violence would have consequences which would be quite different from that which it had in Cuba, China or the Soviet Union:

> In a violent revolutionary situation,if either an Indian guerilla killed an African chile or vice-versa, the guerrillas would start killing each other. We ain't ready for that now. Our people have been struggling for far too long under the serious and oppressive yoke of exploitation, and the ULF should work towards removing those obstacles to a happier life, and seek to give the working-class people a better quality of life. (*Guardian,* August 15, 1977)

Given his view that the Shah clique had "expelled themselves" from the ULF, Panday proceeded to take steps to legitimize his faction of the ULF. A membership meeting was convened on October 2, 1977 at which a decision was taken to expel "anti party" elements. A new Central Committee was also elected. The meeting expressed confidence in Panday's leadership, and voted 'unanimously' that he should not go through with his pledge to resign from Parliament. Panday had told the delegates that he should resign since he had "failed to discover in time the treacherous and ungrateful qualities in men whom I have virtually foisted on you."

A decision was also taken to convene a Party Congress on November 26th and 27th at which time the ideological direction of the Party would be determined. Panday said that his aim was to create a mass political party consisting of people holding divergent political views with the right to urge those on the membership and the electorate. His was preferred to a vanguard party which would proceed by purges and counter purges. What was needed was a loose jointed party of representation, not an élitist party which made spurious claims to scientific purity.

Shah was sharply critical of Panday's decision to call a Congress of his own and to form a rival ULF faction. He felt that such a party would be a "rank Indian party which had no place in this society" (*Guardian,* November 6, 1977). Shah was also scornful of Panday's call for talks with Norman Girwar's Trinidad Islandwide Cane Farmers Association with which both Panday and Shah had fought bitterly since 1973. This was a disingenuous move on Panday's part to prop up a rival to Shah's Islandwide Cane Farmers Union, and clearly suggested that Panday was prepared to stop at nothing to ruin Shah.

Shah admitted that he was not as popular a figure with the sugar workers as was Panday, but insisted that individualism and charisma had no part to play in the "new democracy." The issue was one of principle, and he and his group were willing to "sacrifice their seats in Parliament in four years' time, having already served one, to show that they stood by principles" (*Express,* September 3, 1977). Shah was however not pessimistic about the future. Whereas Panday was stronger among the older sugar workers for whom race was important, he believed that he had greater support among the young of both races who were disenchanted with racial politics. "If Mr. Panday were to take over the entire canefarmers community, it does not matter. My constituency stretches beyond Siparia. My constituency is young Trinidad and Tobago.... I can go to Laventille, Belmont, Caroni or Barrackpore: the young people are behind me, and that's where the future of the country lies. More than sixty-two (62) per cent of the population falls within that age group" (*Southern Star,* September 4, 1977). Shah admitted that race was a reality, but argued that the duty and responsibility of leaders was to "pull people beyond the fetters of race." Shah pledged to continue the struggle for the unity of African and Indian workers "until I die."

The ex-soldier however sought to distance himself from the extremists in the Party. NAMOTI was described as "a little insignificant pocket of extremists who have no control whatever over the Central Committee of the ULF" (*Guardian,* October 1, 1977). It may also be that he was simply denying that NAMOTI was as critical an element as Panday and others claimed.

Panday's reinstatement as Leader of the Opposition eight months after he had been deposed did nothing to heal the rift in the ULF or to stabilize the position on the Opposition benches. Three factors helped to complicate the problem. One was the split in the two man DAC parliamentary representation which came to a head during the "crisis" relating to the issue of self-government for Tobago. The second issue was the dramatic resignation from the Cabinet and the PNM of the Minister of Works, Hector McLean. The third was the Appeal Court's decision to uphold the appeal of Boodram Jattan.[5] With Jattan back in Parliament, the two factions were now evenly balanced, and there was a great deal of speculation as to whether the DAC parliamentarians would do anything to tip the scales one way or another. The DAC at first refused to be drawn into the imbroglio, but McLean's resignation precipitated a series of parliamentary manoeuvres which forced them to change their stance.

The resignation of McLean and the widespread speculation that some members of the PNM whom Dr. Williams had described as "millstones" might follow him forced the Prime Minister to act quickly. The problem however was that the necessary amendment was deemed to require the support of at least three-fourths of the total membership of the House and two-thirds of the membership of the Senate. To obtain this measure of support, the Prime Minister needed the support of some members of the opposition bench. Like the PNM, the ULF manifesto had raised the issue of what to do about "vagrant" MPs. The ULF had however strongly criticized the undated letter formula and was equally opposed to the formula which the PNM had proposed to adopt to make the provision constitutional. Instead of leaving it up to the leadership of the Party to determine when the MP had resigned or that he no longer had the support of his Party, the ULF had opted for the principle of popular recall.

The ULF had in fact introduced a motion in Parliament on February 10, 1978 asking the Government to "take the necessary steps to ensure that the Constitution of Trinidad and Tobago be amended so as to provide for the right of recall of Members of the House of Representatives by a majority of their constituents." Parliament had defeated that motion by a vote of 19-9 and had passed by a similar margin a proposal that "this House agree to provide expeditiously for an appropriate constitutional amendment requiring an elected member of Parliament to vacate his seat in the event he ceased to support or be supported by the Party to which he belonged when he was elected." During the debate, Panday had argued that the recall principle was the only genuinely democratic one and that the PNM amendment was open to abuse.

A number of circumstances however led Mr. Panday to abandon his recall formula and to join Dr. Williams in his plan to insert the PNM formula into the constitution. Both men needed each other and chose to drop their stance of mutual hostility which they had adopted prior to, and following the 1976 election. The new Williams-Panday alliance created a political storm, and public opinion was deeply aroused on the issue. Panday was accused of having sold out to the PNM for a "mess of pottage," of having "gone to bed" with the Prime Minister, and of having condescended to "anoint Dr. Williams with his tongue," a parliamentary euphemism which was not lost on the noisy crowds which listened to the debate in Parliament. Mr. Shah in particular noted that it was more than a mere coincidence that the Prime Minister never felt it necessary to consult with him on any matter during the eight months which he held office, but now found reasons to give Mr. Panday over two hours of his time.

There were however real gains to be achieved by Panday who chose to play the Prime Minister's game because he saw the amendment as a way to force Shah and his colleagues to face by-elections which he was sure he would win. He also calculated that by giving the Prime Minister the support which he needed, he would secure certain gains for the sugar workers for whom he was negotiating. The political crisis broke shortly after the management of Caroni Ltd. had declared that the price of sugar on the international market was low, and that the Company was losing millions. As such, it could not contemplate any wage increase. This was a palpable ploy to induce Panday to make concessions since his political life depended on a favourable outcome to the wage negotiations.[6]

Whatever the reason for his capitulation, Panday explained to Parliament that he and his colleagues had now come to the conclusion that the recall formula was unworkable in practice and that he was supporting the PNM motion, provided there was a guarantee that by-elections would be called within ninety days. He argued that the addition of this amendment to the proposed PNM amendment provided the best possible approximation to the recall formula.

The crisis in the ULF had all the hallmarks of those perennial conflicts which bedeviled left wing parties which participate in bourgeois parliamentary systems. There was conflict between the militant purists who insisted that the "principles of the party" were sacred and had to be safeguarded at all costs, and the compromisers who were more concerned with the party's chances of winning electoral victories and concessions for their supporters on a day to day basis. Conflicts over principles were also aggravated by institutional rivalries between the leadership in Parliament and those who were outside of the leadership circle or who were not in Parliament at all. The leadership, anxious to bargain and negotiate with flexibility within the context of the ongoing political system, was clearly finding it irritating and inconvenient to have to refer continuously to the party outside of Parliament for a mandate to act. One of the reasons for the ULF crisis was Panday's unwillingness to be restrained by the militants on the Central Committee. His aim was to free himself of the cocoon of collective leadership and emerge as the absolute leader of the ULF. His anxiety to place persons who would be loyal to him on local government bodies and in the Senate and to get rid of those who were loyal to the party or its ideology has to be seen as part of this strategy. As we have seen, the crisis was aggravated by race, by personality rivalries, and by memories of past conflicts.

Powerlessness also had its consequence for the integrity of the ULF. Like most parties which are not forced to mute intra-party disputes in the interest of holding on to power, the ULF had ample time to spend on distracting and enervating debates as to "what was to be done." As Ramesh Deosaran aptly notes:

> It has become quite apparent that ULF politicians are falling into the psychological trap or unwittingly constructing a little world of their own wherein they throw in their precious ambitions and delicate egos into the political ring and respond to one another more than they are prepared to respond to the PNM and country as a national constituency. Such has been the history of opposition politics in this country. Such politics has been the politics of disintegration, of displaced aggression wherein opposition politicians, buckling under the tough barriers between them and parliamentary control, turn against their own for reasons more apparent than real. (*Express,* May 8,1977)

The frustrations of the parliamentary game also enervated the ULF. During its first year, the ULF had introduced votes of no-confidence in the government, complained about the partiality of the Speaker, of the suffocating nature of parliamentary rules and regulations, the fact that bills were hastily pushed through Parliament without affording opposition MPs much time to study them, about the fact that research and secretarial facilities were not made available to them by the Government, which was accused of adopting an arrogant and condescending attitude towards them. The Prime Minister in fact openly chided the ULF about its "legislative impotence."[7]

There was a great deal of disenchantment about the plight of the ULF and there were expressions of hope that something would be done to reunite the party. The feeling persisted that a "good opposition party" was essential to stable democratic politics. Typical of this view was the *Catholic News,* the organ of the Catholic Church in Trinidad and Tobago, which in a front page editorial in August 1977 declared that

> ...all of us as loyal citizens, regardless of political affiliations must be concerned about the two party system and our democratic way of life. The ultimate good of the country must be the primary aim, not individual prestige or popularity. Let the ULF recall that a kingdom divided against itself cannot stand. We... urge the ULF to stop all internal wrangling and scoring of points against rival factions, to remove the source of the division within the party and begin the healing process.

Similar appeals were made by many others. Neither faction responded positively. Shah quite bluntly declared that "the time for peace had long passed. There was no making back." Panday was also clearly delighted to get out of the strait jacket of the Central Committee. In February 1978, he flatly rejected an appeal from George Weekes to attend a special COSSABO (Conference of Shop Stewards and Branch Officers) to discuss "the reforging of unity between oil and sugar workers on the industrial front." Panday replied to Weekes that unity on the industrial front could not be reforged unless the question of political unity was first solved. Panday was clearly not interested in the olive branch held out by Mr. Weekes. The split had become permanent, and the broken chain which was once the beacon of hope had now become the symbol of disunity and defeat.

To what extent was the collapse of the ULF inevitable? The NJAC was of the view that it was so. *Liberation,* the NJAC organ, took the position that the split was the inevitable product of the fact that the ULF took the parliamentary road:

> The present ULF split holds absolutely no surprises for us as it follows a most consistent pattern, a pattern based on the old colonial Westminster model, a model which places supreme political power in the hands of a Prime Minister.... It was bound to happen, for the natural outgrowth of conventional politics is rooted in the muck of frustration, in the mire of powerlessnesses, and despite the revolutionary phrases coming out of the mouths of the leaders, the essential factor is still being denied the people; for conventional politics holds one belief as supreme; that decision making comes from the top and filters down to the bottom. And the bottom is where the masses dwell in servitude — at the good of the conventional beasts. (*Guardian,* August 29, 1977)

NJAC argued that "politics is not the road to Parliament, but how to live and create the kind of society we want." To go into Parliament is to "end up crashing on the barren conventional sidewalk, foaming and frothing, twisting in agony by intense political infighting (ibid.).

Tapia also took the view that the ULF crisis was inevitable *given the choices which the party chose to make on the eve of the 1976 election.* To quote Tapia leader Lloyd Best:

> Right from the beginning, the ULF was neither united, nor labour, nor a front, but a regression to an old-time party. At each successive stage of its emergence, in 1973 and 1974 and 1975, right up to the temporary ULF Alliance of the whole Opposition in 1976, there was grave doubt that the method of window-dressing a sugar-worker party could be

> more successful than all the earlier experiments with the PDP and the POPPG, the DLP and the Liberals, the Workers and Farmers Party and the ACDC-DLP. Right from the beginning the ULF's capacity to win a majority and become the Government was limited by its basic communal appeal. A futility of purpose was built into its character. Following all the sugar-belt parties that went before it, Panday, Shah and Weekes tried to break out of this restriction by grafting on an urban wing. And they did it with their eyes open; plenty of evidence confirms they were fully aware that Panday was somehow regenerating the dying fires of the DLP. While Jamadar, Lequay and Capildeo were fiddling, he was acquiring a charisma by reviving a hope. They knew that, as they knew that the other faction was composed of sundry campus radicals and activists-general, largely lacking in popular support and appeal. The bridge between the two were Panday of the WFP and Shah of the February 1970 Revolution. The vain hope, both before but moreso after the election, was that the alliance would have triggered off a mobilization of the urban blacks and youth, opening a way to the politics of change. (*Tapia,* August 28, 1977)

Best argued that the conflict within the ULF was not a "single case of a moderate deviation versus an extremist communist line bent on armed overthrow," nor was the issue merely one of two strong personalities being unable to accommodate each other. The problem stemmed from the fact that the ULF was built from the top down. To quote Best at some length:

> Man-rat Shah and Panday may be, but the issue is really very much larger, and deeply embedded in the history and the recurring errors of movements spawned in the sugar area. But if Panday and Shah are more than mimic-men or man-rat, we will soon see it in their attempt to lift the debate to an articulation of the valid differences over strategy which arises from the choices and the errors of yesterday and from the palpable inexperience of all political leaders and followers and parties, in a land where political starvation daily substitutes for the earlier promise of political education. If Panday and Shah have now split, it was not bound to happen, as NJAC affirms. The fracture has come because ULF took short-cuts with half-ripe organization and half-arsed ideology, setting up explosive contradictions.

> But they could have chosen differently. In 1976 they had the choice to break the PNM monopoly with a UPF along the lines of India: but they preferred backdoor negotiation with ANR Robinson, a tactic exposing their basic pessimism and their congenital deviousness. And were they not helped to make and pursue false choice by the press and the academics and the intellectuals and the public, all programmed by experience to shun the costs of building an effective party that could shatter the traditional base of our politics and set out people free from racial parties?
>
> Mickey Mouse Politics is that politics which functions without any true hope, which repeatedly chooses the path of futility so well expressed in the notion of a "good opposition," always current in ruling party circles. A good opposition party is one which is so clearly doomed to grief that the rulers repeatedly help to recreate it, as they certainly did with the ULF.
>
> And now that futility has become a culture and a habit, a perpetual opposition necessarily selects as its leaders a class of entertainers, charlatans and clowns who survive in the spotlight precisely because they enjoy no relevance to power and therefore need no capacity to manage the State. The consummation of this process of entrenching theatrical irrelevance will come, as it is threatening now to do, when we contrive a special set of elections to select who will be in permanent and ineffective opposition, the final grand acknowledgement that we are dealing with essentially non-competing groups. (ibid.)

It is however difficult to see just how the proposed United Peoples Front would have functioned any better than the United Labour Front. Chances are that the Trinidad version of the Indian Janata would not even have lasted long enough to fight the election, let alone to function after the election with any credibility and competence. Moreover the UPF would have been as fatally flawed as was the ULF since it would have been top down political organization with a vengeance.

There was indeed no inevitability to the ULF split, though as we have indicated, the seeds of disintegration were there from the very beginning. What was missing was willingness on the part of the actors involved to learn from the history of working class politics in Trinidad and Tobago. What was clearly needed was for Indian and African workers to get used to the idea of working together politically to help overcome the suspicions and prejudices inherited from the past. This would of necessity have had to be a slow process which could not be short-circuited by appeals to a "politics of principle." Those who wish to lead the "masses" must remember that it is often necessary to "gaze at their tails" in order to determine how fast and how far they are prepared to go at any one time. The generally held view was that the future was bleak for both factions of the ULF, and that for some time to come, either the PNM or some newer version of it would continue to govern Trinidad.

It was the belief that this was a real possibility which led some former ULF supporters to suggest that traditional opposition politics was futile and that Indians must reconsider their options. "They must either join the PNM, ally with some urban rooted group, or play the role of brokers "whereby the 8 or 10 sugar seats would remain under a party banner but be aligned to another party in the post election phase so as to form a government." Such was the view of Dr. Ramesh Deosaran who in a commentary on the political options open to Indian sugar workers, argued that unless they make the "pendulum swing by getting on the right side," they would continue to occupy the bottom rung in the political and social system. To quote Deosaran:

> The sugar worker is politically emasculated, socially alienated, culturally ambivalent, and psychologically demoralized. Be it in terms of toilets, school places or income per capita, he is always among the last in the country. Today's sugar worker endures an "agouti existence." He dashes in and out of the sugar belt only out of expediency, but quickly returns to revel in his state of helplessness, possibly to play big fish in little pond. He doesn't even have a calypsonian to express his grief.... The sugar worker in Trinidad remains the number one colonial in the Caribbean. (*Express,* March 5, 1978)[8]

Deosaran and other Indian intellectuals argued that the sugar worker was the most exploited, ostracized and psychologically dependent worker in the society. "His existence depends on the paternalism, the charity of the forces that rule but do not identify with him." His life "moves from crisis to crisis." The time had come for Indians to use the vote not merely as an "opposition thing," but as a lever to pry open the corridors of power:

> The free vote is not enough to gain more freedom in a multi-party state. He must now review his political habits, especially if he still wants to play conventional politics. To play radical in a country where race and power are so tightly aligned is to commit political suicide. Twenty-one years of sitting outside in the cold political wilderness could break the will to belong to a nation, and smash any faith in the system whose rules are expected to be obeyed. The sugar vote forms too easily into a ready and convenient masquerade of a political opposition which reaps all the pressures without the privileges. The sugar vote by itself, for all the political savvy of Basdeo Panday, is too predictable and politically ineffective.... This, in essence, is a basis for the perpetuation of the sugar-worker's neo-colonial status. If such options seem opportunistic, it must be understood that the entire Westminster game of politics smacks of opportunism where the players attempt to maximize the returns of their vote. In the case of the sugar workers, his returns have far too long been confined to psychics rewards only. (ibid.)

Although Deosaran canvassed the option of having Indians join urban rooted groups such as the DAC, he was well aware that this had been unsuccessfully attempted in the past. The bottom line of his comment appeared to be an appeal to Indians to join the PNM, and for the latter to welcome them, even perhaps in the context of a one party state. "The PNM, given its base in county St. George would have to appreciate the need for minimizing conflict politics," and see this gesture "as heralding an opportunity for a major breakthrough towards Indian-African unity." As Deosaran concluded:

> This analysis of Caroni in national politics also suggests the inherent justice of multi-party politics, and even raises the possibility of a one-party state if only to minimize racial and cultural conflict and afford a better distribution of state resources.... A very debatable alternative, but one which Trinidadians, in their search for a more viable political alternative, cannot afford to ignore. (ibid)

Deosaran's formula for taking Indians beyond the politics of cultural revivalism and the quest for higher wages and benefits in the sugar industry and into the national mainstream was endorsed by a growing number of Indian professionals and businessmen who believed that Indians had nothing to gain and everything to lose by yoking their fortunes to the bullock carts of the DLP or the ULF. Instead of serving as the basis for a radical alternative, the Indian vote should be used to secure a larger share of the nation's material and psychic resources. Some businessmen in fact argued that if Indians were ever to gain political power on their own, "creole" Trinidadians would not accept it, no matter what ideological colours the party wears. They feared that the ensuing social unrest would make it impossible for them to conduct business in the normal way. Many of them recalled the fate of the PPP in Guyana, and were in fact quite happy with the existing division of authority in the which they were left free to build economic empires while the African element controlled the reins of political and administrative power and take the blame for all the policy errors.

Deosaran's pessimism about the future of opposition politics was also shared by the political leader of the ULF. In a feature address to a ULF Congress in November 1978, Panday celebrated the triumph of his faction of the ULF, but noted that under the first-past-the-post Westminster system, opposition parties were doomed to impotence. This was particularly so in a pluralistic society:

> The result of this system in a pluralistic society is that there is always a significant group in the society that is perpetually alienated from the political processes in the country. With

> time and repetition, this feeling of alienation from political power is so intensified that the alienated group sees itself as outsiders in its own country, un-cooperative and uncommitted to the welfare of the society as a whole. The dominant group, in turn reacts with fearful suspicion and itself becomes uncommitted to the society, preoccupying itself solely with the protection of its own power. Soon both groups are living in a state of subdued antagonism and suspicion, each pulling in different directions to the detriment of the economic social and political life of the country as a whole. (*Express,* December 12, 1978)

Panday told his listeners that the time had come to restructure the political system in order to ensure that power was shared between the two principal ethnic communities in a sort of consociational system:

> The time has come for us to remove our heads from the sand and courageously place on the agenda for national dialogue this whole question of the relevance of our political system. Failure to do so may conceivably result in PNM preaching race and winning the next elections, but it will forever be powerless to get us out of the mess we are in — a phenomenon which affects us all regardless of race colour or creed. We must evolve a system of political power-sharing that has the effect of ending that debilitating feeling of alienation among so many of our citizens. We must create a system that not only allows for, but encourages the total mobilization and commitment of all out human resources in one massive national effort to provide the goods and services that all our people so desperately need. (ibid.)

Panday's suggestion was similar to the one made by Deosaran and bore some resemblance to the political philosophy which underpinned the Report of the Constitution Commission.[9] One could not help but feel that Panday's speech indicated that he had come full circle, and that instead of being one of the principal architects of the politics of succession, he had virtually come to the conclusion that Eric Williams was worth propping up. Panday in fact warned the country that local monopoly capitalists were plotting to remove the Prime Minister by unconstitutional means, and went so far as to call upon the workers to mobilize themselves to abort the planned coup:

> Monopoly capitalists everywhere are vicious, ungrateful, and will go to any extent to protect their privileged positions — even to the extent of treason. You will be surprised to know that at this very moment there is a plan afoot by certain monopoly capitalists in Trinidad and Tobago to stage a coup, depose the Prime Minister and replace him by a more acceptable PNM right winger. The war you have been hearing about between the Government and certain big business elements in the Chamber of Commerce is no joke. According to information reaching me, certain top brass of two companies have already taken a decision that Williams must go and the decision is irrevocable. They are conspiring with certain political persons in the country to stage a right wing palace coup and replace Williams with a Prime Minister who will guarantee protection of their privileged position in the economy. The Prime Minister is aware of this plot and instead of informing the nation of the threat, he has taken his own private precaution by creating a core of palace guards. I feel it is the duty of the Prime Minister to alert the country of this right wing threat to our nation and to mobilize the people in its defence. In any event our greater safeguard against any right wing coup, and the repression against the working people and the small businessmen that would inevitably follow, is to mobilize the working class to meet the attack. I therefore, issue an urgent call for reunification of the labour movement as a matter of immediate urgency in defence of the nation. And I call upon the Cabinet not only to clear the air on this matter but to release the legal and other constraints on the workers to facilitate this mobilization of the labour movement. (*Express,* December 12, 1978)[10]

Panday's speech suggested that he had come to the conclusion that he had more to gain for himself and the sugar workers by working closely with the PNM rather than maintaining an unproductive antagonist relationship. Panday's accommodationist posture also suggested that the "political obeah" of Eric Williams had eventually consumed him as it had others like Bhadase Maraj and Rudy Capildeo before him. Indeed, Eric Williams had not only won another round in the battle for succession but was confidently assuming that he would be around in 1981 to fight yet another election. His minions were also predicting that the PNM would be holding the reins into the 21st century.

End Notes

[1]Even the *Trinidad Guardian* (August 12,1977) which consistently opposed the ULF noted that "there is little cause for joy or comfort among those who do not support the United Labour Front but do possess love for the country. If the ULF will contain their quarrel among themselves and deal with their differences within the bounds of their constitution, the whole crisis may be a good thing for the country in that sooner or later we may have a strictly two-party system based on economic and social considerations, not race." The *Express* was of the same view: "There are many people in Trinidad and Tobago who will welcome the break-up of the ULF. For the Party with its left-wing propaganda has frightened many of our citizens who see a communist under every socialist bed. But the simple fact is that if the main opposition party cannot hold together after a year, our political life would be so much the worse off."

[2]Lloyd Best quite correctly raised the question of just what Weekes, Shah and others considered to be principled politics since they knew full well what Panday stood for when the ULF was created. To quote Best, "in all politics, as in all of life, the principles of today invariably is a convenience." Weekes and the Congress of Progressive Trade Unions had known all along that Panday had become a Senator though he had participated in the "no vote" campaign of 1971, and that he had schemed to become President General of the All Trinidad Sugar Estates and Factory Workers Union through undemocratic channels. As the *Socialist Worker* complained in 1974, "Basdeo Panday had exposed his opportunist streak. What is of concern to us now is the possibility that sugar workers could well be saddled with an educated Bhadase...." The CPTU also met on March 8, 1974 and accused Panday of "betraying the confidence of sugar workers and cane farmers" by

joining the Executive of All Trinidad when he himself had told workers how corrupt and undemocratic that Executive had been (*Socialist Worker,* March 19, 1974). The CPTU was particularly incensed at Panday's tendency to take decisions which affected several unions unilaterally. Shah in particular had good reasons to be suspicious of Panday's commitment to "principle."

[3]Panday had a good relationship with many PNM Ministers and consulted with the Prime Minister on matters of "national concern" — either directly or indirectly. The first consultation with the Prime Minister took place over the issue of the expulsion of MPs who crossed the floor or who were deemed to have lost the backing of their Party.

[4]To quote Panday, "I love George and respect him for his dedication to the working class struggle" (*Express,* September 18, 1977). He also recalled that Weekes had once said that he "had never seen a leader being so brutal to his people to get them off the racial scene" (*Express,* August 17, 1977). Panday said he did not want to lead an Indian party, but would not shirk the role if others forced him into it. As he said, "The ULF is working class and multi-racial. I can lead no other kind of party. If I am forced to choose, I would have to, but with much anguish. This depends not only on me" (cf. *Express,* May 8, 1977).

[5]Mr. Jattan, who was one of the more radical parliamentarians in the Shah faction, was arrested on a wounding charge prior to the election. The incident grew out of the rivalry between the ICFTU of which Shah was President and the pro-PNM, TICFA. Mr. Jattan appealed the sentence, but the constitution (see 49 Sub-section 30) provided that he had to cease functioning as an MP until the appeal was determined. The Speaker also had the power to declare Jattan's seat vacant even before the outcome of the appeal was determined.

During the appeal proceedings, the defence argued that it was wrong for the state to transfer the case from San Fernando to

Port of Spain without explanation. There was also strong criticism of the fact that the state went to extreme lengths to ensure that the jury was selected from outside its natural environment, and that the prosecution took great care by use of its peremptory challenge to make the jury racially exclusive (*Guardian,* June 23, 1978). Jattan was also on another charge of distributing seditious literature and of trying to subvert a jury which was hearing another case.

[6]Panday told sugar workers that they should not go on strike even though the company appeared to be inciting them to do so. Panday was clearly afraid to risk calling a strike which he feared he would lose. As he had told the workers earlier, "we in sugar have begun to realise that whereas the strike weapon was an effective instrument to improve conditions of work when we were fighting private capitalists, we must now devise a new instrument to fight state capitalism" (*Guardian,* January 1, 1977). Panday noted that while profit was the concern of the private capitalist, more was at stake for the state and they were prepared to use the army and the police to crush workers.

[7]The Prime Minister said he was disappointed with the contributions of the opposition and boasted of the executive power "... that has been on the side that has been here yesterday, is here today and will be here tomorrow, and tomorrow and for the foreseeable future." The Attorney General, Senator Selwyn Richardson also told Parliament that the Government had a mandate to rule and that it would declare "500 states of emergency" if it found it necessary to do so in order to rule effectively (*Sunday Express,* October, 1976).

[8]Deosaran was aggrieved by the collapse of the ULF on August 9th, which he termed "Black Tuesday." "The ULF smash-up is not only a disaster for those who braved the batons on Bloody Tuesday, but also for the dark shadows which it now casts across the new dawn of Caribbean politics." Deosaran noted that the broken hopes and dreams of those who had looked to the ULF

for political salvation had led to a "growing impatience and disgust with opposition politicians." Deosaran was particularly angry with Shah whom he dismissed as an impatient romantic who was not fully aware of the responsibilities with which democratic politics burdens its participants and who had now rendered the ULF a "political corpse." To quote Deosaran:

> It is folly to take action based on a dream.... The action against Panday, as desirable as it might have appeared to those around the committee table, had no inherent rightness about it. Democratic politics is not always of the absolute.... It now seems that history would ruefully recall that patience was lacking somewhere.

Unlike Shah, Deosaran saw nothing wrong with charisma which he saw as being necessary in young organizations. "Man's charisma has always shaped and built institutions. It is in some serious respects a psychological defect of the human conditions.... The problem is not how to expel charisma, but how to work it into the orgnization's objectives. And this is a challenge that has little to do with whether one is bourgeois or proletariat. In fact, a charismatic leader is necessary in a young organization or one containing diverse interests.... Political parties need both organization and charisma, organization for continuity and stability and charisma for recruitment and impact. The secret is to marry the two into an effective combination. The ULF failed to do that perhaps through its political experience. It failed to understand the very curious mixture of people and ideas" (*Express,* August 21, 1975).

[9]As the Commissioners noted, "in a small community such as this, rigid confrontation by opposing parties on all issues cannot be for the benefit of the society. Areas of consensus and compromise must be sought and expanded. Some of the procedures which we have proposed are geared towards this goal...." (*Report of the Constitution Commission* 1974:16-17).

[10]For the authors's critical reaction to Panday's warning about a coup (cf. *Express,* December 3, 1978). The suggestion was that the coup talk was not worth taking seriously; "That the rumour should flourish is perhaps the best indication that despair and anguish are deepening among all but the most blindly partisan.... It is in fact difficult to identify a strategic group which does not have a grievance..."

Chapter 7

Indians and the Politics of PNM Succession

Dr. Williams' death on March 29, 1981 and the choice of George Chambers as the new Prime Minister introduced a new element into the political equation in Trinidad and Tobago. One widely held view was that the departure of Dr. Williams was certain to guarantee the defeat of the PNM by the newly formed Organization For National Reconstruction (ONR), led by former PNM Attorney General, Karl Hudson-Phillips, which was widely regarded as a clone of the PNM. Sociologically, the two parties represented the same constituency, though the ONR also attracted added support from Indians disillusioned with the ULF and from the white and "off white" community. This view was based on the assumption that the Hudson-Phillips wing would attract much of the support which the PNM had retained over the years because of personal loyalties to Dr. Williams. Persons who could not bring themselves to "betray" Williams while he lived could now feel free to change their allegiances, or so it was argued. Support for this thesis was to be found in the polling data. When asked which party they would vote for if Dr. Williams were to resign, only 17 per cent indicated they would vote for the PNM, a drop of 11 per cent from the support which had been registered in a poll done just prior to Williams' death. Thirty-three per cent said they would vote the ONR, a gain of 4 per cent, while seventeen per cent said they would vote for "no party" compared to 14 per cent who gave this reply on the previous question.

There was however another possibility, viz., that Dr. Williams could do as much for the PNM in death as he could have were he still alive and that the party and the new Prime Minister could benefit from the enormous groundswell of sympathy and affection which Dr. Williams' death evoked in the public mind. It was possible that Dr. Williams' charisma would in fact become institutionalized in the party itself in the same way in which the charisma of Christ had become institutionalized in the Catholic Church allowing any successor, no matter how insignificant, to partake of that charisma.

The outcome of the elections was however expected to depend on many other things. In part, it depended on whether the PNM was united behind the new prime minister and confirmed him as political leader or whether there was a power struggle in the party. There was in fact no major power struggle, since in critical sections of the public mind, many of the would be successors had eliminated themselves. Indeed, the Presidents's first choice of a successor to Dr. Williams was Errol Mahabir. Clarke was anxious to ensure a smooth transition. Objections were however raised to his proposal on the ground that there were too many rumours circulating which raised questions about Mahabir's dealings with Japanese firms operating in Trinidad. Rather than impose an unpopular choice, the President called the three deputy leaders to President's House and urged them to try and reach an accommodation as to who was to succeed. Chambers immediately declared, perhaps quite cleverly, that he was not interested in the succession and left the issue to be resolved between Messrs. Mahabir and Mohammed, neither of whom were willing to give way. Faced with an impasse, the President decided to appoint Chambers as the new Prime Minister to succeed Dr. Williams. It was understood that the appointment would stand until the ruling party met in Convention to select its new political leader.

The President expressed the dilemma he found on that evening in the following way:

> The view I took academically and the view I still take is that an appointment must be made forthwith. Otherwise, you endanger the country. You must do something about it, fill the gap at once. I used to say no President should go to bed at night without knowing whom he would appoint if he is awakened at the middle of the night and told that the Prime Minister is no longer with us. Most of the time I knew whom I would appoint. On the Friday prior to Dr. Williams' death, I thought I knew whom to appoint. It happened that I changed my mind that night.
>
> The events following Dr. Williams' death caused me considerable problems. I had to choose from among the Members of the House of Representatives [although] there were three deputy political leaders. You could have appointed anybody else. But from a practical point of view, those were the three most likely candidates. And in that setting, one sat all three down and one went through a difficult process, a process in which the one who was appointed was first to eliminate himself, [whether deliberate or not....] I didn't know, but he eliminated himself, and the other two did not eliminate themselves. And the result was that there was a deadlock. I had to resort to the one who had eliminated himself to hold the fort.

The President has indicated that his first choice was Mr. Errol Mahabir. "Notables" in the PNM party, Mr. Francis Prevatt, Chairman of the party, in particular, were however opposed to the latter's appointment, and plumped for George Chambers. Chambers, however, initially expressed disinterest. Many Indians believe that a conspiracy had been cleverly put in place to ensure that an Indian did not become Prime Minister of Trinidad and Tobago.

One of the two passed over deputies, Mr. Kamaluddin Mohammed, does not agree with the former President as to what took place. He in fact denies that there was a stand off between himself and the other deputy leader, Mr. Errol Mahabir. According to Mr. Mohammed, "I was the most senior and experienced man for the job, and it was given to Chambers." Mohammed believes that if he had been made Prime Minister in 1981, "race would not have become an issue in 1995. We would have been in a better position." Mohammed denies that he was involved in any of the transactions which were said to have disqualified him from holding the post of Prime Minister. It seems clear that Mohammed believes he was by-passed because of what he terms "political race" (*Express,* June 16, 1996; *Guardian,* November 21, 1995).

Mr. Errol Mahabir agreed that Mohammed was unfairly by passed. Mahabir was however unwilling to say that race was the deciding factor. When asked whether Mr. Mohammed was by-passed by the President on grounds of race, Mahabir responded as follows:

> I do not know. Knowing Sir Ellis Clarke the way I do however, I do not think that race was a factor in his deliberations. I myself try to avoid making statements about racial discrimination, but I have always wondered what were all the criteria which led to the President's decision. I should point out, however, that the President was not the only actor in the process. On the night when the decision was taken, our discussions at President's House were more with Mr. Francis Prevatt as chairman of the PNM. It was Mr. Prevatt who advised us that the President intended to select one of us for appointment since we were the three deputy political leaders of the PNM at the time. As I believe is now public knowledge, Mr. [George] Chambers indicated that he was not interested in the post and was prepared to work with either Mr. Mohammed or myself. Mr. Mohammed indicated that he was prepared to work with Mr. Chambers or me and I indicated that I was prepared to work with either Mr. Chambers or Mr. Mohammed. We pointed out that this was really a matter for the President and we left it entirely to his discretion. There has been some uninformed speculation about how Mr. Mohammed and I responded. I do not know how that decision of ours was conveyed to the President, but we were advised shortly after by Mr. Prevatt that the President had decided to appoint Mr. Chambers as Prime Minister. (*Sunday Express,* November 26, 1995)

When asked whether he was disappointed with the decision, Mahabir replied as follows:

> I had a very strong case, but I thought that Mr. Mohammed would have been chosen given his 10 years' ministerial seniority. When the provisions of the Constitution are taken into account, it appears that Mr. Prevatt's involvement in the exercise was to assist the President in ascertaining which one of the three of us would have commanded the support of the majority of members of the House of Representatives. It would seem Mr. Chambers was so identified. If I were to guess, I would say that this factor, more than any other, influenced the President's decision. (ibid.)

In the elections which took place following Williams' death, Chambers was faced with a more determined opposition than was the case in 1976. To confront the PNM, three of the established political parties — the ULF, the DAC and Tapia — formed themselves into a National Alliance. The arrangement was that the parties of the Alliance would retain their organizational identities but support each other electorally. There was also an agreement that each would not field candidates in areas which others in the Alliance were deemed to have a good chance of winning. This would mean that the DAC alone would face the PNM in Tobago, the ULF in twelve or 14 seats which that party had either won in 1976 or in which it performed well, and Tapia the remainder.

The problem was that Tapia did not have any grass roots support and was unlikely to gain many votes. The party had obtained a mere 3.8 per cent of the popular vote in 1976 and the results of the poll cited above suggested that it was unlikely to improve its performance. Tapia leader Lloyd Best however believed that the formation of the Alliance would change the chemistry of the problem. The Alliance would represent a qualitatively different formation which would be greater than the sum of its constituent parts. He felt that the "party of parties" represented the first real break away from the old one-man party, something which would embrace all elements and the "tribes" in a fundamental way. "This coalition party... has been organized to give permanent manifestation to the hope for change which the people all over the country see today. The Alliance can make manifest that demand for change and will form the next Government of Trinidad and Tobago." Best expressed the view that the Prime Minister had chosen to make his exit at precisely the moment when it was clear to all the citizens that the political methods of the fifties and sixties could no longer guide the country in the eighties and nineties. "Dr. Williams in the end has cleared the way so that Trinidad and Tobago can advance."

Tapia's agreement to work with parties which its leaders had vehemently criticized in the past was seen as rank opportunism, even though Tapia had in fact indicated as early as 1975 that it was interested in a "Janata" type united front alliance of all the opposition parties against the PNM. Many blacks however did not support the notion of an alliance which had the ULF as one of its constituent units because of their assumption that that party would be the dominant group in any such alliance and would in the end assume the parliamentary leadership. For them the issue was not merely a choice of government and prime minister, but which race would control the citadels of power.

The ONR, for its part, sensed this fact and refused to participate in any coalition. Instead, it called upon all the other political parties "to clear the coast and let there be a straight fight between the enemy and the ONR." Ferdie Ferreira, the party's organization secretary, a former PNM stalwart and confidante of Dr. Williams, insisted that the ONR was the only party which had the "political artillery to destroy the enemy." Needless to say, the other opposition parties did not heed this request. The result was that there were many three cornered contests among the PNM, the ONR and the National Alliance.

The Manifestos

Manifestos are not the critical factor which influence the way in which a majority of voters cast their franchise. Yet manifestos are important aspects of party politics and no serious party ever goes into an election without putting out one. Manifestos are in a sense similar to development plans. No serious government would consider being without one, no matter how rudimentary or unrealistic. Manifestos are put together for a variety of reasons. In part, they seek to include items which appeal to as many sections of the community from whom support is being sought. Manifestos are thus an expression of the type of coalitional politics which normally characterize elections in democratic societies.

The Alliance's Policy and Programme was a good example of this. It consciously sought to incorporate the pet policies of Tapia, DAC and the ULF. Tapia's commitment to radical constitutional reform in general and the large ("macco") Senate in particular was there, as was DAC's commitment to a deepening of the self-government process for Tobago. The ULF's concern for worker participation in industry and national ownership and control of the commanding heights of the economy and a capital gains tax were also highlighted. Other key items included the production of oil and gas in quantities which were just sufficient to meet the country's revenue needs without prejudice to existing levels of employment, the strengthening of parliamentary control over policy making in general and the nation's purse strings in particular, the creation of a Ministry of Manpower and Employment, reduction of the food import bill by means of a radical transformation of agricultural production, including a policy designed to protect local food producers, and the upgrading of agricultural incomes and fringe benefits to levels enjoyed by industrial workers. Also provided for was decentralization of power, the provision of bloc grants to local bodies and to the judiciary, an efficient mass transit system to relieve road congestion and the frustration experienced by commuters at peak travel periods, radical educational reform including curriculum reform and an elimination of the shift system, something which all parties agreed was an imperative.

The Alliance's Programme was one with which most citizens could live. It did not however deal with the question of how its proposals would be translated into effective policy. It merely indicated what the coalition would "play for" if it were to achieve power either fully or in partnership with another party. The Programme was sufficiently broad to allow the Alliance to work with either the PNM or the ONR should the need for this arise.

The Campaign

The election campaign itself was without doubt one of the most exciting witnessed in the history of Trinidad and Tobago. Its importance stemmed from several factors. It was the first election in what might be called the modern period which was not mediated by the powerful charismatic influence of Dr. Eric Williams. The PNM was facing the electorate without him for the first time and there was a great degree of curiosity as to how well the party would perform without its founder and leader of 25 years. The election was important too because the possibility existed that it would witness the breaking up of the great racial coalition which had dominated electoral politics between 1955 and 1980 when it was possible for analysts to predict which constituencies would return candidates supported by Indian or African dominated parties simply by looking at the census data. Ethnic voting was expected to continue being important, but the major cleavage was expected to be white/associate white vs black with the African vs Indian dichotomy being relegated to subordinate significance.

In 1960, Eric Williams proclaimed that "Massa Day Done" and blacks shouted their approval. Unlike many blacks, Eric Williams was careful to note that "massa" was a sociological and not a racial term. Many now felt that the ONR had emerged as the party of the "massas" despite the veneer of social catholicism which the party seemed to display. The party seemed to many to be a wedding cake which had a lot of icing but only a thin layer of black cake. A comparison of the conventions held by the two parties and some of the early meetings in the public squares bore out this analogy. The PNM meetings were unmistakably black and brown working and under class while the ONR gatherings consisted mainly of upscale Africans and Indians, whites and off-whites. This latter community had long felt their exclusion from the corridors of political power, and regarded the ONR as the vehicle through which they would stage a return to what they regarded as their rightful inheritance and place in the political firmament. It would not be true to say that there were no working class supporters of the ONR or upscale elements supporting the PNM. It was however crystal clear that the centre of gravity in the two parties was radically different.

The results of the election came to many as a stunning surprise, especially since one poll had predicted on the eve of the election that the ONR was certain to win 10 seats, with possible victories in another 6 to 10 seats. Least surprised, or so it seemed, was the Political Leader of the PNM who appeared all along to be quietly confident that the PNM would win at least 24 seats and possibly more. Chambers had in fact campaigned on the slogan, "not a damn seat for them." Some members of the ONR had also become worried in the last weeks of the campaign and indeed feared that the party would be comprehensively routed. In their view, the ONR had run a public relations campaign and not a political campaign. It was also felt that Williams' death had robbed them of their visible enemy and therefore their most valuable target.

As it turned out, the PNM won 26 seats, two more than it did in 1976 — and this despite the loss of the two Tobago seats. Five of the PNM seats were however on a plurality rather than a majority basis, essentially because of three cornered contests with the Alliance and the ONR. The party received 218,557 or 52.61 per cent of the votes cast on a national basis and 7,503 or 42.8 per cent of the votes cast in Tobago. The party had lost the two Tobago seats to the DAC in 1976, and the loss in 1981 was a cruel disappointment since it appeared to mark the end of the ruling party's political dominance in that island which had been achieved in 1961. It also signalled the triumph of separatist though not necessarily secessionist sentiment.

As can be seen in Table 1, the ONR ran well in areas where upscale elements predominated as well as in certain districts where Indians were concentrated. Results of voting in the St. Joseph, Port of Spain South and Diego Martin constituencies make the point. In the upscale Valsayn Park residential area, the ONR got 60 per cent of the votes which were cast for the PNM and the ONR. In the heavily Indian Bamboo Settlement area, the ONR won 64 per cent of the votes cast for the two parties, while in the mainly Indian area of Aranguez, it won 60 per cent of the votes cast for the two parties.

Table 1. Votes Cast for the ONR in Rural-Based, Indian-Based Constituencies Compared with Urban-Based Constituencies with Predominantly Black Populations during the 1981 Elections

Constituency	Urban and/or African-based Constituencies	Constituency	Rural and/or Indian-based Constituencies
Point Fortin	26.4	La Brea	19.8
San Fernando West	39.0	Ortoire-Mayaro	13.9
San Fernando East	24.9	Princes Town	17.5
Toco-Manzanilla	22.7	Pointe-a-Pierre	28.0
Arima	27.3	Siparia	13.6
Arouca	22.7	Oropouche	32.6
St. Joseph	41.8	Naparima	18.1
San Juan	21.0	Tabaquite	18.5
Barataria	38.0	Couva South	15.6
Laventille	7.3	Couva North	15.9
St. Ann's East	18.1	Caroni East	14.2
St. Ann's West	17.4	Chaguanas	17.8
Port of Spain East	8.6	St. Augustine	17.1
Port of Spain North	37.3		
Port of Spain South	31.2		
Diego Martin East	31.2		
Diego Martin Central	36.6		
Diego Martin West	24.2		

Source: Elections and Boundaries Commission 1982.

The ULF's support declined precipitously when compared with its performance in 1976 as is revealed in Table 2.

Table 2. Votes Cast for ULF in its Traditional Constituencies - 1976 and 1981 Elections

Constituency	1976 (%)	1981 (%)
Caroni East	48	40
Couva North	62	60
Couva South	66	50
Tabaquite	55	44
Naparima	65	50
Oropouche	67	41
Siparia	63	52
Princes Town	46	32
St. Augustine	47	45
Chaguanas	48	48

Source: Elections and Boundaries Commission 1977, 1982.

The party lost two of its traditional seats, Princes Town and Caroni East to the PNM and a lot of its supporters to the ONR. In terms of the former, which was always a marginal seat for the ULF, three cornered contests ensured the defeat of the ULF candidate. In Caroni East, this factor, plus a change in the demographics of the constituency, affected the outcome. The ULF won the St. Augustine seat as it did in 1976, but with a slightly reduced majority — 44.7 per cent compared to 46.5 per cent in 1976. Table 3 indicates the comparative performances of the Alliance parties between 1976 and 1981 in 11 constituencies in the East-West Corridor.:

Table 3. Votes Cast for Alliance in 1976 and 1981

Constituency	ULF	Tapia	DAC	TOTAL	Alliance	
	1976	1976	1976	1976	1981	
Arima	-	5.7	15.0	20.7	1.2	(Tapia)
Arouca	20	7.0	3.0	30.0	8.4	(")
Tunapuna	24	11.4	2.2	37.6	32.2	(")
St. Augustine	46.5	10.2	1.6	58.4	44.7	(ULF)
St. Joseph	24.8	6.5	3.4	34.7	4.1	(Tapia)
Barataria	20	2.5	4.0	26.5	1.5	(DAC)
San Juan	-	6.0	6.4	12.4	2.6	(Tapia)
Laventille	2.4	2.6	5.4	10.4	4.1	(")
Port of Spain East	4.9	3.2	3.8	11.9	1.3	(")
Port of Spain South	-	6.5	5.0	11.5	1.5	(")
Diego Martin West	5.7	7.0	4.3	11.0	1.7	(")

Source: Elections and Boundaries Commission 1977, 1982.

The figures provide further evidence that race continued to be one of the main variables affecting the election results. What they reveal is that the opposition to the PNM normally did poorly in polling districts and constituencies where Africans were in numerical dominance and did better where Indians (Moslems in particular) were in the ascendancy.

There was a great deal of disappointment in Opposition circles about the PNM's return to power after all that had taken place between 1970 and 1981. Typical was the melancholia forthcoming from Tapia political guru, Lloyd Best. As Best bemoaned, "the country has returned into power the party which had governed us to the brink of the revolutionary upheaval in 1970, which had been squandering a gigantic fortune of petro-dollars since the end of 1973, and which by its errors of omission and commission, had converted our country into a virtual slum, into a den of corruption, indiscipline and immorality, into a desert of desperation and despair."

The ONR leader, Karl Hudson-Phillips, did not accept the results as reflecting the true mood of the people. As far as he was concerned, the ONR and "the majority of the population feels robbed." Hudson-Phillips charged that

> ...the Government is not a properly and fairly elected government and, therefore, does not represent the will of the majority. It is a most dangerous situation for democracy in Trinidad and Tobago. The PNM has brought no change, no hope, no vision to Trinidad and Tobago. The same inefficiencies and corruption will now continue unabated. The PNM will crash under the weight of its own inefficiencies, corruption and dishonesty.

In the opinion of the ONR leader, the PNM used mental violence, fraud and bribery to secure its mandate. The people did not willingly provide it.

Were these remarks merely the splenetic eruptions of disappointed place seekers and disaffected citizens who supported one or other of the opposition parties, or were they views that were shared even by people who voted for or gave silent emotional support to the PNM? This is not an easy question to answer since it involves questions about just how one determines the mood or the neural state of the people of a country. It also involves some understanding about what constitutes a mandate. One dictionary defines the word mandate as "an authoritative requirement as of a sovereign; a command order or charge." It is also defined as an "instruction from an electorate to the legislative body or its representative to follow a certain course of action."

The problem here is that in a general election, as opposed to a referendum on a single issue, an electorate is asked to give a complex rather than a specific response by means of a unique act, the vote. When one goes into a voting booth to exercise one's franchise, one is not asked to tick off the things one likes or dislikes; one is asked to approve a programme, a candidate and a party as a whole either on the basis of what that party has done or what is being promised. The voter is not permitted to disaggregate his decision by saying yes to this or no to that. And therein lies the problem of assessing mandates or electoral moods. It is not even easy to determine what voters have decided in a referendum since the question asked in referenda often become intertwined with other issues. Moods, opinions and therefore mandates are situational, and need to be interpreted in a given context and time frame. It is thus impossible for nay one to say whether the Trinidad electorate voted on November 9th to condone or institutionalize corruption, waste and mismanagement, especially when many (35 per cent according to poll findings) were convinced that the PNM could do a better job than the ONR. Only 28 per cent were of the firm view that the ONR could have improved on the performance of the PNM with 18 per cent saying that they would in all probability perform the same. Twenty per cent in fact felt that the ONR would do worse, with another thirty three per cent expressing uncertainty. In sum, 71 per cent of the sample were unconvinced that the ONR would do better than the PNM.

Given the lack of any unequivocal optimism about the likely performance of the ONR, it can hardly be argued that a vote for the PNM was a vote for "political indecency." The claim is in fact highly subjective. If one were to ask PNM voters, the vast majority would have denied that their vote could be interpreted in the way in which the critics did. There were indeed some persons who had a vested interest in perpetuating some of the negative aspects of PNM rule; but the majority who voted PNM did so because they liked the broad outlines of the system or "way of life" which the PNM had helped to shape and contour over the years though they nevertheless wished to see improvements within the context of that system. Chambers had promised that these improvements would be forthcoming.

The evidence suggests that a majority of PNM members and supporters did not endorse everything that had been done by their party, since it was quite consistent for them to have a positive view towards their party while at the same time disapproving of its negative characteristics and deficiencies. The results suggest that many people were aware that they had to accept part of the blame for the problems faced by the country.

By returning the PNM to power for the sixth term, a tremendous burden was placed on the frail shoulders of the successor to Dr. Williams. In a way, he had become the nation's chief beast of burden. His was a magnificent opportunity to put things right. If he succeeded where his predecessor failed, the country would applaud. If he failed, one could expect the electorate to be merciless, assuming of course that a viable alternative was available. To be successful, Mr. Chambers had to remind himself that there were thousands of people from all strata and professions in the society who had merely given him conditional support and were waiting on him to give a lead in the exercise of reconstruction that most agree had to take place in the next five years while there was still time to proceed incrementally rather than in a cataclysmic fashion. There was evidence that people were willing to accept the call for discipline, hard work and sacrifice if they were made aware that all were being asked to work and sacrifice equally for the general good by a leadership that was itself exemplary.

The nation waited to see whether Mr. Chambers would prove to be a "whale among the sardines" and whether he would in time prove wrong those who characterized Trinidad as a land that was beyond hope and redemption. Chambers was not to achieve the success that many hoped he would. This was in part due to his own idiosyncracies as a leader, the nature of the party which he led, and the fact that it became the prisoner of a clique of placement and office holders. Chambers was also a victim of the collapse of the petro-dollar boom which occurred between 1983-1986 and the economic and political crises to which it gave rise.

Chambers began his stint as a well meaning Prime Minister. He promised to maintain the positive achievements of the PNM and to correct the excesses of Williams' administration. To use his own words, he would "put right that which was wrong and keep right that which was right." Many who had left the PNM over the years rallied back to it in the expectation of change. Many who loved the PNM but hated Williams and his clique, saw in Chambers a man with whom they would work to put the PNM back on its original course. After making a few dramatic interventions in 1981, Chambers retreated behind the cloistered walls of Whitehall and became an adjuster-type politician who brokered policy decisions. He was clearly reluctant to appear to be altering the policies of his predecessor, whether in domestic or foreign policy. Whatever reform instincts he might have had were likewise abandoned as he came face to face with the entrenched power of the vested interests who had captured the party over the years.

Chambers claimed to have found it difficult to prevail against what he called the "wicked" business elements who were opposed to the PNM and the little man. From time to time he inveighed against the power of the interlocking directorates and the pressure that they could bring to bear on those who crossed them. As he told an audience during the 1986 election campaign:

> ...you have no idea how difficult it is to run a straight course in this little Trinidad and Tobago and keep your eyes focussed on your intention [to] uplift the little man in this country. Do not fool yourselves when you elect a man Prime Minister as the people. There are forces in and out of Trinidad and Tobago which, if he [is not] playing a ball to suit them, take the decision long before you that he must go. And that has been my personal experience. My personal experience, as somebody coming after Williams, is that people considered you manipulable. You look small and frail and easy. And when you bowl the first ball, and you say 'you are not talking to me, I am dealing with the people, my authority springs from the people,' they try a second and third time and you damned vex now. And you say: 'if

> you try that again, I will expose you in Woodford Square.' The minute you do that your are earmarked for going. You are earmarked to be removed." (*Guardian,* November 29, 1986)

The PNM Leader also told audiences during the campaign that the aim of the power élite was not "change" of parties in government, but something more fundamental. The aim was to destroy the PNM and the psychological association which that party had established with the people of Trinidad and Tobago. As he declared : "The PNM is part of the culture of this country and the opposition recognized that. The issue in this election is to destroy that. It is not to form the government. It is not to take power. It is to destroy PNM's association and integration into the national life and national psyche of the people of the country." It may well be that Chambers did more to fracture that relationship than did the opposition.

Clearly, however, Chambers was not speaking for the Indian community or the other minorities when he remarked that the PNM had become the essential organizational linch pin of the culture of Trinidad and Tobago and was irrevocably associated with the psyche of its people. They would show him otherwise in 1986, a year in which a coalition of opposition groups calling itself the National Alliance For Reconstruction effectively destroyed the PNM though it would find that it could not sustain itself organizationally once it had achieved that revolutionary feat.

Chapter 8

The National Alliance for Reconstruction: A Dream Betrayed

In December 1986, a coalition of opposition forces calling itself the National Alliance For Reconstruction (NAR) came to power in Trinidad and Tobago, dislodging in the process the People's National Movement which had governed the twin island state since 1956. The victory was a decisive once, one for which many had struggled since 1956. Many predicted the demise of the former ruling party. The NAR won 33 of the 36 seats in the Parliament and 66 per cent of the total votes cast. On the face of it, the defeat was even more comprehensive since two of the three PNM candidates who won did so by a mere 61 and 251 votes respectively. The Prime Minister and Political Leader of the PNM also lost his seat and chose to resign the leadership. The NAR appeared to many to have replaced the PNM as the party that would dominate politics in Trinidad and Tobago for the next twenty five years.

The victory of the NAR was hailed by many as a triumph of democracy in Trinidad and Tobago. It was said that contrary to all expectations and the experience of other Third World countries, Trinidad and Tobago had shown that it could manage the problem of regime change without violence after a long period of one party dominance. It also appeared to have found the formula to ford the racial gap that many had come to believe was not manageable in racially plural societies such as Fiji, Mauritius, Guyana, or Suriname, to name four countries with which Trinidad and Tobago was normally compared. The 1986 victory was characterised as a triumph of "One Love" and ethnic ecumenism since the party included all the major and minor "tribes" of Trinidad and Tobago.

The NAR obtained majority or significant support from all racial groups, religious denominations and social classes, with such support increasing as one went upscale. A SARA Survey revealed that 70 per cent of the Hindus, 69 per cent of the Muslims, 53 per cent of the Catholics and 40 per cent of the Protestants endorsed the party. Taken together, 82 per cent of the Indo-Trinidadian and 41 per cent of the Afro-Trinidadian population supported the party. In terms of class, 70 per cent of the upper middle, 72 per cent of the middle, 58 per cent of the lower middle and 44 per cent of the lower classes endorsed the party.

One newspaper columnist described the campaign and the NAR's victory in the following terms:

> If ever a single, poignant, pleading and deserving message came out of a political campaign in Trinidad and Tobago, or anywhere else for that matter, it was the message of "One Love" emerging from the historic general election of 1986. A look at the crowds, references to the numerous photographs taken, the television footage, and the spoken accounts all state one thing - that at last, a truly integrated and cosmopolitan government has emerged and is fully supported by our richly cosmopolitan population.
>
> All kinds of people voted for the NAR and support and cheer them and justifiably share in their smashing triumph. Black people, white people and every shade in between. All races. Old, hobbling people. Young energetic people. They all came, they all saw and at last they have all conquered. A violated people has triumphed (cited in Ryan 1989b:90).

The collapse of the NAR coalition within months of that pivotal election was perhaps the most traumatic political event in the history of the Indian community in Trinidad and Tobago. The reasons for the failure of that experiment are fully detailed elsewhere (Ryan 1989b). Suffice it to say that the most important factor was the difficulty which the leadership of the coalition faced in its attempt to satisfy the material and symbolic needs of the two major ethnic communities in the context of an economy which had contracted sharply after the collapse of the economic boom, which followed upon the dramatic increase in the price of petroleum between 1973 and 1983. In 1976, the price per barrel of oil was US$26. By 1986 it had fallen to a mere US$9.00.

The strain within the NAR surfaced publicly in the middle of 1987 and led eventually to the formation of a dissident group within the party which called itself CLUB 1988 (Caucus for Love, Unity, and Brotherhood). Later in that year, the caucus transformed itself into a full fledged party which called itself the United National Congress (UNC).

The UNC was formed following the expulsion from the Government of Basdeo Panday and other key members of the United Labour Front (ULF), one of the parties which had dissolved itself to form the NAR. The evidence indicates that Panday *et. al.* contrived to get themselves expelled once they had come to believe that they were being treated as junior members of the coalition and held responsible for unpopular economic decisions which they had no hand in making. Those members of the ULF who opted to stay argued that it would be better for the Indian to stay in the governing coalition. The dissidents however argued that they were not interested in a "mere" exchange of the pews of power with the PNM, but with structural reform designed to change the way in which resources were allocated in the society and to whom. As one of the dissident MPs [Trevor Sudama] wrote:

> It was the fond hope that an understanding and a mechanism would have been forged to induct citizens of East Indian descent into the mainstream of decision, participation and involvement; that a greater sense of belonging and sharing would have been fostered; and that a new awareness of creative possibilities would have emerged. The trauma which attended the failure of that experiment still lingers

> with us. The experiment floundered on the reef of a subsisting majority consciousness of the role, place and functions of Indians as a group in the society. (*Trinidad Guardian,* October 11, 1971)

Opinion polls conducted by St. Augustine Research Associates in June 1988 revealed that the bulk of the Indian community was embittered by the expulsion of the ULF faction from the NAR. Sixty-one per cent of them did not consider the firing of Basdeo Panday justified and 62 per cent wanted him back in the Cabinet; 66 per cent of them wished to see a reconciliation between the ULF element and the NAR. Only 16 per cent of the Indians said they would remain with the NAR if no reconciliation was effected. Moreover, 47 per cent said that they regretted having voting for the NAR.

The figures were much the same when religious affiliation was considered. Seventy per cent of the Muslims, 64 per cent of the Hindus and 56 per cent of the Presbyterians were opposed to Panday's firing, while 70 and 69 per cent of the first two denominational groups wanted to see some sort of reconciliation put into effect. Seventy-four per cent of the Muslims also said they wanted to see Panday back in the cabinet, while 67 per cent of the Hindus and Presbyterians shared this view.

The figures revealed the extent to which Indians across the denominational spectrum felt that the NAR leadership had betrayed them. This anger translated itself into hostility to the NAR leadership in general and to the Prime Minister ANR Robinson, in particular. Indian parliamentarians who opted to remain in the NAR were also singled out for threats and abuse. They were seen as *nemakharams,* people who had betrayed their community and its leader after having received his beneficence.

This feeling of betrayal also expressed itself in a "refugee phenomenon." During 1988, thousands of Indo-Trinidadians "fled" to Canada seeking "refugee status", claiming that they were victims of racially inspired discrimination in their own country.

Indians in fact claimed that they were on the receiving end of rape, robbery and other kinds criminal activity to a greater extent than were other groups. They also alleged that they were not being given their due and just share of material allocations and status recognition in the public sector. Some, like the Indeshian Freedom Party, went so far as to demand that a separate State of Indeshia be created for Indians somewhere in the southern part of the country, a demand that most Trinidadians dismissed as being not only impractical, but grossly ridiculous and designed to buttress claims for favourable consideration for refugee status by Canadian immigration officials.

While it is clear that there was an element of opportunism involved in the claims, there were many who shared and endorsed the feelings of "alienation" which underpinned the demands of the extremists. Indeed, the collapse of the NAR coalition helped to fuel the embers of disenchantment which had long smoldered in the breast of many Indians who believed that the larger society saw them as pariahs and a group apart rather that as fully incorporated members of the national community (cf. Annexe 3).

This feeling was expressed in the writings of Indian novelists, poets, and social scientists prior to 1988. The late Samuel Selvon (Selvon was a *"dougla"*, half-Indian) talked of growing up feeling that "the Indian was just a piece of cane trash" (1987: 31). Selvon also remarked that many Indians feel "oppressed and suppressed" and without a national spokesman:

> ...the biggest insult to his (i.e. the Indian's) pride is that up to today, the Indian community is without a leader, without a voice. We have not had one person, or one party, rising with any degree of power or authority to instill some measure of dignity for him even of mere basic representation. (ibid., 43)

Ismith Khan, another novelist (Khan is a Muslim), likewise remarked that while Indians were responsible for producing the bulk of the locally grown food and many of the services which were consumed in the country without which contributions "all the bureaucracies of power would shut down overnight," they had not been given their due share of power. As he complained:

> The failure of the Indian population to acquire its equal and proportionate representation in the government and governmental agencies of this republic is alarming and disappointing. And if we accept the fact that this is so in what purports to be a democratic state ..., it is shocking because we are speaking about close to half a million people who seem to have little say about their destiny. There are more recent arrivals of immigrant groups to this area than the Indians who have contributed far less to the growth and development of this area, and who have secured for themselves most, if not all, of the advantages that the area promises. The image of the Indian in Trinidad is one of a group of people who should plant cane and tomatoes and watermelons. That is what he was brought here for, and that is where he should stay ... in his place. (Khan 1987: 47)

Khan conceded that Indians have made great strides in the professions, in business, the arts and sciences, but lamented that there had been no corresponding increase in their political status. Interestingly, he was not only critical of non-Indian élites for this "crime", but equally so of upwardly mobile Indians, who in their desire to be accepted by the so called "national" society, had abandoned the rural Indian to their own devices. To quote Khan:

> For the most part, the vast masses of the Indians of the heartland have never been given any thought or consideration by those who managed to rise up out of the squalor and servitude of the sugar cane plantation by those who chose the door of cosmopolitanism. (ibid., 48)

Ignored by the larger society and made to feel unwanted or uncomfortable in the urban bureaucracies, the Indian, who unlike his counterpart in Fiji, Africa, Australia or Java was every whit as entitled to be fully incorporated in Trinidad society, a society in which everyone is an immigrant, turned to the artifice of the entrepreneur as a technique for material survival:

> Unfit for the office of urban life and work, he is a loner who looks out for himself and his family, doing so by wanting to be 'his own boss', whether it is driving his own taxi, or running a *roti* shop or parlour, more recently a snackette, or the traditional dry goods shop ... rice, flour, sugar. (ibid., 50)

For spiritual survival and security, he turned to the comforts and conveniences of his cultural heritage. "In doing so, he absolved himself of the tedium and responsibility that all men have if they expect to exert any clout in the spheres of their lives that have to do with their future and their destiny." In an interesting comment on the behaviour of the upwardly mobile Indian which would anticipate the fate of the NAR in 1991, Khan noted that the coming of independence forcefully brought home to "cosmopolitan" Indians that "democracy deals with numbers, not with small affluent intelligentsia and aristocrats in small clubs" (ibid., 53).

Another interesting perspective on the experience of the Indians in the Caribbean came from Rev. Roy Neehall. In a lecture given in Toronto in 1992, Neehall argued that even though many Indians, as did Africans, surrendered much of the externals of their ancestral cultures, many refused to surrender their souls. Even though some became converts, they retained the essence of their Indianess, the grammar of their culture so to speak. Rev. Neehall, a Presbyterian Minister, admitted that the majority of young Presbyterians pupils were not converted "anyway." Their conversion was instrumental, not essential. Neehall was also correct when he noted that Indians have made an indelible impact in the Caribbean, particularly in Guyana and Trinidad, and that in these two countries at least, "there will never be any such thing as a Caribbean identity that does not bear the stamp of its Indo-Caribbean citizens." India, in his view, had hybridised the Caribbean.

For Neehall, the essential and most valuable contribution that Indians have made to the creation of the Caribbean was resistance. Resistance first took the form of sheer physical survival in the midst of colonial greed and exploitation. Survival was also evident in terms of their determination to retain the validity of their customs and religions in the midst of expressed hostility and disrespect from both Europeans and Africans. The fact that Indians sought to retain the integrity of their family and village life was viewed as reactionary by many, but in Neehalls' view, it also had to be seen as an act of deliberate resistance. Village and family life were mechanisms of resistance. "Their spirit of resistance, fed by their sense of family and religion at the root of their community life, did not protect them from being knocked down, but it saved them from being knocked out."

Neehall (1993:7) noted that just as Pocomania and Rastafarianism in Jamaica served as a vehicles of African resistance to the dominant mainline Christian religions, so too did Indian religions:

> Religion offered to the masses of Indo-Caribbean people a means of expressing protest against the assumed superiority of the mainline Christian Church whose relation to the colonial system was one of accommodation since, for a long time, it did not offer any challenge to the dehumanizing conditions that colonialism and capitalism imposed on the masses of poor people.

Resistance also took the form of class based politics. Neehall is at pains to point out that Indians were involved in at least 5 anti-colonial riots in Guyana, 5 in Suriname and 2 in Trinidad and Tobago. He in fact challenged the myth that Indians were always involved in rearguard political action on the side of the colonial authorities. They too shared the sense of outrage about the colonial exploitation of the peoples of African and Asian descent. It was not, he insists, a problem of division according to race or colour, but of class. The resistance of the Indo-Trinidadian took the form of class based politics, especially in Guyana and to a certain extent in Trinidad and Tobago.

Many saw the Indian parties as "racial parties," but the reality is that "a majority of their supporters were part of a past that had seen itself as being underprivileged and exploited by political and economic forces. Their participation in this kind of politics was an illustration of the persistence of their spirit of resistance." Neehall also claimed was that Indian resistance expressed itself in a fierce desire to own land. "Where land is available to people for food production and other agricultural pursuits, exclusion from the corridors of formal political power does not destroy them" (Neehall 1993:10).

John La Guerre accepts Neehall's thesis that there was resistance. Indians, he says, were better able to resist the encroachments of Western value systems in matters such as what constituted beauty, cultural propriety etc. "Partly as a result of colonial policy which did not seek to strip them of their culture as fully as was the case with the Africans, but also because of the efforts of village pundits, films, missionaries and letters from India, Indians were able to preserve something they were able to call Indian culture even in its very modified form." La Guerre however notes that the fact that many Indians had to exist in a tension ridden relationship between their ancestral culture and the modernizing society in which they found themselves led to a great deal of "malintegration" and "marginalisation." Many, he says were like "Mohammet's coffin," suspended between two cultures" (*The Capildeo Speeches,* Foreword, 1994:xvi).

Not everyone would however agree fully with Neehall's assessment of the political role of the Indo-Trinidadians in the Caribbean. While what Neehall says might be true for some, and in certain contexts for the majority, the overriding concern of the early indentureds were to accumulate enough for the return to India and, where return was not deemed a desirable option, to protect their community from the political radicalism of the Afro-Trinidadian intelligentsia. John La Guerre makes the valid point that despite the later attempt by some sections of the African and Indian intelligentsia to equate them, slavery and indentureship were never perceived as interchangeable. "So that freedom for Indians struck no responsive chord. For the African slaves and their descendants freedom was in fact a major issue; for the indentured immigrants the possession of a contract set a term on his servile status and ensured a return passage to India. It was also only after much hesitation that the Indians finally let down their bucket in Trinidad. The concerns of Indians thus at one level at least differed from those of the African intelligentsia" (ibid.).

La Guerre likewise agrees with Neehall that even Indians who converted to Presbyterianism or who anglicized their names maintained a "fugitive relationship" with the ancestral cultures of Hinduism and Islam. "They also had their sacred books and villages to which they could return to renew their contacts" (ibid.).

Dr. Winston Mahabir, who was a Minister in the 1956-1961 PNM government, also shared the view that Indians in the Caribbean were becoming politically re-indentured, this time to a "factitious" African power élite. Among the evidence adduced to support this claim was that electoral fraud and other forms of political prestidigitation were becoming endemic in places like Guyana. Violence directed towards Indians, scapegoating, and the use of the army and police to silence a potentially "hostile or recalcitrant group" was also said to be on the increase. Mahabir likewise claimed that there was evidence that migration from the smaller islands was being encouraged to Trinidad to offset increased levels of Indian fertility (Mahabir 1987:66).

Like Khan, Neehall and Selvon, Mahabir argued that despite rapid educational gains, the "political interface" between Indians and others was far from what it should be ideally. Indians who had tried to become culturally mainstream or to function within parties like the WINP or the TLP had experienced "the frustrated feeling of being perceived as the internal outsider." These feelings had given rise to the belief that since they were not going to be allowed to "share power", they would have to grasp it, whether by conventional or unconventional means. They had come to feel that after 30 perilously long years of PNM rule, it was now time for the Indians to have "their turn at the cricket crease."

Mahabir was however not prepared to encourage Indians along this path which he saw as self-destructive. "No race in Trinidad," he said, "was entitled to chant with Jessie Jackson that 'our time has come.' A plural society can only thrive if all its members enjoyed equal rights of citizenship and power is genuinely shared." Mahabir was not optimistic that this would happen since "the recorded history of the Caribbean is one of grossly unequal rights." But the effort had to be made. Mahabir also warned that Trinidad and Tobago was home not only to persons of Indian and African descent, but also to Syrians, Chinese, and Europeans, all of whom had made solid contributions to the society. "Certainly, there is no hideous tradition that political power will alternate between the two numerically dominant racial groups" (Mahabir 1987: 74-79).

The demand for the creation of an Indian homeland provoked strong reaction both within the Indian community and without. A group calling itself the Indian Review Committee endorsed the demand, noting that "it is an old issue which refuses to die." One spokesman of the group, Kamal Persad, noted that the issue had been raised by H.P. Singh in 1956 in his pamphlet, *Hour of Decision* which was dismissed as "DLP race propaganda" by the PNM and black nationalists (Ryan 1972: 330-331). Persad noted further that the call for an Indian homeland antedated Singh, and had been on the agenda once Indians had decided that they would make the Caribbean their new home. Poems like the "Kuli Man Has Come to Stay" had called on the larger Caribbean society to recognise the legitimacy of the Indian presence. In Guyana, terms such as "Jahajidesh" and "New Bharatdesh" had also been proposed as alternative names for Guyana. Persad argued that "the ultimate destiny for the Indian nation in the Caribbean and South America ... could be achieved by peaceful constitutional means; if not, Indians should not hesitate to use militant means for ultimate freedom" (Persad 1993: 115-119).

The call for a separate homeland or a union of Guyana and Trinidad was a defensive response to black national assertiveness which emerged after 1945. Fear that Indians would be dominated in the impending Federation of Caribbean States had given rise to calls for a unification of Trinidad and Guyana. The reality of powerlessness in black-dominated states was the major reason for this call for separate Indian states in the Caribbean. The post-Independence experience of Indians in these countries and Suriname also made these fears more real.

Persad noted that two other groups, the *Equality* Editorial Committee and the Indian Arrival Committee, had also issued a statement on January 1, 1991 calling for the urgent creation in the Americas of an Indian homeland consisting of parts of the South American States of Guyana and Suriname and of Trinidad and Tobago. The proposed name of the new state was Bharatiyadesh/Industan and was to be the "realisation of a long deferred dream, a longing and a vision." The demand was to form a "fundamental and central element in the ideological and philosophical system of *Apanghat.*" Those Indians who refused to support this demand or the validity of the identification with mother India were accused of being *nemakharams,* of being ungrateful to their ancestral motherland. Persad linked this demand to what was happening in other parts of the world (Russia, Eastern Europe and the Middle East), where demands for ethnic homelands were becoming more persistent as well as in Tobago where elements saw the results of the 1991 election as Trinidad repudiating Tobago.

Most Indians were of the view that the demand for Indesh or Bharatiyadesh/Industan made no practical sense. Nor was it deemed desirable. Pundit Indrani Rampersad spoke for many when she indicated her opposition, though she did not consider the matter frivolous as many were wont to do. "It is serious, not because there is any real threat of physically dividing an already emotionally divided Trinidad and Tobago, but because it points to more division of our nation, be it physical or emotional." Rampersad agreed that the demand was linked to Indian feelings of political powerlessness. The exclusion from the corridors of power "engineered under PNM rule led to a whole people going into internal exile [as] doors remained shut as the institutionalised exclusion by the state consolidated with time." This exclusion was not only evidenced in state institutions, but in the Caribbean media as well which "contrived to ignore the fact that there is a vibrant ethnic presence in the Caribbean" (Persad 1993: 115-119).

Rampersad argued further that the refugee exodus to Canada in 1988 received its impetus from the collapse of the NAR which she claims "shattered the emotional state of ethnic Indo-Trinidadians who felt all was lost." People, she noted, "felt, and not without justification if you put yourself in their shoes, that Trinidad and Tobago was incapable of getting a government that would treat them equally," and which would allow them "space" to be free to develop. "Such a future for their children, they felt, could not happen under a system that so openly excluded ethnic Indians from all positions in the upper echelons of the administration and the public sector." Rampersad admitted that the economic crisis was also a factor as was "the incredible crime rate and the failure of the Police to protect the lives and property of law abiding citizens."

Indians were thus no longer prepared to go into internal exile and to suppress their emotions in "excessive alcoholism and domestic violence" as their parents and grand parents were minded to do. They were now demanding full incorporation in the society that had traditionally rejected them. "Their's is a traditionally unheard voice that jars the national nerve much as the women's choice for equality did male dominance." Rampersad admitted that the NAR had tried to redress the imbalance in the public sector, but the firing of Panday from the NAR cabinet in 1987 had alienated the support among Indians which that party had gained in 1986. Panday's expulsion was taken as a sign of "oppression" of the Indo-Trinidadian once again. The "Indian ministers who remained therefore had no base." Rampersad however felt that refugee status in Canada or the demand for Indesh was "escapist". Indians, in her view, had to fight for a secure place "right here" (*Trinidad Express,* May 16, 1993).

This determination to fight for a "secure place right here" gave rise to a renewed sense of cultural assertiveness, a new determination to "go back home." This was particularly so in the countryside among the rural population. As Dr. Brinsley Samaroo observed:

> There's a vast ignorance about the rural population — the areas of darkness are so considerable — Indians have become convinced the West has nothing superior to them. Since 1845, they have waited [for recognition], and still feel they don't belong. So there is a resurgence of Indian culture.

Another perspective on the issue however came from Professor Ken Ramchand who addressed the problem in the context of the question as to whether the first arrival of the Indians in Trinidad and Tobago in 1845 should be celebrated as a national holiday. Ramchand argued that Indians should not celebrate their "arrival" in the Caribbean as a unique historical event, but as part of the general arrival process of all immigrants. "Arrival" for him meant developing a sense of self as a Trinidadian person, a process that of necessity excluded any demand for a separate territory that would cradle whatever it is Indians wished to preserve. Ramchand saw no contradiction between feeling pride in one's cultural antecedents and in being part of something else called Trinidadian:

> The necessity people feel to find themselves first as Indian or African or Chinese cannot be dismissed as tribalism. But it would be tribalism, and it could lead to calamity if it wasn't seen as a component for the Trinidadian, or as an intermediate stage on the way to making him up. There is no necessary contradiction between recognising one's ancestral heritage, and being a Trinidadian. You can be Hindu. Muslim, Roman Catholic, or devotee of the Orisha and still be a Trinidadian.

Ramchand's view was not welcomed by the cultural nationalists who saw in his recommendation an anxiety to minimise the real differences which exist between Indians and other groups in the society. As Trevor Sudama observed:

> ... such a suggestion probably springs from a desire to eliminate what is regarded as uncomfortable distinctions between our peoples which were wrought by history and circumstance. It is again an attempt to create another Procustean bed, this time to accommodate all comers.

An interesting question raised by Lloyd Best was whether the sense of alienation felt by the Indians was due to something which was done to them by the creole elements who came before them or whether it was simply due to the facts of geography and history. As Best writes:

> Indians in the Caribbean are indeed in an unequal existential situation compared with Africans. This is not because we wish it so or only (or even mainly) because of the differences in numbers but because there is no way we can escape paying our dues to the logic of history — to the imperatives of timing and sequencing and placing in human affairs. There is such a thing as an Afro-Saxon (which is merely an African in America compelled by his historic location to practice European institutions). What nowhere exists is an Indo-Saxon. The interculturation into which the Indians were inducted at the moment of their entry was by then not even three-sided. By then it had become manysided (so much so that the one thing it could not be was many splendoured). So it is that even if there were no other people in Trinidad and Tobago save Indians, their predicament in the Caribbean, in the Atlantic, and in America would, I suspect, scarcely be different. (*Trinidad Express,* October 6, 1993)

The PNM Government of Trinidad and Tobago "resolved" the question of the holiday by agreeing that May 30, 1995 be celebrated as Indian Arrival Day to mark the anniversary of the 150th year of the arrival of Indians in Trinidad and Tobago. Thereafter, May 1, was to be celebrated nationally as Arrival day, a day with which all ethnic groups in the society could identify if they wished to do so (cf. Annexe 8).

The solution satisfied a few but alienated many. Alienated were some Christians who had to give up Whit Monday to make room for Arrival day and a majority of Indians who felt that the Day should have been named Indian Arrival Day in perpetuity as Indians had demanded. Indians again complained that only grudging recognition was being given to the fact that they had in a fundamental way "arrived". The Political leader of the UNC, Basdeo Panday, argued further though implausibly, that if the holiday had in fact been named Indian Arrival Day, "a fatal blow would have been dealt to the problem of alienation" in Trinidad and Tobago. Panday in fact promised that when the UNC won power, it would proclaim the day Indian Arrival Day, a promise that he would later redeem.

Panday was of the view that Trinidad and Tobago was a plural society and public holidays should thus be truly representative of all its "peoples" including the Baptists and the devotees of Orisha or other African religious belief systems. Others held the view that there were already too many holidays in Trinidad and Tobago and it would be inadvisable to add others to satisfy the expectations of those who were currently making demands and those who might make them in the future (cf. my opinion in *Sunday Express,* May 21, 1995; cf. Annexe 8).

Chapter 9

Racism and the UNC*

I

On Monday May 14, 1990, at a meeting in Princes Town, the Honourable Mr. John Humphrey, Member of Parliament for St. Augustine, told a meeting of the UNC that a high level of racialism is being demonstrated in the United National Congress. Humphrey was quoted as having said:

> Close colleagues of our party are saying that I am too old and that I only like white people. We must cut that nonsense out. These racist elements in the UNC will destroy the party. We must not allow this to happen.... We can no longer allow anyone to ride Panday's back to get into power like Robinson did. A man can only be ridden so much and then he gets tired of being ridden.... If the racist clique should take control of the party, the same thing would happen to the UNC as it did to the NAR.

These allegations were the subject of deliberations within the Interim Management of the UNC which, on the recommendation of the Political Leader of the UNC, appointed a

---

*This chapter is a reproduction of a report which was submitted to the leadership of the UNC by the author who had been asked by that leadership to serve as a one man Commission of Inquiry into the charges made by MP John Humphrey that there was racism in the newly formed UNC.

one-man Commission of Inquiry to investigate the allegations and report on its findings. The author was appointed sole Commissioner by the UNC. The terms of reference subsequently given to the Commission by the Political Leader of the UNC were as follows:

i. to investigate whether there are in fact people at the highest level of the leadership of the United National Congress who are demonstrating a racist position towards the Honourable Mr. John Humphrey M.P. and

ii. to consider whether there is need for setting up an intra-party machinery to deal with similar allegations, and if yes, your recommendations for such a machinery.

There was some question as to whether the terms of reference had somehow been deliberately narrowed and therefore did not allow the Commission to investigate the broader charge made by Mr. Humphrey. The Commission is not aware that there was any deliberate and conscious attempt to narrow the scope of its investigations and was in fact assured that there was no such attempt. The Commission therefore felt free to take notice of any evidence which impinged on the general charge of racism in the UNC levelled by Mr. Humphrey.

In the course of its investigations, the Commission interviewed twenty-four UNC activists who were at the centre of the controversy at the national and constituency levels. Plans to interview more persons were abandoned for two reasons. One was that time was perceived to be of the essence. While no deadline for submitting the Report was ever given, the Commission was aware that there was need to conclude the investigations expeditiously in order to allow the UNC to continue its preparations for the National Assembly which was scheduled for July 22, 1990. The other reason was that the evidence given by those interviewed displayed a recurring pattern. While more detail might have been forthcoming if more interviews were held, it was evident that the basic pattern was unlikely to change. An opinion survey was also conducted to determine how people in general and UNC supporters felt about the suggestion that the party should be open to Indians alone.

In presenting the report, we first detail in full the charges made by Mr. Humphrey and those whose evidence was in general support of the claims made by him. The response of those against whom the charges were levelled follows, after which, the merits of the respective claims are assessed. An attempt has also been made to locate the controversy in the recent political history of Trinidad and Tobago as well as in the general debate about racism and pluralism in societies such as Trinidad and Tobago.

Note should be taken of the fact that unlike what obtains in an officially appointed Commission of Inquiry, the Commission had no power to compel witnesses to appear or to command the submission of documents. Moreover, statements made to the Commission and the reports thereof were not privileged and protected from libel suits as would have been the case if the Inquiry had been established under the terms of the Commission of Inquiries Ordinance. We have thus chosen to avoid as far as possible identifying witnesses and their specific allegations as well as persons against whom these allegations were made.

Mr. Humphrey's Claim

Mr. Humphrey told the Commission that the general problem about which he complained dates back to the founding of the Caucus For Love Unity and Brotherhood (CLUB 88) in February 1988. Mr. Humphrey recalls that at one of the earliest meetings of the CLUB 88, he expressed the view that a new party, if formed, would not get very far if its base extended only to the constituencies which in the past were won by the United Labour Front (ULF). He thus argued that CLUB 88 should seek to attract

National Alliance for Reconstruction (NAR) activists who were disenchanted with Mr. ANR Robinson and the NAR in all thirty-six constituencies. Some of these elements did in fact join CLUB 88 and eventually became members of the UNC when it was formed in April 1989.

We were told by Mr. Humphrey that racial particularism began to rear its head in earnest when the UNC was being established and persons were being selected to form its Interim Management Committee. The composition of that Committee was said to be very different from the old Interim Management Committee of CLUB 88. We were also told that some of the non-Indian activists who were in CLUB 88 began to be marginalised and excluded from some of the house meetings which were sponsored by elements in the leadership structure of the Party.

Racial particularism was also said to have been in evidence when the Constitution for the new party was being discussed. We were told by Mr. Humphrey that during these discussions, he put forward the view that Trinidad and Tobago was made up of many groups and that the leadership structure of the Party should reflect the pluralism in the society. We were told that he lobbied for the principle of collective leadership, arguing that if the leadership of the Party was seen to be collective, greater confidence would be generated in it. His specific argument was that a triumvirate should be established, the members of which would reflect the fact that there were two basic ethnic blocs in the society of roughly equal size, Indians and Africans, and a group which might be described as "others". Decision making in the party would be polycentric and not the preserve of one man or group. This view was rejected as was the subsequent recommendation that there should be two deputy leaders. In making the case for two deputies, it was felt that this formula would also serve to put in place the principle of the triumvirate.

Mr. Humphrey claims that he was told that in discussions which took place in his absence on this issue, some individuals were heard to say that no "white man" should be chosen deputy leader of the UNC since Indians had unique problems in Trinidad and Tobago which only an Indian could understand. Indians, it was said, needed Indians to give voice and leadership to their struggle. Humphrey claims that his response to this was that the UNC was conceived as a *national party* which was to be different from the PNM and the NAR, both of which were "deformations", parties which in their platform rhetoric had made claims to represent the national community, but which in fact were dominated by Afro-Trinidadians. If the UNC was to be truly a national party, "a reincarnation of the original NAR", its leadership must seek to understand the concerns of the entire national community and not one fragment thereof. The UNC's struggle was for equality for all and rather than special privileges for any one group.

Mr. Humphrey believes that there are those who do not share that vision of the UNC's historical role and were surreptitiously campaigning for an Indian party whose leader and deputy leader would be Indian. Their campaign, he alleged, is being organised and orchestrated by persons highly placed in the interim leadership. This clique is said to have supporters in all constituencies, but particularly in Couva South. It is claimed that persons form Couva South have emerged as chairmen of five constituencies and that given the decentralisation of the party into nine regions and the "one man, one vote" formula by which persons are elected to leadership positions in the party, this could hardly be accidental. Humphrey believes that the group's aim is to hijack the party by gaining control of constituency executives and in this way secure a lock on the candidate selection process. The unfair campaign was said to be difficult to counter since it was being waged clandestinely.

The clique, we were told, saw Humphrey, who had openly declared his intention to contest the post of deputy leader, as a threat to its plan to "Indianise" the UNC and therefore sought to marginalise him and his support groups in the constituencies, causing great confusion in the process. The issue was reportedly raised with the Political Leader of the UNC who reportedly took no decisive action.

The incident which triggered the decision to force the issue out into the open arena was the report that a key individual in the Interim Management Committee had instructed an activist in the Pointe-a-Pierre constituency that application forms for party membership should not be distributed to non-Indians. According to Humphrey, he took seriously the views expressed by the Political Leader of the UNC that racism was a stain on the national fabric and that he was embarked on a national crusade to eliminate the scourge of racism from public life. As Panday had said at the Meeting in Aranguez during which the UNC was launched:

> The mandate you have given us to form a new political party is the first step in ensuring the reincarnation of the original NAR — a new vehicle by which we shall continue the struggle for economic prosperity through national unity and national mobilisation, ensuring the widest and deepest participation in the decision-making processes of the people" (see Aranguez Speech in Annexe 20).

Panday, it was recalled, had also campaigned for the creation of an Equal Opportunities Commission. In Humphrey's view, one could not campaign effectively for the creation of such a body at the national level if the instrument of that struggle, the UNC, had persons within its leadership ranks who were themselves guilty of racist and exclusionist practices. Such a campaign would have no credibility. One thus had to first cleanse the "Augean Stables" of the Party.

When asked what he considered to be "racism", Humphrey explained that a refusal to give party application forms to non-Indians was to discriminate on the basis of race. The attempt to have one ethnic group monopolise the party was also "racist". In his view, there was nothing wrong if an ethnic group which felt a sense of identity and pride born of shared experiences, organised to give effect to their concerns within the framework of a party. Freedom of association was guaranteed by the Constitution. Those activities should however be in the open. He nevertheless felt that such a group would have to examine its activities in terms of what the party stood for in its principles and in its Constitution. Group goals would also have to be reconciled with national goals with which they might be in conflict.

Humphrey was firmly convinced that Panday was not part of the clique which was seeking to Indianise the UNC and that the latter were acting without his support and quite contrary to the principles to which he was committed. In his view, this clique was seeking to ride Panday's "political back" just as others had been accused of doing. The clique was also accused of seeking to use non-Indians to achieve their goal of Indian domination.

Humphrey was not alone in levelling these charges at the "anti-party" clique. Others made similar allegations before the Commission. We were also told *inter alia:*

- that the clique was not really motivated by "race but by religion and that it was a group of "super Hindus" who were creating mischief in the party by seeking to "Bhagwatise" it. Considerations of casteism (or its residues thereof) were also said to be relevant

- that persons with certain ideological perspectives were also being marginalised

- that in its membership drive, the group was in the main seeking out and courting Indians in the hope of securing and consolidating an Indian base in the party

- that attempts had been made to relocate constituency election meetings previously scheduled for ethnically neutral sites to venues where Indians were numerically dominant

- that some members of the group felt that Africans had had their turn to run the country over the last thirty years and that Indians should now have their turn
- that some members of the group felt that non-Indians had shown that they could not run the country, that Indians were more competent to do so and should therefore seek to gain control
- that the group felt Indians were now the largest single group in the population and perhaps the wealthiest and could go it alone
- that members of the group saw themselves as Indians rather than Trinidadians
- that the group felt that given its control of constituencies in south and central Trinidad and pockets along the East West Corridor the UNC could "come through the middle" in three cornered election contests and either win the next general election outright or hold the balance of power
- that individuals in the UNC had expressed the view that "help" packages paid for by monies raised by UNC "Help Clubs" should not be given to Afro-Trinidadians who never "help" Indians
- that activists in the Pointe-a-Pierre constituency were going around asking supporters of non-Indian political aspirants whether they knew of any "creole" who helped Indians and that these activists had said they wished to put up an Indian in the area
- that complaints were openly made by the Head of the Party Organisation and Formation at a meeting

in Chaguanas that in the Constituency of Diego Martin Central over 200 members present at an election meeting and yet only 2 Indians were elected to the Constituency Executive out of a slate of 10. The organiser was heard to say: "we will deal with that later"

- that candidates and their backers either paid the membership fees for persons whom they had co-opted to support them in their bid to be elected, paid people and provided transportation for them to vote, or made illegal use of membership cards or computer print-outs in order to engineer outcomes in constituency elections favourable to Indians

- that the same things which they left the NAR for were becoming evident in the UNC

- that Mr. Kelvin Ramnath is a silent partner of the clique although he is the real leader, the real strongman

- one of the chief mischief makers was said to be Dr. Rampersad Parasram who wished to be Chairman, Secretary, Chief Election Officer, Chief Rule Maker and Public Relations Officer of the UNC. Both Ramnath and Parasram were accused of having their own agenda and were said to be using Panday, without whom neither would have any political future. It was felt that they should both resign from Party

- that the leaders of the clique, which had previously been warm towards non-Indian activists in the Party, had now cooled towards them

- that Mr. John Humphrey was not the leader of any group in the party as alleged and in fact always disavowed those who referred to him as "the next Prime Minister." Instead, he always sought to project the Political Leader, Mr. Basdeo Panday

- the political culture of the East West Corridor differed from that of Central and South and members of the clique were not sufficiently experienced in the "folkways" of Corridor politics

- that the UNC's decision to have an office in the capital city was a positive move in that it had helped to remove the "stigma" of it being an Indian party. The move symbolised the fact that the UNC saw itself as a national party. Elements were however giving contradictory signals by their behaviour.

The activists who testified before the Commission in support of the allegations were firm in their belief that only a few persons in the UNC were guilty of racism. In their view, Indians as a group did not want an Indian party. Those who joined the UNC did so because of its campaign for equality and genuine multiracialism or non-racialism. They were thus of the view that the UNC should now purge itself of those elements who were betraying its ideals and continue to work towards the fulfillment of the goals which it set for itself. Racism should be "nipped in the bud" and discouraged by the party leadership at all levels. As one witness advised: "the cancer should be excised before it spreads."

Like Mr. Humphrey, they were also firm in their view that Mr. Panday was not part of the racist clique and speculated that his hesitancy to act decisively might have been motivated by his desire to keep the group together. They however argued that he must now choose. As one witness put it: "If he chose "right", God would open doors for him that were now closed." He would become a "national hero" rather than an object of unfair suspicion. Some indicated that if the right decisions were not made, they would walk out of the UNC in protest as they had done with respect to the NAR. Others however said that they would stay in and fight for their ideals and principles because of their commitment to building a nation in which the children of every race and creed would find an equal place.

The Charges Rebutted

Persons against whom these allegations were directed have generally deemed them unfortunate and untrue. They have replied, *inter alia,* that the incidents and occurrences which gave rise to the "crisis" within the party are linked to the UNC's decision to democratise the process of recruiting persons for party office and for candidate selection. In the past, a small group of people in the leadership of the ULF or the NAR handpicked those persons who would hold office or carry the party standard in local and national elections. The "new political culture" now enshrined the principle of decentralisation, the use of the primary for candidate selection, and the one man one vote formula as opposed to the use of the delegate system which obtains in other parties.

The Commission was told that in the exercise of their democratic right to mobilise support for office at the constituency level, party members have used all the strategies normally used by office seekers, and it may well be that some grassroots elements have appealed to communal sentiment. It was however denied that there was any clique at the centre which was masterminding any campaign to monopolise office for persons of one ethnic extraction to the exclusion of others.

The Chairman of the party's Division of Organisation and Formation, which deals with party organisation, admitted to the Commission that he had the support of a team of workers, most of whom were based in the constituency of Couva South. He and his team travelled all over the country organizing the party in the constituencies in the course of doing party work, and it would be thus quite normal for him to be in contact with aspirants for office. Persons well known to him might well have emerged victorious in some of the elections. This might have led some, especially those who were potential rivals, to believe that there was a conspiracy afoot and that unfair practices were used. The allegations about conspiracy were however vigorously denied.

It was further noted that at its inception, the party lamented the fact that non-Indians were not supporting it. As such, deliberate steps were taken to strengthen its support base in the East-West Corridor. It was agreed that it would take the Party a long time to break the historical barriers that were the by-product of slavery and indentureship as well as those created by post-independence politics. It was nevertheless regretted that Mr. Humphrey had not succeeded in using his influence to attract much of a following of non-Indians along the Corridor. Humphrey was also accused of not having raised any funds for the UNC as he had done for the PNM and the NAR.

The principal organisers of the party claimed that they made and would continue to make a determined effort to mobilise support along the East West Corridor in the hope of recapturing the spirit of the NAR and that the thrust had paid dividends. It was their view that by dint of hard work, significant and encouraging breakthroughs have been made in terms of recruiting members in all 36 constituencies, and that no leader worth his salt would put this newly found support at risk by doing or saying anything which would signal to non-Indians that they were not welcome in the UNC. It was considered sheer "madness" for the leaders of a young party to do any such thing.

The Interim Chairman of the Party also drew the attention of the Commission to several statements which he had made on various platforms and which were quoted in the daily press to the effect that "it was time to put an end to the politics of race and discrimination on the basis of colour, creed and class." To quote him:

> People must really begin to feel a genuine sense of belonging and no group in the society should feel they are left out of the mainstream of national life. Whether they are from Laventille, Tobago or Caroni, they are all entitled to equal treatment.

Evidence was also submitted by the Party Chairman that he had personally sponsored and endorsed the applications for membership by non-Indians. He too agreed, as did the Head of Party Organisation and Formation, that Indians do not want an all Indian party and that any party which sought to define itself in this way was certain to lose the support of many Indians. Indians, it was said, know that such a party would be ineffective and they would not support it. It was recalled that in the 1977 Local Government Elections, Indians voted against the ULF and for the PNM because they felt that a "pure" Indian party would be ineffective in terms of delivery of needed community resources.

With respect to the allegations made by Mr. Humphrey, it was claimed that he might well have been somewhat naive in believing that he would not be challenged. No legislator, whether at the national or the local level, had automatic privileges. One's election or re-election would depend on what work one did in and for the constituency. The people and not the leader would decide. The claim was that Humphrey and a few other incumbents began to experience feelings of political anxiety and insecurity when they saw teams with which they were associated defeated in constituency elections. The Party was also said to be attracting new blood and that its support base was now very different from that of the ULF. In the process, no one's office was secure. People would have to engage in a competitive struggle for the people's vote since they could no longer count on "free rides". There was no longer any charismatic umbrella to shield one from the unpredictable fortunes of democratic politics.

The claims made by Humphrey were said to be prompted by feelings of desperation, possibly prompted by his fear of losing control of the constituency of St. Augustine, or losing the contest for the post of deputy leader. It was suggested that his outburst was a studied attempt to preempt possible defeat. The Commissioner was also told that Mr. Humphrey was extremely popular with Indians and often got more popular applause than either Mr. Panday or Mr. Ramnath and would easily have won the contest for the post of deputy leader, in part *because he was white.* It was even suggested that if a prominent and well credentialed Afro-Trinidadian were to endorse the party, he too would have a very good chance of being elected deputy leader, so anxious were Indians to have outstanding non-Indians validate their activities.

Strong objection was taken to the allegation that "super Hindus" in the party were seeking to dominate the party, though it was agreed that Dr. Rampersad Parasram, a prominent Hindu pundit, was an indefatigable party worker who had played a major role in the miraculous vitalisation of the UNC. It was said that he had brought to the UNC human and material resources which were hitherto unavailable to the ULF which had a more radical image.

Concern was expressed about the tendency on the part of many to see pundits in politics as something unusual and illegitimate when similar strictures are not brought to bear on clergymen of other denominations. No one thought it unusual for Baptist, Catholic, Presbyterian or Anglican Ministers to be involved in politics. Some, it was noted now serve in the Senate. Reference was also made to the roles of persons like Bishop Tutu, Martin Luther King and radical Catholics who were in the frontline of political struggles the world over.

One witness also bemoaned the fact that Hindus were always stereotyped and seen as a threat in Trinidad and Tobago. In his view, Hindus had now become "like the Jews in Europe." Everything which they did was viewed with suspicion and seen as part of a hidden agenda. As one complained, "Why they want to extinguish them, I do not know. Why do they always wish to choke and chastise them so? Is it because they have come too late on the stage"? Hindus, it was noted, made no "uproar" when they were excluded from political power during the years of PNM rule. Why should anyone feel threatened if they now seek to exercise their democratic right to organise politically and build coalitions to advance their group needs? This was seen as a healthy development and not evidence of racism.

The Commission was assisted by a few witnesses who were able to identify the errors of both groups even though they might themselves have generally been sympathetic to one group or another. The Commission was told, for example, that Mr. Humphrey provided openings for his detractors by failing to return to his constituency to thank the voters following his election victory in 1986. It was also said that as the Minister responsible for the DEWD Programme, he did little to provide jobs in that programme for his constituents, arguing that he had national obligations. It was also said that he did not open a constituency office. It was however reported that Humphrey had sought three months leave from his constituency responsibilities to attend to the onerous duties which had devolved upon him as Minister of Housing, Settlements, Infrastructure and Public Utilities. We were also told that when he was accused of neglecting his constituency by those who were challenging him, he said that "if one constituency did not want him, thirty-five others did." This was viewed as a regrettable statement.

We were also told that Humphrey had a tendency to over-react at times. More than one witness told the Commission that Humphrey was a "risk-taking" politician and that his outbursts often put him and the party in positions of embarrassment. Humphrey was also described as someone who often took controversial positions without consulting his colleagues. It was recalled that he had to be chided for saying during the run up to the 1986 General Elections that "Trinidadians were not yet ready for an Indian Prime Minister" and that Panday should give way to Robinson. In their view, if this was indeed true, this was also a case of racism. It was speculated that he had come to regret making that statement and that he might now be regretting the statement which he made about racism in the UNC.

The Commission's View

Having considered the evidence of those who gave testimony, the Commission is of the view that elements in the party have been guilty of using dirty tricks, including appeals to race as a strategy of mobilisation in some of the constituency elections which have taken place so far within the UNC. This possibility was in fact admitted by some of the leading members of the party who observed that the "new political culture" which the UNC [was] seeking to put in place and to which it [was] firmly wedded ideologically, [was] a new plant which [was] struggling to survive in an environment which [was] hostile to its growth. It was also agreed that the new electoral system, with its one man one vote principle, was new to many and that no ground rules or code of ethics had been put in place to regulate the conduct of elections. A free for all existed, and power seekers were using all the artifices known to political operatives in democratic systems to achieve victory. This caused a great deal of turmoil and confusion in the party as the Party's Political Leader himself acknowledged. Mr. Panday in fact expressed the hope that the fierce campaigning for office in the Party would not "smash it to smithereens." To quote him, "We hope that the fall out would not traumatise the Party and that the losers would accept the democratic process and its results. We hope the UNC will be strong enough to handle it."

What is not clear is the extent to which elements at the grassroots level of the party who engage in unethical practices are being deliberately encouraged to do so by a clique consisting of some of the most senior members of the Interim Management Committee. Such evidence that was offered to the Commission is speculative and circumstantial. Some of it is clearly not true. We are satisfied, for example, that there is no substance whatsoever to the allegation that the Interim Chairman of the Party instructed a party activist to ensure that membership application forms were not to be given to non-Indians. The person who allegedly received this instruction advised the Commission that there was a misunderstanding as to what happened. What he was told by a fellow activist (not the Party Chairman) from the Pointe-a-Pierre Constituency was that he ought not to give "help rations" to non-Indians.

One recalls that it was this charge which led the Honourable John Humphrey to complain about racism in the party at an open meeting of the UNC. The charge of racism does not however hang entirely on the truth or falsity of the allegation about the distribution of forms. There is the additional claim that those who use race as a strategy of mobilisation were being encouraged to do so by a clique in the Interim Management committee. We were not supplied with any hard evidence which allowed us to say with conviction that such a conspiracy existed. All that one can say is that given their overarching responsibilities for party management and party organisation, opportunities were provided for certain individuals to build networks in constituencies which would be of value to them as political resources when needed. Every serious party leader or would-be leader seeks to rally support and build networks. The question is whether the rallying cry was that Indians ought to be put in all key positions in the party. The evidence which was presented to support this claim was inconclusive.

It should be recalled that the Party openly debated the question as to whether it should, as a matter of policy, go out of its way to attract non-Indian "notables" to its ranks. Some felt that this was necessary since some persons might be unwilling to get openly involved in party politics in general or UNC politics in particular. One thus had to recruit aggressively across the ethnic board in order to have the party present itself to the electorate with an acceptable national image. The argument was that parties in plural societies must ensure that their "slate" was ethnically balanced.

This position was opposed on the ground that it was tokenism and window dressing. It was also seen as being discriminatory, since one was inviting carpet baggers (Johnny come lately) to come in, *via* parachutes, to the very top of the party, displacing people who had worked hard to build the organisation from scratch. It was argued that the Party should be declared open to all and that those who believed in what it stood for and who wished to join should walk in rather than be ushered in as part of any deal which guaranteed them a position of leadership. If others did not come in, that would not be the fault of the Indians. In any event, there was nothing wrong or shameful about an Indian party since Indians were citizens of Trinidad and Tobago and entitled to form parties if they so wished. The question was also asked as to whether individuals or groups which flatly refused to associate with the UNC might not themselves be guilty of prejudice and racism.

There was speculation that those who opposed the recommendation that "notables" of other ethnic groups should be specially brought in were afraid that they would lose control of the party if this were to be done. One had no way of proving this since the arguments which were advanced against the proposal were quite plausible.

There was also an understandable concern about "backriders", people who ride the backs of communal or working class heroes only to abandon them once they got into power. Trinidad's political history is replete with such occurrences. The very circumstances which gave rise to the formation of the UNC would also have led these persons to argue that the only way to avoid the "neemakaram" phenomenon is to disavow "praja" politics and allow the people to choose in as direct a way as possible those persons whom they felt they could trust and whom they felt would best represent their community needs.

The question of "whom to trust" appears to lay at the root of the crisis. More than one witness, on both sides of the argument, agreed that many Indians feel a deep sense of hurt about what happened to some of their leaders in the NAR fold and that much of what is now taking place is the "backlash" which those events generated. Whether justifiable or not, the feeling exists that Indians contributed immense material resources and worked very hard with others to wrest power from the PNM and that they were not given a commensurate share of that power. They were marginalised and given cosmetic roles which disguised the fact that the critical areas of political decision-making are monopolised by representatives of other communities. Reference was frequently made to two articles which appeared in the *Trinidad Express* entitled: "THE INDIANISATION OF THE GOVERNMENT" and "THE ULF GRAB FOR POWER" which was said to have given grave offense to Indians.

One is not dealing here with the truth or falsity of the assertion that Indians have been marginalised and treated as political pariahs. The perception that they have been is however deeply and widely felt. One would thus be very surprised if there were not individuals, at all levels of the UNC, who have taken vows that that must never be allowed to happen again and that Indians must become part of the mainstream of national politics. No one in fact specifically denied that such views had been heard from time to time within the counsels of the UNC. Persons against whom allegations were made also admitted that the view had been expressed in party discussions that it was possible that given the numerical dominance and strategic location of Indians in the community, the UNC could pull off an election victory. It was however noted that the Party's considered position was that it was not in the national interest to replace "Afro-Trinidadian hegemony" by "Indo-Trinidadian hegemony." The party was committed to equality and power sharing based on the principle of individual and group equality. The case of Fiji was referred to and the view was expressed that the lessons of Fiji had to be heeded if the society was not to become embroiled in irreconcilable ethnic conflict.

The Commission's considered view is that there is good reason to believe that remarks that might loosely be termed "racist" have been uttered within UNC circles at all levels, and that some individuals have gone further and behaved politically in accordance with the views on race which they hold. It is also likely that these individuals have said that Indians must rally behind their own leaders and that some of those remarks were made in the context of John Humphrey's declared candidacy for the post of Deputy Leader of the UNC.

Given the official "protocol" about the irrelevance of race which informs political behaviour in Trinidad and Tobago, and the disjuncture between what is held privately and said within the confines of the "kin" and what is said and done in public, these views would in all probably have been expressed "sotto voce" to members of the Indian community rather than on public platforms, and it would therefore be difficult to find concrete evidence that they were ever uttered.

Despite what is officially proclaimed, racial stereotyping and behaviour based on those stereotypes are embedded in the society, and express themselves particularly though not exclusively at election time. It would thus be unreasonable to assume that they do not express themselves in mass political parties which engage in the raw struggle for political office and community resources.

One of the complaints levelled against Mr. Humphrey is that at no time did he air his complaint about the alleged instruction that membership application forms should not be distributed to non-Indians before a meeting of the Interim Committee or any of the institutions of the UNC even though he had at least 48 hours to do so. This was seen as unfortunate. Mr. Humphrey claims that the matter was discussed with Mr. Panday on the very day that he aired the matter openly, and other witnesses have confirmed that these and other complaints about what was happening at the constituency level was brought to Mr. Panday's notice.

The Commission is of the view that the Political Leader of the Party erred in not responding to the complaints promptly by summoning a meeting of the Management Committee to discuss the issue raised. The Commission is also of the view that Mr. Humphrey would have been on stronger ground if he had called for a meeting of the Interim Management Committee to discuss the issue and the latter had refused to do so. Mass political parties, by their very nature, are coalitions of people with different views, interests, ideologies, emotional needs, and behavioural patterns, and as such there must be conflict. Such parties invariably have mechanisms to resolve or broker conflicts and minimise the washing of dirty linen in public. It may well be that the UNC is not yet fully institutionalised and that the new political culture is weakly internalised. The Political Leader is still seen as the "institution" which referees group conflict and makes all critical decisions.

The Commission has been asked to advise as to whether there is need to set up intra-party machinery to deal with allegations such as those made by Mr. Humphrey. The Commission is of the view that the party should quickly put in place the code of conduct which is provided for in its Constitution and that full use should be made of the Disciplinary Tribunal which is also provided for in the Party's Constitution. The Commission is of the view that there is no need to create any new institutions to deal with allegations about racism. What is needed is a deliberate effort to clothe existing institutions with a set of precepts with all deliberate speed. The UNC is a new political party seeking to introduce a "new culture" to govern political behaviour in Trinidad and Tobago. The effort is commendable. The institutionalisation of that new political culture will however not come overnight and without sustained effort. The struggle, though an uphill one, is however worthwhile, and should be pursued. One should not expect progress to be linear. Contradictions are the stuff of life in general and political life in particular.

II

A national opinion survey was conducted to try and determine the extent to which the view prevailed that the UNC should be an Indian Party or whether membership in it should be open to all. Eighty-eight per cent of the Indo-Trinidadian respondents in the sample who were UNC supporters said that the UNC should be open to all. Only 9 per cent of them said it should be an Indian party, while 3 per cent said they could not decide. By comparison, 65 per cent of the Afro-Trinidadians who responded to the question felt that the Party should be open to all, while 29 per cent said it should be open to Indians only. Six per cent were unable to decide. In sum, while a majority in both groups felt that membership in the UNC should be open to all, Indo-Trinidadians were less inclined to want membership restricted ethnically than were Afro-Trinidadians by a margin of 20 points. One wonders whether those Afro-Trinidadians who felt that membership in the UNC should be restrictive were stereotyping that Party as an Indian party and taking the view that people of African descent should have nothing to do with it.

Reference might also be made to another survey conducted by SARA in October 1989 in which respondents were asked to indicate whether the ethnicity of the leader of a political party was important in their calculation as to which party they should vote for. Seventy-three per cent of our respondents said that they believed it was indeed an important consideration, while 15 per cent said they did not think that it was. Six per cent could not say for certain, while 6 per cent chose not to say.

Close to three quarters of the respondents from all ethnic groups agreed that the ethnicity of the Political Leader was an important consideration. The same response pattern emerged whatever the age, the social class, sex or the educational level of the respondent. In no group other than the upper middle class did the percentage agreeing with the proposition fall below 70 per cent. In that particular case, 62 per cent agreed, 31 per cent disagreed and 6 per cent claimed they did not know.

What these figures suggest is that the concern about who leads the political party of one's choice cuts across party lines and is not limited to the members or supporters of the United National Congress.

III

The analysis and evaluation of what is taking place within the fold of the UNC and in the society at large leads us to conclude that it is simplistic to say that certain elements within the leadership structure of the UNC are "racist" while the majority of Indians are not, or that non-Indians within the UNC or in the society at large are not racist. Clearly, the nature of the relationship between Indians and non-Indians inside and outside the UNC is a dynamic one which varies from time to time and the context. It is the context and the arena in which the relationship is situated which determine how the groups behave towards each other. The context may be economic, social, or political or all three combined. The arena may be a public one — the market place or the work place — or it might be within the private sphere of the family.

Racism can be defined as racial prejudice in action, prejudice which is expressed in systematic attempts to dominate or exclude a group or groups from high status or well paying jobs, educational opportunities, places of residence, clubs, places of entertainment, roles etc. In the context of contemporary Trinidad and Tobago, it is a moot point whether one can say that racial prejudice is strongly felt but weakly (or subtly) expressed in social behaviour, whether racial prejudice is weakly felt and weakly expressed, or whether it is weakly felt but strongly expressed.

Some argue that while racial prejudice appears to have declined in Trinidad and Tobago, the society is nevertheless "mortgaged" to the past, and prejudice and racism have become "institutionalised" and continue to affect the way the society is ordered. Some however deny that race prejudice exists at all.

Some are of the view that we are all "racists," though most would agree that "racism," Trinidad and Tobago style, is benign and protean compared with the deeply entrenched and perverse strains found in places like South Africa. One might in fact argue that what some refer to as "racism" in Trinidad and Tobago is qualitatively different from that which is seen in South Africa where race is an officially sanctioned criterion for social stratification and resource allocation and that that which obtains in Trinidad and Tobago should be given a different label. Indeed, one has to distinguish between consciousness of and pride in "race," the creation of political and social organisations to advance the fortunes of that "race," and behaviour which systematically seeks to exclude other groups from a legitimate share of national resources.

Yet others argue that so much miscegenation has taken place in Trinidad and Tobago that it is meaningless to talk about race at all. While the concept of "race" based on somatic, genetic or physiological criteria has no scientific validity, most people in racially encysted or segmented societies regard themselves as belonging to one "race" or another and act towards each other, not on the basis of how scholars might classify them using technical criteria, but in terms of how they "see" each other and in terms of the traits and characteristics which are assumed to define them whether these characteristics are inherent, mythical or the result of social conditioning. The images which groups have of each other, especially in rapidly changing societies, are not static, however. They become transformed in the wake of dramatic events or dramatic occurrences which arouse emotions such as the emergence of charismatic leaders or mass parties, or as a result of changes in the economic or social circumstances of the respective groups and the fears, anxieties or expectations which are generated by these developments.

Rapid social change might lead individuals or groups which are hitherto subordinate and which had entertained a certain image of themselves, to seek the route of assimilation or emulation of the superordinate group or to segregate themselves further and emphasise their uniqueness or difference and develop a posture of anti-racial racism. The celebration of "Negritude" by Africans in the Diaspora is one example of this phenomenon.

Invariably, members of the group react differently, with some seeking to conform and integrate while others opt for separation which might seem to them to provide greater security and group solidarity. The processes might be attended either by militance or quiescence. Changes in the society may provoke yet another orientation, one that is neither assimilationist nor separatist. Groups and individuals often develop feelings of ambivalence. Their loyalties and orientations towards the superordinate group or culture or the host society become split. Unable to forswear the advantages and attractions which might be seen to come from integration, or unable to sustain a full existence in the context of the separate society and culture to which they feel emotionally attached, they "flip-flop" from one to the other leading dual lives.

Writing in 1903 W.E.B. Dubois *(The Souls of Black Folk: 1965:13)* drew attention to the ambivalence which he witnessed in fellow American blacks:

> The Negro ... is gifted with second-sight in this American World. It is a peculiar sensation, the double consciousness, this sense of always looking at one's self through the eyes of others, of measuring one's soul by the type of a world that looks on in amused contempt and pity. One ever feels his twoness — an American, a Negro; two souls, two thoughts, two unreconciled striving; two warring ideals in one dark body.... The blackman's turning hither and thither in hesitant and doubting striving has often made his very

> strength to lose effectiveness, to seem like absence of power, like weakness. Any yet, it is not weakness — it is the contradiction of double aims.

Herbert Blumer and Troy Duster (*Theories of Race and Social Action* 1980:233) describe the problem of group ambivalence in the following way:

> The split tends to be unstable in that the racial group wavers back and forth between two directions, shifting between the leadership offered by the proponents of one or the other direction. Even the leaders themselves may reflect this ambiguity in their positions and views at differing times.... The subordinate racial group is caught in the recurring dilemma of whether to move in the assimilationist or the separatist direction or the dilemma of how to adjust these two opposing orientations. The superordinate group, on its side, is caught in the contest between the exclusionary tendency and the gate-opening disposition, a contest which can become profoundly political under certain sets of circumstances and in response to certain kinds of events. The play of these sets of antagonistic forces constitutes the core happenings in race relations.

It is often in the context of these fluid political and social situations that race becomes a "problem." When the groups involved "know" their places and stay in them — either because they have internalised the values of the superordinate group and "accept" their roles or the subordinate group is forcibly repressed, there is no "problem." It is when the social order is upset and the subordinate group begins to challenge the protocols of the society and clamour for full incorporation that the society is said to have a "racial problem." The superordinate group which is seeking to maintain its hegemony is usually among the first to claim that it is the subordinate group which is responsible for creating a racial problem where none existed before.

Indeed, it could be argued that individuals and groups who proclaimed most loudly that there is no racial discrimination in

Trinidad and Tobago are those who are most satisfied with the prevailing allocation of resources and the patterns of office holding. These elements wish to maintain the status quo by pre-empting the challenge of others who are not satisfied that national resources are allocated equitably and who therefore wish to have the social pie cut differently. One man's harmony and balance is seen by others, differently situated, as disharmony and imbalance.

The problem within the UNC and in the larger society can perhaps be explained in terms of some of these considerations. Indians who were assigned pariah status in the 19th and much of the 20th century have made enormous economic and social gains in the last two decades, and this has prompted them to make demands for fuller political and social equality. They believed that they were about to achieve their goals as a result of the defeat of the PNM in 1986. The dramatic events of 1987 and 1988 which culminated in the expulsion of Messrs. Panday, Sudama, Humphrey and Ramnath from the NAR Government forced many of them to reassess their orientation towards the society. Some continued to maintain an overt integrationist posture and chose to remain within the fold of the NAR. Many who transferred their loyalty to CLUB 88 and to the UNC were however, ambivalent. They wished to create in the UNC a party that was more socially egalitarian and democratic than either the PNM or NAR were seen to be. In this quest they were more "integrationist" than were either the PNM or the NAR. Yet it is clear that in the very bosoms of many of these same people, there existed an urge to reject the universalist orientation and to create a political instrument that would safeguard and advance the goals of the community. The two orientations — the communalist and at times racist and the other universalist and hyper-democratic — exist not only in the souls of a "clique" at the top but among many.

Whether the communalist/racist orientation or the universalist thrust becomes dominant or not will depend on a great extent on what happens in the next few years. Much will depend on whether the country's economic fortunes improve. A great deal would also depend on the form the General Elections take in 1991 and its outcome. In the short run one expects an intensification of racial consciousness and conflict. It remains to be seen whether those who have the responsibility for managing the country's affairs in both the official and private spheres, recognize the danger facing the country and take steps to manage the conflict in an effort to moderate its intensity.

SUMMARY AND CONCLUSION

Some United National Congress (UNC) political activists at the constituency level have used strategies of a "racist" nature in their recruitment and campaigning activities.

Some UNC activists and parliamentarians have been marginalised as the party grew and contests for office developed.

The attitude shown towards non-Indians by some elements in the UNC was not one which was calculated to making them feel welcome and comfortable within the fold of the party. They were made to feel that they were in the UNC to "get something" rather than to contribute to the building of the party and the country.

The charge that a leading member of the Interim Management Committee instructed an activist in the Pointe-a-Pierre constituency that membership application forms should not be given to non-Indians is false. While there have been reports that other activists have refused to give application forms to non-Indians, no evidence was led on this issue by anyone who testified before the Commission.

There is good reason to believe that uncomplimentary remarks concerning the ethnicity of Mr. John Humphrey and his suitability or otherwise for the post of deputy leader of the UNC have been made by members of the UNC leadership. It was not made clear whether the remarks were made in the context of "old talk" or represented firm positions taken by such persons. One notes that Mr. Humphrey himself had also publicly expressed the view that the ethnic identity of a political leader was important to voters and that Trinidadians in 1986 were not ready to entertain the prospect of having an Indian as their Prime Minister.

The evidence led made it difficult to prove conclusively that a conspiracy existed involving leaders of the UNC to prevent Mr. Humphrey from being elected to the post of deputy leader of the party by reason of his ethnicity or age. We are however satisfied that some individuals believe that Mr. Ramnath is better suited to the post, either because of his ethnicity, his "seniority" as a parliamentarian or because of the work which he has done to build the party.

At the time of writing, the Commission was not aware as to whether Mr. Ramnath intended offering himself as a candidate for the post of Deputy Leader. He did however indicate that he was unsure as to whether he was "ready" for such a role. He was also uncertain as to whether he would defeat Mr. Humphrey if he did offer his candidacy. Mr. Humphrey, it should be emphasised, did not implicate Mr. Ramnath in the alleged plot to make the UNC an "Indian" Party or to exclude him from leadership positions in the UNC. He agreed that he was a "hard worker."

Mr. Humphrey is a popular figure among UNC supporters and activists but he has his critics and detractors as well. Some of these might well have used his ethnicity as the wedge with which to discredit him. It is an asset as well as a hindrance to his leadership aspirations.

No new institutions appear to be needed to deal with ethnic conflict within the UNC. The Constitution provides for a Disciplinary Tribunal which could be used to deal with such developments. What is needed is the elaboration of a code of conduct about what might be deemed appropriate or inappropriate political behaviour and the vitalisation of the existing machinery when disputes arise. The Political Leader of the Party, Mr. Basdeo Panday, is held in high regard by all factions of the Party and has an important role to play in helping to elaborate the code of conduct which will inform party behaviour.

Chapter 10

Indians and the 1990 Crisis

The attempted overthrow of the NAR Government on July 27th 1990 by a group of Afro-Trinidadian Muslims, the Jamaat al Muslimeen, provoked an extremely hostile reaction within the national community generally and in the Indian community. Surveys done by the author showed that 75 per cent of the population felt that the attempt was unwarranted despite the unpopularity of the NAR government. Sixteen per cent claimed otherwise. The difference between Indo-Trinidadians and Afro-Trinidadians on the issue was marginal. Seventy-three per cent of the Indo-Trinidadians felt that the Jamaat were wrong to attempt to use force to overthrow a constitutionally elected government while the corresponding figure for Afro-Trinidadians was 75 per cent. There was however a significant difference in the way the Muslim community reacted. Only 54 per cent of them condemned the attempt compared to 74 per cent for the Hindus, 77 per cent for the Anglicans and 79 per cent for the Catholics. It should also be noted that 44 per cent of the Muslims felt that Bakr should be pardoned compared to 29, 23 and 21 per cent of the Hindus, Anglicans and Catholics respectively.

It is clear therefore that while Indians generally, like most other Trinidadians, were hostile to the Jamaat al Muslimeen's assault on the constitutional order, and wanted them to pay the ultimate price for their urgency, Muslims were badly divided. Indeed, they had been divided in their response to the arrival of an

African Muslim presence in the Caribbean in the sixties and thereafter, both on racial and religious grounds, since many found it difficult to come to terms with the challenges posed by both the radical Arab brand of Islam being espoused by Abu Bakr and his followers as well as by the fact that Islam, which was generally assumed to be an "Indian" religion in the Caribbean, was now becoming vocally endorsed by an underclass Afro-Trinidadian element.

Views differed sharply among Indian Muslims as to whether Bakr was a "true believer" or one who merely spouted Islamic rhetoric without understanding the inner essence of the Islamic ideology. Some dismissed him sneeringly as a "Muslim by rote," a pseudo Muslim who used Islam and the Qua'ran selectively, choosing only those parts of the ideology which suited his purpose and personality — its tolerance of polygamy and its tolerance of militancy and the bearing of weapons to defend the faith. As one Muslim put it:

> Many converts have accepted Islam after deep and searching study; others have made a cursory study of it or seek to interpret its teachings themselves or misunderstood the teachings of this noble religion... If the action of those persons [on July 27] was a result of religious conviction, then they do no understand the faith. (*Guardian,* August 12, 1990)

Yet there were others who insisted that Bakr was an Islamic liberation theologist who was very serious about Islam and that he was a votary of the orthodox Wahhabi or its Libyan variant, the Sanasya Movement, which differed fundamentally from that which was practiced by most Indian Muslims in Trinidad and Tobago. The Islamic Trust described the Jamaat al Muslimeen as a "genuine and committed group whose beliefs and practices conform to the teachings of Islam as outlined in the Qua'ran." It was also noted that after some initial skepticism, the traditional Islamic establishment had begun to accept him as a genuine religious leader, one fit to share public and religious platforms with them.

The reactions of Muslims to an African Islamic presence have been told more fully elsewhere (Ryan 1991: 84-122). The early history of Islam among Africans in Trinidad has also been recorded by Brinsley Samaroo's account (1995: 201-213). What we seek to do here is merely to record the views of two spokesmen who in our view represented typical views that were being articulated by conservative Hindus following the coup. The first came from the Secretary General of the Maha Sabha of Trinidad and Tobago, Mr. Satnarine Maharaj. According to Mr. Maharaj:

> The Hindu community is by its nature non-violent and peaceful. We regard family life as sacred. We worship Mother Earth. We believe in the free enterprise system and have had parliamentary democracy as part of our culture.

Maharaj also declared that the Hindu community could not condone the destruction of Port of Spain by fire. "According to our ancient law giver *Manu,* among the most horrendous of crimes is that of arson." Maharaj compared the role which the Hindus played in 1970 with that of 1990 and criticised the leadership of the NAR and the Christian Churches for marginalising the Hindus. To quote him further:

> The alienation of the Hindu community by ruling groups in the society was never more evident, and at a peak even, during the six-day crisis. While other groups in the society have at times resorted to "violence" to achieve their goals, Hindus have never done so... in fact the behaviour of Hindus during the hostage crisis was the same in 1970. They acted as "counterweights." In 1970, when a group of people attempted to change the fabric of national life through violence and intimidation, the Hindu community held its ground and while others were marching the streets and shouting slogans, our people were in the field tending their crops and animals so that the nation could be fed. Again in 1990 when armed revolutionaries held hostage our Parliament and its occupants and the national television station, and when looters ran off with all the foodstuff they could lay their hands upon, the Hindus were in the fields

> tending their crops an animals and on the highways selling food to our nation which was on the verge of panic. In Central Trinidad, there was no looting and burning as there was in the East West Corridor, and this is due to the philosophy of the Hindu religion. In spite of the food they supplied and sold, the Hindus have not been recognised and given their due place on the national agenda. No government minister had come forward to officially acknowledge the role Hindus played in feeding the nation during the crisis. We are yet to see this happen. In fact I am waiting to see it. However, we will continue to agitate vigorously for recognition of our contributions to the national well being but we will never resort to violence to achieve this. During the hostage crisis, the views of the religious leaders of the Hindu community were not sought, and it was as though Hindus were "inconsequential" in the scheme of things. Instead, everything was left to the control of the *St. Clair Mob* — Roman Catholic Archbishop Anthony Pantin; Anglican Bishop Clive Abdulah; and Canon Knolly Clarke. From the night of July 27th and the next five days, the only three religious heads occupying the centre spot were the R.C. Archbishop, the Head of the Anglican Church and Canon Knolly Clarke. The media and others in authority pretended that Hindus — who form 27 per cent of the population — did not exist. It is only belatedly that the IRO has been called into session and the media remembered that there is a Hindu community and that their views should besought. Even though it was Abu Bakr who asked for these leaders, Bishop Abdulah should have approached all members of the IRO for a "joint approach." But then that is the approach of the *St. Clair Mob* who like to pretend that this is a Christian country. And everytime these people sneeze, it is on the front page of both papers. When we make attempts, they are used as secondary stories. (*Guardian,* August 15, 27, 1990)

Another typical view came from a younger group of Hindu fundamentalists whose basic criticism of the Jamaat al Muslimeen, as well as some Indian Muslims, was that they were seeking to de-emphasise their Indianness and to establish an African Islamic state. The authors of the *Indian Review* in fact saw the Jamaat al Muslimeen not as an Islamic group but as an extension of the Black Power Movement of the seventies. As the *Review* puts it:

> The Friday July 27th, 1990 attempted coup d'etat by the Black Muslim group, the Jamaat al Muslimeen directed against a constitutionally elected and legitimate government, represents the second attempt by Afro-Trinidadians to forcibly seize power from a black government. The first attempt was in February-April, 1970. After twenty years, history has repeated itself. The areas of similarity are too numerous for one to fail to draw this obvious conclusion. The Islamic and religious nature of the Jamaat al Muslimeen would tend to mask the fundamentally African nature of this entire event. But for the Jamaat al Muslimeen, race was as, and even more, important than religion... Imam Abu Bakr sought to create a Black Islamic State, an element that was central to his ideology of Black Power... For the Black African Muslim, Islam has a revolutionary effect. He has a new Islamic personality. He has a feeling of superiority and an increase in African pride, pride in self and race, pride in his Africanness. He develops self-reliance. There is absolutely no contradiction between Black African consciousness and Islam. In fact, it increases this Black African consciousness to its highest level. It gives the African a new world view that is both African and Islamic. As the Black African Muslim experienced this personal transformation so he wants to transform this environment. Hence the Jamaat al Muslimeen's attempt to overthrow the government and to establish an Islamic state by the use of force which is justified by its theology. The new state would of course be a Black African Islamic state. (*Indian Review* August-September, 1990)

The Editors of *Equality: The Journal of Ethnic Studies* also insist that Bakr's movement was pro-black and anti-Indian. As they wrote in their August 1990 issue:

> Muslim Indians ... are unanimous in their view that the African Muslims have brought a bad name to Islam. Apart from being used merely to fund the group, the Indian Muslims have had to suffer the humiliation of seeing their wives, sisters and nieces being seduced by irresponsible Black males in the name of Islam. Abu Bakr and his followers had never sanctioned nor promoted Indian cultural practices like Hosay, beating *dholaks* (hand drums), sing-

ing of *Kasidas* (hymns) and wearing of Shalwars (2-piece dress).

The Jamaat newspaper, *The Light,* funded by Indian Muslim, Kayma Hosein, carried mainly photos of and articles of Africans. Tubal Uriah Butler, Makandal Daaga, Canon Knolly Clarke and Abu Bakr were highlighted in the latest issues, No. 5, May 1990 and No. 6, June 1990. The ideology formulated and the names chosen, were slanted towards Black African states like Ethiopia.

It is not surprising,therefore, that Abu Bakr's choice of negotiators on the hostage crisis was non-Indian, that is neither Muslim nor Hindu. For him, it was Black first and Muslim afterwards.

Interestingly enough however, Ramesh Lawrence Maharaj, then the Attorney for the Jamaat, claimed that the Jamaat al Muslimeen were victims of PNM generated "alienation." To quote Maharaj:

> The failed coup of July 27th, 1990 was also a reaction to alienation, discrimination and injustice in the society. The Jamaat members felt that they were not being treated equally because other religious bodies were benefitting from land given to them by the State. On the other hand, land which the state had converted from mangrove swamps, and upon which the Jamaat had constructed several buildings was being seized by the State which was prepared to use force against members of the Jamaat. They felt oppressed, alienated and discriminated against. There was no speedy or effective machinery to deal with their perception of injustice. Thus allegations of discrimination come from all levels of society. (*Indo-Caribbean Resistance* 1993:39)

Mr. Maharaj is now the Attorney General of Trinidad and Tobago and now appears to hold views that are different from those expressed above (cf. Chapter 14).

Chapter 11

The Elections of 1991: Challenging PNM Dominance

The results of the general elections held in December 1991 indicated that the UNC had not succeeded in crossing the ethnic divide. With 45 per cent of the votes, the PNM won 21 of the 36 seats. The UNC won 13 seats and the NAR 2, both of which were in Tobago. The NAR was completely shut out in Trinidad. The PNM won all of its seats in constituencies where Indians were in the minority while the UNC won theirs in areas where Indians were in the majority (Tables 1 and 2). The UNC came close to winning a 14th seat in another constituency (Point-a-Pierre) which the PNM won by 192 votes. By the same token, they came close to losing another (Fyzabad) constituency which they won by a mere 177 votes. The UNC claims that it was deprived of victory because of a flawed electoral list and slow voting procedures in polling divisions where they expected to win. While there were indeed flaws in the list and voting was slow in certain polling divisions, these difficulties affected all political parties rather than the UNC alone.

Panday claimed that the UNC lost the election by a mere 7,000 votes in closely contested constituencies. Victory in these would have allowed the party to hold the balance of power. To quote Panday:

> ...the UNC had more votes than was necessary in order to win those constituencies. Had we been able to bring out those votes on election day, the UNC would have had 18 seats, the PNM 16 and NAR 2 seats. And had the NAR not divided our votes in 1991, we would have won 19 seats. (*Trinidad Express,* October 11, 1993)

This claim is arguable since some NAR votes would have gone to the PNM. The UNC did as well as it did largely because its leader had convinced a majority of the Indian community that the time had come for it to take over the reins of power, though he consistently maintained that should the UNC win, it would share power with others. Panday's success was also due to the fact that he had successfully stigmatised those Indian MPs who stayed with the NAR after the collapse of the coalition in 1988 as *nemakharams,* persons who had betrayed those who had struggled for the upliftment of the Indian community over the past decades. Using the power of rhetoric for which he is justly acclaimed, Panday almost single handedly transformed the UNC, which many were prepared to dismiss as a failure just months before the election, into a party which the bulk of the Indian community, especially those at the lower end of the social class spectrum, came to regard as the only legitimate vehicle that could fulfill their aspirations for political power.

That the party did not do better was due to several factors. The first was that the Indian gentry generally chose to support the NAR while some 10 per cent of the Indian community supported the PNM. The party suffered too because the NAR did not take away as many votes from the PNM as the UNC expected. The party also lacked the financial, technical and organisational resources to compete with the PNM and the NAR, both of which were better funded and managed. As one of its defeated candidates reflected, "the UNC was unable to translate its popular support into an organisation. If we had an efficient and well oiled electoral machinery, we would have won that election with a safe 20 seats. But our party constitution was a bit loose and limited. Our party's activities were haphazardly organised" (*Trinidad Mirror,* February 14, 1993). In the final analysis, however, the party failed to win because it was still widely seen as an Indian party with an Indian agenda and not as the "national" party which its leaders claimed they wished it to be. The fact that 15 of the party's candidates were non-Indian did not convince many that it was the genuinely multi-racial party it claimed to be. Most of the non-Indians were in fact nominated to contest seats that were non-winnable.

Following the elections, the party boasted that it had made inroads among the non-Indian electorate in constituencies like Ortoire-Mayaro and San Juan-Barataria. The UNC did obtain 34 per cent of the vote in the latter constituency, but 43 per cent of the voters in that constituency were Indian and it is safe to assume that the UNC's support came mainly from that source. Similarly, the party gained the support of 37 per cent of the electorate in Ortoire-Mayaro. But that constituency was 47 per cent Indian. There was in fact no constituency in which the UNC got more votes than there were Indians on the electoral list (see Tables 1 and 2). Polling data have consistently revealed that the UNC, like its predecessors, receive little or no support from non-Indians, and its performance at the polls in 1991 provide no evidence whatever to support the "break through" thesis. The UNC began its formal life as a party which sought to regroup Indo-Trinidadians following the crisis in the NAR, and notwithstanding efforts at ethnic ticket balancing, and rhetoric about equity and class struggle, the election results indicated that it remained an Indo-Trinidadian party.

The NAR, the party which in 1986 had been widely viewed as the crucible par excellence of multiracial unity, obtained a mere 126,919 votes or 24.43 per cent of those voting. It won two seats in Tobago and none in Trinidad. The party came third in 16 constituencies and second in 18 constituencies. The constituencies in which it came third were those in which Indians were dominant i.e., over 60 per cent. The only exception to this rule was in Chaguanas where its candidate narrowly defeated the PNM candidate by 358 votes and in Oropouche where another defeated the PNM candidate by a mere 74 votes.

Table 1
Ethnic Profile of Constituencies Won by PNM - 1991

Constituency	Ethnic Profile		Performance of Parties in Constituencies won by PNM		
	Non-Indian	Indian	PNM	UNC	NAR
Laventille West	96	4	81.08	1.56	15.07
Port of Spain North	92	8	63.45	1.80	31.72
Diego Martin West	91	9	60.71	2.01	35.87
Laventille East	90	10	74.23	4.45	19.52
Diego Martin East	89	11	54.98	2.90	40.82
Diego Martin Central	88	12	60.12	2.83	35.81
Port of Spain South	86	14	59.70	3.90	34.44
St. Anns East	85	15	70.16	5.53	22.56
Arouca South	83	17	69.71	8.42	20.33
Arima	79	21	61.48	8.07	28.52
Arouca North	72	28	58.83	14.21	25.59
Toco Manzanilla	71	29	55.26	21.58	21.02
Point Fortin	70	30	56.45	11.76	29.85
La Brea	69	31	59.37	22.19	17.88
San Fernando East	66	34	62.61	12.04	24.97
St. Joseph	61	39	41.30	32.16	24.37
Point-a-Pierre	59	41	36.26	35.01	26.84
San Fernando West	58	42	48.72	14.57	35.74
Tunapuna	58	42	46.81	28.42	22.24
Barataria/San Juan	57	43	44.44	34.43	19.28
Ortoire Mayaro	53	47	46.66	37.03	15.78

Source: EBC 1992.

Table 2
Ethnic Profile of Constituencies Won by UNC - 1991

Constituency	Ethnic Profile		Performance of Parties in Constituencies won by UNC		
	Non-Indian	Indian	PNM	UNC	NAR
Siparia	18	82	18.60	65.59	13.48
Oropouche	18	82	16.03	62.61	20.82
Chaguanas	23	77	18.14	59.19	20.50
Naparima	24	76	21.47	56.60	19.40
Tabaquite	29	71	25.78	44.81	28.85
Caroni East	33	67	28.27	54.39	19.87
Couva South	33	67	32.20	53.10	12.56
Caroni Central	35	65	30.32	51.27	16.36
Couva North	35	65	21.21	61.09	15.20
Princes Town	37	63	37.47	44.73	15.04
St. Augustine	37	63	29.32	45.86	22.78
Nariva	44	56	30.23	45.88	15.55
Fyzabad	45	55	36.65	37.76	15.97

Source: EBC 1992.

Following the election, the UNC leadership vowed that the organisational and mobilisational errors which it believed cost it victory in 1991 would not be repeated and that 1996 would see it holding the reins of power. As one of their spokesmen expressed it: "the party is not content to be in a position of opposition. We are preparing to take the government, and if we are really to mobilise our forces, we need to strengthen our structure" (*Trinidad Mirror*, February 14, 1993). The report of the 1990 Census which indicated that Indians constitute the single largest group in the country (40.3 per cent) as opposed to Afro-Trinidadians who accounted for 39.6 per cent of the population, gave a psychological boost to the leadership of the party which boasted that Indians were now in a position to win power. As Panday concluded:

> That simple fact has put the PNM on the horns of a dilemma from which it seems unable to extricate itself. This dilemma arises from the history of the elite in the PNM, which has, for more than 30 years, ridden the backs of the African masses by appealing to race in order to win the elections. That strategy worked well for them as long as the African electorate was in the majority. Now that that is no longer so, Manning realises that he cannot win the elections without substantial Indian votes, votes which the PNM has studiously alienated over the years in a long history of discrimination, vilification and humiliation. (*Trinidad Guardian,* October 11, 1993)

Panday's statement seemed to assume that Indians were an undifferentiated lot and that all would support an Indian dominated party regardless of class or religion. Past voting trends indicated that this did not occur. Some supported the PNM and some the NAR. It also ignored the fact that the mixed population and the minority elements, which together constituted some 20 per cent of the population, were more likely to throw their electoral weight behind either the NAR or the PNM if they believed that a vote for the former was likely to be a wasted vote (cf. Annexe 6).

Panday conceded that Indians had not yet come to appreciate the power which the new demographic reality conferred on them. As he lamented:

> ...when in 1945, Indo Trinbagonians celebrated the 100th anniversary of Indian Arrival Day, Indians constituted 27 per cent of the total population. They accepted the fact that against a background of racial voting, they could not and would not participate in any meaningful way in the governance of the country. Today, Indians constitute the largest single ethnic group in the country, yet many of them are of the same view still.

According to Panday, the minority syndrome has sunk so deeply into the psyche of Indians that even when the minority had become the majority, they refuse to accept that fact, and continued to behave as though they are still a minority (cf. Annexe 7).

Panday was however convinced that the age of PNM dominance was over, and that with the demise of the NAR, the rights of succession belonged to the UNC. After close to 150 years of being in the wilderness and of genuflecting to others on the question of national political leadership, the time had come to mobilize the Indian population to make a bid for political power. Those who opted not to be so mobilized thus had to be demonised and called *nemakahrams,* people who were prepared to sell their souls and betray their ancestors for a mess of pottage from the new oligarchy. Panday denied that this was his strategy, and sought to mask his game plan by stigmatising those whom he called pseudo racists in the Afro-Trinidadian community who pretended that they were ruling in the interest of the Africans when in fact they were governing in the interest of the "parasitic clique." It however seemed clear that while the main text of Panday's message articulated a cross racial appeal against the "parasitic oligarchy" and their spokespersons, the sub-text represented an unambiguous communal appeal.

In saying that Indians "were their worst enemy," willing to sell their birthright for a jacket and tie, a wig and a gown, a seat in the Senate, or a little contract here and there, Panday was clearly attacking elements within the Indian bourgeoisie who were forging links with the wider community in various ways and in the spaces that were being opened up as the state became more ethnically neutral. He was telling them that they had a "higher" responsibility to support their *jhat* in its quest for a turn at the crease. Panday also told the NAR that it had to purge itself of the French creole element in the party as a condition of any unity arrangement with the UNC. According to Panday:

> What is left of the party is dominated by the French creoles. It is the same group which dominates the PNM. The French creoles support both the PNM and the NAR. But they don't really want the PNM to lose the elections. They use the NAR as a counter-weight and tool to threaten the PNM that if it don't do so and so then they will stay with the NAR. They don't want the NAR to join in any political party. But the NAR will have to make up its mind if it will continue to be used to win elections rather than a counter-weight. (*Express,* May 2, 1993)

Panday however did not formally shut the door on unity talks since, as he boasted, "the history of my political career is trying to forge unity. The opposition's position is that unity is critical and crucial. What I have learnt from 1986 is that there must be mechanisms for the resolution of disputes." As was his wont, he indicated that the "people" would have to decide what the nature of the UNC-NAR relationship would be. The final judge of what the "people" would do of course would be Mr. Panday himself, and it may well be that Mr. Panday had concluded that the "people" had spoken loud and clear in a bye-election in which had been held in May 1994 in Pointe-a-Pierre which indicated that the UNC had neutralised the NAR except among the "French creole element."

Panday's comments served to amplify the anxieties of those in the non-Indian population who, for a variety of reasons, were fearful of the political ascendancy of the Indian community and who indicated that they would support the PNM or any other political party as an alternative to what they considered to be their more "immediate political enemy." Many who were pro-NAR in sympathy vowed to support the PNM instead of the party of their first choice if this was seen as being likely to ensure the defeat of the UNC. Many dissident PNM supporters also indicated that if an anti-PNM vote or abstention was seen to make a UNC victory likely, they would continue to support the PNM even though they were extremely unhappy with many of the economic and other policies which their party was pursuing. In sum, as occurred in

Guyana, race would be allowed to function as an override to policy or ideological considerations.

The white and mixed business community which regarded Indian businessmen as fierce economic competitors and who also endorsed the basic structural adjustment policies being pursued by the PNM government, were prepared to support and finance the latter's electoral campaign and to denigrate the UNC whenever possible. They deeply resented being characterized as a "parasitic oligarchy" which, in conjunction with a black political élite, exploited the non-white elements in the society. As Panday had complained:

> It is becoming clearer to the masses in the East/West Corridor that they are being used by the parasitic oligarchy to win power which they use in their own interest. The poor, the hungry, the unemployed, the destitute and the desperate of Laventille, Belmont, Cocorite, Waterhole, Gonzales and the rest of the corridor are slowly but surely coming around to the view that they are not the PNM, but the beasts of burden of the PNM, whose backs are ridden election after election by a small French Creole clique supported by a black managerial élite. (*Trinidad Guardian,* October 11, 1993)

The UNC leadership was of the view that their best option for the election which was due in 1996 was to seek to enter into some sort of formal or informal electoral arrangement with the NAR. Some elements in the NAR were also of the view that such an arrangement was the only way for the former governing party to revitalise itself. The NAR leadership in fact entered into a "common platform" agreement with the UNC to contest a by-election in Caroni East in September 1994 as a prelude to a fuller alliance in time for the 1996 election. The then Political Leader of the NAR, Mr. Selby Wilson noted that he was under pressure from UNC-NAR floaters to enter into the electoral *entente* with the UNC. To quote Mr. Wilson:

> Because of the structure of the NAR and because the UNC, as it were, splintered off from the NAR, both parties have a significant number of people whom I call "floating voters" between the UNC and the NAR, people who are sympathetic towards the NAR and sympathetic towards the UNC as demonstrated in the Point-a-Pierre elections where we saw the UNC's majority come by the movement of persons who voted for the NAR in the 1986 elections switching their allegiance to the UNC. And there are floating sympathizers of both parties. Indeed, some of the pressure for the movement toward joining up with the UNC came from these supporters in that they are always advocating that the parties must get together again and try to recreate 1986. (*Sunday Express,* October 2, 1994)

Many members of the NAR party, especially the white and mixed element, however strongly objected to the *entente* and forced the leadership to withdraw from the arrangement. The collapse of the *entente* also led Mr. Wilson to resign from the leadership of the NAR. Wilson however indicated that he too was suspicious of Panday's motives for joining the *entente.* Panday was described as being "fluid" and more concerned with electoral success than national unity (cf. Annexes 4, 5).

The collapse of the "common platform" forced the UNC to adopt a "united front from below" strategy. That strategy was one that sought to attract as many of the NAR's Indian supporters as was possible. It also sought to appeal to the black underclass which was known to be disenchanted with the PNM government which was pursuing policies that had given rise to increased unemployment and a reduction in welfare services which, given the dramatic reduction in available tax revenues, the economy can no longer afford. The strategy was given a "trial run" in the by-elections held in May-July 1994 in the constituencies of Laventille and Pointe-a-Pierre. The results in the latter constituency indicated that the UNC did in fact capture the bulk of the Indian vote which had gone to the NAR in 1991. It however failed in its bid to win over the support of the black underclass in Laventille.

The UNC received a mere 340 votes in the latter constituency compared to the 3,854 won by the PNM.

Despite persistent complaints by Indian spokesmen about underrepresentation in the political system, Indians were well represented in the 1991-1996 Parliament. Seventeen of the 36 Members of the 1991-1996 Parliament were Indian (47 per cent), while in the 31 member nominated Senate, 17 or 55 per cent were Indian. In the 1986-1991 Parliament, there were only 10 Indians out of the 36. The Indian community was however not proportionally represented in the governing party or in the government itself. The Political Leader of the PNM indeed expressed concern about this and indicated a wish to redress the imbalance. The party had sought to achieve this goal by including more Indians on its slate of candidates. Of those who did contest, only 4 were however elected. Three of these were appointed to the cabinet. The Prime Minister publicly expressed regret that more Indian PNM candidates did not win seats and indicated that he was anxious to compensate for this by appointing Indians to the Senate and making them ministers thereafter. Only 1 Indian, the Chairman of the party, was however made a minister *via* an appointment to the Senate. Another, who was invited to join the Cabinet, declined out of concern that he might be viewed as a "token" Indian, and perhaps even a *nemakharam* (cf. Annexe 9).

Indians accused the Prime Minister of "patronising" the Indian community, but the Prime Minister was genuinely committed to the policy of incorporating Indians in positions of executive responsibility within the PNM and did not rule out the possibility that the Political Leader of the PNM could be an Indian. While the policy was informed by the goal of continued PNM dominance, it was also seen as being essential if future ethnic conflict is to be avoided.

There were those who believed that the only way to avoid conflict arising from the seeming intensification of ethnic competition was to reconstitute the National Alliance For

Reconstruction or some such combination or to find some formula to ensure that political power was shared between the two equally balanced ethnic communities. The experience of the NAR between 1986 and 1991 however made the recreation of such experiments unlikely for several years to come. That experience had in fact led to a hardening of political tensions between the two major communities. Ethnically based political competition became sharper and more shrill, and threatened to escalate even further as the general election grew closer. There was in fact a growing fear in the Afro-Trinidadian community that Indians, who were dominant in the commercial sector and were gaining ascendancy in the bureaucracy, would also win political power, thus concentrating in their hands all the critical levers of power. A Report entitled *Ethnicity and Employment Practices in the Public Sector* (Ryan and La Guerre 1994:25) had in fact concluded that while Indo-Trinidadians were underrepresented at the higher end of the Central Public Service for historical and other reasons, they were well represented in the clerical, judicial and professional sectors where merit and criteria prevail. It also went on to indicate that it was not "inconceivable that the Public Service may eventually become dominated by Indo-Trinidadians" (cf. Chapter 12).

It was of course true that the Indo-Trinidadian community, like its Afro-Trinidadian counterpart, was differentiated along cultural, class and denominational lines, and that as was the case in the past, it may not vote as a solid bloc. Survey data however indicated that the UNC had in fact begun to enjoy considerable support among Presbyterians, Indian Catholics and Muslims.[1] Given the right set of circumstances, it was possible that more upwardly mobile Indians who in the past supported the NAR or the PNM could be induced to support a restructured UNC. As we shall see, this is precisely what occurred in 1995.

The UNC leadership however formally endorsed power sharing and was seeking to force the PNM to concede it. Mr. Panday called for the creation of a government of national unity, and promised that when he won control of the Government, he would put such a united front in place. Having experimented unsuccessfully over the past 15 years with a number of strategies designed to force pre-election accommodations, formal alliances or coalitions, Panday believed that a post-election power sharing strategy would provide the mechanism needed for effective governance in Trinidad and Tobago since, in his view, neither the PNM nor the UNC had the legitimacy to govern on their own. One thus had to be concerned not only with how to win elections, but how to govern after winning. Only a national government, he argued, would have the moral authority to govern Trinidad and Tobago effectively. The Guyana experience had fortified Panday's thinking on this issue (Ryan 1992: 47-49).

Panday's refusal to cooperate with the PNM to enact fundamental legislation which required a qualitative majority was thus designed to force the latter party to concede that it could not govern Trinidad and Tobago effectively without UNC concurrence given the fact that the two dominant parties represented two entrenched clusters which not only had rough numerical parity, but which also had effective veto power over the other in many spheres of national life. In his view, Trinidad and Tobago's political system was bi-polar rather than uni-polar, and as such, its political system and culture should reflect this reality.

End Note

[1]Data collected in a 1993 (November) SARA poll indicated that while 42 per cent of UNC support came from Hindus, a quarter came from Catholics who were Indian. Twenty per cent of the Catholics in the sample were Indian. Fifty-six per cent of them supported the UNC. The UNC also did well among Indians belonging to other Christian denominations, i.e., Presbyterians, Assembly type churches, etc. Twenty-nine per cent of them supported the UNC. The data, taken together, indicated that in spite of the attempts of the UNC to vault the racial divide, the UNC was still essentially an Indian party (83 per cent of its supporters were Indians) dominated by the Hindus. The party however had considerable support among Muslims and Christian Indians. In sum, the party was becoming multi-denominational, if not multi-racial.

Chapter 12

Indo-Trinidadians and the Labour Market in Trinidad and Tobago

I

The conventional wisdom in Trinidad and Tobago is that Indians are dominant in the private sector, particularly in the manufacturing, distributing and agricultural sectors while Afro-Trinidadians are dominant in the bureaucratic and securocratic sectors. There are Indo-Trinidadian spokesmen who challenge this generalisation and argue that Indo-Trinidadians are marginalised in all sectors, especially the financial and petroleum sectors and that they have been victims of the parasitic oligarchy in the private sector generally. Minister of Planning, Trevor Sudama, in his former role of opposition parliamentarian, authored a number of articles in which he challenged the view that Indo-Trinidadians were dominant in the economic sector as is widely believed. This he sees as a convenient myth which had several functions. To quote Sudama:

> The propagation of this myth, has impacted on the society in three ways:
>
> a. Any economic policy or initiative which was envisioned to unduly benefit those areas of the economy where the Indians presence was strong had to be discontinued simply because it was viewed

as accentuating an already acceptable imbalance in favour of Indians

b. Africans were persuaded to restrict the influence and participation of Indians in the political sphere, allegedly in order to pre-empt Indian domination in all spheres of the society

c. Indians are seen as economically self-sufficient and are in a position to create employment opportunities for themselves. Africans, on the other hand, could only look to the state and public sector for employment and the state and public sector ought to be under their control as a matter of right and distributive justice. Discrimination practiced against Indians with respect to recruitment in the public sector was thus given justification. (*Trinidad Express*, April 30, 1991)

Similarly, Basdeo Panday, argued that the NAR government, of which he was once a part as Minister of External Affairs up until the split in the coalition in 1987, was very miserly in the allocations which it made to the Indian community. Panday accused the NAR of spending only 3 per cent of the Budget on agriculture. Infrastructure and food technology, he complained, were stifled, while the conglomerates were being given licenses to import food. Panday noted that between 1988 to mid-1991, 248 small businesses collapsed. "Many of these were agriculture based, and went down the chute because the conglomerates had monopolised large sectors of the economy by a series of interlocking directorates" (*Express*, December 6, 1991).

Panday was lamenting the economic alienation of the agricultural and agro-processing community, the majority of whom are Indian. Panday of course did not detail how many businesses of other ethnicities suffered as a result of structural adjustment and whether Indians were in fact among the majority. Insofar as there were more Indo-Trinidadian businesses, this might have been the case. Proportionately however to those which existed, research conducted done at ISER indicate that more firms belonging to persons of Afro-Trinidadian ancestry went to the wall in the post-boom era. But saying all this gets us ahead of our account which has an historical foundation (Ryan and Barclay 1992).

Trinidad and Tobago has always had a segmented labour market. For historical and other reasons, the white population occupied the top managerial and technical job positions in the private sector, the "off white" and mixed elements the middle level positions, while Africans and Indians were relegated to manual occupations in the agricultural, industrial and service sectors. Within this broad framework, there was further segmentation. Whites were dominant at the upper levels of the national and foreign owned private sector in which were located the major financial, commercial and industrial enterprises, and retained hegemony in these sectors well into the post-independence period. By then, they were being challenged by business élites from the Indian, Chinese and Syrian-Lebanese communities. Indians were dominant in the agricultural sector generally, but primarily in the sugar and rice industries and in market gardening. The descendants of the enslaved African population, better educated generally than all the other sectors, were dominant in the public services, the teaching, medical and legal professions,the security services and in manual occupations in the non-agricultural sector. There were of course people from all ethnic communities in each of these sectors, but the broad occupational pattern sketched above is fundamentally accurate (cf. Braithwaite 1953; Ryan 1991).

The historical reasons for this pattern of labour segmentation are generally well known, but bears repeating, if only briefly. On the sugar plantation which was the dominant economic institution for most of the 19th century, whites were owners and managers, while Africans planted and reaped the canes and manufactured sugar under the supervision of white overseers and technocrats. Following emancipation, Chinese, Portuguese and Indian labourers were brought in to replace the Africans who deserted the plantations for self-employment in agriculture and various craft undertakings. Those who remained in the sugar industry did so as independent cane farmers or as employees in the sugar factories. Africans also sought employment as peasant proprietors, contractors or labourers in the cocoa industry which emerged in the late 19th century to challenge the dominance of the sugar industry (Phillips-Lewis 1988).

On leaving the sugar plantations, the Chinese and Portuguese moved into market gardening and petty commerce in both the rural and urban areas, catering to the needs of co-ethnics and the general population at large. The Chinese became dominant in the grocery trade, the clothes laundering industry and in the food retailing sector. The Portuguese too became dominant in the grocery trade and in the retailing of alcohol and food. In these sectors, they competed with the Europeans who remained economically dominant in the major urban centres and with the emergent Indian business class which, unlike the African educated element, opted for the most part to take the route of self-employment rather than pursue careers in the public service.

This career choice was informed by a number of considerations, the main one being the structure of the education system. For most of the period following emancipation, the primary and secondary schools were owned and controlled either by the state or by the Christian denominations. Indians, both Muslims and Hindus, were generally unwilling to send their children to these schools out of concern that they would be alienated from their religions which the Christians deemed pagan and heathen. The Presbyterian Church of Canada, which embarked on a special proselytizing mission to the Indians in the 19th century, succeeded in persuading some Indians to enter their schools and to convert to Presbyterianism, but the majority remained outside the school system until the mid-twentieth century when Hindus and Moslems started establishing schools of their own, in the teeth of hostility from the Christian denominations. Indian families were also generally unwilling to have their offspring mix socially with African children out of concern that they would be socially and ritually contaminated in the process. Some became converts to Catholicism, Anglicanism and Presbyterianism in order to secure jobs which required school certification, but the majority remained alienated from the Western dominated educational system.

Following the political withdrawal of the British in 1956, Afro-Trinidadians considered the public sector to be their preserve. As Harewood and Henry (1985:73-74) explain:

> The black intellectuals, who came to power in 1956, saw education as the major avenue for economic mobility and or the escape from poverty from their mass base. Concurrent with the thrust given to education, was the substantial expansion in the Public Service to serve the needs of a modernising state in respect of high level professional, skilled technicians and a host of educated clerical and administrative cadres. All these new positions provided opportunity at the same time as it provided mobility and justification for the faith in education. Blacks who previously dominated the lower and middle orders of the Public Service, as well as an ever increasing number of Indians could look to employment in the Public Services as providing channels for mobility primarily on the basis of merit deriving from educational qualification. The expansion of the black middle class was directly related to the opportunities created in the Public Service until the late 1960's. The oil boom of 1973 and beyond allowed for the further growth along the continuum, albeit on a higher trajectory, as employment in the Public Service jumped by over 33 per cent between 1973 and 1978.
>
> The oil boom created a new phenomenon, that of a truly well-off black elite, enjoying in some cases a life-style and income comparable to the older established economic or comprador elite. This new parallel elite was to be found in the highest echelons of the State Service Sector and as well in new State Enterprise Sector as managers and top bureaucrats. It would be remembered that with the entry of the Government through public sector participation, not only in the utilities, but also in the

Productive Enterprises, there was room for employment as high-level functionaries for the better-educated and technically trained from among the supporters of the ruling party in what were deemed to be politically 'sensitive' positions.

Among the parallel black elite, must be included the professionals whose scarce skills at the beginning of the oil boom allowed them to earn substantial rental income. The people were to be found in accountancy and auditing, in the legal profession, and in a range of professions and consultancies in the Construction Industry. The boom generated an inordinate increase in demand for certain professional services relating to construction, real estate and areas of high finance. Some of these professionals used their new riches to acquire substantial real estate and other prime assets thereby guaranteeing even higher income flows and higher real assets rating in the buoyant economic climate of the middle and late 1970's.

While this entire group became an elite parallel to the traditional elite in terms of life-style and income, their relationship to the means of production was still discretely different and their condition was more directly tied to the resources of the state sector. In any event, they benefitted from the high private returns to formal education noted by Henry (1974). This lent further credence to the efficacy of credentials.

At the other end of the spectrum, the lower income Blacks, who in their dispossession, unemployment and underemployment of the 1960's, rioted and adopted militant postures in the early 1970's, were also to benefit from the boom through the direct transfers by the Government ... but also, and more importantly through indirect transfers in the form of make-work schemes, and sometimes by totally unproductive unemployment on the Special works Projects or latterly in the Development and Environmental Works Division (DEWD). As resources permitted this programme to be transformed from an occasional to a more regular guaranteed source of income, the poorest Blacks were relieved of the direst forms of poverty.

The dramatic growth of schools catering specifically to Hindus and Muslims in the fifties served to initiate a basic shift in the labour markets of Trinidad and Tobago. By the 1970s, when Africans began to challenge the whites for greater incorporation in the job markets of the private sector, especially in those occupations previously dominated by whites and "off-whites," Indians also began demanding greater incorporation in job markets in the public sector previously dominated by the African and mixed elements. While Africans were raising their fists in anger to the ruling political and economic elites and shouting "black power," Indians were raising their voices and making claims for fairer treatment in the allocation of public resources, especially in the area of scholarships and jobs in the teaching establishment, the central civil service, the municipalities and in the rapidly growing state enterprise sector. Many had begun to return to Trinidad and Tobago following self and family financed schooling in Canada, Britain and the United States only to find that while they did benefit, they fared less well than others in competition for jobs in the public sector which had rapidly become the prime provider of jobs. The result was a silent and sometimes not so silent struggle between the whites and the Africans on the one hand, and Indians and Africans on the other for rents.

Harewood and Henry note once more:

> The Indian community, which in the first phase of self-government and independence, was comprised largely of rural dwellers living on small and medium sized holdings or as estate and plantation labourers, did benefit also from the democratisation of education and, to a lesser extent, from the mobility increasingly afforded by less particularistic criteria in hiring in the Public Service. Furthermore, the traditional quest of upwardly mobile Indians for independent professions, especially in medicine and law, or for proprietorships in small business and commerce, as a protective measure in a hostile social environment, allowed the group to benefit from the major boom in the 1970's, when the returns in such fields climbed astronomically.

> Moreover, the withdrawal from a declining agriculture into more lucrative occupations is fully corroborated by the more than average increase in the income of Indians... While there continued to be pockets of abject poverty within this group, especially in the more depressed sugar-growing areas, the economic strides were substantial. At the same time, the ownership of assets, particularly of land, and their substantial appreciation in the 1970's, provided the collateral for the start of a number of small businesses. The Indian community with a higher participation in small business than the Blacks at the beginning of the 1970's were better placed to take advantage of the new opportunities in the private enterprise sector in the buoyant economic conditions then extant. Some of the businesses were to blossom into medium and in some notable instances, into very large conglomerates: the high income elasticity of demand for services in distribution and commerce at the onset of the oil boom in the 1970's provided great opportunities for the growth of such enterprises. Some of them now rival the traditional commercial or comprador establishments. The reversal in position in average income between the Black and Indian communities over the short period 1971/72 to 1975 is related to the differential nature and distribution of the assets held. (ibid., 75-76)

II

Given their delayed entry into the Civil Service, it is hardly surprising that in 1957, there were no African permanent secretaries in the Civil Service. By 1965, three years after the achievement of independence, there was only one. He was Permanent Secretary in the Ministry of Finance. There were then 9 non-Indians holding such posts. In 1966, when there were 15 non-Indians holding these posts, there was still only 1 Indian permanent secretary. If the figures between 1957 and 1977 are aggregated, we find that only 25 or 10 per cent of the 210 posts at this level were held by Indians, a period when Indians were 35 to 40 per cent of the population (Table 1).

Table 1. Numbers and Percentages of Permanent Secretaries, by Ethnicity, 1957-1977

Year	Indian		Non-Indian		Total
1957	-		100.0	(5)	5
1960	-		100.0	(11)	11
1961	-		100.0	(9)	9
1962	-		100.0	(11)	11
1963	-		100.0	(8)	8
1964	-		100.0	(7)	7
1965	10.0	(1)	90.0	(9)	10
1966	2.2	(1)	93.8	(15)	16
1968	8.3	(1)	91.7	(11)	12
1969	14.3	(2)	85.7	(12)	14
1970	12.5	(2)	87.5	(14)	16
1971	17.6	(3)	82.4	(14)	17
1972	18.8	(3)	81.2	(13)	16
1973	18.8	(3)	81.2	(13)	16
1974	18.8	(3)	81.2	(13)	16
1975	30.8	(4)	69.2	(9)	13
1977	18.2	(2)	81.8	(9)	11

Source: Civil Lists 1957-1977.

When Indians make the charge that they were not adequately represented in the public sector, the response of non-Indians is that they either did not apply or that they did not have the requisite entry qualifications or seniority to be recruited or promoted. As suggested above, there is some truth to this counter assertion. The fact remains, however, that Afro-Trinidadians and the mixed element regarded the public service as their preserve once the Europeans had been dislodged following the achievement of self-government in 1956. Indians were seen as being less than congenial as co-workers and social partners, and were not generally welcomed in what was deemed the fortress of creole bureaucratic power.

What was perhaps true in the pre-independence era was however no longer so in the sixties and seventies. More and more Indians were achieving certified status at all levels of the educational hierarchy and more were applying to fill jobs in the public sector. By 1988, more than half — 51.8 per cent — of those applying to enter the clerical grades were Indians. Between 1988 and 1991, 48.8 per cent of all applicants to this class were Indian. The remainder came from all other groups (Table 2).

Table 2. Applications for Entry into the Clerical Class for, 1988-1991 (Grade of Clerk 1)

Years	Total Applications	Indian Names	Non-Indian Names
1988	1,179	611 (51.8%) m. 232 f. 379	568 (48.2%)
1989	1,150	578 (50.3%) m. 230 f. 348	577 (49.7%)
1990	1,273	608 (47.8%) m. 222 f. 386	665 (52.2%)
1991	1,576	732 (46.4%) m. 282 f. 450	844 (53.6%)
TOTAL	**5,178**	**2529 (48.8%)** **m. 966 f. 1563**	**2649 (51.2%)**

Source: Register of Applications, Service Commission Department.

By February 1993, there were slightly more Indians employed in the Clerical grade I class (1,038) than non-Indians (1,029). At the level of Clerk II, there were 531 Indians to 446 non-Indians. At the level of Clerk III, there were 219 to 225 non-Indians. The profile at the level of Clerk IV was however different. There were only 77 Indians to 160 non-Indians, a situation that was probably a function of blocked mobility. As persons in this range move up the ladder or move out of the service, this disparity will no doubt be redressed and Indians would come to occupy more posts in the clerical grades at all levels than all other groups combined. As it is now, if all grades are aggregated, they hold 1,945 of the 3,805 posts in this class or just over 50 per cent (Table 3).

Table 3. Ethnic Composition of Clerical Class (All Grades) at February 1993

	Clerk I	Clerk II	Clerk III	Clerk IV
Total of Indian Names	1,038 m. 276 f. 762	551 m.166 f.385	279 m.122 f.157	77 m.22 f.55
Total of Non-Indian Names	1,029	446	225	160
TOTAL	**2,067**	**997**	**504**	**237**

Source: Establishment and Seniority Lists, Service Commission Department.

When the current status of these clerical grades is examined in percentage terms, Indians are 54 per cent of Clerk I, 59 per cent of Clerk II, 49 per cent of Clerk III and 32 per cent of Clerk IV. The data clearly indicate that during the period 1980-1992, Indians were appointed to clerical level posts at accelerated rates in comparison with appointments in the period before, as well as by comparison with the appointment of individuals belonging to other racial groups.

The data also reveal that Indians are doing as well or better than all other groups in the open competitive Civil Service Examinations. Between 1980 and 1991, 72 of the 140 top places in those examinations were secured by Indians (Table 4).

Table 4. Number of Indians Passing Civil Service Examination for Entry to the Grade of Clerk 1 and Ranking - Top 20 (Selected Years)

Year	Number of Indians in Top 20	Ranking in Examination
1980-1981	9	2/6/7/10/13/14/15/17/18
1983	10	3/4/5/9/10/11/12/13/18/20
1984(1)	12	1/3/4/7/11/12/13/14/15/16/19/20
1984(2)	12	2/4/6/7/9/10/11/12/13/15/16/20
1085	9	2/3/5/9/10/12/14/18/20
1990	10	1/2/3/6/7/8/11/17/18/20
1991	10	1/4/5/10/13/14/15/16/18/19

Source: Examinations and Testing Section, Service Commission Department.

The data also show that Indians were appointed to 34.8 per cent of all permanent posts in the central public services between 1981 and 1991. In 1984, they secured 41.7 of those appointments. The percentage however dropped to 24.3 per cent in 1988 when few such appointments were made (Table 5).

Table 5. Appointments to Posts in the Public Service, 1981-1991

Year	Total Appointments	Indians Appointed	Indians as a Percentage of Total Appointments
1981	1,500	498	33.2
1982	1,552	601	38.7
1983	1,582	499	31.5
1984	1,718	711	41.4
1985	904	241	26.7
1986	713	279	39.1
1987	311	111	35.7
1988	70	17	24.3
1989	360	133	36.9
1990	1,529	463	30.3
1991	1,028	371	36.1
TOTAL	**11,267**	**3,924**	**34.8**

Source: *Trinidad and Tobago Gazette* (Various Issues).

Indians however did less well in securing temporary appointments (29.9 per cent) and acting appointments (28.2 per cent) during the decade under consideration (Tables 6 and 7).

Table 6. Temporary Appointments to the Public Service, 1981-1991

Year	Total of Temporary Appointments	Indians Appointed Temporarily	Indian Appointees as a Percentage of Total
1981	748	229	30.6
1982	794	209	26.3
1983	594	138	23.2
1984	343	130	37.9
1985	521	161	30.9
1986	123	37	30.1
1987	248	90	36.3
1988	210	64	30.5
1989	126	61	48.4
1990	80	30	37.5
1991	341	87	25.5
TOTAL	**4,128**	**1,236**	**29.9**

Source: *Trinidad and Tobago Gazette* (Various Issues).

Table 7. Acting Appointments in the Public Service, 1981-1991

Year	Total Acting Appointments	Indians Appointed to Acting	Indian Appointees as a Percentage of Total
1981	2,185	595	27.2
1982	2,156	532	24.7
1983	1,611	467	29.0
1984	1,383	370	26.8
1985	1,319	371	28.1
1986	763	219	28.7
1987	704	178	25.3
1988	349	125	35.8
1989	223	67	30.0
1990	132	60	45.5
1991	440	193	43.9
TOTAL	**11,265**	**3,177**	**28.2**

Source: *Trinidad and Tobago Gazette* (Various Issues).

Indians complain that they are discriminated against when it comes to promotions. The figures for the 1981-1991 period show that they secured fewer promotions than all other groups combined – 31.3 per cent – but given their late start, it is not clear that the figures provide unequivocal evidence of overall discrimination whatever might be true in individual cases. Interestingly, in 1989, 51.7 per cent of all promotions were secured by Indians (Table 8).

Table 8. Promotions in the Public Service, 1981-1991

Year	Total Promotions	Indians Promoted	Indians as a Percentage of Total Promotions
1981	2,072	623	30.1
1982	1,504	444	29.5
1983	1,419	471	33.2
1984	1,261	435	34.5
1985	1,235	363	29.4
1986	358	91	25.4
1987	330	87	26.4
1988	24	7	29.2
1989	232	120	51.7
1990	1,371	445	32.5
1991	1,011	300	29.7
TOTAL	**10,817**	**3,386**	**31.3**

Source: *Trinidad and Tobago Gazette* (Various Issues).

It is widely believed that Indians tend to opt for and succeed in getting appointments in certain critical sections of the civil service. One hundred and eighty five of the 346 accounting posts (40 per cent) are held by them. One hundred and fifty-nine or 44 per cent of the 379 posts in the Customs and Excise division are also held by them. In the Budget division and in the Treasury a third of the posts are held by them. In Inland Revenue, 48 per cent of the posts are held by them.

Indians are also in a majority or hold a significant share in the state sectors of the following professions shown in Table 9. (Table 9).

Table 9. Indians in Professions in State Sector

Medicine	-	34.8%
Engineering	-	43.7%
Ambassadors	-	37.5%
Judiciary	-	45.8%

Four of the 7 Justices of Appeal are Indians.

Data obtained from available professional lists (which are not always up to date) show a mixed pattern in terms of the status of the Indo-Trinidadian community in the following professions as a whole (Table 10).

Table 10. Ethnic Composition of Professions

Profession	Indian	All Others	Year
Engineers	20	80	-
Dentists	29	71	1994
Lawyers	38	72	1994
Medicine	44	56	1986
Architects	5	95	1993

Indians were however less well represented in some areas of the Public Service in relation to their numbers in the population.

Only 25 per cent of the research and planning officers were Indian. They were also underrepresented in the senior administrative class. As of October 1992, they held 29.4 per cent, 9.5 per cent and 12.5 per cent of the Administrative II, IV and V posts in the service. The same picture obtains at the level of Head of Department. In 1970, 17.3 per cent of the headships were held by Indians; in 1980, the percentage was 15.2. In 1992, the figure was 13.9 per cent. This underrepresentation at the senior level is partially explained by their late entry into the Public Service.

Indians are also generally less well represented in the state owned enterprise sector in relation to their numbers in the population. As Table 11 shows, in only four of 17 enterprises examined did Indians hold 40 per cent or more of the jobs. These were Caroni Limited (59 per cent), Trinidad Cement Limited (52.1 per cent), Tanteak (42.5 per cent) and PTSC (40.2 per cent). At the management level, only in five enterprises were Indians to be found in proportions comparable to their numbers in the general population. These were Caroni (62 per cent), National Gas Company (71.4 per cent), Trinidad and Tobago Methanol Company (50 per cent), Petrotrin (44.4 per cent), Trinidad and Tobago Electricity Corporation (40.0 per cent).

Only in 5 of the enterprises was there a significant Indian presence at the level of the Board of Directors. These were the Public Transport Service Corporation, Trinidad Cement Limited, the Agricultural Development Bank, Trinidad and Tobago Television Limited and Caroni Limited. In six of the enterprises, there were no Indians on the Board.

Indians were also found to be grossly underrepresented in the Security Services. In 1970, there were only 9 Indians in the top officer corps of the Police Service. Of the 149 who held the rank of sergeant, only 6 were Indian. Ten years later, only 22 of the 244 sergeants were Indian. There were 108 constables among the 581 persons holding that rank. Looking at the service as a whole which then numbered 1,102, 180 or 16.3 per cent were

Table 11. Comparative Diversity in Selected Public Enterprises (1993)

	Bord of Directors		Total Lab Force	% Non-Indian	% Indian	Management		General Labour Force	
	% Non-Indian	% Indian				% Non-Indian	% Indian	% Non-Indian	% Indian
WASA	83.3	16.7	3280	75.8	24.2	100.0	0	75.8	24.2
ADB	50.0	50.0	220	68.2	31.8	85.7	14.3	68.9	31.1
BWIA	100.0	0	2045	76.0	24.0	81.7	18.3	75.6	24.4
PTSC	57.1	42.9	1491	59.8	40.2	100.0	0		
TTEC	77.8	22.2	3184	66.1	33.9	63.6	36.4	66.1	33.9
TCL	50.0	50.0	359	47.9	52.1	...	...	...	...
TTMC	66.7	33.3	235	66.8	33.2	50.0	50.0	67.6	32.4
CARONI	23.1	76.9	964	40.2	59.8	38.0	62.0	40.5	59.5

Source: Ryan and La Guerre 1994.

Table 11. Comparative Diversity in Selected Public Enterprises (1993) - Cont'd

	Bord of Directors		Total			Management		General Labour Force	
	% Non-Indian	% Indian	Lab Force	% Non-Indian	% Indian	% Non-Indian	% Indian	% Non-Indian	% Indian
NP	80.0	20.0	528	78.5	21.5	100.0	0	76.3	23.7
NFM	100	0.0	423	82.3	17.7	85.0	15.0	82.1	17.9
LASCO	100	0.0	223	91.5	8.5	75.0	25.0	92.0	8.0
NCB	100	0.0	811	73.7	26.3	75.9	24.1	73.5	26.5
AATT	100	0.0	630	80.5	19.5	89.9	11.1	80.0	20.0
TTT	55.6	44.4	148	80.1	19.9	60.0	40.0	82.6	17.4
TANTEAK	83.4	16.6	146	57.5	42.5	62.5	37.5	57.3	42.7
NGC	87.5	12.5	331	68.6	31.4	28.6	71.4	32.6	67.4
PETRO-TRIN	72.7	27.3	5455	66.3	33.7	55.6	44.4	66.3	33.7

Source: Ryan and La Guerre 1994.

Indian. In September 1992, the percentage had grown to 25 per cent.

Despite their growing numbers in the Police service, Indians continue to complain that they are discriminated against both in terms of recruitment and promotion. In response to assertions by non-Indians that their underrepresentation is a reflection of the fact that many did not apply to join the service in the pre-independence era and in the years immediately following, Indians assert that they did not do so because they were of the view that the society did not welcome them in such positions. There is some truth in this assertion. Colonial police authorities and their successors were of the view that Indians lacked the physical attributes for the job and disqualified many on the basis of height and chest expanse. It was also said that they were heathen and therefore untrustworthy. It was likewise believed that ethnic considerations would not dispose them to arrest co-ethnics. A popular prejudice held that a "coolie could not be trusted to arrest a coolie." It was also said that the few who joined soon abandoned the service.

It is true that jobs in the Police Service were low paying and arduous and that the Indian community (as did others) looked upon careers in the service with disfavour. Indians also found the environment of the service challenging in what they were required to eat, drink and do to be considered good colleagues. Thus their reluctance to enlist. Whatever the truth of the matter, Indians are no longer disinclined to pursue careers in the Police Service. This change of attitude has also begun to be evident among Indian women, many of whom now apply to join the ranks without much success, however. In 1992/1993, 40 women were recruited into the Police Service. Only 2 were Indians.

Both males and females complain that discrimination still prevails in recruitment and promotional practices and that even though they score highly on written examinations, interview panels, which are manned almost exclusively by Afro-Trinidadians who have the required seniority to sit on those panels, adjudge them unfairly. They allege that nepotism and other non-achievement criteria still inform recruitment and career advancement, a conclusion that is supported by evidence adduced by the Centre For Ethnic Studies. While the announced recruitment policy is informed by equity considerations, policy and practice do not converge.

Much of what is said of the Police Service is also true of the Fire Service, the Armed Service and the Prison Service. In 1970, only 7 (4.6 per cent) of the 155 Fire Service officers were Indian. In 1980, the percentage had increased to 12 per cent. In 1992, this had increased to only 14.1 per cent. The figures for the Defence Force are much the same. Only 9.7 per cent of the Commissioned Officers in the Defence Force are Indian. In the Coast Guard, the percentage is 17.4 per cent.

Looking particularly at the Trinidad and Tobago Regiment, there were 104 Indians (8.3 per cent) in the 1,135 member body. In 1990 the percentage had dropped to 7.6 per cent. The number of Indians remained constant, but the number of non-Indians had increased by 234. The percentage of officers had dropped from 13.6 to 6 per cent.

The Prison Service also revealed Indian under-representation. In 1970, Indians accounted for 2.9 per cent of the Prison Service. By 1980, this had increased to 7.6 per cent. More Indian officers were recruited in the following decade. By 1992, there were 235 of them out of a total of 1,016. The relevant percentage was 23.1 per cent. Predictably, they are grossly under-represented at the senior officer level. They occupy only 13.5 per cent of those posts. Despite the improvements achieved, there still continues to be the view that given the dominance of Afro-Trinidadians in the prison population, Afro-Trinidadians make more suitable officers. (Of the 2,697 persons in penal or corrective service institutions in 1990, 1,775 or 66 per cent were Afro-Trinidadian, 19 per cent were Indian and 15 per cent were other or not stated. The age group 25-34 accounted for 46.7 per cent of the prison population (CSO 1993)). The concern is that the race factor would complicate the problem of discipline within the prison system.

What the foregoing analysis indicates is that for a variety of reasons, public sector careers and jobs which were once considered the near exclusive preserve of Europeans, the mixed population and Afro-Trinidadians, are being increasingly sought after by Indo-Trinidadians. Increasing levels of educational achievement, increased deculturalisation, the general increase in population, growing urbanisation and the narrowing of job opportunities in the private sector have led Indians to demand equity in employment in jobs in the public sector. As Indians move from the rural areas to urban centres and surburbian enclaves, as they become more cosmopolitan and embourgeoisified, they no longer view farm related actives or even commerce as their primary avenues of economic activity. They have also become less deferential, less inclined to accept the roles to which the colonial and post-colonial society relegated them, and are clamouring for full economic citizenship. The political élites who speak on their behalf have also become more strident, much to the chagrin of creole élites who accuse them of "having a plan" to add political and bureaucratic hegemony to that which they currently enjoy in critical areas of the private sector.

The current thrust by Indians for full incorporation in public sector job markets is being greeted with much anxiety by Afro-Trinidadians. This concern was dramatically articulated by a former Public Service Commissioner, James Alva Bain who felt that social balance required that their rate of entry into the Public Service should be slowed down. To quote Bain:

> With the introduction of compulsory primary education, the East Indians have increasingly acquired education and have been increasingly invading the fields of the Civil Service, the professions and government. As their numbers must now reach parity with the people of African descent,

> there is a real possibility that, in the not too distant future, they will get control of the Government. Should this time come when the East Indian sectors own most of the property, business and wealth of the country as well as control of the Government, an imbalance could develop in our society that would not be good for the nation. It is an urgent necessity, therefore that all of us give serious though to these matters and like sensible people make a conscious effort to counter any undesirable consequences that could develop from such a possible situation. (*Express,* April 26, 1976)

The *Report on Employment Practices in the Public Sector* (1994:25) also comments on the reactions of Afro-Trinidadians:

> That the Public Service might one day become dominated by Indians is not in itself a problem. The real problem is the possible response of Afro-Trinidadians to the increasing Indo-Trinidadian presence in what has traditionally been the preserve of the Afro-Trinidadian population. Already there are signs of tension and disquiet. In any Department or Ministry presided over by an Indo-Trinidadian, there is talk of discrimination against Afro-Trinidadians. The Afro-Trinidadian public servant feels particularly insecure in the knowledge that the current Chairman of the Public and PoliceServices Commissions is an Indo-Trinidadian. These feelings of insecurity stem from the perception – nay, belief – that once an Indo-Trinidadian is put into a position of authority, he/she will naturally, automatically, instinctively, without really thinking about it and not necessarily with any malicious intent, favour his/her own kind in all matters. This perception is very strong, and can be discerned widely among Afro-Trinidadian public servants. Indians are characterized as "cliqueish", "clannish" and "openly racist"; and non-Indo-Trinidadians genuinely fear what might happen if an Indo-Trinidadian were to become head of their department.

Whatever the empirical data from this study might reveal, there is other material which indicate that both major ethnic groups earn levels of incomes from the state in rough proportion to their demographic status in the population. In a survey conducted in June 1990 by St. Augustine Research Associates, an attempt was made to determine the extent to which jobs in the public and private sectors were distributed among Indians and non-Indians. Respondents (989) were asked the following questions: Is your income earned mainly from Government employment or private sector employment? The latter included own account workers. Of those who were earning an income at the time of the survey, 30 per cent said they received most of their income from government sources while the remaining 70 per cent said that they earned theirs in the private sector. When source of income was cross-tabulated with ethnicity it was found that 55 per cent of those who earned their income primarily from state and parastatal agencies — (including the teaching service, utilities, state-owned corporations and local government bodies) — were non-Indian, while 45 per cent were Indian. Turning to those who earned their income primarily from private sector sources, 56 per cent were non-Indian and 44 per cent were Indian.

In another study conducted by the Institute of Social and Economic Research in 1990 in which 3,583 persons were interviewed, 40.3 per cent of the Afro-Trinidadians in the sample said that their fathers were or had been employed by the state, while the remainder, 59.7 per cent, were in the private sector (either paid or self-employed). By comparison, 38 per cent of the Indo-Trinidadians said that their fathers were or had been employed by the state while 62 per cent were in the private sector. These two sets of figures suggest that quite apart from what might have been the case in the Central Civil service, the Protective Services and some utilities, Indians were not and are now not discriminated against in terms of employment in the public sector taken as a whole. The figures suggest that Indians and non-Indians are represented in the public sector in proportions that approximate their numerical status in the general population.

III

Claims to the contrary, notwithstanding, all the available quantified data indicate that there are more Indian owned businesses than businesses belonging to any other group. Data from studies done by ISER in 1990 reveal that of the businesses in Trinidad and Tobago employing 5 persons or more, 42.5 per cent are owned by Indo-Trinidadians. The visual data are also compelling. More recent data collected by ISER (1996) reveal more or less the same — 54.2 per cent, 23 per cent and 11.4 per cent are controlled by Indo-Trinidadians, Afro-Trinidadians and other groups respectively. The pattern varies from sector to sector. In the distribution sector it is 60, 23, 17 per cent respectively in favour of Indo-Trinidadians. In the manufacturing sector it is 51, 31 and 17 per cent respectively.

There are also differences in the sizes of firms owned by the ethnic groups. While 27 per cent of all self-employed groups are Afro-Trinidadians, only 16 per cent of firms that employ 10 employees are owned by Africans. Indians are evenly spread throughout all classes of firms whereas the Chinese, Europeans and the Syrians are running the larger firms (cf. *Sector Assessment Study for the Small Business Development Programme in Trinidad and Tobago 1996).*

There are also critical sectors of the economy where there is almost an exclusive dominance of Indo-Trinidadians. The heavy vehicle transport and the vehicle parts industry, sugar and agro-processing, road surfacing, the movie distribution industry, and fishing and forestry for example, are dominated by Indo-Trinidadians. The same would not of course apply to banks and the major insurance and financial companies, but below the very top level of the banks and insurance companies, Indians are dominant. The fast food business is shared with the new international food chains, Kentucky Fried Chicken and McDonalds, and competition is keen with the Chinese and the Syrians, but in terms of sheer volume, the Indians are dominant. The same would hold in the fabric, drug trafficking and racing pool industries where the Indians are in sharp competition with the Syrians, particularly in the key urban areas of Port of Spain, Arima, Tunapuna, San Fernando and now Chaguanas.

Indian political leaders have generally endorsed the call for an Equal Opportunities Commission which they assume would further their quest for equity in the public sector. As Ramesh Lawrence Maharaj (1993:40), the current Attorney General, explained in a lecture given in Toronto 1992, "whatever arguments may exist against the creation of a Equal Opportunities Commission, such a Commission will serve a useful purpose in allowing persons who felt alienated or discriminated against to have their complaints investigated speedily without any complicated legal formalism or machinery" ("Challenges to East Indians in Trinidad and Tobago," in *Indo-Caribbean Resistance,* 1993:40). Afro-Trinidadians and other non-Indians have either resisted this demand or insist that its writ must extend to the private sector as well since it is widely believed that Afro-Trinidadians, who for a variety of reasons are not major owners of private sector institutions which employ large numbers of people, are victims of discriminatory recruiting practices. Indians are widely believed to be especially guilty of recruiting co-ethnics. Chinese, Syrian-Lebanese and Europeans are also said to be guilty of ethnic exclusivism, through less so than are Indians. Investigations conducted by the Centre For Ethnic Studies (CES) confirm these beliefs, but show that Afro-Trinidadian employers are not as free of prejudicial recruitment as they believe.

The survey found that there was almost as much co-ethnic recruiting in firms owned by Afro-Trinidadians as there was in firms owned by Indo-Trinidadians. In the sample of 512 firms surveyed, 40 per cent were owned by Indo-Trinidadians, 25 per cent by Afro-Trinidadians, 20 per cent by people of mixed descent, 5 per cent by whites, 3 per cent by Chinese, and 2 per cent by Syrian/Lebanese. Six per cent were not easily classified in ethnic terms. These percentages compared very favourably with those yielded by a similar study conducted by the Institute of Social and Economic Research (Ramsaran 1993).

There were 1,869 senior managers in the firms surveyed. Indians constituted 37 per cent of the management group, the mixed group made up 27 per cent, Africans 21 per cent, whites 8 per cent, Chinese 5 per cent and Syrian/Lebanese 1 per cent. Indians were represented in the managerial class in proportions that roughly matched their numerical status in the general population. Africans were somewhat underrepresented in managerial positions in the firms surveyed, a finding that was consistent with their low level of ownership of business. They were, however, more highly represented at the professional level than any other ethnic group, at 44 per cent. The figure for Indians was 29 per cent, for mixed 18 per cent, whites 6 per cent and other — that is, Chinese and Syrian/Lebanese, 3 per cent.

Looked at in greater detail, the CES data revealed that professionals were more frequently employed in firms owned by "co-ethnics." Ninety-three per cent of the firms owned by Indians excluded African professionals altogether. Sixty-nine per cent of the firms owned by whites had no African professionals. Indian professionals fared little better in firms owned by Africans or whites. Eighty-nine per cent of the firms owned by Africans, most of which were small, had no Indians employed at the professional level. Seventy-seven per cent of white-owned firms also employed none.

The study also revealed that no Africans were to be found in 22 per cent of all the firms sampled. By the same token, no Indians were to be found in 18 per cent of all the firms in the sample. Thus, in 40 per cent of the firms surveyed, one or other of the numerically dominant groups in the population was unrepresented at any level. There were also no whites or Chinese in 85 per cent of the firms sampled and no Syrian/Lebanese in 98 per cent of them. The picture that emerges is thus one of extreme ethnic concentration in a majority of the firms in the sample.

The portrait becomes even more frighteningly monochromatic when we look at employment patterns at the senior level in firms owned by the various groups. There were no Africans at the senior level in 88 per cent of the firms owned by Indians, in 93 per cent of the firms owned by Chinese, in 82 per cent of the firms owned by Syrian/Lebanese, and in 77 per cent of the firms owned by whites. Indians fared no better. There were none at the senior level in 79 per cent of the firms owned by Africans, in 64 per cent of the firms owned by Chinese, and in 75 per cent of the firms owned by mixed elements, whites and Syrian-Lebanese respectively.

The picture revealed by the data shows clearly that ethnicity plays a major role in recruitment in all firms at all levels, but especially in senior management. Africans were mainly found in the manipulative and unskilled areas in most organisations, but particularly so where physical strength was a natural requirement of the job.

In spite of this, only 2 and 6 per cent of those who responded to the questionnaire on behalf of the firms in the sample admitted that race or religion respectively were considerations when employees were being recruited. Most indicated that experience (58 per cent) was the most important factor, followed by gender and age.

The survey also clearly revealed that groups are stereotyped by key decision-makers within firms (as indeed they are in the wider society), and that these stereotypes help to inform recruitment decisions. While a plurality, or in some cases a majority of the reporting officials declined to single out any group which they viewed as being better performers or producers at the work place, a large block of them had views on the subject and were prepared to articulate them.

Indians were seen by reporting officials to be more punctual than Africans by a margin of 21 points. Indians were also seen to be more hard-working by 36 per cent of all reporting officials. They were likewise seen as being more reliable by 25 per cent of those reporting. Africans, however, were deemed to be more honest by 13 per cent of the reporting officials, while Indians were considered thus by 10 per cent of them.

When the responses were cross-tabulated with race, we found that close to a third of the reporting officials in each ethnic category were unwilling to deem any group as being better performers. What was interesting, however, was that many of the African reporting officials agreed that Indian workers were more punctual, productive and harder-working than their co-ethnics. A significantly high proportion of managers of African origin also selected Indian employees over Africans in respect of the attributes of profitability (37.8 per cent), productivity (38.6 per cent), more hard-working (37 per cent), reliability (29.9 per cent), punctuality (33.6 per cent) and dedication (33.3 per cent). Indian workers were selected almost equally with Africans in respect of the attributes of team spirit, dedication to work and high achievement. They were less esteemed on the score of interpersonal relationships and honesty by African managers.

The assessments made by managers of other ethnic backgrounds, whites and those of mixed ancestry, were also instructive. Indian workers were regarded by a higher proportion of mixed and white managers as being higher achievers, more hard-working, more reliable, more punctual, more dedicated, more loyal, more likely to contribute to the profitability of the firm, more productive, and as having a better and more dedicated attitude to work. African workers were the choice of only a very small proportion of the managers in almost all instances.

One suspects that considerations of this sort, reinforced by factors such as obligations to family, extended kith and kin, friendship networks, *praja* relationships, geographical location and historical circumstances, go a long way towards explaining why, in spite of all the changes that have taken place in the job market in the sixties and seventies in both the public and private sectors, and all the talk about Trinidad and Tobago being a "rainbow" society, or one in which national unity is within reach, job recruitment patterns are still as skewed as they are.

IV

Some of the data provided above are reinforced by data generated in the 1990 Census relating to levels of education achieved, levels of income earned, and occupations held by the various ethnic groups in the society.

An examination of the data relating to highest level of educational attainment received by the various ethnic groups reveals that there are 27,809 persons in the population who received no formal education (Table 12). Seventy-two per cent of them were Indo-Trinidadian and 19 per cent were Afro-Trinidadian. There are obvious historical reasons for this imbalance. Most of these people are in the older age cohorts of the national population.

At the nursery/kindergarten level, there were fewer Indo-Trinidadians in school than there were Afro-Trinidadians. The percentages were 31 per cent for Indo-Trinidadians, 43 per cent for Afro-Trinidadians and 25 per cent for those who are mixed. The mixed element in this age cohort were 21 per cent of the total population. What these figures indicate is that in 1990, Indians were starting formal schooling later than other groups in relation to their proportion of the population. It may well be that more Indo-Trinidadian parents or grand parents are available at home to baby sit their progeny. The urban-rural spread of the population may also explain the disparity.

At the primary, secondary and university levels, the percentages for the two major numerical groups are almost identical, while in terms of "other" types of educational credentials, Afro-Trinidadians exceeded Indo-Trinidadians by a whopping 16 percentage points. One is not clear as to what explains this significant difference.

An examination of the information which respondents gave to census enumerators about the cash income which they earn indicates that Indo-Trinidadians are more likely to be found at the lower end of the income scale, with the reverse being the case at the middle and upper ends of the scale (Table 13). Looking first at persons who were earning $1,299 per month or less in 1990, we find that 46 to 47 per cent of the Indo-Trinidadian community making this claim as opposed to 37 per cent of the Afro-Trinidadian community.

Table 12. Educational Attainment, by Ethnicity (%)

Ethnic Group	None	Nursery/ Kinder-garten	Primary	Second-ary	Uni-versity	Other
African	19	43	42	39	34	46
Indian	72	31	41	39	34	30
Chinese	1	-	-	1	2	1
Syrian/ Lebanese	-	-	-	-	1	-
White	-	1	-	1	5	2
Mixed	8	25	16	20	22	20
Other Ethnic Group	-	-	-	-	1	-
Not Stated	-	-	-	-	-	1

Source: CSO 1994, 63.

When we look at those who claimed to be making between $1,700 and $2,499 per month, Afro-Trinidadians also do better. In the $4,000 to $5,999 range, Afro-Trinidadians as a group are also ahead by 7 percentage points and the same obtains in the $6,000 to $7,999 range by 5 percentage points. In the $8,000 and above range, Indo-Trinidadians are only 1 percentage point below Afro-Trinidadians, 28 to 29 per cent. The mixed group also does well in the upper brackets. Although they are only 16 per cent of the total income earning group, 24 per cent of them claim to be in the $4,000 to $5,999 bracket, 28 per cent in the $6,000 to $7,999 bracket and 26 per cent in the $8,000 and above bracket. Eleven per cent of those in this upper bracket are white even though whites account for 1 per cent of the total income earning group. Three per cent of the Chinese are in this high income group. The data in some cases seem to contradict what appears to be the case, and one is not clear as to whether what respondents reveal to census takers represents their full earnings. We also note that the CSO does not seem to have a high degree of confidence in the income data which is generated by its surveys, particularly when they are disaggregated.

Turning next to the occupations held by the various ethnic groups, the data suggest that there continues to be a great deal of segmentation in the labour market. At the managerial level, for instance there are more Indo-Trinidadians than Afro-Trinidadians. The percentages are 39 and 25 per cent, respectively. Twenty-three per cent of the mixed population occupy managerial type positions in the society, a per cent that exceeds their share of the labour force. The figures seem to represent what is indicated by visual experience and data from the CES study cited earlier.

Afro-Trinidadians are ahead of Indo-Trinidadians in jobs classified as professional by 4 percentage points (37 per cent to 33 per cent) with the mixed group accounting for 22 per cent of those jobs. The gap is even wider at the level of technicians. Forty-one per cent of this group are Afro-Trinidadian, 34 per cent are Indo-Trinidadian and 22 per cent are mixed.

Table 13. Income Levels, by Ethnicity (%)

Division and Ethnic Group	Under $500	$500-$1299	$1300-$1699	$1700-$2499	$2500-$2999	$3000-$3999	$4000-$5999	$6000 $7999	$8000 and Over
African	37	37	42	45	45	43	38	33	29
Indian	46	47	42	39	34	34	31	28	28
Chinese	-	-	-	1	1	1	2	3	3
Syrian/Lebanese	-	-	-	-	-	-	-	1	1
White/Caucasian	-	-	-	1	1	1	4	7	11
Mixed	16	15	15	16	19	19	24	28	26
Other Ethnic Group	-	-	-	-	-	-	-	-	1
Not Stated	-	-	-	-	-	-	-	-	1

Source: 1990 Census.

Table 14. Occupation, by Ethnicity

Occupation	African	Indian	Syrian/ Chinese	White Leban/ ese	Cauca- sian	Mixed	Other	Not Stated
Managerial	25	39	4	1	7	23	1	-
Professional	37	33	2	-	4	22	-	-
Technicians	41	34	1	-	1	22	-	-
Clerks	40	35	1	-	1	22	-	-
Service Workers	47	35	1	-	-	17	-	-
Agricultural	24	57	-	-	-	18	-	-
Craft	50	34	-	-	-	15	-	-
Plant and Machine	37	49	-	-	-	14	-	-
Elementary Occupation	40	47	-	-	-	13	-	-
Not Applicable	39	40	-	-	1	19	-	-
Not Stated	43	39	-	-	-	16	-	-

Source: 1990 Census.

Table 15. Industry, by Ethnicity

Industry	African	Indian	Chinese	Syrian/ Leban-ese	White Caucas-ion	Mixed	Other	Not Stated
Sugar (Cultivation)	6	92	-	0	-	3	-	-
Other Agriculture, Forestry, Fishing & Hunting	25	56	-	-	-	18	-	-
Petroleum & Gas Prod.	47	32	-	-	2	18	-	-
Other Mining & Quarrying	55	30	-	0	-	14	-	-
Manufacturing & Refining of Sugar	13	82	-	0	-	4	-	-
Petroleum Refineries	42	42	-	0	1	15	-	-
Food, Beverages & Tobacco	38	41	1	-	1	19	-	-
Textiles, Wearing Apparel and Leather Goods	43	39	-	1	1	16	-	-
All other Manufacturing	38	41	1	-	1	19	-	-
Electricity, Gas & Water	49	33	-	-	-	17	-	-
Construction	50	36	-	-	-	13	-	-
Wholesale & Retail Trade, Restaurants and Hotels	34	46	1	-	1	17	-	-

Source: 1990 Census.

Table 15. Industry, by Ethnicity - Continued

Industry	African	Indian	Chinese	Syrian/ Leban-ese	White Caucas-ion	Mixed	Other	Not Stated
Transport, Storage and Communication	42	38	-	-	1	17	-	-
Financing, Insurance, Real Estate & Business Service Sector	43	27	1	-	2	26	-	-
Public Administration	53	29	-	-	-	17	-	-
Sanitary & Similar Services	39	48	-	-	-	11	-	-
Social & Related Community Services	48	33	1	-	1	17	-	-
Personal & Household Services	44	39	-	-	-	16	-	-
Other Services, Inter-national and other extra-territorial Bodies	43	28	1	-	3	25	-	-
Not Applicable	39	40	-	-	1	19	-	-
Not Stated/Not Adequately Described	43	39	-	-	-	17	-	-

Turning next to those who are in jobs defined as clerical, 40 per cent are Afro-Trinidadians, 35 per cent are Indo-Trinidadians and 22 per cent are mixed. A dominance of Afro-Trinidadians and the mixed is also to be found among service workers (47, 35, 17 per cent respectively) and craft workers (50, 34, 15 per cent respectively) (Table 14). Indo-Trinidadians are however dominant in agriculture (59, 24, 18 per cent respectively) and in what are called "elementary occupations" (47, 40, 14 per cent respectively).

Although there is an element of overlap and ambiguity in terms of how jobs are classified, what these figures tell us is that the Afro-Trinidadian, mixed, and "neo-European" population seem to be dominant in white collar type jobs, and in the service sector, while Indo-Trinidadians are dominant in agriculture. They however have shares that are roughly proportionate to their numbers in the labour force at the managerial level and exceed their share in jobs defined as "plant and machine" type and elementary occupations.

Much has changed since this data were collected in 1990. Several thousand persons have lost jobs in both the public and private sectors and one is not aware of any data which have classified job losses in terms of the categories used above. Both Indo-Trinidadians and Afro-Trinidadians however claim to have suffered more than the other from down-sizing and poverty inducing structural adjustment policies. The latter claim that job losses in the public sector, especially in the utilities, have hit them harder, and that being more urban, they are unable to fall back on subsistence or commercial agriculture as many Indo-Trinidadians were allegedly able to do. We however have no empirical data to prove or disprove these claims. Similar claims have been made in Guyana by the two groups (see my "Guyana: Beyond Ethnic Paramountcy," 1992).

End Note

[1] Much of the data for this chapter were drawn from *Ethnicity and Employment Practices in Trinidad and Tobago* 1994, Centre for Ethnic Studies, UWI., eds. Selwyn Ryan and John La Guerre.

Chapter 13

Anatomy of an Electoral Revolution: The General Elections of 1995

I

The outcome of the Trinidad and Tobago General Elections of November 1995 constituted a veritable social revolution in that what emerged was not merely an alternation of élites or a changing of the guards, but a fundamental change in the ethnic composition of that ruling élite. The former ruling party, the People's National Movement (PNM), which had its centre of gravity in the Afro-Trinidadian population, and which had been in power since 1956 with a brief 5 year interregnum, secured 254,159 or 48.74 per cent of the votes cast and 17 of the 36 seats; the main opposition party, the United National Congress (UNC), which draws its support largely from the Indo-Trinidadian population, amassed 240,372 votes or 45.74 per cent of those cast and also won 17 seats, while the National Alliance for Reconstruction, (NAR) the cross-ethnic coalition which had governed the country between 1986 and 1991, obtained 24,933 votes, a mere 4.76 per cent of the votes cast and 2 seats, both in Tobago. Neither of the Trinidad based national parties could thus govern without the support of the two Tobago based members of Parliament.

The election was called some 17 months before they were constitutionally due.[1] The Prime Minister told Parliament that his decision to advise the President to dissolve Parliament and call elections was informed by his belief that he could not govern effectively. The PNM, which had won 21 seats in the 1991 election, had lost one of them in a by-election in May 1994. The party's majority was further reduced when another of its parliamentarians, the former Minister of Foreign Affairs, resigned his seat after a highly emotional break with the Prime Minister.[2] The Government's decision to remove the Speaker of the House and replace her with the Deputy Speaker, who was an elected PNM member of Parliament, also effectively meant that the Government could only count on the routine support of 18 of the 36 members of Parliament.[3] The Government's claim meant that no elected parliamentarian or minister could fall sick or travel on private or official business for any extended period without running the risk that the Government's legislative schedule would be seriously affected. The Government also argued that it ran the risk of being overthrown following a successful vote of no confidence. This was hardly likely however, since a specific resolution dealing with confidence would have had to be introduced and the Speaker would have been able to exercise his right to cast the deciding vote. A vote of no confidence required the Opposition to persuade a majority of all the members to support the motion and the UNC simply did not have the 19 votes required (cf. Annexes 11 and 12).

As important as were some of the reasons formally given, the ruling party's decision to call a general rather than a by-election to fill the seat vacated by the resignation of the member for San Fernando West was prompted by concern that it could lose the seat because of low turnout among its support base. The UNC had been boasting that they had organised San Fernando West with "military precision," and that the constituency was theirs for the taking.[4] The Party was also aware that, for much the same reason, it might not do as well as it wished in the local government elections which were then due and for which it was preparing. If either or both of these developments occurred, it was feared that it would provide a major boost for the opposition which could serve to generate a bandwagon effect which it might have been difficult to reverse in 1996, a year in which the government was also expecting to have tough negotiations with public sector unions. The decision to call a general election was thus seen as a way to circumvent all of these difficulties.

Following the elections, the former Prime Minister let it be known that the party leadership feared that if the elections had not been called when they were, the PNM might have lost at least two more seats, a claim that is hotly disputed within PNM circles by elements who feel that if the election was scheduled when they were due, both the party and the Government would have been better prepared (*Mirror,* January 12, 1996; also *Guardian,* January 13, 1996). Those who subscribe to this latter view believe that the Government would have been better advised to present a populist budget, which was already substantially prepared, before calling the election. They also believed that the Government would have been the beneficiary of the numerous job creation projects which were in the pipeline and which were scheduled to come on stream in 1996 (cf. Overand Padmore, "Manning's Gamble," *Guardian,* October 15, 1996).

The Prime Minister however calculated that the PNM faithful and the floating vote were more likely to rally to the party in a general confrontation with the UNC which he was advised was in a state of organizational disarray. He firmly believed that the PNM could not possibly lose a general election, and that it indeed stood a very good chance to win the 24 seats which it claimed it required to govern effectively. The PNM had in fact accused the Opposition of refusing to cooperate with it in making changes to the Constitution which it deemed necessary to restructure the Police and other Service Commissions and to pass legislation which abrogated the rights of persons charged with repeated criminal offences.[5]

It is of course now "history" that instead of winning the election with an increased majority, the PNM won only 17 seats in Trinidad, the same number as the UNC, which left the two NAR members of Parliament from the sister isle of Tobago effectively holding the balance between the two major parties. This was exactly the result which the NAR had hoped to achieve. The NAR in fact did not expect to win the election, and had contested only 19 seats. The party in fact hoped that the result in Trinidad would be a stalemate and that the NAR would thus "make the difference."

It therefore came as no surprise that the leader of the NAR, former Prime Minister ANR Robinson, chose to give his support to the United National Congress rather than enter into a post-election alliance with the PNM which had signalled its willingness to consider some sort of accommodation with the NAR, even though its Political leader had made it very clear during the election campaign that the Party would "fight alone, win alone or lose alone" since it considered coalition governments inherently unstable. Robinson clearly relished being sought after by both the PNM and the UNC. As he chortled, "the stone which the builder rejected had now become the corner stone of the new edifice."

There were several reasons for the outcome of the election. Some had to do with failures of the ruling party and its leader; others had to do with the general state of the economy, while yet others had to do with what the opposition parties were able to achieve. Also important was the state of race relations which had been dramatically transformed in the period following the 1991 election and more particularly in 1995, the year in which the Indian community marked the 150th Anniversary of its arrival in Trinidad and Tobago. The burden of our argument however, is that while several factors contributed to the outcome of the election, the ethnic factor by far is the one with the greatest explanatory significance. For Indo-Trinidadians, the capture of political power was the jewel, the crowning achievement for which many had laboured and dreamt.

This claim has been challenged by some observers. Dr. John La Guerre, for example argues that claims about the salience of the race factor are asserted and not proved and that race has been used merely as a "loose description of a number of variables."

,a Guerre argues that "issues" were far more important and undamental in the election as was the fact that the UNC had nanaged to transform itself into a party that seemed able, for the irst time, to function as an effective alternative to the PNM overnment. In sum, the UNC had an organisational weapon that vas more vital than race. La Guerre argues further that culture, eligion, and geographical location were also important eterminants of voting behaviour, all of which, is of course true *Guardian,* March 13, 1996). These can however all be subsumed nder the broad concept of ethnicity (cf. Annexe 2 for a further iscussion of this issue). Then too, ethnicity is a first order issue vhich informs one's cosmology and how one constructs and erceives "reality" and the issues (Hintzen 1996). It is true in ontemporary Trinidad, there is a great deal of fluidity and that ndividuals are cross pressured and straddle a variety of overlapping thnicities. For many, ethnicity is only symbolic, cosmetic, or ostalgic, and does not express itself in everyday behaviour. For thers however, it is more than symbolic. The context often etermines which orientation is relevant. Our argument is that in 995, ethnic pride was the dominant factor that drove many Indo-'rinidadians many of whom had voted PNM, ONR or NAR before nto the UNC fold, even though many had reservations about how vell that party might perform in terms of addressing certain policy sues, especially those relating to the economy. To most of them, e overriding view was that the time had come for Trinidad and 'obago to have an Indian Prime Minister. The dramatic swing in oter allegiance among Indians of all classes and creeds to the JNC cannot possibly be explained otherwise.

Those who challenge the view that race was the critical ariable also argue that the PNM had lost its appeal to many voters f all ethnicities and that the party was rejected on grounds other an race. The Party, they assert, had shown that it was incapable f solving the many critical problems facing the country-spiraling rime rates, high unemployment, persistent poverty and ispossession, the drug trade, a growing coarseness in the society nd a general decline in its institutional fabric and in the standard of governance, and that many had come to believe that it was tim to ignore the race factor and give the UNC the chance for which was asking. It is also argued that the UNC had succeeded i restructuring and re-imaging itself and was now attractive to th Indian middle class as well as to others who were not Indian. Whil it is true that the UNC had been able to re-engineer itself, the fac is that it failed to attract any significant support from the Afro Trinidadian community. What happened, in the main, was tha Indo-Trinidadian voters of all confessional allegiances and classe who in the past had split their votes among several competing partie — the PNM, the ONR and the NAR — solidified behind the "new UNC. In their view, the election promised to provide them with a unprecedented opportunity to deal with the problem of politica peripheralisation about which they had long complained. As on put it, "we just wanted people to treat us like we are part of th country."

Afro-Trinidadians who were disenchanted with the PNM for the reasons given above, as well as for other reasons, eithe continued to support that Party out of fear for what a UNC victor might mean in terms of the reallocation of material and symboli resources — the so called "fear factor" — or withheld their suppo from all parties. Some abstained in the belief that the PNM woul win anyway. While it is true that none of this can be prove conclusively, the correlation between voting behaviour and th ethnic composition of polling divisions clearly points to th conclusion that most Indo-Trinidadians voted for the UNC an most Afro-Trinidadians voted for the PNM. One understands wh some would wish to resist this conclusion. For ideological reason it is important to establish that race and/or ethnicity has ceased t be a major factor in the politics of Trinidad and Tobago. Th evidence however suggests that both parties used and wer beneficiaries of the race factor. It is also interesting to note tha most of the commentators who asserted in public that race wa not a factor in the election were Indo-Trinidadian rather than Afro Trinidadian.

II

The PNM and the Election

Despite its loss of power, the PNM's overall voting support actually increased from 233,950 in 1991 to 255,855 in 1995. The Party increased its vote in all but three constituencies, Arima, Laventille West and Tobago East. This increase in support came from new voters, 43,255 of whom were added to the 1995 electoral list, as well as from upscale elements who previously supported the NAR. Of the 102,397 votes which the NAR lost in the election, approximately 21,935 or 13 per cent went to the PNM. The other 88,770 (87 per cent) went mainly to the UNC. The split was largely along ethnic lines as was foreshadowed by the results of the two bye-elections which were held in 1994.[6]

The party however appeared to have suffered a corresponding loss of support among the constituency which normally provides it with much of its political muscle, a loss which neutralised some of the gains which it achieved among upscale elements and which might have proved critical in the marginal constituencies which the party lost. Voter turn out rates among the black urban working and under class population, especially the younger cohorts, were much lower than they were in 1991 when the PNM's campaign theme was "we care" and when the Party had popular figures in its ranks such as the late Morris Marshall, the MP for Laventille West. A SARA Survey conducted in October 1995 indicated that only 52 per cent of the Afro-Trinidadians aged 18-21 wanted the PNM to win the election. Seventeen per cent had no party preference, while 10 per cent chose the NAR. Seventy-nine per cent of their Indo-Trinidadian counterparts wanted a UNC victory, while 10 per cent endorsed the NAR. Significantly, while 84 per cent of the Indo-Trinidadians aged 18-21 said they would "definitely" (75 per cent) or "probably" vote (9 per cent), only 68 per cent of their Afro-Trinidadian counterparts were of this disposition. Significantly, only 50 per cent said they would "definitely" vote.

The view that the PNM suffered a loss of support from the black underclass has been challenged by some analysts who claim to have seen no evidence of this in the voting figures which show that the PNM's support actually increased. According to Bishnu Ragoonath, "only in one constituency, namely Nariva, did the PNM percentage of the votes cast see a decline in comparison with the 1991 value. What this therefore suggests is that the PNM was able to maintain and even increase its traditional support base at the 1995 election" (cf. Bishnu Ragoonath, "The 1995 Elections How the Votes were Really Shared." Mimeo, Department of Government, UWI 1996). My own view is that the PNM would have done better if more of its supporters had turned out to vote. It is to be noted that only 6,757 (or 10 per cent) more persons voted in 1995 than did so in 1991 though 43,255 new names were added to the electoral list.

Constituencies in which Afro-Trinidadians were numerically dominant or in which they were in high concentration tended to have lower voter turnouts than constituencies in which Indo-Trinidadians were dominant. The average voter turn out in constituencies won by the UNC was 68.1 per cent whereas for the PNM the figure was 59.4 per cent. The turnout in all 17 constituencies won by the UNC exceeded the national turnout rate. The following are some examples of the turnout in the two sets of constituencies:

Table 1
Voter Turn Out, by Ethnicity - 1995 General Elections

Indo-Trinidadian Dominant Constituency	Percent	Afro-Trinidadian Dominant Constituency	Percent
Fyzabad	70	Laventille West	48
Naparima	70	Laventille East	53
Nariva	69	Arima	59
Oropouche	67	Port of Spain North	55
Point-a-Pierre	70	Port of Spain South	54
Siparia	68	Diego Martin West	55
Princes Town	69	Diego Martin East	57
Chaguanas	69	Diego Martin Central	55
Couva South	69	St. Anns East	57
Couva North	68	Tobago East	48
Oropouche	67	Tobago West	50

Source: EBC 1996.

There were however seven constituencies which were won by the PNM in which turn out approximated that of those won by the UNC and exceeded the national turn out rate of 63.2 per cent. These were Tunapuna (67 per cent) San Fernando East and West (65 and 67 per cent respectively), Toco-Manzanilla (64 per cent), Point Fortin (64 per cent and La Brea 66 per cent). All of these constituencies however had high concentrations of Indian voters and the contests were therefore keen. Only in one constituency won by the UNC did the voter turn out fall below two-thirds. This however occurred in 12 constituencies won by the PNM.

It is also worth noting that in 15 of the 17 constituencies won by the PNM, there was a decline in the percentage of the electorate that turned out to vote and that in 11 of the 17, the *absolute numbers* of those voting also declined. The reverse was the case in the constituencies won by the UNC. In 14 of these constituencies, the absolute number of persons coming out to vote increased over the 1991 figures. There was however a decline of percentage turn out in 9 and an increase in 7 as opposed to only 2 for the PNM constituencies (*Trinidad and Tobago Review*, December 1995).

Part of the reason for voter apathy among the black underclass had to do with the policies of structural adjustment which were being pursued by the Trinidad and Tobago Government. These policies involved downsizing the public sector, privatization or policies related to planned privatization of the public utilities and the state enterprises, cut backs in the amount of employment generating project work available, and the reduction or cancellation of subsidies and welfare services, all of which impacted heavily on the poor. The general economic policies being pursued by the Government were applauded by the international financial agencies, the local financial community and the élite strata, but the poor generally, and the urban poor in particular, were not persuaded that the policies were in their interest, promises and assurances to the contrary notwithstanding.[7] The opposition leader Basdeo Panday put his finger on the PNM's dilemma when he observed that

> ... former Prime Minister made the awful error of abdicating the responsibility of the Government to deal with unemployment. That's where the former government went wrong. They were concentrating on liberalisation and the trends in the world which they could not escape, and which we cannot escape either. We accept that we have to live within the context of the World Bank and conditionalities. But at the same time, the government has a positive role to play in the removal of poverty and destitution. (*Express*, January 3, 1996)

Manning conceded that the PNM made mistakes which hurt it politically. He agreed that the structural adjustment policies affected the party's traditional supporters who had lost their jobs in the public sector. He however felt that many of the victims had come to see the wisdom of the policies after they had found alternative employment. Not enough of this reassessment had however occurred by the time of the election (*Express,* November 11, 1995). Many traditional PNM voters made it clear to party activists that they were without work, whether permanent or temporary, and were therefore without the wherewithal to live or to look after their families and would therefore "punish" the party by not voting. It was not that they did not value their vote as others (meaning Indians) do, as some complained. They felt they had nothing meaningful to vote for.

The PNM's Political Leader chose to ignore these signals, believing as he did that once the bell was rung, the faithful would come marching home as they had done in the past. Platform speakers in fact sought to reason with the unemployed, telling them that even if they did not get a "little ten days" (temporary project work), there were collateral benefits to be obtained from the PNM's macroeconomic policies — low inflation, jobs in the future (the Prime Minister had boasted that his Government would eliminate unemployment completely in the near future) — and that they should therefore take the long rather than the short term view (*Express,* June 13, 1996). Light was being seen at the end of the tunnel, he assured electors. They were also told, albeit in coded language, that a victory for the UNC would in all probability witness either a cessation of the Unemployment Relief Programme (URP) or a shift of projects from the urban to the rural areas which would be to their disadvantage. Deputy Political Leader Keith Rowley pushed the "fear factor" button for all it was worth. As he told a meeting in Laventille, " if voting for the PNM means getting a ten days, then you could vote for the UNC and you will see how many ten days you would get" (*Newsday,* November 2, 1995). The UNC, it should be recalled, had always complained that "Laventille," which was used as a metaphor for urban depressed areas inhabited by the Afro-Trinidadian community, was being given more by way of project work than rurally based communities. The PNM defended this by arguing that "Laventille" was a threat to the social stability and security of the rest of the society, and therefore had to be "pacified."[8] It was said that the suburbs of Port of Spain would become unliveable if Laventille's social needs were not catered to.

The PNM's message that the black community was in danger and was in need of support got through to some, but clearly not to all of its followers in this strata, many of whom stayed away from the polls (see "The Fear Factor," *Express,* November 1, 1995). This was particularly true of younger blacks who do not relate to the PNM in the manner in which their elders did. Some blacks were also heard to say that the opinion polls were predicting that the PNM would win anyway, or that the PNM would get their vote "automatically" whether they did or did not vote, not realizing that by not voting, they were indirectly helping the UNC to win those constituencies in which the numerical balance between the two ethnic groups was close.

It is worth recalling here that the likelihood that the black under class would stay away from the polls was clearly indicated in the Laventille West by-election which was held in May 1994. Only 22 per cent of the potential electorate of 25,126 bothered to vote then, compared to 57.39 in 1991. The PNM's vote dropped from 10,947 or 81.08 per cent of the votes cast in 1991 to 5,527 or 70 per cent in that by-election. The signals were clear then, and while they were recognized and addressed — promises were made to build soup kitchens, relief centres and housing complexes in East Port of Spain and elsewhere, as well as to introduce all sorts of job creating projects — the effort was less than adequate given the time available and severe resource constraints (*Express,* November 12, 1995).[9]

Part of the problem was that the PNM leadership had been advised by "official spies" that the UNC (mistakenly, as it turned out) and the NAR were in a state of political undress and that the PNM could not possibly lose the election. The Prime Minister had also asked protesting supporters in Laventille "if not the PNM, who?" His assumption, like that of other PNM leaders, was that the party was permanently integrated into the psyche of the Afro-Trinidadian, and that that bond could never be broken. As Mr. Manning in fact boasted during the campaign, "it is either the PNM or chaos. The choices facing the population are the opposition and its bacchanal or the oasis in the middle of the desert — the cool, calm stability that is the PNM" (*Express,* November 21, 1994). Much that was done or not done was informed by this overconfidence. Thus, even when the UNC showed that it had not in fact been caught completely unprepared by the calling of an early election and that it was in fact expecting it, the PNM took long to get into political over drive. The Prime Minister's snap election call in fact caught the PNM electoral machine unprepared, even though it had been put on notice that a local government election was imminent. The PNM also seemed to have focussed its election efforts in strongholds which it could not lose rather than in the marginal seats as the UNC did.[10] PNM campaign managers complained that unlike the UNC leader, the PNM leadership did not walk about the marginal seats or hold spot meetings in any of them.

Party stalwarts are now convinced that the PNM was not ready for a general election. The Party's Election Officer had in fact submitted a report to the Political Leader advising him that party groups were not functioning, and that disenchantment was rife. The Political Leader inexplicably did not share that report with his three deputy leaders who only learnt of its existence after the election. In his pre- and post-election report to the Political Leader of the Party, the Elections Officer detailed a number of factors which, in his view, were crucial determinants of the electoral outcome. Among these was the decision of the Finance Minister, who was also a deputy leader of the Party, not to stand for re-election, public controversy over the choice of certain candidates, and the decision of the General Secretary to contest the election, which, in his view, had a negative impact on the ability of the central party machine to service the needs of the constituencies. Field officers were also said to be inactive. So too were many party groups. The Elections Officer was of the view that government policies were hurting the party and alienating its support base.

The Election Officer was likewise sharply critical of the party's intelligence machinery for totally underestimating the financial strength and the level of operational preparedness of the Opposition as well as for overestimating the strength of the PNM. The result, in his words, was a "volcanic eruption" which took the PNM's political high command completely by surprise. The official noted that in the constituency of Fyzabad which he oversaw, while the PNM increased its vote by more than 1,000 over that which it obtained in 1991 — 6,886 to 5,867 votes, the UNC's vote of 10,097 was 1,400 more than the combined opposition vote in 1991. Something fundamental had caused this dramatic shift in voter allegiance.

The Political Leadership was also criticised for the weaknesses that were manifest in the central party apparatus, the intermittency of its propaganda machinery, its tendency to defer to managerial types rather than politicians ("we must not saddle the party with political non-achievers"), its division of the "Grand Old Party" into "new" and "old", its stifling of criticism, and its tendency to victimise those who dared to criticise. Warned the Elections Officer: "members must be free, within reasonable limits, to criticize both party and government when in office without fear of victimization and/or inappropriate retaliation from the leadership"[11] (cf. Annexes 14 and 15).

Mr. Manning denied that his leadership style was autocratic and indicated that in one respect at least, he ought to have been more so. He was referring to the fact that he "consulted" his three deputy leaders about the date on which he proposed holding the election. He has since charged that the date was leaked to sources close to the UNC which enabled them to be prepared. He vowed that the "next time round," he would take action which was "autocratic," since he would not share information about the date with anyone (*Express,* February 11, 1996). There is however no incontrovertible evidence that there was in fact a deliberate politically inspired leak, (though it is difficult to assume that a "secret" of that nature could remain a "secret" for any length of time especially since some pre-election arrangements would have had to be made) and Mr. Manning may have been looking for scapegoats. It also appears that the consultation about the proposed date was formalistic and that the decision was not enthusiastically endorsed by some of those with whom it was shared. Given the structure of power within the leadership, they had little choice but to go along.

Constituency neglect was also one of the major factors which explained the performance of the PNM. Few PNM candidates had serviced their constituencies, perhaps assuming that there would be time in 1996 to mend fences. Early elections thus caught them unprepared. Three candidates paid dearly for this neglect — the representatives from the critical constituencies of St. Joseph, Ortoire-Mayaro and Barataria-San Juan.[12] While the withdrawal of black underclass support was national in scope, the ethnic balance in these marginal constituencies was such as to make their negligence meaningful. The party also lost and came close to losing another marginal seat, Tunapuna. Prime Minister Manning exonerated himself from blame for not being aware of the weaknesses of the party in these constituencies. He told members that they were the "eyes and ears of the leadership" and had to be careful about the information they supplied. If the information was flawed, the decisions made on the basis of that information would also be flawed. Manning complained that constituency groups had endorsed the sitting candidates in the three marginal seats which the PNM lost and that he was only now being told that they were not effective. Manning however admitted that he had spent too much time on governing and that the party was neglected (*Express,* February 11, 1996). Given the experience of the election and what he now knew about the mood of the country and the party, he felt he was now better prepared to "walk the middle road as the PNM prepares to govern Trinidad and Tobago [again]" (*Guardian,* January 13, 1996).

Constituency neglect did not however have the same significance in UNC held constituencies. In Pointe-a-Pierre, for example, the ethnic factor served as an override which swept away the PNM candidate who had been nursing the constituency for several months and was generally liked by constituents. He was told that he was on the wrong side of the ethnic divide. In the UNC constituency of St. Augustine, the sitting candidate acknowledged that he had not serviced his constituency. He was nevertheless carried to victory by the surging tide of ethnic support for the UNC.

The PNM leadership also made errors which were responsible for the Party's performance, though it is difficult to quantify this factor. Mr. Manning's political stocks were quite high up to May 1995 when he returned from a visit to Hong Kong and made a number of serious political blunders from which he had not recovered when the election was called. The errors involved firing his Foreign Minister during a television address to the nation without advising the Minister before hand; firing the Honorary Consul for Trinidad and Tobago in Hong Kong by fax and then telling the nation that he did so in order to re-appoint him to another post; using the might of the State and the Emergency Provisions of the Constitution to detain the Speaker of the House of Representatives whom the Government had asked to resign because of allegations about her inappropriate behaviour; and perhaps the silliest gesture of all — making the claim in a national address that he was the "Father of the Nation" and thus must speak to it in a certain way about matters of national importance. Very few persons were prepared to forgive Mr. Manning — aged 46 — for this impertinent political claim. Following the election, Mr. Manning made things worse for himself among PNM supporters by claiming that he was the "Father of the PNM," if not the nation (cf. Annexes 11 and 12).

Polling data and comments heard on radio talk shows had provided ample evidence that Mr. Manning's stocks had taken a nose dive and that withdrawal of affect and respect was massive within the national community generally, and within the Indian community in particular. In a survey carried out by the author in June 1995, 67 per cent of the Afro-Trinidadian and 79 per cent of the Indo-Trinidadian population gave Mr. Manning a negative rating in terms of his performance as Prime Minister. Mr. Manning's "cocky" political style also alienated many. Following his break with the PNM, Mr. Ralph Maraj, the Minister of Foreign Affairs accused Mr. Manning of being "petty, insecure and dictatorial." He complained further that he was a "victim of political thuggery and hooliganism," and went so far as to compare the Prime Minister to Idi Amin. Maraj argued that Manning was a "liability to the PNM" and predicted, prophetically, that he would destroy that party and cause it to lose the forthcoming elections (*Guardian*, August 8, 1995; also August 27, 1995). Few in the PNM believed Maraj at the time. It is now clear that ministers other than Maraj disliked the Prime Minister's leadership style and his tendency to rely more on the Chairman of the Party, an appointed official, Senator Lenny Saith, than on his three elected deputy political leaders. Manning and Saith, it was said, operated like "Bim and Bam." While more open discussion of issues was allowed than was the case in the cabinets of either Dr. Williams or Mr. Chambers, the debate was structured so that Mr. Manning's views invariably prevailed.[13]

Pre-election surveys done by St. Augustine Research Associates (SARA) on behalf of the *Sunday Express* in June 1995 and by Market Facts and Opinion on behalf of the *Sunday Guardian* in the run up to the elections may also have served to convince leaders of the PNM and many of their supporters that they were invincible. The Party had also commissioned polls of its own which might have informed the decision to call the election early. The collective results of the various polls bred a sense of complacency which proved to be counter productive. Ironically, the SARA polls which were published in October following the calling of the election were criticized by both UNC and PNM supporters for different reasons. UNC leaders and supporters claimed that the poll was a deliberate fabrication which sought to demoralize their supporters Those who did not allege mischief nevertheless told their supporter that the poll was "wrong" in that it did not reflect the suppor which they knew their party had on the ground. The PNM's Politica Leader was also of the view that the poll was "wrong." He believec that it underestimated the support of the PNM in that it gave the party only 15 sure seats and saw only 4 or possibly 5 more as bein likely to fall into its column. The party leadership was confidentl expecting to win between 21 and 24 seats. Both leaders thus founc it tactically necessary to discredit the poll (cf. Annexe 19).

The SARA polling data had however indicated that there would be a high voter turnout among the Indian population anc that in the absence of a third party, the Indian vote, which previousl went to the NAR or the PNM, would solidify behind the UNC Given this, it was accurately predicted that all constituencies in which the Indian population was in a majority would be won by the UNC. There were 14 such constituencies. This meant that 5 seats, the so-called PNM marginals, would determine the outcome of the elections in Trinidad. The two Tobago seats were expected to go to the NAR although the PNM leadership believed it could win one of them, Tobago East.

A summary of the major findings of the highlights of the October 1995 SARA poll is provided in the box below for the record:

HIGHLIGHTS OF SARA POLL CONDUCTED OCTOBER, 1995*

- Seventy-six per cent of the electorate considered the forthcoming elections to be either "very important" or "important."
- Unemployment was seen to be the most important issue in the campaign 29 per cent – followed by crime – 19 per cent – and the ethnic identity of power wielders (12 per cent).
- Seventy-five per cent of the Indo-Trinidadians generally and 81 per cent of the Hindus in the sample said that they would definitely vote. Sixty-six per cent of the Afro-Trinidadians said they would do so.
- Seventy-seven per cent of the Afro-Trinidadians in the sample would give the PNM another chance to govern. Sixty-eight per cent of the Indians wished to see the UNC in power.
- Fifty per cent of those polled were of the view that the PNM should be given another chance to govern the country. Not all of these were unequivocal in this view, however. Thirteen per cent reported that they were disposed to return the PNM to power because they saw no alternative to the ruling party. The UNC was deemed to be politically illegitimate and unviable. Thirty-nine per cent were however minded to give the UNC a chance at the crease.
- Patrick Manning was the choice of 64 per cent of the Afro-Trinidadians in the sample as the person preferred to be Prime Minister, 41 per cent of the mixed group, and 9 per cent of the Indo-Trinidadians.
- Seventy-five per cent of lower strata black females endored Manning as Prime Minister compared to 51 per cent of black lower strata males. Only 2 percentage points separated Indo-Trinidadian females and males of this rank.
- Forty per cent of the sample said that they preferred to see the PNM form the next government, 30 per cent the UNC, 11 per cent the NAR, and 1 per cent the MUP.

- Sixty per cent of black lower class males and 78 per cent of black lower class females reported that they would prefer to see the PNM form the new government.
- Sixty-eight per cent of the Afro-Trinidadians preferred to have the PNM form the next government, 10 per cent of the Indo-Trinidadians and 40 per cent of the mixed group.
- Basdeo Panday was the choice of 64 per cent of the Indo-Trinidadians and 74 per cent of the Hindus as the person preferred to be Prime Minister, 8 per cent of the mixed group, and 4 per cent of the Afro-Trinidadians.
- Indo-Trinidadians were more than 3 times as likely than were Afro-Trinidadians (70 to 19 per cent) to say that the PNM had no significant achievement to its credit since it came to power in 1991.
- Sixty-six per cent of the Indo-Trinidadians generally and 72 per cent of the Hindus specifically preferred to have the UNC form the next government, 8 per cent of the mixed group, and 4 per cent of the Afro-Trinidadians.
- Forty-one per cent of those who said they would vote UNC reported that they were doing so because of who the leader was. Those who were voting for the PNM tended to stress party (30 per cent) and policy continuity (29 per cent) rather than who the leader was (11 per cent).
- Sixty-three per cent for the Hindus in the sample were of the view that the presence of Lawrence Maharaj in the UNC enhanced that party's chances of winning the election. Only seventeen per cent of the Afro-Trinidadians in the sample and 21 per cent of the mixed population agreed with this assessment.
- Support for NAR comes mainly from Catholics (12 per cent) and agnostics (17 per cent). Eight per cent of the Muslims and 5 per cent of the Hindus reported that they would support the NAR.
- Seventy-one per cent of the Afro-Trinidadian population picked the PNM to win the election. Fifty-six per cent of Indo-Trinidadians picked the UNC to win.

*Sample Size 1002.

III

The UNC and the Election

The UNC started off the election campaign seemingly at a decided disadvantage. It was widely regarded as a political underdog with an electoral machinery which was rudimentary at best. In previous elections, the UNC had no political machinery or financial backing to talk about. It had never won more than 13 seats in a general election and those only in areas where a clear majority of the population was Indian. The party remained entrenched in areas that lay behind the rice and sugar cane "curtain." To use calypsonian David Rudder's phrase, it remained "locked up in the sugar cane jail." The party espoused a working class ideology and was deemed politically untouchable by the urban gentry of all ethnicities. Its leadership was also widely regarded as being less than suitable for high office. Indeed, the PNM had considered the UNC leadership to be its most valuable electoral asset.[15] Its political leader, Mr. Basdeo Panday, was charismatic as he was quixotic, and had said and done much to upset Afro-Trinidadians, particularly by his repeated changes that Indians were "alienated." The European business community was also offended by Panday's reference to them as a "parasitic oligarchy" which, in conjunction with the black and Indian managerial elite, was exploiting the community.[16]

When asked what was responsible for the change which took place in the fortunes of the UNC, Mr. Ramesh Lawrence Maharaj, the UNC's Policy and Strategy Officer, indicated that preparations for the 1996 election campaign had begun as early as 1992 since the Party had come to the conclusion that only 7,132 thousand votes in 5 constituencies stood between it and victory in the 1991 election. These were:

San Juan - Barataria	1,363 votes
Ortoire - Mayaro	1,565 "
Pointe-a-Pierre	192 "
St. Joseph	1,312 "
Tunapuna	2,699 "

As Mr. Maharaj reflected:

> After the General Elections of 1991, it became clear to us that if we had a more effective election strategy and election day machinery we would have been able to translate our mass support into votes and would have won the General Elections. The leadership of the Party decided that the necessary machinery had to be put in place for the Party to win the General Elections of 1996. The Party started preparing for a 1996 Election in 1992.

Mr. Maharaj had also made a similar statement in a lecture given in Toronto on June 6, 1992. To quote him:

> The results of the last general elections indicate that the UNC made gains along the east west corridor in what were predominantly PNM strongholds with a strong African base. The seats of St. Joseph, Tunapuna, San Juan, Barataria, Oropouche and Point-a-Pierre were won by the PNM. If the UNC had received a total of just under 7,000 votes in these seats they would have obtained 18 seats in the Parliament, and would have won the elections. The UNC was therefore denied forming the Government of Trinidad and Tobago by only 7,000 votes. It is interesting that the PNM polled 233,950 votes, the UNC polled 151,046 and the NAR 127,335. In other words, the combined votes of the UNC and NAR show that a majority of the people of Trinidad and Tobago voted against the PNM. *(Indo-Caribbean Resistance:* 1993:40)

According to Mr. Maharaj, the Party's mobilization strategy involved, *inter alia,* changing its behaviour in Parliament in an attempt to convince the electorate that it was a disciplined organization which could provide the country with an alternative government. The process of creating and approving a new party constitution was also designed to mobilize supporters and convince them that power could be won. The alleged attempt on the part of the PNM to discredit the party's Political Leader by laying 5 charges of sexual harassment against him was also said to have backfired in that it created sympathy rather than disgust for the accused.

The meetings that were called to discuss the state's action in fact provided a useful platform around which to rally support for the UNC. Panday was projected as a martyr who had struggled for the oppressed in the UNC and who was now being targeted because he had attacked the "parasitic oligarchy" and had exposed its links with the Mafia, the drug lords and the PNM.

Panday, who was given bail in the sum of $75,000, had denied all allegations of sexual impropriety involving women employed in the UNC office and instead countercharged that he was being politically persecuted by those who were frightened by the prospect of a UNC victory and who thus wished to discredit him and the UNC just when the SARA polls were indicating that the party could win the next election.

The population was divided in its opinion as to whether Panday was guilty as charged or not. Forty-four per cent of the Indo-Trinidadians generally and 54 per cent of the Hindus believed he was falsely accused. Ten per cent of the Afro-Trinidadians and 37 per cent of the Muslims were of this view. Those who believed in Panday's guilt felt that he should give up the leadership of the UNC and make way for someone who was more acceptable to the national community. It was also felt that if Panday gave up the leadership, it would be easier for NAR elements to join with the UNC and create a grand coalition against the PNM as had occurred in 1986 (*Mirror,* October 16, 1994).

Panday refused to resign and managed to emerge from the crisis with an enhanced status among the Indian population (cf. *The Harassment of the Hon. Basdeo Panday* 1995). Panday in fact blamed UNC MP for Chaguanas, Hulsie Bhaggan, whom he described as a "loose cannon," for helping the PNM and the defendants to orchestrate the campaign against him. As he complained, "just as we reach the pinnacle, look what this woman come and do." Bhaggan, who had been expelled from the UNC after having had the Whip withdrawn, denied being a PNM agent. Her complaint was that there was no democracy within the UNC and that the Party was dominated by an oligarchy led by Messrs. Panday and Maharaj, both of whom she accused of trying to silence and marginalize her.

The UNC claims that when the election was eventually called, "the Party had the necessary election machinery in the marginal seats" and felt sure it would have captured 19 seats. Mr. Maharaj also disclosed that a US election public relations team had conducted analyses in respect of the marginal constituencies long before the election was called and that structures were put in place to secure victory in the said seats. Maharaj's comments suggest that the UNC's ready response once the election date was set was not the by-product of a leak from a PNM source — assuming that there was in fact any such leak — but the result of careful pre-planning. It also appears that promises of significant funding were made well in advance of the calling of the election. The PNM was however completely unaware of these developments and was taken completely by surprise.

One week into the campaign, reports began to surface that three businessmen who were previously very closely linked to the PNM — one had in fact served as the Minister of Industry and Trade in the PNM Government of the day — had decided to make substantial sums of money available to the UNC to fund a massive advertising campaign to re-package, reposition and legitimize it in the minds of the electorate.[17] It later became public knowledge that Mervyn Dymally, a former member of the United States House of Representatives, who had become closely associated with the UNC, had recruited a number of public relations experts from the United States to assist the UNC in its campaign operations.

Using the human and material resources available from these and other sources, the UNC mounted an "air power" offensive the likes of which had never been seen in Trinidad and Tobago.[18] The media, both print and electronic, were saturated with political messages which sought to portray the PNM as being politically inept, especially in the critical areas of crime and unemployment, two areas where several surveys had shown the party to be most vulnerable (*Express*, October 16, 1995). The irony was that previous to this blitz, the UNC leadership was widely seen to be the party that was soft on crime. One of its key members, Mr. Lawrence Maharaj, had defended the Jamaat al Muslimeen which had sought to overthrow the government in June 1990 as well as a number of persons charged with serious drug and other offenses (Ryan 1991). The UNC had also blocked the Governments' efforts to change the Constitution in order to put in place what the latter deemed to be a more efficient administrative structure and policies to deal with crime.

The Political Leader of the UNC had taken the line then that as Leader of the Opposition his role was not to make the Prime Minister look good, but to get his "backside" off the seat of Government. Additionally, he charged that the legislative and constitutional changes which the Government was seeking to introduce infringed civic liberties and were designed to transform the Prime Minister into a constitutional dictator. What was needed, in his view, was a more effective system of crime detection and apprehension of criminals as well as improved machinery for the speedy administration of justice.

There is some question as to how effective the UNC's advertising campaign was in changing voter intentions. In a survey conducted by the author, 75 per cent of those sampled claimed that they had made up their minds as to how they would vote prior to the advertising campaign. Seventeen per cent however indicated that the advertising campaign had helped them to make up their minds. This is a credible claim. The advertising thrust, which was assisted by the fact that there are three radio stations which cater specifically to the Indian community, served to raise the profile of the election and clearly helped to convince UNC supporters that victory was within their grasp. It may also have had a pro-UNC effect on some undecided voters.

The campaign, which had as its theme "give yourself a chance," succeeded in consolidating and bringing out Indian voters who were firmly persuaded that this was the best chance ever offered them to deconstruct what took place in 1956-1961 when the African descended population captured political power and led Trinidad and Tobago to Independence. Many Indians who were not previously committed to the UNC, or even sympathetic to it, chose to openly identify with the party, in some cases because they wanted "change", but more often than not, because they wished to see an Indian dominated party in power. Many who supported the PNM in the past also voted for the UNC. This was particularly true of Muslims to whom a special appeal was made for unity of all Indians, all *jahajibhais.*[19] Indians were also told by ex-PNM Minister Ralph Maraj that they would "not have another opportunity like this for a very long time. Now that you have it, you should take advantage of it and ensure that the UNC is elected into government. If the UNC gets those five odd marginal seats and picks up one or two others which are relatively close, then the UNC can end up with 19 seats and maybe as many as 21 seats in the new Parliament" (*Newsday,* November 1, 1995).

Hulsie Bhaggan, who had broken with the UNC to form the cross-ethnic Movement for Unity and Progress (MUP), was correct when she observed that many Indians voted UNC because they wanted to give Panday a chance to be Prime Minister. "The overwhelming sentiment among Indians was that they wanted to give Panday his last chance to be Prime Minister. All the Indians united.... People did not vote against me. They voted for Basdeo Panday to be in power" (*Mirror,* November 24, 1995). Bhaggan, who blamed SARA for her defeat because it showed her as having no chance of winning, also argued that Panday's call for "national unity" was a euphemism for "Indian unity." As she observed:

> This national unity thing is merely PR. I see it as Indian unification. I don't think they have been able to pull into their ranks high profile people of other races. The UNC has done what the PNM did and it is now time for an alternative. We cannot continue with these types of ethnic parties. (*Guardian,* January 4, 1996)

Bhaggan further argued, with justification, that former Minister of Planning in the NAR administration, Winston Dookeran, and the NAR, were used opportunistically by the UNC. Both were used as part of the Indian unification process to support Panday. Dookeran was in fact told by the UNC that if he did not commit himself openly to the UNC, his silence would be interpreted as "part of a conspiracy to foist the PNM on a beleaguered population" (*Guardian,* October 9, 1995).

Following the election, the UNC's Policy and Strategy Officer complained that the party's election machinery did not function as well as he had hoped. To quote him:

> Just as in 1991, our election machinery was not as effective as we hoped it would be, and there was a breakdown in some constituencies. It could not be that we could not get 1,000 more people to vote for us in San Fernando West. Our predictions for marginal seats like San Fernando West and Tunapuna almost came true. We lost out on votes because we failed to identify our voters and take them to the polling stations. (Maharaj, February 2, 1996)

Some UNC activists had banked on winning 20 seats. That hope was however not realistic, and the most that the party could reasonably have hoped for was 19 seats, 5 more than it had when the elections were called.

There were many other factors which explained the performance of the UNC. The Indian community had been mobilized and readied for political combat by the year long celebration of the 150th Anniversary of the Arrival of Indians in Trinidad and Tobago and the national debate as to whether the country's highest national honour should be called the "Trinity Cross," a term which has Christian significance. Trinidad, it was noted, was a multireligious society and as such its honour system should be religiously neutral (cf. Annexe 8).[20]

The Arrival Day celebrations were marked by the visit of the President of India to Trinidad and Tobago and by a number of local and national events which showcased Indian achievement One week before the elections, the Hindu community also celebrated the festival of Divali in grand style. One day before the election, that community also celebrated *Kartik Nahaan*, an event which involved the ritual cleansing by water of the body and spiri of polluting influences. Hindus were told by Panday and their Pundits that on election day, they should complete the process of cleansing by voting the demonised PNM out of power. The spectacle of *murtis* (statues) of Lord Ganesh "drinking milk" also had its effect on the minds of Hindus.[21] The timing of the elections thus coincided with a series of activities which pre-disposed Indians of all confessional groups to come out and vote in order to bring into being the "jahajibhai republic" and the end of PNM hegemony which this author had anticipated would take place around the turn of the century rather than in 1995. The "real" election campaign, the battle to achieve "political arrival," was in fact fought in the mandirs and mosques rather than in the public squares where policy issues such as crime and unemployment were debated.

The UNC leadership was however very aware that given the way in which its support was concentrated in Central and South Trinidad, it would not only be difficult for it to win power unequivocally, but also to govern on its own. It did not control any of the main towns other than Chaguanas in Central Trinidad It thus had to reach out and forge links with urban based non-Indian interests in the society. This was a strategy which had been pursued by its leader, Basdeo Panday for over three decades (Ryan 1989). It is in this context that he openly invited other groups and interests in the society to join him in pursuit of a "government of national unity." As he declared:

> It is time to revive the "One Love" theme again so that African and Indian communities could work together to build the country and take it forward into the 21st Century. They say love is better and sweeter the second time around. (*Guardian,* October 15, 1995).

Panday was in fact making a virtue out of necessity.

Moves to forge links between the UNC and the NAR (or at least one section of it) had in fact been in process since 1994 when efforts were made to establish common platforms to contest by-elections in Caroni East and Pointe-a-Pierre. Panday was anxious to bring on board those whom he had previously alienated by referring to them as their "own worst enemy," *nemakharams* (ingrates), or as associate members of the "parasitic oligarchy."[22] As election day approached, he also declared himself anxious to structure a consensual decision making process that would allow capital and labour to make meaningful contributions to policy making. Panday had consistently expressed the view that the country would never succeed in mobilizing its considerable human resources to alleviate poverty because of the division between business and labour and between Indians, Africans and others. Members of the All Trinidad Sugar Estates and General Workers Union of which he was President were thus advised that they should not expect special favours since "we are on the threshold of merging government, business and labour." The consensual approach was necessary, he opined, because "Trinidad and Tobago is a most highly plural society. Because of our smallness and diversity, we live in crucible-like conditions" (*Mirror,* November 3, 1995).

Even though he was ideologically committed to the principle of "national unity," Panday had become firmly convinced that the UNC had to be the vessel within which unity was to be forged. In the past, he and the parties which he led had abdicated leadership in favour of others deemed more acceptable to the larger society. Now the vehicle had to be the UNC. As he remarked at the launching of the UNC's election campaign:

> UNC means "U Need a Chance". Today you have got a little bit of that chance. Remember for the past several years we have been crying out for unity in our country, crying out to unite our people. We have done all kinds of things, sacrifice our political careers, hand up the leadership, hand up everything, we have done everything; we have even slept with the devil, all of it in the interest of national unity; and we continue to talk of national unity, and therefore I came

> and told you come my brothers and sisters that it is time to love again.
>
> And so when I said it is time to love again, a lot of our cynics sniggered and laughed at us. Well when today you look at the slate of candidates that were presented to you, some from the PNM, some from the NAR, some from the UNC — you will see that in fact we are loving again. You see, when I said it is time to love again, they did not wait for me to finish my sentence; they went and jump into all kinds of things. I meant that this time the loving is going to take place in the House of the Rising Sun, but even more important it is going to take place on the UNC bed....
>
> This is a team that will take you to government; it is a team that will give you the chance that you deserve. You deserve a chance ... and the UNC will give you that chance. The time has come for us all to give ourselves a chance and I am assured that when we go to the polls on elections day, we will give ourselves a chance. I have no more life on this stage and my position now is with you, and I intend to come among you and we shall both give each other a chance. (*Guardian,* October 18, 1990)

The UNC team of 36 had 18 Indians and 1 White. The remainder were mixed or of African descent. All but two of the latter were however in unwinnable seats. The same was however the case with respect to the Indians who contested the election on behalf of the PNM (cf. Annexe 9).

The "Dookeran Factor" and the Election.

One of the intriguing aspects of the campaign which served to give it its peculiar character was the division within NAR and the so called "Dookeran Factor." Dookeran, a former member of the United Labour Front (ULF) and one of the ministers in the NAR government who had chosen to remain in the Cabinet following the split in the coalition which took place in 1987, had been promoted by some elements in the NAR as a less "threatening"

Indian leader than Panday. He was regarded as being acceptable to all ethnic groups and classes, and in fact often emerged ahead of Panday in a number of leadership popularity polls. Given this, he was urged by NAR elements to accept the leadership of the party following the resignation of Mr. Selby Wilson in 1994.

Dookeran's cross-ethnic acceptability however constituted both a strength and a weakness. It was a weakness in the sense that he had no secure political base and could not win any constituency on his own. Indeed, he was humiliatingly defeated in the 1991 general election by the then UNC candidate, Hulsie Bhaggan. Aware of his basic electoral weakness as well as that of the NAR, Dookeran refused the invitation to lead the former ruling party. All parties were however aware that he could add value to their ticket in that he was attractive to detribalised floating voters, particularly those who were Indo-Trinidadian. Dookeran's endorsement was thus sought by the PNM, the UNC and the NAR.

Dookeran was however of the view that there was no room for a third party in the politics of Trinidad and Tobago. He was also of the view that he could not win if he ran on a NAR ticket. Fearing that he would be tagged as an opportunist if he joined either the PNM or the UNC as he was being urged to, Dookeran vacillated and finally chose to attempt the role of regime maker. His strategy was to try to be all things to all men by supporting the call for national unity. Dookeran argued that while there were "good people in all three parties," given the political crisis and the racial polarisation prevailing in the society, no single party was adequate to the task of governing. Unity was thus an imperative however difficult it might be to achieve in the wake of what had happened to the NAR in 1987-1991. In Dookeran's view, the society "had to focus on the issues of the moment rather than on the personalities and errors of the past." It should likewise strive to fashion an accord that would recapture the ecumenical spirit of 1986. Dookeran however gave his hand away when he noted that "the vehicle may change its name, but the movement and intent of the people remain consistent" (*Newsday,* October 14, 1995).

Dookeran's unarticulated goal and that of the Committee of National Unification of which he was a member, was to broker an accord between the UNC and the NAR. The conversations which were held with the PNM were thus part of an elaborate charade to disguise the game that was being played. According to Ernie Ross of Ross Advertising Ltd., who handled the public relations work for the Committee of National Unification, Dookeran's involvement in the campaign was carefully choreographed and planned. Dookeran believed that the UNC was the only viable political vehicle through which he could promote the programme of national unity which he hoped to advance. Since he could not openly join the UNC, he was advised to promote the unification theme from the periphery. What actually happened is well described by Ross:

> We were validating the concept of national unity by the credibility of Winston Dookeran, by the credibility of Clive Pantin and by the sensationalism of Brian Kuei Tung coming out from the shadows. [It was] carefully, carefully planned. It was done through the commonality of the UNC's public relations team working in conjunction with what had become the national unification public relations team because we were running on parallel lines. Brian Kuei Tung represented the business community, Winston Dookeran and Clive Pantin represented the floating NAR vote and the ambivalent voter who perhaps did not believe the vacuous verbiage, perhaps, of the UNC camp in the heat of an election battle. (*Guardian,* November 12, 1995)

Ross' statement makes it clear that Dookeran's actions and those of former NAR Minister Clive Pantin and former PNM Minister Brian Kuei Tung, and other NAR notables were coordinated with the UNC for maximum impact. As one former NAR Minister commented, "the campaign was being fought on two tracks, one you see, and the other you don't see." The PNM and those who sympathised with it saw the call for an accommodation and unity, for what it was, a patent ruse to widen the support base of the UNC. The PNM was also resolutely opposed to the unity formula being proposed. According to the PNM leader, bringing the parties together in the manner proposed would be like "putting crabs in a barrel." Manning was also of the view that the principles of the Trinidad Constitution assumed checks and balances and a formal opposition.

The NAR and the Election

The NAR was split in its view as to what it should do in relation to the unity platform. One faction felt that its best chances for success lay in joining the UNC and did its utmost to get the NAR Executive to forge some sort of accord with the UNC. These efforts had been made throughout 1994, particularly in the months preceding the bye-election in Caroni East. The initiatives however failed for a variety of reasons. Among them was the fact that neither of the dominant elements in either party was willing to give way to the other. At its meeting on October 8th, 1995 which endorsed ANR Robinson as its new leader, the dominant element in the NAR formally indicated that it was contesting the election as a separate organisation. "Time For One Love Done. We are going it alone, sink or float," was how one member put it (*Guardian,* October 10, 1995). One former NAR Minister, Anthony Smart, was blunt in his opposition to any alliance with the UNC: "There must be absolutely no question of an alliance or an accommodation between the NAR and the PNM or the NAR as led by Basdeo Panday and Ramesh Maharaj" (*Express,* October 9, 1995).

The Interim Chairman of the NAR Mr. Robert Mayers dismissed as mischief, reports that the NAR was going to join the UNC in bed. "There is no accommodation or arrangement. They [the UNC] are trying to give an impression that they are recreating "One Love." But it is political mischief" (*Guardian,* October 19, 1995). Continued Mayers:

> The elections will not be an intellectual exercise but ... a raw vulgar campaign based on race; and they are going to beat the tribal drums at fever pitch. If the NAR were to stay out of this election, the country would be split asunder. It would be totally irresponsible for the NAR if it did not

> intervene. One has to be a voice of reason in the madness that surrounds us.... In the prevailing cacophony of bongo against tassa in this campaign, the NAR concept of One People must ascend. For make no mistake about it, the elections of 1995 is not who can best govern this twin island. No, it is about the so-called dominant race. (*Guardian,* October 18, 1995).

The UNC, for its part, felt that power was well within its grasp, and as such it was only interested in that extra increment that the NAR might bring, particularly in the marginal seats. It therefore wished to secure NAR support without conceding too much as it had done in 1986 in respect of the ONR. As the Chairman of the NAR complained in respect of the accord talks which he had held with the UNC, "they called us and we met with them waiting to hear what they had to say. But on their end, there was nothing much; so the meeting was quite short. They were not interested in unity it appears; they seemed more interested in power (*Guardian,* October 17, 1995). With respect to Mr. Panday's comment that "'Love' must take place on a "UNC bed", Mayers quip was that "love based on a shallow relationship will never stand" (ibid.). Mayers indicated that he would have been happier if Mr. Dookeran had been identified as the person to lead a government of national unity. "The NAR would be prepared to respond to that" (*Guardian,* October 27, 1995).

Mr. Panday was unhappy that the NAR had chosen to contest as many as 19 seats in the election. He noted that the UNC did not put up any candidates in Tobago in opposition to the NAR in its contest with the PNM, but that the NAR did not reciprocate by not putting up candidates in Trinidad against the UNC. The UNC did not however have any support in Tobago. In Panday's view, however, the NAR was trying to split the UNC vote to allow the PNM to win: "We have been trying to find the NAR strategy, and we can only conclude that they are putting up candidates to make us lose. We have no electoral arrangements with them — *at least that element of the NAR.* But we know that there are several NAR people at the top who are totally dissatisfied with their putting up candidates the way they did" *[sic]* (*Guardian,* October 23, 1995). Panday nevertheless expressed hope that some accord could be worked out with the NAR. "We need a national front government to mobilise our human resources even for four or five years rather than adversarial government.. We have opened our arms to the NAR. That has not worked. Our job is to keep on fighting for national unity.... While the electorate might be polarised on race, politicians must not exacerbate what has been a historical tragedy." (*Newsday,* November 1, 1995).

The failure of the accord prompted some NAR elements to cross over to the UNC, which they saw as being the stronger of the two parties. Two members of the NAR executive and one NAR appointed ambassador even agreed to join the UNC election team. They and their supporters were highly critical of the NAR high command for failing to respond to Panday's call for national unity. In the words of one, "those in favour of national unity should not "just talk the talk, but should walk the talk" by joining the UNC platform (*Guardian,* October 28, 1995). The NAR chairman was however critical of the behaviour of this element whom he accused of "political prostitution" and of seeking opportunistically to get a "tan in the rays of the rising sun" (*Express,* October 16, 1995).

Former NAR Minister, Lincoln Myers, was equally critical of those whom he said believed that "harmony in diversity means being able to flip from here to there to make their political point. I think if you believe in certain principles, whether your organisation is up or down, you have to fight it out unless your organisation is so corrupt and decadent that you do not see your way to do that" (*Express,* October 27, 1995). Myers suggested that some of his former colleagues were "not fit to be peoples representatives."

The Political Leader of the NAR, ANR Robinson, was less harsh in his criticism of those who defected to the UNC. He felt he could not blame them for their choice since the NAR decided to contest the election rather late. "They were anxious to participate and did not think the NAR would be ready in time for the election. What is important, however is what they stood for now and in the future." Robinson however declared himself opposed in principle to going into bed with any one. That "turned him off." The NAR, he said, had held no talks with anyone about any alliance. "We sought to have a peace accord with the UNC whereby we would not contest against each other in certain seats. They did not agree to that" (*Express,* October 25, 1995). Robinson however noted that the NAR's involvement in the campaign was not about seats. Its aim was to bring a "moral focus" to the electoral process and governing" (*Express,* November 25, 1995).

The MUP leader, Hulsie Bhaggan, also claimed that it was important for both the NAR and the MUP to be involved in the election in order to ensure that at the end of the day, neither the UNC nor the PNM controlled the Parliament. As she put it, "ANR Robinson became Prime Minister in 1986 with just two seats. In this election, nobody can tell what will happen, not even [pollster] Selwyn Ryan, since the situation is so fluid" (*Express,* October 27, 1995).

In the end, there was no accord between the NAR and the UNC. Even though they criticised each other during the campaign, the attacks were benign. The sharper attacks were reserved for the "common enemy," the PNM. Both parties got much of what they had hoped to achieve. The UNC was able to attract the bulk of the NAR vote — some 87 per cent of it — while the NAR, with its two seats in Tobago, was able to "make the difference" in that the UNC was unable to govern without its support (cf. Annexe 21).

The "political frog hopping" or "political whoring" that was characteristic of the campaign was the subject of much adverse public comment. The UNC was however not the only beneficiary of this movement of persons seeking a political base. There were also a number of persons who expected to be endorsed as candidates by the UNC who, after failing to do so, switched to the PNM in he hope of gaining whatever resources were available for distri-ution should that party win. The former UNC member for Nariva vas perhaps the most visible UNC individual to defect to the PNM. There were also several NAR activists who abandoned the UNC and the NAR to join forces with the PNM. In sum, both major parties were beneficiaries of this process of criss-crossing, a levelopment which raised serious questions as to just what party nembership and loyalty meant in the contemporary Trinidad olitical environment (*Guardian,* October 27, 1995).

One candidate who belonged to neither ethnic group and vho joined the UNC after having spent many years being critical f its leadership made the point that if one wanted to become nvolved seriously in the political process at the national level in Trinidad and Tobago, one's only alternative was to join one or ther of the two major parties. In his view, the decision had to be aken entrepreneurially and pragmatically and not on the basis of ny overriding principle. Such actions were also legitimized by he argument that if one did not like what one saw in the existing thnically based political parties, the thing to do was to get inside f them and seek to transform them into trans-ethnic organisations, abian like. If one did not do that, one was not entitled to complain (*Express,* October 17, 1995).

The UNC and the Jamaat al Muslimeen

The UNC was also actively supported by the Jamaat al Muslimeen, the group which had attempted to overthrow the NAR government in July 1990. The Jamaat had supported the NAR in he 1986 election in the hope that its expectations in relation to the ands at Mucurapo for which they were seeking to obtain legal itle from the state would be realized. By 1990, they had come to he conclusion that the NAR was seeking to destroy their rganization, and attempted the coup in the hope of creating a ostage situation which would topple the government (Ryan 1991). The Jamaat supported the PNM in the election of 1991 in the hope hat the PNM would settle both the land issue and the claims which they were making for compensation from the state for the destruction of their property that took place following the coup. The Court had made an award of $12m to the Jamaat which the State had appealed. Instead, the PNM Government counter sued for $65m for damages done to state property, and had opposed any settlement of the land issue on the terms desired by the Jamaat (*Express,* October 13, 1995). What was more, the PNM had used the military apparatus to keep the Jamaat under close scrutiny (*Guardian,* October 15, 1996). Thus their decision to support the UNC.

During the election campaign, Yasin Abu Bakr went so far as to claim that the Political Leader of the PNM had prior knowledge of the 1990 coup and was in fact a co-conspirator. Manning, he said, called the Jamaat twice on the day the coup took place. He swore on the lives of his wife, his children and the heads of Muslims nationwide that he was speaking the truth. The name of Allah was also invoked. Another member of the Jamaat, Loris Ballack also corroborated Bakr's claims, saying that he met Manning clandestinely on several occasions (*Express,* October 14, 1995). Manning denied these allegations and sued for libel and slander. The charge was not widely believed, however, and did not seem to have affected the election in any way. There is however neex to have this matter clarified (*Guardian,* October 20, 1995).

The UNC denied that there was any alliance or *entente* with the Jamaat (*Express,* October 13, 1995). But some of the leaders of the UNC were known to have a cordial or at least a good working relationship with members of the Jamaat. The Deputy Leader of the UNC in particular was known to be a sympathizer, while the UNC's Chief Whip was their counsel in the legal matters which they had with the State. The Jamaat in fact had openly signalled as early as 1994 that they wanted to become a legitimate part of the political process by creating a political party, the New Vision Movement which participated in the Laventille bye-election.[23] They had also indicated that they would in future use the UNC as a vehicle for that involvement. Their boast, made ı conversation with the author, was that they controlled the young ıderclass vote along the East-West Corridor and would either eliver it to the UNC or discourage it from voting for the PNM. hey in fact campaigned along the Corridor as well as in the ıarginal seats of San Fernando West and Ortoire-Mayaro seeking • delegitimize the PNM and Mr. Manning, and to project Mr. anday and "our Asiatic brothers" as the more likely champion of ıe cause of the black masses.

In various campaign speeches, Bakr told Afro-Trinidadians, hom he described as "stupid niggers", that they would "drown" they supported the PNM. The latter were advised to forget race ıd ally with an element that would work in their interest. To quote ıe speech at length:

> Show me what you own after 39 years of keeping the PNM in power. You have given your loyalty and support to the party, and all you have received in return are empty promises. You're like slaves on a plantation, and Manning and them are like overseers. And still you're saying that you're going to die PNM. Well, you done dead already. You should get a coffin now. You Africans are considered as no people. If you were considered as people, the Prime Minister would not have given you soup as a diet. Manning can't go to Goodwood Park, Valsayn, or Maraval and open any soup kitchen. That would be an insult to those posh people. If the government had considered you as people, they would know that you have to eat everyday. But what you now have after 39 years of blind loyalty, is a bowl of soup. You stupid people, if you were to line up all the races in a bank to get a loan, the Africans would be the last to get it. So you now saying that the Indians are trying to take over the country? But the Indians have already taken over, you dotish people. Go home and turn on your radio ... the Indians already have three radio stations operating. All Africans like you have is police stations. While you're out in the night partying, wining and dining, the Indians are at home teaching their kids their school work. While disrespectful PNM women, who should know better, are wining in the streets in front of Manning and the boys who have been applauding them, the Indian women teaching

> their children at home. When next you go to the hospitals, look at the doctor. The majority of them are Indians. And look and see who are the lawyers too. But when you go to jail, you see where the African is world class ... they make up 90 per cent of the prison population. Manning doesn't care about you. When Africans and Indians are killed, he doesn't care. But when two White women were killed in Westmoorings, Manning quickly intervened by taking over Russell Huggins' portfolio as Minister of National Security. (*Sunday Mirror,* November 5, 1995)

In a post-election statement, Bakr claimed that the Jama had helped to win votes for the UNC and openly thanked all tho along the East-West Corridor, San Fernando, Mayaro and Morug to whom he had spoken at pre-election meetings "for th manifestation of their support and understanding of the theme those meetings as was reflected in the results on polling day Tunapuna, St. Joseph, San Juan-Barataria and Ortoire-Mayaro (*Mirror,* November 12, 1995). In sum, Bakr was claiming cred for UNC victories in those key constituencies in the hope that h would get the "pay back" which he dearly needed. Bakr also urge the business community, PNM supporters, and the less fortuna ones in the society to put the national interest above party loyalt and support the new Government.

There is some question as to whether Bakr's open embrac of the UNC helped or hurt that party. Some who were famili with what took place in the Tunapuna constituency assert that th open and public association of key elements in the Jamaat's securi arm with the UNC's campaign, alienated potential supporters an may have helped the PNM to retain that seat by the narrowest margins — 247 votes. It is however claimed that the Jamaat helpe the UNC in Ortoire/Mayaro by intimidating some influenti individuals who were being encouraged to endorse PNM candidat from doing so. Allegedly, they were also the vehicle through whi bribes were offered to influentials in this constituency to deliv votes to the UNC — $500 up front and $500 if the UNC won.

Following the elections, the Jamaat was accused of making vertures to successful PNM candidates, particularly in the 'unapuna and Arouca South constituencies, urging them to cross ver to the PNM. The Political Leader of the PNM in fact alleged ıat members of the Jamaat offered one M.P. $1.5m and another anything he wanted" to change allegiance. Six other candidates /ere reportedly approached (*Express,* November 17, 1995). The ⁄IP for Tunapuna confirmed that efforts were made to buy him ut. The Jamaat admitted that it urged PNM Members of 'arliament to cross the floor, as they had a constitutional right to o, but denied that they offered money. The matter was reported) the police, but nothing came of it. It was also alleged by UNC ıfluentials that some impecunious PNM members had signalled ıat they were disposed to switch sides for a consideration or in rder to avoid languishing in opposition. This was however denied.

There were persistent reports that in addition to their xpectation that the outstanding matters dating back to 1990 would e quickly settled, the Muslimeen were seeking to capture the Jnemployment Relief Programme on which some TT$140m is pent each year, and to use such control to deliver black underclass upport to the UNC. The Jamaat denied this, but the evidence ndicates that a bid for control was in fact made in Tunapuna, Arouca and Nariva in the week following the election as it had een in Laventille and elsewhere before (*Mirror,* November 17, 995). The Jamaat al Muslimeen hoped to be allowed to function s the *de facto* power broker or praetorian guard for the UNC mong the Afro-Trinidadian underclass in the East West Corridor ince the UNC itself lacked capability in these areas. The Jamaat's fficial position was that they had been given no authority to pproach or bargain with anyone. Neither did they want any osition in the new regime. They however claimed the right to upport any party that they believed was working in the interest of Trinidad and Tobago [*Mirror,* November 24, 1995]. They insisted hat they were free men and no one had the right "to push them outside the citizenry."

The UNC and the Baptists

Another Afro-Trinidadian who campaigned for the UN(was Archbishop Barbara Gray-Burke who claimed that she wa speaking on behalf of the Spiritual Baptist community. Burke who claimed that she was a "traditional PNM," expressed the vie that the "pro-black" disposition of people like herself had gotte the Baptist community nowhere. "The African Government neve did anything for us. The UNC is an asset to this country. Some o us just have to put the racial bogey to rest and get to work (*Mirror* December 10, 1995). Burke was particularly upset that Mr Manning had reneged on a promise, allegedly made while i Opposition, to support the Spiritual Baptists' demand for a publi holiday to celebrate their survival as a group in the face of th hostility of the colonial authorities. The holiday was to be celebrate annually on March 30th to mark the repeal in 1951 of the 191 Shouters Prohibition Ordinance and was to be called Liberatio Day. Instead, the former Prime Minister offered the Baptists lan on which to build a cathedral, a primary school, and $1.1m fo social programmes which he deemed more meaningful than a holiday which people would only use to go to the beach (*Guardian* January 26, 1996).

Mr. Panday, ever one to seize an opportunity to positio the UNC as a defender of underprivileged blacks, endorsed th call for a public holiday for both the Spiritual Baptists and th Orisha group which also wanted a holiday to be proclaimed i June which would be named Lord Shango Day. Panday in fac appointed spokespersons of these groups to the Senate to make their case during the debate in that Chamber on the issue. He argued that Trinidad and Tobago was a plural society and that its institutions and symbolic arrangements should reflect this diversity There was however little support among the Afro-Trinidadian community for either of these holidays since few of them adhere to any of these groupings. According to the Annual Statistical Digest, (1992) there are only 33,689 Baptists in Trinidad and Tobago.

Archbishop Burke was persuaded to be the UNC's candidate in Laventille West and polled 637 votes to the PNM's 10,447. There is however little evidence that those who voted for her were Afro-Trinidadian since the constituency had close to 867 Indian names on its electoral register. Archbishop Burke was in fact not able to deliver the Baptist vote in Laventille or in Point Fortin and elsewhere to the UNC as the party had hoped, and if anything, her association with the UNC led to her marginalization among Baptists who in the main remained attached to the PNM. Burke however claimed that she did not lose "fair and square" and that she was prevented from holding meetings by young blacks who resented her argument that the UNC would replace 10 days project work with long lasting jobs for all (*Sunday Mirror*, November 12, 1995).

PNM: Old and New

It was widely believed that the PNM lost a significant number of votes because it failed to use the good offices and network assets of persons who belonged to its "old guard." The Political Leader of the PNM reportedly refused to endorse a request to allow members of the old guard to speak in support of PNM candidates. The cleavage between the "new PNM" and the "old PNM" had been a matter that had given rise to a great deal of acrid controversy following the defeat of the PNM in 1986. Some of the ex-Ministers complained that they were scorned by the new leadership. The new leadership for its part took the view that the old guard had been badly discredited by the reports of corruption which were in circulation after that election. It was felt that if the party was to return to power, it had to be repackaged and repositioned. This required that the old élite be delinked from the party and kept out of view. This was deemed to be an important part of the strategy of selling the party to the floating vote that lay in the middle class community of all ethnicities. As Mr. Manning put it, "we do not like to use the term "new."" We are now reorganising the party so that it is truly reflective of the various compositions of the society (*Express*, May 16, 1988).

The party was then eagerly seeking to achieve toeholds in the Indian community and the leadership made many a visit to Hindu and Muslim notables while it was in opposition. Even after the party regained power in 1991, one of the first things the Prime Minister said was that he was "looking for Indians" to appoint to his Cabinet, a statement which gravely offended both Afro-Trinidadians and Indo-Trinidadians. The one felt he was capitulating to the southern based Indian power brokers in his party, while the latter felt he was guilty of tokenism.

Critics however felt that the "opening to the Indians" strategy had been taken too far and had become counter productive. The Political Leader was told that it was imperative to reunite the Party as part of the 40th Anniversary celebrations which were being planned for January 1996 as part of the effort to mobilise the old PNM base for the coming elections. Mr. Manning, who had been humiliated by some members of the old guard when he was a junior Minister, particularly Mr. Errol Mahabir, however remained resolutely opposed to any proposal to bury the hatchet, though he did so on a very selective basis. Since the election defeat, steps are now being taken by the leadership to reattract the old guard to the party fold. Some have however said they would only respond positively if Mr. Manning were to change his leadership style. Some have insisted that he must resign as leader of the PNM (*Express*, February 8, 1996).

While there is no evidence that the old guard campaigned openly against the party, there is some evidence that those who supported it did so weakly and quite late in the game. Their failure to provide open and enthusiastic support may in fact have been critical to the PNM's defeat in the marginal constituencies of Barataria/San Juan and Ortoire/Mayaro.

The UNC and Afro-Trinidadian Voters in the East West Corridor

Following the election, there was a great deal of debate as to whether Afro-Trinidadians who were not wont to vote for the

NC did so on this occasion. During the campaign, many dvertisements had been directed to Afro-Trinidadians urging them forget race. They were told to consider the "issues" and give ne UNC a chance to show what it could do to address their roblems. Basdeo Panday had been focussing on this question of ne "African vote" for quite some time and the UNC had contested bye-election in Laventille in 1994 to test his theory that the era of acial voting was over. The party in fact boasted that it would win ne bye-election. The UNC did not however do well. It received mere 327 votes but promised to continue working in the onstituency in order to prove that it was possible to build a class ased national party.

By 1995, Panday claimed that he was beginning to see light t the end of the darkened tunnel. In his view, the PNM no longer ad the resources which were available to it in the "petro boom" ra to bribe the electorate, and peoples of African descent were eginning to view politics in terms of policies and programmes ather than in terms of race. As Panday exulted:

> Issues [are] now being looked at instead of the blind appeal to race. If this trend continues, the question will no longer be who we go put, but what we go put. The politics seems to be moving in the direction of issues as race is put on the back burner. Soon this topic will be of historical and academic significance only, and there will be no such thing as the Indian, African or Chinese politician. Politicians will be judged by their works and not by their race. (Address to UWI Conference Marking 150th Arrival of Indians in the Caribbean, 1995).

The results of the 1995 election seems to have convinced anday and others in the UNC that the much hoped for reakthrough to non-racial voting did in fact occur. The evidence or this claim is said to be the fact that the UNC received more upport than it usually did along the East West Corridor — 2,506 otes in Diego Martin Central, 1,536 votes in Diego Martin East, ,737 votes in Diego Martin West, 1,916 votes (6,000 in some accounts) in Port of Spain South, 2,371 votes in St. Anns Eas 1650 votes in Laventille/Morvant and 827 votes in Laventille Wes The assumption is that these voters were Afro-Trinidadian. Whi it is of course difficult to determine with absolute certainty th they were not in fact Afro-Trinidadians, it is relevant to point ou that there are hundreds of Indians on the voting lists in all of thes constituencies, and that there is an extremely close correspondenc between the numbers of votes received by the UNC and the India names on the voter list. The comparable figures are 2,269 in Dieg Martin Central, 2,206 in Diego Martin East, 1735 votes in Dieg Martin West, 2,765 in Port of Spain South, 2,945 in St. Anns Eas 1,979 in Laventille East/Morvant, and 870 in Laventille West. Many of these votes went to the NAR in 1986 and 1991 while few went to the UNC in 1991.

An examination of aggregated voting data for selecte polling divisions in five marginal constituencies reveal interestin patterns (Tables 2 to 6). Before commenting on them, howeve we need to indicate that the data relating to the ethnic distributio of the divisions are based on the 1991 electoral list. The elector list used in 1995 contained some 41,000 additional names. W however assumed that the basic ethnic character of each pollin division did not change significantly. It should also be noted th the polling divisions in the 5 constituencies were not random chosen. The ones selected were those in which one ethnic grou was unequivocally dominant and the differences in the number o votes cast for one party or another correspondingly wide. Or could however have chosen other polling divisions to make th essential point, viz., that there was a marked correlation betwee the demographics of the polling division and the votes cast for th two major parties.

The figures also provide evidence that rates of voting we invariably much higher among Indians than among those who we not. It is also evident that in most cases, the proportion of th votes cast for the UNC exceeded the proportion of Indians in th selected polling division. The overall difference was 12 per cent

St. Joseph, 10 per cent in Barataria/San Juan, 7 per cent in Tunapuna and 4 per cent in Ortoire/Mayaro. In San Fernando West, however the PNM won 4 per cent more votes than there were non-Indians in the selected polling divisions.

A post-election survey conducted by the author in January 1996 indicates that there might have been some cross over voting, though not as much as claimed by the UNC. Seven per cent of the Afro-Trinidadian population and 19 per cent of the mixed population claimed that they voted for the UNC. In SARA's pre-election polls, 5 per cent of the Afro-Trinidadians and 10 per cent of the mixed population had reported a disposition to vote for the UNC. One can expect that the UNC would seek to use the machinery of the State to expand its share of the Afro-Trinidadian vote during its stint in office since it would need to do so to maintain its lien on power.

Table 2. San Fernando West Constituency

Address	Polling Div. No.	Indians	% of Indians	Non-Indians	% of Non-Indians	UNC	%	PNM	%	NAR	%
Rambert Village	3790	450	78	126	22	456	72	160	25	22	3
San F'do/Siparia/ Erin Road	3795	768	68	356	32	602	55	447	41	41	4
Marabella	3995	133	21	500	79	56	14	317	81	19	5
Paradise Pasture	4151	205	30	490	71	158	21	572	77	18	2
San Fernando	4180	103	45	126	55	109	31	230	65	14	4
San Fernando	4181	242	37	410	63	139	33	262	62	24	6

Source: Elections and Boundaries Commission 1996.

Table 3. Ortoire/Mayaro Constituency

Address	Polling Division Number	Indians	% of Indians	Non-Indians	% of Non-Indians	UNC	%	PNM	%
Barrackpore	3480	961	99	7	1	953	96	42	4
Barrackpore	3485	436	89	56	11	381	87	55	13
Naparima Mayaro Rd.	3425	249	88	35	22	205	88	28	12
Table!and	3510	419	86	69	14	392	87	58	13
New Grant	3505	534	78	146	22	445	81	105	19
Naparima Mayaro Rd.	2560	298	77	89	23	280	74	100	26
Tableland	3515	539	71	226	29	469	74	162	26
Rio Claro	2580	536	67	270	33	431	70	186	30
Mayaro	2430	116	17	582	83	108	24	349	76
Moruga Road	3545	117	15	668	85	77	13	538	87

Source: Elections and Boundaries Commission 1996.

Table 4. Barataria/San Juan Constituency

Address	Polling Division Number	Indians	% of Indians	Non-Indians	% of Non-Indians	UNC	%	PNM	%
San Juan	1095	150	20	596	80	93	22	325	78
Saddle Road	1130	40	7	546	93	53	14	328	86
Barataria	1320	68	14	409	86	66	22	234	78
Barataria	1335	159	19	697	81	173	26	482	74
Barataria	1355	53	21	201	79	92	29	223	71
Barataria	1365	101	20	400	80	87	28	220	72
San Juan	1400	333	55	273	45	312	68	149	32
San Juan	1405	871	63	520	37	850	77	257	23
El Socorro Rd.	1415	981	70	409	29	875	84	168	16
El Socorro	1416	238	70	100	30	211	77	64	23
El Socorro	1436	482	67	234	33	375	70	157	30
El Socorro	1440	401	80	103	20	280	76	89	24

Source: Elections and Boundaries Commission 1996.

Table 5. Tunapuna Constituency

Address	Polling Division Number	Indians	% of Indians	Non-Indians	% of Non-Indians	UNC	%	PNM	%	NAR	%
El Dorado	1755	685	89	82	11	628	95	29	4	3	1
Tacarigua	1765	724	67	353	33	603	71	233	28	9	1
Five Rivers	1780	981	61	620	39	805	64	441	35	17	1
Curepe	1535	608	59	430	41	560	71	214	27	12	2
El Dorado Rd.	1695	158	24	497	76	127	23	420	76	8	1
El Dorado Rd.	1710	142	23	477	77	95	26	268	72	7	2
Tunapuna	1685	96	23	313	77	75	27	203	72	4	1
Tunapuna	1680	102	22	356	78	70	20	268	76	13	4
St. Augustine	1625	257	21	985	79	246	29	578	68	21	3
Tunapuna	1715	94	21	352	79	70	25	206	72	10	3
Tunapuna	1690	102	17	483	83	83	21	302	76	11	3

Source: Elections and Boundaries Commission 1996.

Table 6. St. Joseph Constituency

Address	Polling Division Number	Indians	% of Indians	Non-Indians	% of Non-Indians	UNC	%	PNM	%
St. Joseph	1030	100	21	373	79	112	28	293	72
Mount D'or Rd	1031	83	9	826	91	111	20	452	80
Champ Fleur	1035	287	22	1038	78	226	28	570	72
Mt. Hope	1041	31	5	618	95	35	8	418	92
Mt. Hope	1042	66	12	477	88	49	15	285	85
Mt. Hope	1046	63	12	473	88	59	16	307	84
San Juan	1055	111	19	469	81	80	24	249	76
San Juan St	1085	348	69	159	31	282	80	71	20
Aranguez Main Rd	1455	256	81	59	19	187	86	30	14
Aranguez	1460	789	79	205	21	612	87	88	13
Aranguez	1465	1190	90	139	10	997	95	52	5
Aranguez	1470	512	92	45	8	409	97	14	3
Aranguez	1475	234	89	29	11	210	94	14	6
Mt. Lambert	1480	87	17	412	83	66	22	232	78
Mt. Lambert	1495	192	21	714	79	83	26	242	74
BS No 1	1500	738	87	106	13	399	91	39	9
St Joseph	1530	74	18	327	82	64	25	193	75

Key: BS No.1 - Bamboo Settlement No. 1. **Source:** Elections and Boundaries Commission 1996.

End Notes

[1]The elections were constitutionally due in December 1996 but could have been deferred for an additional 3 months.

[2]Ralph Maraj was summarily relieved of his portfolio by the Prime Minister because of differences which the two were having over the conduct of foreign policy and whether he or the Prime Minister should be the one to take credit for the decision taken to locate the headquarters of the Association of Caribbean States in Trinidad and Tobago. There were also personal differences between the two San Fernando members of Parliament which generated tension between them. The Minister learnt of his demotion during an national address given by the Prime Minister. Public opinion was savage in its reaction to the manner in which the firing took place and the Prime Minister was forced to reassign Mr. Maraj to another Ministry, that of Public Utilities (see "Five Options for Mr. Maraj," *Guardian,* July 28, 1995). Mr. Manning clearly disliked Mr. Maraj and was determined to humiliate him. He had in fact been trying to force him to resign from the Cabinet before taking the decision to fire him and had to be restrained by Cabinet members.

[3]The Speaker, who was the sister of the Foreign Minister, was accused of engaging in business transactions which were unbecoming for a person holding such an office. Some of these transactions came to public attention in a matter before the Courts in which the Speaker was accused of being a "stranger to the truth." The Speaker insisted that the matter was a private one and refused suggestions that she should resign, forcing the government to introduce legislation to give it the power to remove the Speaker by a majority vote. Emergency legislation was subsequently

introduced by the Government to prevent the Speaker from presiding over Parliament out of concern as to what she might do to derail the proceedings that were being put in place to remove her from office. See Appendix II for the Government's case against the Speaker. The Opposition, which had hitherto been openly critical of the Speaker, accusing her of bias, chose to rally to her defense in what many regarded as a triumph of ethnic politics over principle. The Government in fact feared that if it had not moved against the Speaker, the Opposition would have accused it of condoning impropriety. "Blood" however proved to be thicker than water. Many saw the government's actions as evidence of heavy handedness against someone who was a woman and an Indian woman at that, and wondered as to why others who were male were not similarly dealt with. The reference was to Senator Lenny Saith, the Minister of Planning who was experiencing difficulties servicing his loans with several commercial banks which agreed to write them down. The allegation was that the loans were forgiven because of who the borrower was.

It would not have been easy to bring down the government, however, since the Speaker retained his casting vote. The incident served to further polarise the two major racial groups in the society and helped to shape attitudes towards the election. The author opposed the Government' decision to declare the state of Emergency. As he wrote (*Express,* August 5, 1985), "The government overreacted and did not count the political cost, the impact on the population or the impact on our image. The sound bite that went around the world is that we detained the Speaker in order to deal with a political matter.... Even admitting that the Speaker was trying to stage a "coup" of her own, in politics, timing is important and the weaponry appropriate to the situation."

[4]The UNC said it viewed San Fernando West as a "crusade," the outcome of which would send a message to a "beleaguered" country (*Express,* September 4, 1995).

[5]Some sections of the Constitution are entrenched and required a two-thirds or a three-fourths majority to amend them. Proposals to remove the power to discipline police officers from the independent Police Service Commission to an executive appointed agency were opposed by the UNC on the ground that the power would be abused. The Government argued that if management was to be held accountable, it had to have the responsibility to discipline. The Government also wished to disallow repeat appeals to the Privy Council by persons found guilty of murder who then seek to relitigate their sentences by filing constitutional motions claiming that the delay in carrying out the sentence constituted cruel and unusual punishment.

The UNC also claimed that legislation aimed at denying bail to repeat offenders would be abused by the Police who might have an interest in putting away certain individuals by falsely accusing and incriminating them.

[6]Indians who supported the NAR in 1986 and 1991 in the main went to the UNC while the white, mixed and Afro- Trinidadian element either remained with the NAR or went over to the PNM. A few of the latter however switched to the UNC on the eve of the election. This split first became evident in 1994 during the bye-elections which were held in Caroni East and Point-a-Pierre. The Leadership was pulled in two directions. The Indian element wanted to effect a platform agreement with the UNC while the mixed-white element wanted to maintain the organisational independence of the Party.

[7]Among the positive indicators of the economic turn around were a growth rate of 4.7 per cent in 1994. The petroleum sector grew by 8.3 per cent after 3 consecutive years of contraction. National gas production rose by 13 per cent. The non-petroleum sector grew by 3.5 per cent in 1994 compared with 0.8 per cent the previous year. Growth was also strong in manufacturing (7.6 per cent), agriculture (12.6 per cent) and construction (15.6 per cent). Unemployment also fell from 19.8 per cent in 1993 to 16.5

per cent in 1995. Inflation also dropped from 10.8 per cent in 1993 to 8.8 per cent in 1994. The external current account surplus expanded from US$102m in 1993 to US$214m in 1994. Exports grew by 15 per cent mainly due to high prices for exports in the petrochemical sector.

Foreign direct investment also grew dramatically from US$178 in 1992 to US$521 in 1994 (which represented 10 per cent of GDP). Despite these positive indicators of economic wel being, not much of it was trickling down. The employment figures in fact masked a great deal of underemployment in that many were deemed to be employed who were only seasonally or temporarily so. This was particularly the case among the young. The unemployment rate also excluded the "discouraged poor" who had stopped looking for jobs. A currency devaluation of 26 per cent in April 1993 increased prices as did the removal of subsidies on a number of basic commodities and services. Real wages also fel for the 11th year in a row and real wages in 1994 were one-hal what they were in 1982. (cf. "Trinidad and Tobago," in *Overcoming Volatility: Economic and Social Progress in Latin America,* 1995 Report. IDB, October 1995. Washington: 69-171).

[8]The fear of what "Laventille" might do if it were no provisioned was brought home quite dramatically during the events that followed the attempted seizure of power in July 1990 when commercial establishments in Port of Spain and along the East West Corridor were looted and torched. Protests over the non delivery of project work also took place during the by-election campaign in the Laventille constituency in May 1994. Groups blocked a major highway which passed through the area, demanding that they be given "10 days." Crime, most of which was directed outside the community, was also on the increase. While much of it was drug related, a great deal was fuelled by poverty as youths sought ways to earn income for themselves and their families. The euphemism for much of this activity is "putting down a wuk." (For a fuller discussion of the politics and the problem of poverty in the

Laventille community (cf. Ryan, St. Bernard and McCree, eds. *Politics, Patronage and Community in Laventille* (forthcoming)

[9]Cf. *Leadership That is Working: The PNM Manifesto*, 1995. Promises were made to transform the East Port of Spain area into a modern extension of the city.

[10]The 10 marginal constituencies were those in which the ethnic balance was such as to allow either party to win. There are those in which the Afro-Trinidadian and mixed population is larger — the so called PNM marginals — and those in which the reverse is the case, the UNC marginals. Because of the virtual solidarity of the Indo-Trinidadian vote, the UNC won all of its marginals as well as three of the 5 PNM marginals.

Pre- and post-election surveys done by the author clearly revealed evidence of the extent to which the Indian vote solidified behind the UNC. Studies done by the *Trinidad and Tobago Review* (December 1995) came to similar conclusions. As the *Review* noted:

> Such gains as the PNM did enjoy may very well have come in significant measure from persons who do not customarily vote for the party but who chose to do so on this occasion for tactical reasons. But if there was in fact a slackening of traditional hard-core support for the PNM, we may see in that a critical factor in the loss of the so called "PNM marginals" of Barataria/San Juan, St. Joseph and Ortoire/Mayaro.
>
> As can be seen from the figures for the percentages of the vote cast for the winning candidates, low voter turnout will not affect the ability of the PNM to win seats in certain areas, assuming that no party emerges to challenge it in those places. The significance of high rates of abstention among those who form its "natural" constituency, however, is that, as was demonstrated in this election, in the event of a straight ethnic face-off, the party is rendered vulnerable in those electoral districts where there is rough parity between the two great ethnic blocs. Three such were lost

in 1995 and Tunapuna and San Fernando West were only barely saved.

> In a longer perspective, high rates of abstention in the urban constituencies, overwhelmingly PNM, suggest intensification of a development to be noticed in elections since 1986 — that is, the fact that the PNM has taken a smaller percentage of the popular vote than have the major parties arrayed against it. When these parties have been united, as in 1986, or when one of them has united the major element in the electorate that is antagonistic to it, as in 1995, the PNM has lost.

[11]Election Officer's Report, "General Elections — November 6, 1995." Other post-election reviews confirm that the party was woefully unprepared for the election (cf. Annexe 14).

[12]A majority of party groups had rejected the incumbent candidate proposed for Barataria/San Juan. The political leadership however overrode them and persuaded the favoured challenger to withdraw. The feeling was that the incumbent, an Indian, would attract cross ethnic support while the challenger would not. The gamble of playing the race card was however lost. Interestingly, the leadership listened to protesting groups in Laventille and Port of Spain South where it was felt that changes of candidate would not be electorally expensive.

The candidate for Ortoire-Mayaro later explained that had the election been held when it was constitutionally due, he might not have contested (*Independent,* July 26, 1996).

[13]Mr. Manning defended his leadership style by saying that a Prime Minister needed to take certain unorthodox steps to maintain discipline. Ministers were free to challenge his views, but when they challenged his authority, he had a problem. Maraj and the late Morris Marshall were accused of doing so. "Things were getting out of hand". Manning noted that running a government is a "tricky business," and one could not use orthodox

methods to contain fission. One could not suspend a Minister nor cut his pay. One could only fire him. But one could not dismiss Ministers for everything; "so that in between there, each prime minister has to define the mechanisms by which he will maintain discipline in his own government" (*Guardian,* December 3rd, 1995).

Mr. Manning also defended his choice of Mr. Saith to act as Prime Minister during his absence from the country. He indicated that he did not wish to create rivalries among his three deputies (*Guardian,* January 1, 1996).

[14]St. Augustine Research Associates, of which the author is managing director, conducted a poll the first week of the campaign. It was published on October 22, 1995. The Report had the PNM ahead of the UNC and the NAR. The percentages were 40, 30 and 11 respectively. The author did not however forecast that the PNM would could win 24 seats as the calypsonian, the Mighty Chalkdust alleged in his hilarious calypso, *"Adam [Selwyn] in the Garden Hiding — From Manning,"* sung during the 1996 calypso season. Indeed, the PNM was publicly advised that 20 seats was the maximum number of seats which the party could win (cf. Annexe 19).

Another mini-poll conducted by SARA one week before the election in four urban marginal constituencies had the PNM further ahead of the UNC and the NAR. The percentages were 48 per cent, 30 per cent and 5 per cent respectively. The PNM however only won two of the marginals while the UNC captured the other two. In retrospect, it is clear that there was a last minute swing to the UNC following upon publicised "defections" to the UNC on the part of high profile persons formerly associated with the NAR.

A post-election survey conducted in January 1996 by SARA corroborated what was evident in the official voting data. Eighty-nine per cent of the Indo-Trinidadians in the sample reported that they voted for the UNC, 7 per cent for the PNM, and 2 per cent for the NAR. Fifty-six per cent of Afro-Trinidadians claimed that they voted for the PNM, 7 per cent for the UNC and 6 per cent for the NAR. These figures however suggest that there was more cross ethnic voting on the part of both Indo- and Afro-Trinidadians than normally occurs in General Elections. Previous surveys suggest that no more than 1 or 2 per cent of the African population voted for the UNC or its earlier manifestations.

[15]Panday was widely regarded as an "Opposition" politician who lacked the "credentials" for high office. It was even widely believed that the job of Prime Minister was one to which he neither aspired nor had the competence to handle. In 1994, Panday, who was known to have a drinking problem, was charged with a number of serious sexual harassment offences which were said to have taken place at the offices of the trade union of which he was President. These matters were before the courts at the time of the election. Panday was cleared of the charges after election day. Many were of the view that the charges were politically inspired. Others believe that Panday was in fact guilty as charged, but that the prosecution failed to prove the charges. In any event, the issue raised additional questions about Mr. Panday's suitability for Prime Ministerial office (cf. *The Harrassment of Hon. Basdeo Panday* 1994).

Mr. Maharaj too had a reputation which was of concern to many. He was accused of several very serious criminal offences. These include incidents which involved, inter-alia, the disappearance of court documents and witnesses. Maharaj's role as a criminal lawyer also involved defending persons charged with drug offences and attempts at an unconstitutional seizure of power. Given all this, many were concerned about the close ties which existed between Panday and Maharaj and were even more concerned that Maharaj might be made Attorney General if the UNC were to win the election. An opinion poll conducted by SARA sought to measure the "Maharaj factor" in the election. The poll showed that Maharaj was widely discounted by non-Indians generally, but was less so by Indians. Fifty-four per cent of the Indo-Trinidadians in the sample felt his presence in the UNC enhanced that party's electoral chances while only 17 per cent of the Afro-Trinidadians felt this way. Twenty-five per cent of the latter were uncertain while 19 per cent of the former were of this view.

Maharaj accused this author of being responsible for orchestrating the PNM's campaign against him. The author was responsible for no such thing (*Mirror*, December 3, 1995). Maharaj may well be right when he argued that the PNM's strategy of focussing on him helped the UNC in that the spotlight was taken away from Mr. Panday. The evidence indicates that both UNC leaders were targeted equally, but that Maharaj was more so.

[16]Panday first used the term to described the white "French Creoles" (the term is loosely used to define all local whites) whom he said used their strategic positions in the society to enrich themselves at the expense of the people. The term was later broadened to include the non-white élites who work for the "French Creole" owned organisations and the major economic conglomerates.

[17]The involvement of the businessmen with the UNC seemingly had to do with the fact that all three believed that they were unfairly treated by the Government in terms of what they sought to do as businessmen. All three blamed Prime Minister Manning and committed themselves to destroying him at all costs. The commitment was made several months before the elections were called but only became public knowledge 3 weeks before election day. The Prime Minister has hinted that the election date was leaked by one of his ministers to one of the three with whom he was known to have close personal and business links.

[18]The UNC claims that it had booked millions of dollars worth of advertising in advance of the election date to prevent the PNM from blocking their advertising campaign.

[19]Muslims, especially those in the urban areas, normally gave their support to the PNM rather than to the Hindu dominated political parties. The PNM for its part, always sought to ensure that elements of the Muslim élite were well placed within its ranks. The UNC often accused Muslims of being Party In Power (PIP) supporters. Over the past few years, however, the UNC sought to imitate the PNM as part of its strategy to broaden its religious base. The strategy worked well. The evidence suggests that there was a massive switch of loyalty among Christian Indians and Muslims from the PNM to the UNC. This was especially the case in the constituency of Barataria-San Juan where many Muslims live. The PNM candidate for this constituency was of the view that she lost the election "across the highway, in El Socorro and through the floating NAR votes" (*Express*, November, 1995).

[20]The debate as to whether naming the country's highest honour the "Trinity Cross" in a multi-religious society also helped to fan the embers of race conflict as did the debate as to whether May 30 should be called "Arrival Day" or Indian Arrival Day.

[21]This phenomenon occurred in several parts of the world and was said by some to be due to absorption of the milk by the porous material used to make the elephant headed icon. Many Hindus however believe that it was a miracle (cf. "Milk-Drinking Murtis," Miracles or Just Strange," *Express*, March 22, 1996).

[22]The term is a Hindu expression used to describe the ultimate in ingratitude. One Indian spokesman remarked that being a nemakarham constitutes an "unbearable blemish." Panday was thus being very pointed in castigating Indians for not supporting their own Party. To quote him:

> We are our worst enemy. We are too easily prepared to sell our birthright and that of our follow men for a mess of pottage from the tables of the new oligarchy. Some will sell it for a jacket an tie and a ministry, some for a wig and a gown, some for a seat in the Senate, some for a little contract here and there. Our detractors say we are the victims of a curse, which like a virulent plague, threatens to engulf the entire community (cf. Annexe 7).

The statement was made at a rally of 30,000 celebrating the 150th Anniversary of the arrival of Indians in the Caribbean (*Guardian*, March 5, 1996).

[23]This election and the Jamaat al Muslimeen's role in it is more fully discussed in my *Politics, Patronage and Community in Laventille* (forthcoming)

[24]Calculations done by author from voting lists using a name recognition formula.

Chapter 14

Triumph and Trauma

The results of the November election in Trinidad and Tobago benchmarked a significant shift in the balance of ethnic forces in the society. The results were greeted with great jubilation by the Indian community which felt that it had finally arrived politically after having been marginalised for 150 years. This was so even though the UNC did not win a clear majority and had to share power with the NAR. As one Indian put it, "we have reached.... For the first time, Indians in Trinidad have put their differences aside and rallied together. We have been ruled by others all our lives; [now] we are in a different time. We have given ourselves a chance with Panday at the helm" (*Mirror,* January 16, 1996).

The Sanatan Dharma Maha Sabha well articulated the manner in which the election campaign and the results were viewed by the Hindu community. As it declared:

> The year 1995 saw at least 50,000 "Indians" assembled at Skinner Park to commemorate, and to commiserate; to succour dreams of grandeur and to brood on the anguish of remembered humiliations. It was a celebration of citizenship, the joy of triumph. It was a claim on the land and an affirmation of citizenship. It was a sharing of love with "African" school children and Orisha worshippers and Shouter Baptists. It was a call to national; unity in every sphere of existence.

> On May 30, we marched, mile upon colourful mile of joyful descendants, sweating in the sun, from Tacarigua to the Maha Sabha headquarters at St. Augustine. Why? The enigma of arrival. There were mountains of achievements yet unclaimed, even as every cultural, legal and economic obstacle lay removed from the path to greatness. So we sweated joyfully, smiling, laughing, touching ... and sharing the sweet libation of triumph which covered our every pore. We were more than 25,000 protected by our household deities ... and blessed.
>
> As we daily share the prosperity for which our ancestors toiled, we annually journey to the beaches and rivers to perform *puja* and make offerings of our best fruits and flowers as tokens of gratitude as reminders of our good fortune, as obligations we must not abandon. Katik 1995 was different. It was 150 years after arrival and the next day we were to choose a Prime Minister! From the ends of the island they came. We arrived at Manzanilla to perform *puja,* to bathe and to brood on the momentous hours ahead which would allow us the possibility of our country giving its confidence to a Hindu, a Trinidadian of Indian descent, as our Prime Minster.
>
> We felt the beauty of achievement. We felt the force of pride in our achievements which none can deny; and we know that in this our Land, the land of our birth, our *Janam Bhoomi,* we can become the President of our Republic, the Prime Minister, the Attorney General or anything that we choose to be. The year 1995 is indeed the one of arrival. (*Express,* November 18, 1995)

Indo-Trinidadians had always resented the assumption of Afro-Trinidadians that they had a prescriptive right to succeed the British, and that any attempt on the part of the Indo-Trinidadians to become more fully incorporated in the political system was subversive of the order and equilibrium which obtained in the society. As former MP Hulsie Bhaggan puts it:

> There appeared to be a sentiment among some Afro-Trinidadians which suggested that they had the divine right to political office. Most Indo-Trinidadians felt that it was

> their time now and they should be given a chance. (*Guardian,* March 17, 1996)

The Afro-Trinidadian community, for its part, was stunned, tearful and traumatized. As the calypsonian Cro Cro put it in his prize winning calypso, *They Look For Dat,* "November 7th, I see Black Man Cry; Look blood still running from Black People Eye." Few assumed that such an unbearable and unforgivable "trespass" would ever have taken place in their lifetime or at least in the near future. To most, it was neither desirable nor sustainable (cf. Annexe 17).

The PNM Political Leader was disinclined to entertain any suggestion that he should seek to enter a coalition with the NAR since he had openly stated that the PNM would "fight alone, win alone or lose alone" (*Guardian,* November 7, 1995). The General Council of the Party however authorized the leadership to open negotiations with Mr. Robinson. While Manning ruled out any prospect that the Prime Ministership would be offered to Mr. Robinson, he agreed to entertain discussions with the former Prime Minister on the ground that the PNM did not really lose the elections. To quote Manning:

> The PNM got about 230,000 votes. All the other political parties combined got considerably less than that; it would therefore appear that the will of the majority of the people of Trinidad and Tobago is that the PNM be part of the government of Trinidad and Tobago. If the PNM takes the position that we are staying out of any government, we are in fact disenfranchising some 230,000 people. If we are responsible as we have to be, then we just have to find a solution. (*Express,* November 8, 1995)

The Chairman of the PNM also said that the PNM could "not just pick up its marbles and walk away. It had a role to play and should play a role in the national interest" (*Guardian,* November 8, 1995). It is perhaps worth noting that while the 256,159 votes which the PNM actually got was larger than that of the UNC which got

240,372, the combined tally of the UNC and the NAR, which got 24,983 votes, exceeded that of the PNM by 9,196 votes.

The UNC-NAR Coalition

The Political Leader of the NAR, Mr. ANR Robinson, has given his own account of how and why he acted the way he did following the November 6th election, and how and why he behaved in the manner in which he did in the succeeding six months. Efforts were made to persuade Mr. Robinson to work with the PNM rather than with the UNC. These efforts came from many quarters. Some businessmen who were either sympathetic to the PNM or concerned that the change of government would lead to a loss of business confidence, sought to persuade Robinson and the NAR to enter into a coalition arrangement with the PNM instead of the UNC, as a holding arrangement until such time as new elections could be scheduled. This arrangement would have had the advantage of leaving the PNM in a position to determine the date for new elections. Some elements in or close to the PNM likewise felt that "any means necessary" should be used to persuade Robinson not to be the instrument by which a *Hinduraj* was established in Trinidad and Tobago. Robinson was accused of "betraying" his race. The calypsonian Cro-Cro, for example, felt that Robinson had plunged the "sword in his hands" into the breast of the African man.[1]

Concern was expressed that what was taking place in Guyana and Suriname in respect of the political dominance of the Indian community in those two countries would eventually take place in Trinidad and Tobago. Some also saw the possibility of formal political links being established between the three Hindu controlled states, and feared that these would eventually lead to the creation of an Indian "homeland" in the Americas, and the progressive marginalization of the African descended elements in the area, a goal which some Indian fundamentalists had long cherished. These had talked about the "ultimate destiny for the Indian Nation in the Caribbean being achievable either by peaceful constitutional means or, if not, by the use of militant means for the achievement of ultimate freedom."[2]

Robinson however resisted the appeal to form a partnership with the PNM, preferring instead to deal with the UNC. This move was clearly dictated by his belief that he could get a better deal, both for himself and Tobago, from the UNC than he could from the PNM. The heated exchanges during the campaign between Robinson and Manning over the Tobago self-government issue, the events of 1990 (Robinson had accused Manning of being a co-conspirator with the Jamaat when it sought to effect a seizure of state power in 1990), and Robinson's own experiences with the PNM dating back to 1969-1970 had clearly made it difficult for the two men to work together. Robinson may well have welcomed the opportunity to humiliate the PNM as Dr. Williams had humiliated him.[3] It is also possible that even though the UNC and the NAR were seemingly at "war" during the election, it was a "phony war," and that the NAR *entente* did not materialize immediately following the election and that they had in fact been signalling in advance to the effect that if no party won a clear majority, the UNC and the NAR would have to work together. One recalls Panday and Robinson flirting politically on television, *flagrante delicto,* in the week before the November 6th election.

Robinson has insisted that his decision to work with the UNC was driven by principle and concern for the national interest. The NAR, he told the 8th Annual NAR Convention in April 1996, was placed in a position of highest responsibility. Experienced statesman as he was, he chose not to exploit the position for any selfish purpose which might have had catastrophic consequences for the country, both politically and economically. This might have happened, for example, if he had attempted to follow the strategy used in St. Vincent by James "Son" Mitchell who demanded and got the Prime Ministership as the price for his tie breaking cooperation with the People's Political Party in 1972.

In Robinson's view, the electorate had rejected the appea of both the PNM and the UNC for a mandate to rule. Robinson however claimed that the electorate's rejection of the PNM's demand was politically and sociologically more compelling, even though the PNM got more votes in Trinidad than the UNC. One is not clear how that judgement was arrived at. Were there forces at work which suggested to Robinson that the "zeitgeist" wa moving in favour of the Indians and that he had to recognize the "necessity" of moving with it? What indeed would have happened if Robinson had decided to embrace Manning and re-unite the PNM? Would the Indian community have swallowed it as they had done in 1981 when George Chambers was chosen by the President before Errol Mahabir or Kamaludin Mohammed following Dr. Williams death in office? (cf. Ryan 1989a). Would there have been a renewed refugee phenomenon, such as occurred in 1987, both psychically and physically? (Ryan 1989b). Would there have been open protests on the streets as there were in St Kitts and Guyana in 1992?

We of course have no answers to these questions. Nor do we know whether they ever entered Robinson's mind. According to Robinson, the PNM's record in power over the past 35 year was there for all to see. In the last year of its most recent term, it record was particularly dismal. To quote Mr. Robinson:

> The ruling party, the PNM, had chalked up a dismal record, particularly in its fourth year of governance. It had adopted a confrontational stance with almost every major institution in the country; Police Service Commission, Public Service Commission, Teaching Service Commission, Police Commissioner, the Court of Appeal and even the Privy Council. It incarcerated the Speaker of the House of Representatives under a state of emergency and its leader thereupon declared himself to be father of the nation.... In its final year, 1995, the leadership of the party exhibited precipitate and alarming deterioration. (*Express,* April 23, 1996)

In Mr. Robinson's view, there were also serious concerns about the Opposition UNC, in general and Mr. Maharaj in particular. On balance, however, he felt he had to give the nod to Mr. Panday since there was no question of re-installing Mr. Manning as Head of Government after his call for a "renewed mandate had been rejected by the electorate." Robinson also tells us that he "rejected out of hand" the appeal to race to resolve the tie in favour of the PNM. His claim was that his own political history and his contemporary involvement in attempts to set up an International Tribunal which was seeking, *inter alia,* to try individuals for heinous crimes against humanity such as genocide, would have made such an act "politically incorrect."

One is however not entirely certain that Robinson's decision to work with the UNC was driven solely by concern for the national interest and that "selfish" considerations were also not operative. It is clear that Robinson sensed that he could work more easily with Mr. Panday than with Mr. Manning. Mr. Robinson must also have calculated that his political interests in Tobago would have been better served by an arrangement with the UNC which had no base in Tobago, than with the PNM which was still a viable party in Tobago.

Interestingly, Mr. Robinson tells us that the NAR Council had initially decided to avoid forming a formal coalition with any party and that it had decided instead to give the UNC "critical support," i.e., judge the latter on the basis of what it sought to do in Parliament. Those who were anxious to share in the allocation of spoils or who felt that the Indian community should not be frustrated, however opposed that decision. Mr. Robinson and the Council went along with this change of position and advised the President that he, and the other elected MP from Tobago, would give their support to Mr. Panday for the post of Prime Minister. The country was on the edge, and Mr. Robinson felt that they had to act decisively:

> We could have dillied; we could have dallied; we could have,as some adamantly held we should, negotiated — if necessary with both sides — in order to extract the best deal — in senatorial and ministerial appointments and settled quotas, not omitting the Prime Ministership. As a former Finance Minister, I had no doubt that the interest of the country required a clean break out of the deadlock and in the direction of stability in order to avoid deepening tension, uncertainty, economic deterioration and possible violence and a free fall of the Trinidad and Tobago dollar. (*Express,* April 23, 1996)

During the days preceding the decision to form a "co partnership," there were numerous reports that in seeking to "mak the difference," some members of the NAR sought to force th UNC to appoint several of its key members to positions in th Cabinet, the Senate, boards of statutory authorities, and stat enterprises as the price for its cooperation. The names of severa high profile persons from both Tobago and Trinidad were bruitec about. Mr. Robinson has however insisted that neither he no Miss Nicholson were ever party to those negotiations. As h reports:

> I want to make it abundantly clear... that while I made proposals to Mr. Panday on behalf of the NAR, I never have at any time bargained or negotiated or sought to impose terms and conditions. All such allegations are completely false and absolutely without foundation. Miss Nicholson's hands and mine, and by extension the NAR's, are free of any such arrangements. I consider that the electoral and parliamentary statistics would speak for themselves and the Prime Minister would think fit to be guided accordingly. (ibid.)

Many NAR members were angry with Mr. Robinson for not insisting that NAR stalwarts be given key offices as the price of cooperation. Mr. Robinson tells us that he chose not to do so, since he was anxious to avoid any confrontation that might prove divisive:

> It is tempting for members of parties in a coalition government to feel that the role of the parties is to share

> between their members the fruits and benefits of power. The PNM did it among its own members with a vengeance. And there are members of both the UNC and NAR who feel "is we time now." They want to be the flip side of the PNM coinage. But if it was wrong under the PNM, it is wrong also under the UNC/NAR coalition. If it was wrong for the PNM to engage in acts of corruption, then it is wrong for the UNC/NAR to do the same. Do not ask me to support you in that line of conduct. Do not tell me because X did it before me that is reason or justification for me to do it. If it was wrong for X, it is wrong for me, and no justification for me to do it. (ibid.)

A party, he insisted, is not a trade union seeking to realize the "unrealistic welfare expectations" of its members. A proper party is one that has a vision that encompasses the fundamentals of the entire society. More importantly, plural societies, more than others, require leaders to act responsibly rather than confrontationally:

> In multi-cultural societies and societies that are divided on ethnic and racial lines, confidence building is a necessary process to the resolution of conflict situations. A high degree of patience, skilful and sensitive management and understanding are all required for long-term success. (ibid.)

Mr. Robinson, who was given the post of "Minister Extraordinaire" in the new regime with ministerial responsibility for Tobago, tells us that since the election, he has chosen to speak softly and even avoid carrying a big stick. His experience in the 1986-1991 regime had chastened him, and made him recognize the importance of settling differences internally, rather than to resort to public posturing as Panday *et al.* were minded to do in 1987-1991 (Ryan 1989b). He was equally aware that there were forces which were anxious to pry open every crack that appeared in the coalition. More importantly, he felt that it was necessary to let all and sundry — both nationally and internationally — know that Trinidad and Tobago had one, and not two Prime Ministers. Apologizing for his caution and silence, he assured his listeners who thought his actions "foolish," that they would in time discover that his actions were in fact wise.

While expressing certainty that the coalition would last the NAR felt that there were problems which needed to be sorted out. Mr. Robinson himself observed that given the inexperience of the new Ministers and the complexity of government, mistakes were unavoidable. There was however a patent need to review the post-election arrangements which were made. There was need for more political will to be devoted to improving communication and consultation between the co-partners in the interest of the two parties, the Government, and in the national interest.

Robinson's statement was clearly an important one, not only for what it said in the text, but in the sub-text as well. Robinson was speaking to his supporters and detractors in Trinidad, those in Tobago, to Mr. Panday and the UNC, to people like calypsonian Cro Cro who accused him of selling out, and for the historical record. To his supporters who were very angry with him for playing Pontius Pilate by not seeking to ensure that the NAR got a fairer share of the disposable spoils, he was telling them that in the context of Trinidad, if not in Tobago, he was not a machine politician who would soil his hands in the pork barrel.

Mr. Robinson was also telling Mr. Panday and the rest of the UNC team that he should not be taken for granted and that he should be properly consulted before key and potentially far reaching decisions and statements were made. He also warned the UNC that no race should seek to construct an hegemonic edifice. That way lay disaster. Mr. Robinson was however clearly aware that while he had some leverage which could be used in this evenly balanced political game, he had to act with restraint. If he overplayed his hand and his bluff was called, the coalition could collapse, and with it all his hopes for settling the Tobago question and perhaps inheriting the Presidency, which some believe was the ultimate spoil to which he aspired.

The First 200 Days

The leaders of the two parties were aware of the mistakes which had been made in the 1986-1991 period of NAR rule and were determined that these should not be repeated. They had thus agreed on a code of conduct that would govern relationships between them. The *Heads of Agreement* provided, *inter alia,* that the two parties would work together to broaden and deepen the process of unity throughout the country, and that they would seek to include in this process all groups and individuals comprising the national community, including the Members of Parliament. The parties also agreed to ensure that the decision-making process with respect to the governance of the country embraced the principles of the rule of law, transparency in public affairs, and morality and integrity in public office. They also agreed to establish and sustain a code of conduct for cabinet ministers (see box).

The parties likewise agreed to "review the existing political and legislative framework with the objective of integrating the unity process into existing structures and to establish appropriate mechanisms to initiate and foster dialogue and programmes to make the best use of the energy, talents, skills, and enterprise of the entire population in the nation-building process." There was also agreement to utilize existing mechanisms of conflict resolution and to develop new ones on a consensual basis (*NAR Conference Agreement Documents,* April 1996).

Heads of Agreement

Whereas the United National Congress and the National Alliance for Reconstruction held discussions with the view of forming the Government of Trinidad and Tobago following the general elections held on the 6th November, 1995 the parties hereby agree as follows:

1. To take measures progressively for the purpose of confidence building between the United National Congress and the National Alliance for Reconstruction with a view to facilitating, promoting and strengthening collaboration between the two parties. Towards this end the parties will place emphasis on decision-making by consensus, particularly at the level of the Parliamentary caucus.

2. To work together to broaden and deepen the process of unity throughout the country including in this process all groups and individuals in the national community as well as Members of Parliament. The parties will expeditiously introduce legislation to implement the national consensus agreement on Tobago contained in House Paper No. 6 of 1978 with appropriate constitutional and other legislative safeguards.

3. To utilize and where necessary view the existing political and legislative framework with the objective of integrating the unity process.

4. To take immediate initiatives to utilize the Human resources of the United National Congress and the National Alliance for Reconstruction in the formation and continuance of the new government of Trinidad and Tobago.

5. To establish the legislative provisions and/or mechanisms to ensure that the decision-making process with respect to the governance of the Country embraces and gives effect to the principles

of Truth, the Rule of Law, Transparency in Public Affairs and Morality and integrity in Public Office. The Parties will establish and maintain Codes of conduct for cabinet Ministers, Parliamentarians, Members of The Tobago House of Assembly and local government representatives.

6. To restructure the political system to afford representation to sections of the electorate who by reason of non-alignment with major political groupings are denied participation in the governance of the Country.

7. To strengthen and deepen the decentralization process at all levels of Government.

8. To establish appropriate mechanisms and institutions to initiate and foster dialogue and programmes designed to harness the energy, talents, skills and enterprise of the entire population in the nation-building process.

9. To utilize existing mechanisms and to create appropriate ones for conflict resolution between the affected parties.

The principal partners in the coalition which some had deemed improbable because of the "compulsions of the culture," were aware that there was a widespread belief that the new government would collapse under the pressures that would be brought to bear on it by place seekers, contract hunters and by those who, having been long in the wilderness, wanted to advance ethnic and community concerns which could only be secured at the expense of incumbents and current consumers of available resources. As Panday himself puts it:

> By becoming Prime Minister, I have evoked all kinds of feelings and released many pent-up and deep seated hopes and aspirations; but unfortunately it has exposed many trepidations as well. That is to be expected in a society such as ours. (*Guardian,* December 4, 1996)

Mr. Panday's way of addressing this problem was to signal that he was not a "Caroni Prime Minister," and to urge his followers to cease displaying signs of vengeance, arrogance and triumphalism, and to accept their victory with dignity, humility and a sense of responsibility. "Be careful what you do and say," he warned. Panday advised his supporters that his success as Prime Minister would be determined by how they behaved (*Express,* November 20, 1995; see also *Guardian,* March 28, 1996).

The new Prime Minister also called for the establishment of a "government of national unity," arguing that the society was "difficult to rule" and could not be governed effectively or productively without it. Interestingly, former UNC Member of Parliament, Hulsie Bhaggan, felt constrained to make the point that "those most vociferous for racial unity are in fact rabid, closet racists, [whilst] those who speak out in an open manner and call a spade a spade are likely to have worked through their prejudices" (*Guardian,* March 17, 1996).

In pursuit of the unity goal, Panday invited the PNM to collaborate with the UNC in forming an all party government, perhaps knowing full well that the PNM would refuse. As he put it:

> Because of the highly plural, divisive and fragmented nature of our society, no single group can run Trinidad and Tobago successfully to the exclusion of other groups. And based on that analysis, I have always argued on the need for national coalition government. But God disposes and what you want may not be what you get and so those who do not want unity, unity will be forced on them. (*Guardian,* November 7, 1996)

He also urged the creation of a consensual decision making process which would enable Government, labour and capital to participate as partners in the resolution of critical policy issues affecting the economy.[4] The UNC likewise signalled to the community that it did not propose to change everything overnight, including the memberships of statutory boards and the executives of state enterprises, as the NAR did in 1986, and, much to the chagrin of some of its supporters, stressed that it would maintain most of the economic policies that the PNM had put in place between 1991 and 1995 in the interest of continuity.

In his choice of Cabinet, Mr. Panday was sensitive to the anxieties of the non-Indian community who were not used to seeing cabinets which consisted mainly of persons of Indian ancestry. Seeing that there were only 4 elected members in the coalition who were not of that extraction, four others were brought in via the Senate. The Cabinet of 21 thus contained 8 non-Indians and 13 Indians, which was not an unreasonable balance having regard to the ethnic basis of the UNC and the need to tie all the elected parliamentarians to the Government in the interest of survival. Four of the Ministers were Hindus, as were two parliamentary Secretaries. Three were Muslims while the remainder were Christians.

Many Afro-Trinidadians, among them artist/poet Le Roi Clarke and the National Joint Action Committee (NJAC), were unhappy with the appearance of the Cabinet which, in the view of Clarke, made him feel he was in Pakistan.[5] NJAC felt there was need to alter the physical appearance of the Cabinet. "In making his decision, Panday should let himself be influenced by historical experience and not the satisfaction of a few persons to whom he feels indebted" (*Guardian,* November 11, 1995). NJAC urged the new Prime Minister to avoid the mistake with respect to appointments to the boards since this would only aggravate existing apprehensions and fears. NJAC and others who made similar observations were however reminded that PNM Cabinets always over-represented Afro-Trinidadians.

The PNM welcomed the UNC's initial endorsement of its policies, many of which had been criticized during the election campaign. It however rejected the invitation to form a national government which it viewed as being contrary to the Constitution and its conventions which require an active Opposition. The PNM was aware that the UNC was in fact using the unity formula to conceal its weakness or to perpetuate itself in power. It thus argued that while the PNM believed in unity, such unity would have to take place within the framework of the political parties. In Mr. Manning's view, both parties should re-engineer themselves so that they become more attractive to people of all ethnicities. To quote Manning, who described the PNM as the "alternative government":

> What is emerging from all of these things is that the government appears to be systematically seeking to undermine the position of the Opposition and therefore it is not the Opposition that suffers but the public. I have the responsibility to resist these attempts. Everything the government has done is to subvert the role of the Opposition under the guise of national unity. The population ought to watch very carefully what is happening, the net effect of which is to divide the society. It is for that reason we have not joined a government of national unity. The approach is dangerous... Since 1987 when I became Political Leader, I said we need to bring the whole country together. We believe the way to do it is at the level of the political party. All parties should be broad based reflecting the composition of the society in which we operate. It is in fact a coalition of interests. In this way the integrity of the Westminster system as we have it in Trinidad and Tobago is maintained. (*Guardian,* November 10, 1995)

Notwithstanding the superficial peacefulness of the transfer of power, there were numerous incidents, particularly at the grass roots level, which created tension in the society following the election. In a survey conducted by SARA in January 1996, Afro-Trinidadians and persons of mixed ancestry were asked to indicate whether they had either direct or hearsay evidence of any incident which served to confirm the concerns which had been articulated during the campaign as to what might happen if there were to be a change of regime following the election (Table 1). As many as 19 per cent of the Afro-Trinidadians and 12 per cent of the mixed persons in the sample reported that they had personally experienced incidents of one kind or another which made them feel that the concerns expressed during the election campaign were justified.

Table 1. Post-Election Experience Relating to Racial Behaviour (%)

Response	Afro-Trinidadians	Mixed
Personal Experience	19	12
No Personal Experience/ Hearsay Evidence only	26	20
No Personal Experience or Hearsay Evidence	19	32
Too Early to Make Judgement	29	29
Refuse to Say	6	5
Other	1	3

Twenty-six per cent of the Afro-Trinidadians and 20 per cent of the mixed said that while they themselves did not have any personal encounter which gave them concern, they had heard of incidents which suggested that the fears expressed were not exaggerated. Nineteen per cent of the former and 32 per cent of the latter were however of the view that the fears were overblown;

yet another 29 per cent of the both groups felt that it was much too early to say whether that was the case or not. If the figures are projected onto the national plane, it would mean that some 50,000 of the 256,014 Afro-Trinidadians and 12,000 of the 101,412 persons of mixed descent, 20 years and over, personally experienced incidents of a racial nature which gave them cause for concern and anxiety. No attempt was however made to discern what the incidents were, or how serious they were considered to be.

There were a number of decisions taken during the first 200 days of the new regime which generated controversy and negative political fall out in the minds of some groups in terms of gender and race. Among these were the removal of Mrs. Kamla Persad-Bissessar as Attorney General and her early replacement by Mr. Ramesh Lawrence Maharaj. While most expected that this appointment would have occurred at some time, the fact that it seemed to have been fast forwarded suggested to many that the explanation given for deferring the appointment was fictive, and that the 3-month postponement was stage managed in order to avoid ruffling the feathers of those known to be upset about the prospect that Mr. Maharaj would be appointed to the post of Attorney General.

The Jamaat Imbroglio

Also provoking concern was the perceived closeness of the Jamaat al Muslimeen to the regime, a perception that remained for a long while inspite of the efforts which were being made by the new Government to put some distance between itself and the Jamaat.[6] Shortly thereafter, the Jamaat sought and received an audience with the Prime Minister at which it presented a five point agenda. They requested that

- the 8.8 acres of land granted by Dr. Eric Williams to construct an Islamic Cultural Complex at 1 Mucurapo Road be regularised by a deed to the Jamaat al Muslimeen

- the $2.1 million offered by the State's lawyer during the recent hearing before Justice Best as compensation for the destroyed Jamaat buildings be paid without further complications as an act of good faith, the remainder of the assessment to be completed by arbitration
- the settlement of the "hijab" issue so that Muslim women and men who have been debarred from employment and schools for wearing the garment which covers the head and shoulders will face no further discrimination
- the Jamaat al Muslimeen be considered for State assistance in the construction of schools at 1 Mucurapo Road and that their teachers be admitted to teachers' training colleges and be paid by the State as is done with other denominational schools
- skilled and qualified members of the Jamaat al Muslimeen are not discriminated against for employment (*Express,* December 6, 1995).

Following the meeting, Bakr expressed optimism that their demands would be heeded. "There is a change in the atmosphere," he opined. "I have no reason to doubt Mr. Panday at this time. Down the road ... we don't know" (*Express,* December 6, 1995). Bakr later indicated that the UNC had given them the assurance that the court award would be paid (*Guardian,* July 28, 1996). The general public however made it very clear to the UNC that it would strongly oppose any effort on its part to legitimize the Jamaat al Muslimeen. The UNC thus sought to distance itself from the Jamaat. The general public however remained convinced that a clandestine link existed. It was noted, for example, that the brother of a key Jamaat activist had been the manager of the UNC campaign in the Tunapuna constituency and was made a supervisor on the Unemployment Relief Programme.

Comments made by the Jamaat in March 1996 however suggest that the group had lost patience with the Government which it accused of stonewalling on its commitments. To quote Bakr:

> I have my problems with the UNC. I am giving them a little chance, but time is running out. Before the election, Panday said he was going to obey the rule of law. And the court has ruled that the Jamaat should be paid compensation for buildings and property which were damaged by the State. But we are not hearing anything about it. (*Express,* March 3, 1996)

Bakr was angry with the Attorney General, the Jamaat's former attorney, for failing to appoint a team to meet with the Jamaat as promised, and chided Mr. Maharaj for being the only person to have benefitted financially from the crisis in that he had received millions of dollars in legal fees from the Muslimeen. "Meanwhile, we have no schools and our children can't go to other schools. When a government does not obey the rule of law, anarchy steps in because nobody is under compulsion to obey it" (*Mirror,* March 3, 1996). Bakr in fact gave the Government a 7 day deadline to meet with his new attorney, Mr. Subhas Panday, the Prime Minister's brother (*Guardian,* March 14, 1996).

When asked whether he felt comfortable negotiating with the Jamaat, the younger Panday, who was known to be at odds with his elder brother and the Attorney General, observed that his brother had spoken to them and there was thus no reason why he should not do so (*Guardian,* March 17, 1996). The Prime Minister was also asked about his brother's role in the matter. His retort was that "he was not his "brother's keeper" and had therefore taken "no note" of what he had done (ibid.). It is also worth noting that Mr. Maharaj took offense at being given a deadline to meet the Jamaat's new lawyer. He insisted that he was not going to be "terrorised" by anyone in matters like these" (*Express,* March 18, 1996). Mr. Subhas Panday, he advised, should deal with the state's lawyers and not the Attorney General, since the latter had previously dealt with the matter.

Mr. Subhas Panday's reaction to the Attorney General's comment was instructive for what it indicated about the politics of the problem. Mr. Panday dismissed Mr. Maharaj's comment as "emotional ranting and raving designed to gain acceptability in the eyes of the population ... because he wants to be in the good books." He indicated that he was not dealing with personalities, but with the Attorney General who just happened to be the former Attorney of the Jamaat (*Guardian,* March 17, 1996). Panday was of the view that "the Jamaat was being sacrificed on the altar of political expediency. They have been betrayed by Ramesh Maharaj who, in their view, had now become the chief defendant. A conflict of interest clearly existed. As such, they felt that the matter should be handled by an independent tribunal. Failure to do so would induce a breakdown in the rule of law and mark the introduction of anarchy" (*Mirror,* May 19, 1996).

Clearly, the pressure of public opinion on the Jamaat had made the Government in general, and Messrs Panday and Maharaj in particular, politically uncomfortable. The Government was clearly caught between the proverbial rock and a hard place. It wanted to placate the Muslimeen and eliminate the threat which it posed to social peace, the constitutional order, and perhaps to themselves. It however feared that doing so could be politically expensive since majority opinion was opposed to the payment of compensatory damages to those who had attempted to seize control of the state unconstitutionally, destroying many lives and much public and private property in the process.

The leader of the Jamaat expressed further annoyance with the Government when his organisation was denied permission by the Police to hold a public meeting in the town of Couva as part of its public education campaign. Fumed Bakr:

> ...this is the same UNC we supported and put in Government. That is public knowledge.... We made our application and we were stopped.... Just now, nobody will be able to say anything in the country. (*Mirror,* May 12, 1996)

The Muslimeen were also angry with the Government for enacting legislation (The Military Training [Prohibition] Bill) to control the training of paramilitary forces. The Muslimeen claimed that their men were doing nothing more than running and doing push-ups and insisted that no one was going to prevent them from training (*Mirror,* May 26, 1996).

The UNC was clearly concerned about the Jamaat, and was taking steps to forestall a coup attempt. There was in fact a report that the leaders of the UNC and the NAR had entered into a secret side deal to the one which had been made public on November 11th when the coalition was being formed. According to that report (*Mirror,* June 2, 1996), Clause 4 of the Agreement reads as follows:

> The United National Congress hereby acknowledges that it is not now, nor shall it during the pendancy of this agreement, become engaged in any association or arrangement with Abu Bakr and the Jamaat al Muslimeen of any nature whatever.

There had been earlier concern in NAR circles about links between the UNC and the Jamaat, and this alleged link was one of the reasons given for the fracturing of the common platform that elements from both parties had sought to put in place for the Caroni by-election in August 1994 (cf. Annexe 4). Having regard to the fact that the 1990 coup effort was directed against an NAR government led by Mr. Robinson, it was plausible to believe that the latter would have inserted such a provision in the Heads of Agreement. Mr. Robinson however denied ever seeing such a provision. Nor did he know anything about it. He however indicated that "several people, on their own tried to put forward something on behalf of one party or another, and that might have been one of them. But it was never put up" (*Mirror,* June 2, 1996).

The UNC leadership did not make any official statement as to whether such a clause exists, and it has to be assumed that it does not. The party is however clearly at odds with the Jamaat, and has increased the security presence around ministers in general and the Attorney General in particular.*

Despite his quarrel with the UNC, Abu Bakr refused to have any dealings with the PNM and he continued to insist that the PNM's Political Leader and the MP for La Brea had met with one of their members at his home 5 weeks after the election to try and get the Jamaat to break with the UNC. Bakr however insisted that he would not allow the Jamaat to be used by the PNM to create any disharmony between itself and the UNC. That posture also included relationships between the Syrian and Indian communities who were known to be fierce economic competitors. To quote Bakr:

> Under the PNM, the Syrians benefitted. But now that the Indians are in power, the old colonials feel threatened. The Indians have all the infrastructure in place to get lucrative contracts. The only people who did not benefit from all this were the Africans. The Syrians are hoping that media hysteria will scare the UNC, and so they will not obey the law and pay us the money. They hope to be able to benefit from a NAR and UNC conflict. But we have practical experience now, and that scheme will not work again. They are hoping to drive a wedge between us, but we are the last of the Mohicans. The last of the resistance (*Sunday Mirror,* March 10, 1986).

Bakr also recalled his pre-election criticisms of the PNM and its leaders and predicted that the "African people would wander in the wilderness for 40 years until a new leader comes forward from amongst the people, cross them over the River Jordan, and liberate them for the first time (ibid.)

---

*Abu Bakr claimed that two weeks prior to the election, he secretly taped a conversation with Mr. Maharaj in which the latter promised that the UNC would give the Jamaat legal title to the land at Mucurapo if it were to win power. Bakr has threatened to release the tape if the AG denied making the promise. No denial was made at time of writing though Maharaj has dared Bakr to play the tape.

The Baptists

As promised, the UNC moved to give the Baptists their promised national holiday. The decision to do so by substituting Easter Monday was not politically cost effective in the sense that while the Baptists were pleased, fulfilling the promise came at the expense of many more who considered Easter Monday an important national calendar event and were thus unhappy that their long weekend was being taken away to appease a religious minority. The fact that the UNC was forced to reconsider the proposal at the request of Mr ANR Robinson, its "co-partner," in the coalition, also generated a belief that it was acting without due deliberation and consultation. Tobagonians argued that Easter Monday was an important calendar event for them in their tourism schedule.

The issue of the holiday split the Baptist community along religious and political lines. The PNM was negotiating with one group — the West Indian United Spiritual Baptist Sacred Order Incorporated (WIUSBOI) while the UNC dealt with another element, the Shouters. The latter were banned by the 1917 Ordinance while the WIUSBSOI were not. Liberation Day thus meant little to the WIUSBSOI (*Express,* February 2, 1996). Both groups claim to be about 200,000 strong, a claim that is clearly nonsensical (WIUSBOI is part of the National Congress of Incorporated Baptist Organisations). Archbishop Douglas indicated that members of the Congress were not opposed to the holiday, but felt that the things promised by the PNM were more meaningful. After the holiday was celebrated, what would happen to the Baptists? He was of the view that the growing number of Baptists and their children would benefit more from the construction of a cathedral and a primary school (*Mirror,* January 1, 1996).

The Shouters countered by asking the Government to give them a state aided school in addition to the holiday (*Mirror,* March 3, 1996). They also asked for the table of precedence to be revised to recognise the Baptist's presence in the country, representation of Baptists in organisations which deal with social planning and development, an annual allocation of funds for social welfare projects, and the renaming of Woodford Square after Archbishop Elton Griffith. The Prime Minister merely promised that the Government would consider these requests (*Express,* January 27, 1996).

The Civil Service Debt

The Government also ran into initial difficulty in its attempt to meet its campaign promise to pay Civil Servants the debts that were due to them in cash. Having told the Minister of Finance to "rake and scrape" to find funds to enable the government to fulfill this promise, the Government was having difficulty meeting its obligations. A provision of some TT$90m was however made in the 1996 Budget as a gesture of its good faith. Mr. Panday's comment, made during the budget debate, that after allocating 65 percent of the budget of TT$10b to pay public servants and service the public debt, less than TT$4b was left to provide for other essential services that the people required, and that something had to be done about it "no matter what the consequences," was however seen by the Public Service Association (PSA) and public servants as a smokescreen behind which the Government was seeking to renege on its promise (*Express,* February 26, 1996). It was also seen as a signal that Government was planning to downsize the public sector further.

Panday's comment did not endear the Government to public servants who resented what they saw as an attempt to cut their income further or throw some of them on the breadline. The Government however reached an agreement with public servants, agreeing to pay them partly in cash and in bonds, a sum equal to one quarter of the outstanding arrears of TT$2b in 1996 (*Express,* April 25, 1996). The settlement was not radically different from that originally agreed to with the PNM prior to the election. Panday however claimed that the UNC did a better job at marketing the offer than the PNM (*Newsday,* June 7, 1996).

The Public Service Association had a somewhat different interpretation to that of the Government as to what was the status of the negotiations as of June 1996. To quote Mr. Weatherhead, PSA Secretary:

> Mr. Panday knows, from his own intimate involvement in the issue, that this debt is only partially settled. He knows that the agreement to pay bonds applies to the parts of the debt already quantified, and that the remaining portion of debt is still being quantified. Mr. Panday also knows that his government has failed to meet their legal obligations — based on the government's withdrawal of its appeal in the increment-suspension case last October — to pay correct salaries from May 1996.
>
> He also knows that as long as public officers are not paid their correct salaries, the debt continues to accumulate every month. He should also report that his government accepted the position of the PSA with respect to payment of bonds and quantification of increment arrears. He knows that his government did not convince the PSA to accept that position. It was they who accepted our position and only after four months of resisting it.
>
> In presenting his government's "achievements" to the electors, the political leader of the UNC must also tell the truth about his party's promise to pay the debt in cash. He must explain that the promise of cash has been severely reduced to a mere $900 per person, before tax, while almost all public officers are owed at least $20,000.

The "Assault" on Black CEOs

There were a number of other policy decisions and developments which served to aggravate the concern that, notwithstanding assurances about national unity, Afro-Trinidadians were being displaced in public sector organisations to make room for Indo-Trinidadians. There was concern that the chairmanships of the boards of the more important utilities and state enterprises — The National Gas Company (NGC), The Water and Sewerage Authority (WASA), Petroleum Company of Trinidad and tobago (Petrotrin), Point Lisas Development Company (PLIPDECO), Tourism and Industrial Development Company (TIDCO), International Communications Network (ICN), Trinidad Flour Mills — were being handed to Indo-Trinidadians. More worrying and less understandable was the fact that several Afro-Trinidadian CEOs of some of these bodies were being "constructively dismissed." It was also noted that of the non-executive directors who were retained, few were Afro-Trinidadians. Mr. Ken Valley, former. Minister of Industry, Trade and Commerce, had the following to say in Parliament on the matter:

> When we look at the appointments of chairman of boards made so far, we see that the last chairman of ICN was Anna Mahase: the new one is Mr. Rambachan. In the case of the Petroleum Company of Trinidad and Tobago, the last chairman was Trevor Boopsingh; the new one is Donald Baldeosingh. In the case of the National Gas Company, the last chairman was Ken Julien; the new one is Steve Fergusson. In the case of TIDCO, the last chairman was Robert Bermudez; the new one is Ishwar Galbaransingh — part of the three. Plipdeco: last chairman, Peter Quentrall-Thomas; new chairman, Nirmal Rampersad. Quite simply, in the last, government — when you look at even these boards, you would see that there was a mix representing national unity, that the chairmen of the boards — that is extremely important, that we see that the chairmen of the boards appointed so far represent one sector of the population, and I ask that you take note of that, because when you talk about national unity, you must carry it out in practice. (*Express,* March 29, 1996)

Valley noted that only one of the 12 Boards filled up to the end of March had a non-Indian chairman. During the tenure of the PNM administration (1991-1996), 11 of the 39 chairmen were racially mixed, 10 were Afro-Trinidadian, 10 were Indo-Trinidadian, and 8 were "what we would call white."

The UNC responded to these charges of political victimisation of CEOs by counter charging that the incumbents had shown partisanship to the PNM. As the Minister of Finance declared, "the UNC-NAR administration intends to keep vigil over the heads of state organisations to ensure the delivery of justice, fair play and professionalism to the public" (*Guardian,* March 5, 1996).[7]

The Minister of Finance however denied that race was responsible for the firing of any CEO or for any request that they go on leave. Waste, corruption, mismanagement and political partisanship were at the root of the problem. As he declared:

> It is not by accident that you find all the CEOs, or the majority of them... are of a particular ethnic or racial origin. I have no difficulty with that. [But] the country is not going to be easy with this Government if it has evidence of wastage, mismanagement, [and] of corrupt practices and chooses to ignore it merely because of political pressure being put on it by saying that if you touch some of these people, because of their ethnic origin, you would be accused of race. *[sic]* (*Express,* June 21, 1996)

The Minister noted that while he was not going to "chase every ghost," if he was sent information about waste and corruption, he had a responsibility to send it to the boards for their attention and for investigation. The decision as to whether any individual was fired or suspended was left to the board, a claim also repeated by the Prime Minister. Few believed the claim especially since the Minister of Finance had publicly declared that "heads will roll" and that the UNC/NAR administration planned to "keep vigil over the heads of state organisations" (*Guardian,* March 5, 1996). The Minister in fact agreed that the Government had a political agenda, and advised anyone who was unwilling to be part of that agenda that he or she was free to negotiate termination arrangements with the government. Other ministers claimed that they had been victims of either sabotage or, in some cases, a lack of cooperation. One Minister was quite blunt about the need to put "one's own in certain posts." As she put it:

> When you are a party and you win a government, [it] is you and your people to march in. When you lose, you must know how to pack your bags and move out. (*Express,* June 14, 1996)

The Minister noted that several top public and quasi-public servants had heckled opposition politicians while cheering those whom they supported. Some had even managed campaigns for political parties. If the parties which they supported lost, they sought to undermine the new administration in various ways. The NAR was said to have been a victim of this in 1986. The PNM was also accused of having fired several NAR appointees in 1991. The shoe was now on the other foot.

The PNM however insisted that the firings were both politically and racially inspired, and the UNC was accused of having brought racial feeling to a boil. During the local government elections, the Leader of the Opposition claimed that race relations in Trinidad and Tobago were at their lowest ever. Manning attacked the UNC for imposing on the population some of the "worst racists acts ever perpetrated by any Government in Trinidad and Tobago" (*Mirror,* July 14, 1996). The charges were somewhat exaggerated, but were widely shared among the Afro-Trinidadian population.

Unemployment Relief Programme

The decisions which were made in respect of recruitment for unemployment relief work also alienated many PNM and NAR supporters. Typical was the *cri de coeur* of PNM MP for Diego Martin East, Colm Imbert:

> In complete contradiction of the underlying philosophy behind public works programmes such as the Unemployment Relief Programme which are specifically designed to provide a social safety net for persons in

> depressed urban and suburban areas, where alternative forms of employment and income generation, such as agriculture, are simply not available, the UNC has shifted the focus of job opportunities almost completely to the rural areas. As an example, in a suburban/urban region such as Diego Martin, which encompasses three separate constituencies, stretching from Carenage to Maraval, with an overall population in excess of 120,000 persons, the new government started the 1996 URP with a total of only six projects in the entire area, providing employment for barely 75 persons.
>
> Under the PNM, in recognition of its urban characteristics, the Diego Martin region would normally start the year with 20 URP construction projects, and six women's projects, employing in excess of 300 persons per fortnight. This total would increase later in the year so that eventually over 500 persons would be employed in the URP at any given time in the Diego Martin area.
>
> And despite all of the glib rhetoric that we hear on a daily basis about "national unity," the allocation of employment opportunities is equally disastrous in the depressed areas around Port of Spain and along the East West Corridor, while on the other hand rural areas in Central and South Trinidad are being given special attention by the UNC. This ill-advised strategy of the UNC is showing the seeds of social discontent in North Trinidad and is weakening the social fabric of the country as more and more people are beginning to perceive that their areas are being deliberately targeted for political discrimination simply because they voted for the PNM. (*Express,* April 5, 1996)

The NAR's National Council also passed a resolution unanimously accusing the UNC of showing "open discrimination [against] NAR members in respect of URP job placements." The NAR called upon the UNC to honour its agreement with the NAR made on November 11, 1995 in respect of utilizing the human resources available to the coalition.

A spokesman of the Jamaat al Muslimeen likewise accused the UNC of discriminating against urban areas and of having precipitated the rioting and looting which occurred in downtown Port of Spain, and the shooting and arson which took place in the Morvant/Laventille area in April and May 1996. The Muslimeen Head of Security was of the view that the upheaval in the URP was driven by poverty and a struggle for bread rather than by race or politics. While it was a Caroni vs Laventille issue, it was not so much racism or politics as it was a bread and butter issue. Continued Hassan Anyabwile, who denied that the Jamaat was fuelling the crisis:

> The UNC is making it very difficult for an Indian to ever become Prime Minister in this country again. If the UNC really wanted to win hearts on the East/West Corridor, they would have given the [Laventille] area 29 URP projects to Caroni's 34. (*Mirror,* May 19, 1996)

Similar complaints came from the San Juan/Laventille constituency where there were protest demonstrations. PNM elements there were resentful of the fact that more jobs were being allocated to the El Socorro/Barataria area in which levels of unemployment were said to be lower than in the San Juan area (*Mirror,* July 12, 1996). One angry militant described what was taking place as a "race war" and accused the UNC of "dividing the people":

> All the Blacks have been put to work on the job sites north of the Eastern Main Road, while is only Indians working in the El Socorro and Barataria districts. We want the UNC leadership to know while it is talking national unity, there is only division in San Juan/Barataria. (ibid.)

The UNC however denied that it was discriminating against anyone and claimed that it was seeking to depoliticize and transform the URP into an agency that trains and equips people to find jobs in the private sector. To quote the UNC Minister responsible for the URP programme:

> The aspirations of this Government of national unity is to depoliticise the URP because it has not been so in the past. It cannot be right for it to continue to be a source of political patronage. But this Government of national unity has not breached any agreement with anybody, because the aspiration of this Government of national unity is to be fair to all concerned. (*Guardian,* April 4th, 1996)

Critics were however not convinced, and argued that there was a gap between ideology and reality. Ironically, UNC supporters also complained that they were being dismissed arbitrarily from URP projects in the El Socorro/Barataria Area (*Guardian,* July 24, 1996). Concerned that job allocations to URP projects were a major source of conflict which could be politically costly, the Prime Minister warned MPs to avoid becoming involved in job placements on the Programme (*Guardian,* July 26, 1996).

The policy decision taken by the Government to postpone or cancel development or renewal projects which were earmarked for urban areas and to accord instead a higher priority to rural development also served to arouse anxieties among urban based Afro-Trinidadian development elements. The decision to defer building the National Library complex also generated great anxiety.[8] The planned shift of focus and of resources from urban to rural communities was however predictable.[9] Having regard to all that the Political Leader of the UNC had been saying over the years about discrimination in the allocation of public sector resources and alienation, one would have been surprised if a UNC Government had taken no steps to redress this perceived imbalance. While there was and continues to be a lot of talk about meritocracy, careers open to talent, and equal opportunity, the reality in resource scarce societies like Trinidad and Tobago is that politics becomes clientelised, and resources allocated on the basis of ascriptive as opposed to achievement criteria. Those are facts of the political life, no matter what regime is in power.

The Media Crisis

Perhaps the most significant event which served to define and colour the first 200 days of the new regime was its attack on the *Trinidad Guardian* which served to unnerve elements in the society as well as the financial markets. In the first week of February 1996, the news media carried stories to the effect that the Prime Minister had been waging an undeclared war with the *Trinidad Guardian* which he accused of being unfairly critical of him and the new UNC/NAR Government. Mr. Panday demanded that the *Trinidad Guardian* should dismiss its news editor, Mr. Jones P. Madeira. He also indicated that he would debar the *Guardian's* reporters from attending official functions until this was done.

Panday was particularly upset about a *Guardian* editorial, "Panday Alarum," which called upon him to produce evidence that the Leader of the Opposition had declared at a public meeting that the PNM would "heat up the streets" in an attempt to bring down the UNC Government. According to Mr. Panday:

> I want to put this country on alert that the vibes coming out of the Opposition is an intention to resort to violent demonstrations in order to bring this Government down. I want to warn the PNM leader that he shouldn't start anything he cannot stop; he shouldn't start anything that he cannot control. More importantly, he should not start anything that will divide this country beyond repair.... It is clear that this Opposition does not know how to deal with this Government. It cannot criticize it for its measures. We are doing everything that is right. In order to get back on this side, it seems prepared to resort to violence, violent demonstrations. Not only has the statement come to us in the House today, but I have information that on January 4, 1996, at a meeting at the Malabar Community Centre, the Honourable Leader of the Opposition is reported to have said that there will be heat in this Parliament, and there will be heat in the streets of this country after the honeymoon period of the new Government is over. (*Trinidad Guardian,* January 17, 1996)

In commenting on what it called Mr. Panday's "desperate allegations," the *Guardian* (January 17, 1996) suggested that Mr. Panday should have more regard for the public's intelligence. It noted further that

> The PNM had laid the foundation for the country's democratic system and would therefore not deliberately set out to destroy it by violent means.

The *Guardian* told Panday that Manning and the Member of Parliament for Diego Martin West — the latter had promised to get parents to come out in protest against the Government's decision to cancel plans to build a school in that constituency — were simply doing what he did while in Opposition. Moreover, opined the Guardian, the UNC, both while in Opposition and during the recent election campaign, "was linked to an organization which had attempted a violent overthrow of the Government in 1990, an event whose repercussions are still worrying us today" (*Trinidad Guardian,* January 18, 1996). Mr. Panday was clearly stung by this attempt to link the UNC with the Jamaat al Muslimeen.

Criticism of the *Guardian* was also levelled by Mr. Wade Mark, Chairman of the UNC, and the Minister of Information. According to Mark:

> There is a group in this country bent on subverting the party, the Government, as well as the PM, and they are using everything in their power to achieve their goals. If you look at the Guardian for the month of January, you see there is an effort to promote the Prime Minister as an alcoholic. Every time you see the PM, you see him with a glass in his hands.... There is a subtle attempt at undermining the Prime Minister and the Government. If you have this projection, within a year or two without us responding .... [people] will begin looking at the Prime Minister Basdeo Panday as an alcoholic, and this is not accidental. It is subliminal, psychological. It is warfare

that has been declared by this particular newspaper. (*Trinidad Guardian,* February 5, 1996)

Mr. Mark called upon the UNC's National Executive and the members of the Party

> ... to use every means within their power to defend itself against all predators. The UNC is prepared to take whatever steps necessary to defend its political leader and party against these vicious attacks. (*Trinidad Guardian,* February 5, 1996)

The Government was clearly determined to "police the press," to employ a term used by a minister in an unguarded moment. There was a great deal of speculation as to why the Government chose to engage in this self-destructive conflict with the *Trinidad Guardian* on this matter, knowing that the consequences of so doing would be serious. Clearly, the Government seemed to feel that its protest and planned actions were justified. It may well be that the Government was of the view that having regard to the ownership structure of the established press and the antecedents of those who controlled editorial policy, the UNC, unlike either the PNM or the NAR, would not get fair treatment from the two established media houses, and as such had to intimidate and regulate them in order to get "respect."

The comment made by UNC activist, Mr. Unanan Persad, seemed to reflect UNC thinking on the question of the vexed relationship between the established print media and the Government. Mr. Persad's position was that the UNC was being unfairly criticised for alleged abuses of press freedom, but that the criticisms were a mere mask for a devilish power play which was inspired by the "mongrelised" élite and their surrogates. To quote Mr. Persad:

> It is clear that the centre of gravity of political power has shifted and there are minority sections of the population that cannot bring themselves to accept this fact. They feel that this is only a temporary situation; a limbo, so to speak,

> in their political existence. It is this context and in the spirit of the realignment of the various forces and areas in the community that this power play is unfolding. The subliminal messages are intended to polarise the population in these instances and portray the government as racist and sectional in an attempt to bring it down. This type of journalism is intended to intimidate the legitimate government and put them on the defensive on issue after issue. If no action is taken by the Prime Minister, the irresponsible reporting will continue until the government is put with its back to the wall, at the mercy of its detractor. Now that we have stripped bare the hypocrisy of the surrogates for what they are, and uncovered the virulent bile that they spew for their mongrelised principals, and have shredded their cloak of sanctimony; now that we intend to heighten the level of confrontation with them as well as the contradictions that they suborn and the inequities and duplicity that they proselytise; now that we intend to obtrude their patrons and spotlight them upon the public gaze in their naked viciousness, they have hit the button to eject. But we will catch them and deal with them before they hit the ground. (*Guardian,* February 9, 1996)

Faced with strongly critical reaction from significant sections of the society, the UNC regime seemed anxious to find a face saving formula to retreat. In a meeting with the publishers of three leading newspapers in the region, the Barbados *Nation,* Guyana's *Starbroek News* and the *Trinidad Express,* the Government agreed, after heated argument, to discontinue the boycott of the *Guardian* unconditionally. The publishers, for their part, agreed "to work towards establishment of a mechanism in Trinidad and Tobago within three months to consider complaints by and against the media that was consistent with what exists in other democratic societies" (*Express,* April 12, 1996).

The Attorney General however later denied that the Government had ever agreed to self-regulation, though the records indicate that this did happen. Mr. Maharaj had in fact indicated that it was only if the Government felt that the self-regulatory regime was not working that it would resort to a statutory body with coercive powers (*Express,* April 3, 1996). Mr. Maharaj subsequently held otherwise, and went on to reopen the issue by again alleging that "some owners of the media are promoting division of the society, undermining national unity and destroying national cohesiveness (*Guardian,* March 11, 1996). He further alleged that the "media moguls were hypocrites who had their own agendas and were prepared to pursue them at all costs." Mr. Maharaj indicated that the Government was preparing a "Green Paper" on the issue of press regulation. At time of writing, this had not been done.

While Indians generally seemed to support the Government on the press issue, the other ethnic groups and the Media Association of Trinidad and Tobago (MATT) were suspicious and violently critical. The PNM leadership argued that the media was the first bastion being attacked, and that the Election and Boundaries Commission would follow. The Leader of the Opposition also claimed that the November 6th election might have been the last free contest in the country, and insisted that given the threat, fresh elections should be called immediately (*Express,* April 5, 1996). He also indicated that the government seemed bent on exercising "power for the sake of power" (*Express,* June 22, 1996). The former Prime Minister also indicated that he had reason to believe that the Government had plans to place him under "house arrest," an allegation that most dismissed as being absurd and paranoia driven (cf. my "Media Row Hits Raw Nerve" *Express,* April 14, 1996).

The UNC regime denied all allegations that it was seeking to muzzle the press. In its view, it was only seeking to ensure greater balance and greater fairness in the coverage that was given to government programmes and political personalities. As the Attorney General noted:

> ... the press has a social responsibility, a public duty, because the freedom of the press is not for the benefit of the press; it is for the benefit of the public. We are not seeking to interfere with a media organ's right to support a political party. What we are concerned about is that if there are

> untruths, falsities or if there is unfair treatment of matters, there should be some mechanism to give a right of correction or another view. (*Guardian,* April 4, 1996)

It is however clear that elements within or sympathetic to the UNC were determined to bring the established media, which was viewed as being hostile to the Indian community and its cultural and political ambitions, to heel. They complained that most of the commentators and columnists were not of Indian descent, and that the media neglected groups and events that were outside the East West Corridor, the bastion of "creoledom" (cf. *Express,* April 12, 1996). In the view of one critic, "the national press is a creole vehicle to maintain, protect, and defend the [creole] order of things, the sacred "calypso land", their view of what is national. The media men and women are simply not prepared to tolerate alternative views and perspectives" (*Indian Review,* May 1996: 45).

Having just won political power that had long been denied them, Indians were clearly anxious to retain it, and were prepared to do whatever was necessary prophylactically to achieve that goal. The media helped bring down the NAR and the "new" PNM after just one term, and UNC political strategists were seeking to ensure that this did not happen to the newly elected regime.

Party politics apart, it is clear that the crisis in the media was a by-product of the social revolution that followed in the wake of the election. As Burton Sankerali sagely asserted:

> What we need to recognize is that the media, like politics or carnival, is an arena of ethnic contestation. The media provides a space where these different interests may define themselves. Perhaps the most significant instance of such ethnic contestation in recent times has been the Indian breakthrough in the dominant media. This was achieved largely due to economic power and certainly not because the media elites (in general) like the Indians. The dominant media, therefore, is not a neutral space.

> This brings us to the "politics of definition." Why is it that certain branches of the media — Radio 103, Radio Sangeet, the *Catholic News* — are defined as ethnic or sectional while others are not? More important, who does this defining? I put it to you that every media institution in this country is ethnic-based. Every newspaper, every radio and television station represents the interests of a particular group or groups. In the case of the dominant media, it largely represents the perspectives of the more Eurocentric groupings. Where necessary such interests need to be unmasked.
>
> .... The aftermath of the last general election signified a shift in the balance of power at the level of the society's elites. Following on this, the Indocentric political elite perceptively recognized that it could successfully rough up a basically unsympathetic Eurocentric media elite knowing that the latter would back down, it not having the gumption to escalate the conflict for fear of plunging the country into Indo-Afro civil war. Here we may notice how brilliantly the Prime Minister played the "race card." (*Sunday Express,* April 14, 1996)

Similar observations about ethnic imbalance in the media, at least prior to the seventies, were made by the author (Centre For Ethnic Studies 1995). If the Government's unarticulated plan was to intimidate the press and force it to be more sensitive to the concerns and expectations of the Indian community and the UNC, it is arguable that the UNC had achieved its aim. The short term price was however very high in that the regime attracted a great deal of hostility and suspicion about its agenda. In time, however, the gain to the UNC might exceed the cost paid to achieve greater balance.

The "media crisis" took place amidst a general feeling of insecurity in the country. Indeed, the press "war" which saw 7 editors and several columnists resigning from the *Trinidad Guardian* in protest against what they viewed as attempts by the principal shareholder of that organ to force them to take actions which in their view compromised their own professional judgement, helped to fuel fears that public unrest was likely.[10] So too did staff protest at the State owned ICN television station against the attempt on the part of the newly appointed Chairman to contract a former UNC parliamentarian to become the station's news anchor, commentator on debates in Parliament, and host of the programme, "The Issues Live." The protest succeeded in forcing the cancellation of these plans. Those concerns were aggravated when the Minister of National Security decided to increase security presence around the Parliament and other public buildings because of what he saw as "general public tension in the country." While denying that the tension had anything to do with fears as to what the Jamaat al Muslimeen might do, the Minister noted that he had to react because of the security risk of having all these Cabinet Ministers in one building without an [adequate] security presence (*Guardian,* April 4, 1996).

Tobago

The NAR Political Leader articulated demands for a more favourable deal for Tobago in its quest for greater autonomy. Robinson was of the view that Tobago should be given self-governing status and that the Tobago House of Assembly (THA) should have the constitutional authority to make policy for Tobago. He claimed that their exists an all party agreement in 1978 that Tobago should have self-governing status. That agreement was the ""Bible" for Tobago's Independence." Manning was accused of tearing up that agreement (*Guardian,* October 23, 1995). Robinson has however never been explicit as to what he considers self-government to mean in the context of Trinidad and Tobago.

The PNM's position was that such authority should recognise that Trinidad and Tobago is a unitary rather than a federal state, and that policies defined by the THA should in no way be inconsistent with national policies and as such should be approved by the Cabinet and Parliament of Trinidad and Tobago. The PNM had in fact negotiated an arrangement with the Assembly just prior to the election. That Agreement, which became the subject of intense controversy during the election (it was described as a "meaningless bribe" by Mr. Robinson), provided that the THA should be constitutionally entrenched, that revenues generated and collected in Tobago should be retained there, that the policy making powers of the Assembly should be clearly enunciated, and that there should be better coordination between the THA and the Central Government through the Prime Minister. It also provided that the THA was empowered to make bye-laws for Tobago, but that these bye-laws shall operate "in addition to and not in derogation of any law of the Republic of Trinidad and Tobago. It also provided that such bye-laws should not come into force before the expiration of 30 days after their publication and that they were subject to a negative resolution the national Parliament (Draft Bill, September 30, 1996).

The question of what powers the THA would be given by the UNC/NAR had not yet been determined at time of writing and it remains to be seen what the outcome of such determination would be. One suspects that when the ink is dry, the final settlement would not differ much from what was agreed to by Mr. Manning and the THA.

The Dynamics of the Coalition

There was speculation in the society that the UNC-NAR coalition was in a state of "pre-collapse" (Lloyd Best's term) and that it would not last out the five year term. This view was informed by the fact that the coalition had a mere two seat majority, and as such might not be politically sustainable over time. This pessimism was reinforced by the fact that the coalition included individuals who were part of the NAR regime which had come to political grief in 1987. Much bitterness had followed that coalition, especially between Messrs Panday, Humphrey and Sudama on the one hand, and Mr. ANR Robinson and Mrs. Pamela Nicholson, the two Tobago MPs on the other. The question to be determined was whether the players had learnt from their past "one love" experience, and whether in fact love was in fact going to be sweeter, to use Mr. Panday's phrase, the second time around.

Up to the time of writing, relationships between the two parties seem to be "fluid." Both parties however insist that no new general elections would be held before they were due in the year 2000. The NAR leadership expressed satisfaction with the number of appointments to boards which it had so far received, but there continued to be strong protests at the grass roots level that NARites were being passed over for jobs under the URP. Indeed, some NARites insisted that since the NAR was responsible for the UNC being in power, NARites should receive half the appointments to jobs and offices in the gift of the state. One activist in fact declared that if the Panday Government did not "respect the NAR 100 percent, it would be the shortest government ever" (*Guardian,* March 4, 1994). The UNC was accused of "deceit" and of seeking to put its own people in place to the exclusion of NARites. Worse, they were seeking to create a "Hindu State" surreptitiously, and of showing no gratitude for the role being played by the NAR in the coalition. It was said that the aim of the UNC was to annihilate the NAR by forcing its members to take out UNC cards to get jobs (*Sunday Express,* April 25, 1996). These outbursts led one NAR stalwart to declare that "if the main focus of the party is to fight for jobs, let us fold up the party and go home" (ibid.).

The then Chairman of the NAR, Mr. Robert Mayers, agreed that all was not well with the manner in which the coalition was functioning, and that "structural" problems existed. He indicated that the Agreement between the two coalition partners was not being adhered to by the UNC, especially as it related to the "utilisation of the country's human resources" and the functioning of the new government. Mayers argued that "the stability of the coalition did not depend on the NAR alone," and that the "UNC [had] a greater responsibility to ensure that stability" (*Express,* April 9, 1996). Mr. Panday indicated a willingness to review the unity pact and appointed a team to address those issues that were causing difficulty (*Express,* April 23, 1996).

The Political Leader of the NAR likewise admitted that there were strains in the relationship, but chose not to be articulate about them. A "still tongue keepeth a wise head," he cautioned. Robinson noted further that the NAR "had triumphed in a way that hardly any of us expected." As such, the situation imposed critical responsibilities on the party. To quote him:

> We are now participating in and forming part of the new government. But it is true that the situation in the country and in the government is vastly different from what it was between 1986 and 1991. We are in a dramatically different situation from our first term, so to speak, in office. In addition, coalition governments are not often found in this part of the world. Trinidad and Tobago needed and voted for a coalition government. Trinidad and Tobago, from the point of view of stability and order, needs a coalition government, and the NAR happens to be in a crucial role in respect of that coalition government.
>
> So I want you to understand that you are perhaps in an even more critical role than you were between 1986 and 1991. Certainly the uncertainty is much greater now than it was then. We were confident then that we would survive for the five years. We are confident we will survive for the next five years, but in much more uncertain, much more hazardous circumstances. Consequently, this requires from the NAR and from all those who are participating in the government a degree of thoughtfulness, a degree of commitment, a degree of dedication, and a degree of skill such as has never been required before in government in the history of Trinidad and Tobago. (*Express,* April 12, 1996)

Robinson noted that there were "mischief makers" who did not want the coalition to work, but that he was determined that it would (ibid.). He however urged the UNC and its supporters "to desist from seeking to monopolise power." That way lay disaster (*Express,* April 15, 1996).

All of these issues came to a head during the run up to and the events following the June 24th local government elections.

All three parties needed to perform well in order to vindicate their claims. The PNM Political Leader needed a good showing to vindicate his claims to continued leadership of the party while the party itself needed a victory to prove that its "defeat" in 1995 was an accident and that it was not terminal as some claimed it was. The UNC for its part, wanted a victory to signal that its "arrival" was sustainable and that it was the party of the future. Mr. Panday had in fact asked voters to give the party a "sign" which would tell him "well done, good and faithful servant."

Following the election, supporters of both major parties claimed victory, and praised God for the outcome. Both parties vigorously disputed the claims of the other. The only matter on which there was universal agreement was that the NAR lost comprehensively and that the party's hope that its showing at the polls would allow it to make claims for enhanced status and power within the coalition were completely smashed. The NAR secured a mere 20,698 votes (5.8 per cent of the total cast) in the 34 seats which it contested. While this represented a doubling of the number of votes which it received in November, 1995 the fact is that the party failed to win a single seat.

In seeking to obtain UNC agreement that it be allowed to contest a meaningful number of seats, both within and outside the East/West Corridor, the NAR was clearly hoping to use the "leg up" or "life support" which it felt it had secured by being in the coalition, to rebuild its political muscle in the East/West Corridor and elsewhere to a point where it would one day be able to challenge both the UNC and the PNM for national dominance. NAR activists, who were hoping to ride on the backs of the UNC, were thus deeply disappointed that the latter did not allow their party to contest winnable seats, relegating it instead to districts in urban Trinidad where the PNM was still supreme. As one activist complained, "Panday has kept all in Central and is fighting us tooth and nail for the East/West Corridor" (*Express,* June 6, 1996).

The NAR was clearly unhappy with the manner in which its coalition partner had treated it in the negotiations over seats, and there was many an angry voice calling upon the party to go it alone or even change the party with which it was allied in government rather than "sell out" to the UNC. During the campaign, NAR leaders often declared that the NAR was the only authentic bearer of the flagship of national unity and political decentralisation, and that all other versions were counterfeit. Robinson had in fact blasted PNM and UNC politicians alike for being political chameleons. As he declared:

> You will hear all of them [the politicians] trying to mouth and give lip service to the principles of the NAR. Everybody talking unity today.... Everybody talking [about giving] people power... decentralisation, devolution. [But] that is what the NAR was founded on. When Robinson was asking for that for Tobago, his throat was to be cut. (*Guardian*, June 5, 1996)

Robinson called upon NAR supporters to "watch politicians carefully; [watch] how people can change their positions from government to opposition and opposition to government. You can never predict what they will say... As time goes on, it is going to tell more and more that it is the NAR that stands for principles that will save this country from chaos and destruction" (*Guardian*, June 5, 1996).

The NAR was hopeful that it would have been able to capitalise on the mood of disenchantment which prevailed among Afro-Trinidadians in the East/West Corridor and that it would win a few seats here and there. As one of its platform speakers put it:

> ...it is wrong to say that the NAR is dead in Trinidad and only alive in Tobago. There are people all over Trinidad who are just awaiting the call to rally behind the NAR. The NAR has to take control of the East/West Corridor for starters. That is where the new foundation of the party would be laid. (*Independent*, June 7, 1996).

The election results showed that the NAR remained a politica corpse in Trinidad.

The UNC, for its part, was clearly anxious to gain a foothold in the Corridor and was not prepared to cede all these areas to the NAR. Some UNC activists were known to be secretly hoping that the NAR would be routed by the PNM, and one assumes they were happy that the NAR was politically mauled The NAR complained bitterly that the UNC did not support it or the ground as it had done in terms of the UNC, and alleged that its partner had in fact campaigned against its candidates in some constituencies. The NAR specifically claimed that the UNC's support of two independent candidates (who were pro-UNC) in the Arima Corporation caused the party to lose those seats (*Express,* July 2, 1996).

Following the elections, the National Executive of the NAR indicated that it proposed to re-examine its relationship with the UNC. One of the options for the party was a complete merger with the UNC. Prior to the June 24th election, the party's new Chairman, Anthony Smart, hinted that it should in fact do so. According to Mr. Smart:

> In 1986 we came together. In 1988, for one reason or the other, we separated. We have learnt from our mistakes and as we seek to come together again, as we say in the (coalition) agreement to broaden and deepen the process of unity, we will tread carefully, cementing and building block by block so that when we are one again, we will stay together till the end of time. That is what we are seeking to do. When we are one again, we will stay together 'til the end of time. (*Express,* June 14, 1996)

Some NAR supporters were however strongly opposed to this course of action, and in fact believe that the NAR was being hurt by its relationship with the UNC. Some of these individuals were of the view that the party should consider a link with the PNM in order to stop a UNC, which, to use Lloyd Best's phrase, was becoming "rampant." In Best's view, one had to stop the political pendulum from swinging too far in the direction of the UNC.[11] Mr. Manning in fact invited prodigal NARites to come back home to their "father's house" in the PNM (*Express,* June 14, 1996). In reality, however, most of NAR's supporters had already gone either to the UNC (these are Indians in the main) or to the PNM, leaving only few who considered it impossible to associate with either. This element believes that the party should retain its organisational integrity and continue standing for the principles which it espoused while playing a balancing role in the political system. Some would even have welcomed a NAR withdrawal from the coalition arrangement in order to allow for the more effective performance of that role.

Typical of this point of view was Lincoln Myers, one of the founders of the NAR, and a former Minister in the NAR regime. Myers was extremely critical of the relationships which developed between the coalition partners. He was also quite disenchanted with ANR Robinson whom he believed had abdicated his responsibility to lead the NAR as a Trinidad as well as a Tobago party. Myers indicated that he was among those who supported the move to enter into a coalition with the UNC in November:

> That community's political moment had come, and it ought not to have been deprived of the opportunity of being in government. [But] it is clear to me that if there is to be any meaningful level of resurgence on the part of the NAR, there has to be distance put between itself and the UNC. (*Independent,* July 15, 1996)

Myers was in fact of the firm view that the "aim of the UNC was to exterminate the NAR from the politics of Trinidad." Everything they have done since November points in that direction.

Commenting specifically on the UNC's attitude towards the allocation seats for the local government elections, Myers felt that the UNC was never interested in sharing any seats with its coalition partner. The UNC "was literally dragging the NAR down to Nomination Day. That was perhaps sound tactics on the part of the UNC if it was engaging an adversary." But the two parties were partners. If the UNC had any genuine regard for its political ally and in the concept of national unity, "then the NAR ought to have been represented throughout the country. If the UNC believes that the NAR is important to the coalition, then it ought not to have posed any difficulty in ensuring that at least one seat in each of the regions, at least one winnable seat, would go to the NAR." (*Independent,* July 12, 1996). Instead, UNC's actions in some electoral districts caused the NAR to lose. Myers also felt that a joint UNC/NAR motorcade in Diego Martin on the eve of the election had the negative effect of galvanizing PNM voters to the detriment of the NAR. The evidence however indicates that the motorcade had no such effect.

Like Myers, ANR Robinson was also disturbed by the UNC's electoral tactics which he said constituted a "disturbing development for the relations between the two parties." Robinson was concerned that there were independents appearing with the perception on the part of people that they were being supported by the UNC" (*Express,* July 10, 1996). Myers, Robinson and others in the NAR had now come to appreciate that the UNC considered the coalition arrangement to be a transitional one, and that its aim was to secure complete paramountcy if it was able to do so. The party has in fact decided that it will maintain its independence and organisational integrity and not rely on the UNC or join with the PNM. It likewise declared that though two of its members now support that party in the government "the NAR as a party is not part of the Government. All we have are two of our members who serve in Government" (*Guardian,* August 2, 1996).

Turning next to the question of which of the two major parties won, the local government election, the PNM's claim was that it won 63 of the 124 seats and controlled 7 of the 13 corporations where there was a clear result, and had achieved a tie in the remaining corporation. Clutching at straws, the party claimed that 63 seats and control of 7 corporations meant that they had "won" the referendum and that the UNC had not been able to drive the party into "permanent exile" as it had boasted it would. The Balisier remained fresh rather than "withered," as the UNC had hoped it would become.

. The UNC, for its part, argued that it had not only retained control of the four corporations over which it had control prior to the election, but had wrested control of two others from the PNM, and also shared the honours in a third which was previously controlled by the PNM. Moreover, whereas they had only won 41 seats in the previous local government election, they had now won 61. What was more telling in the UNC's view was the fact that the UNC won 178,800 votes compared to the 154,307 won by the PNM — 24,493 more — even though the UNC only contested 91 seats whereas the PNM contested all 124. If one assumes that the pockets of UNC supporters in areas not contested by that Party supported the NAR, then the UNC total might in fact be somewhat higher. Then too, if one were to add the votes secured by the NAR to that of the UNC, it would be seen that the two coalition partners had secured 199,498 votes, which was 45, 191 votes more than the PNM. If the election was indeed a referendum which would either register a vote of confidence in the UNC or indicate that the population agreed with the PNM that "enough was enough," then the only conclusion that could be drawn was that the UNC had won. The UNC's claim that it had asked the electorate for a pat on the back for a job well done so far and that it had received a "big hug" seemed to have some validity.

It is true that there were major boundary changes in 8 of the regional corporations, many of which, on the face of it, were not in favour of the PNM. There were also 15 fewer seats in 1996 than there were in 1992. One is therefore comparing grapes and apples when one attempts to make a one to one comparison between the two results. While these might help to explain why the PNM lost certain seats and control of a number of corporations, the brute fact of the matter is that the votes of the UNC separately and the coalition collectively exceeded that of the PNM. What this indicates is that the PNM was in greater trouble than it cared to acknowledge publicly.

It could be argued that the PNM had suffered a major trauma just 7 months ago, and that its leadership was still in shambles and in the process of being rebuilt. From this perspective it could be argued that the PNM did well to hold on to seven corporations and to increase its vote from the 149, 363 votes which it received in the 1992 local government elections when it was in power to the 154,307 which it received in June 1996. The UNC on other hand was in power, had access to seemingly unlimited supplies of public and private money and what money could buy politically. The Party was on a "roll" and should arguably have done much better than it did and the PNM worse.

Following the elections, the question arose as to whether the UNC had made any significant "breakthroughs" in areas which were once held by the PNM. By "breakthroughs," one understands that the UNC would have won in areas where Afro-Trinidadians and mixed elements predominated with the reverse being the case in areas in which Indo-Trinidadians predominated. The UNC claims that it did make significant "breakthroughs" in the November 6th election, and did even better on June 24th. Mr. Panday also became verbally inebriated when the results of the elections became known. He talked about the impending success of the plan to encircle the PNM with a pincer movement directed from the East and the South which would eventually drive the PNM into the Gulf of Paria and the Atlantic Ocean to rendezvous with its founder, Dr. Eric Williams.

The Chairman of the UNC was likewise of the view that the party had broached the walls of creoledom though he admitted that despite its scientific planning, the UNC's election day machinery had shown certain weaknesses. These he ascribed to "complacency" and "human error." Had these not occurred, the UNC would have made greater inroads into the urban areas. He nevertheless felt that the UNC had gained ground in such areas and that "no one looking realistically at the voting could say things remain the same. We have gone ahead of the PNM... We made inroads in PNM controlled councils from the east and in the south." These gains were made even though the party had to fight against great odds. To quote Mark:

> ...we have had to fight against several odds: one being the fact that this coalition is a new political entity led by an Indo-Trinidadian PM, a situation which has understandably sent the counry into culture shock. We've had to weather the attack and the spreading of racial tension by the PNM — every action by Government is interpreted by them as being based on race — we've had to cope with the so-called "media war," plus criticism by detractors. Despite all that, the UNC has performed well. (*Guardian,* June 30, 1996)

The election data do not however support the extravagant conclusions drawn by the UNC. There was little evidence of any meaningful breakthrough. It might in fact be more accurate to talk about "trickle through." The evidence indicates that voting behaviour on June 24th was remarkably similar to that of November 6th. Anxious to complete the journey began in 1845, and convinced that they were supporting winners rather than losers for a change, Indo-Trinidadians turned out to vote in large numbers. The turn out rates for Indo-Trinidadians averaged 67 per cent while that for Afro-Trinidadians averaged 36 per cent. Actual rates in some electoral districts were considerably less. Given this, the UNC was able to win in districts where Indo-Trinidadians were in a minority. Normally, these seats would have been won by the PNM.

Sated with formal political power which they held for 35 years, and seeing little forthcoming from its possession, Afro-Trinidadians, particularly those in the cities and the western peninsula, were disenchanted, and stayed away from the voting booths in large numbers. The fear that they would lose what little they had proved insufficient to rouse them from their lethargy.

What the data in fact suggest is a massive withdrawal of affect rather than political apostasy which is implied in claims about breakthrough (For details, cf. my "Little Evidence of UNC Breakthrough," *Sunday Express,* July 7, 1996). As Lloyd Best also observes:

> The lead story is clearly the greater enthusiasm which is evident in the UNC catchment. It is underpinned by the 73.6 per cent increase registered for the party in the 1996 vote when compared with 1992 and with a corresponding figure of only 3.3 per cent for the PNM. The participation rate of 43.9 per cent makes this the highest ever for a local election — the first over the 40 per cent benchmark. The breakdown shows that the five corporations which had participation rates just equal to or below the average were all won by the PNM. Of the five that approached 50 per cent or were above it, four were won by the UNC.
>
> It is this factor of UNC ascendance and PNM stasis which has to be carefully placed in the scales of history. It is the dynamic currently at work in Tunapuna, San Fernando West and Toco-Manzanilla (Sangre Grande). It reflects the pincer movement to which Mr. Panday referred in his address. The UNC has already laid siege to the once impregnable citadel along the East-West Corridor. The aim is to drive PNM right back into the Gulf. (*Sunday Express,* June 30, 1996)

Following the elections, PNM supporters again raised questions as to whether their party could re-engineer itself under Mr. Manning's leadership, or whether a fundamental restructuring of the leadership is called for. They were aware that while in a head to head political confrontation with the UNC in a general election, the bulk of the PNM core would probably hold as it did in November 1995 and June of 1996, any party which hoped to win a clear majority in the year 2000 had to depend on more than its core to break the gridlock that has put the country's electoral system in thrall. As recent elections in Quebec, Israel, India, Spain and elsewhere have shown, minorities which are detached from the major voting blocs could make the critical difference in an election. As one Indian politician opined in the context of India where the Congress Party was recently defeated, "the age of coalition politics has begun." The same is likely to be the case for some time to come in Trinidad and Tobago. Given this, both parties need to look for leaders who could retain the loyalty of their core support, but who could also appeal to minority parties or those who are detached from homeland and tribe.

Findings of Local Government Elections Survey Conducted by Vishnu Bisram in mid-June 1996 n = 710 Adults

- The PNM was the choice of 43 per cent of the sample, the UNC 45 per cent, and the NAR 3 per cent. Nine per cent were undecided.

- The UNC-NAR coalition was approved by 88 per cent of the Indo-Trinidadians in the sample, by 38 per cent of the Afro-Trinidadians, and by 46 per cent of the Mixed and other group.

- The UNC-NAR coalition was disapproved by 3 per cent of the Indo-Trinidadians, 50 per cent of the Afro-Trinidadians, and 15 per cent of the mixed and other groups. The approval/disapproval ratings for Minister Panday were roughly the same.

- Eighty-seven per cent of the Indo-Trinidadians interviewed disagreed with Opposition Leader Patrick Manning that the UNC-NAR Government was discriminating against Afro-Trindiadians compared to fifty-one per cent of the Afro-Trinidadians who disagreed. Thirty-three per cent of the latter agreed while 16 per cent were unsure.

- Eighty-four per cent of the Indo-Trinidadians said they would vote for the UNC while 82 per cent of the Afro-Trinidadians said they would vote for the PNM.

- Eight per cent of the Afro-Trinidadians said they would vote for the UNC while 7 per cent of the Indo-Trinidadians said they would vote for the PNM.

- Less than 2 per cent of the Baptists said they would support the UNC.

- Few Hindus or Muslims said they would vote for the PNM. (cf. *Asia Online,* July 1-7, 1996)

End Notes

[1]The chiefly title, Igbaro, was given to Robinson by the Yoruba Chief the Oooni of Ife, Nigeria, in 1991. Robinson replied to Cro Cro's charge that as an African, he had betrayed blacks when he chose to "marry" Panday, and that Tobagonians had "looked for dat" when they supported that NAR instead of the PNM. Robinson argued that in "matters of state" it was always his goal to act on the basis of principle rather than on race (*Express,* February 24, 1996).

[2]Cf. Kamal Persad in the *Indian Review,* May 1995; May 1996. Persad, H.P. Singh and others in this organisation have been known to express some extreme views on the issue of an Indian homeland in the Americas.

[3]Mr. Manning accused Mr. Robinson of acting out of spite in his dealings with the PNM and Trinidad. To quote Manning: "It may well be that the people of Trinidad are being victimised for the way they voted in 1991 when he was given no seat in Trinidad. We have always known it; vindictiveness and spite stare us in the face again.... That coalition is in power today because of the actions of the Minister Extraordinaire. All things that you feel could be brought to an end in this country could easily be brought to an end if the honourable gentleman acts responsibly; but vindictiveness is the order of the day" (*Express,* June 15, 1996).

[4]To quote Panday further: "Trinidad and Tobago is the most difficult land to rule because of its highly plural nature. This, however was not the problem. In Trinidad people are forced to live in conditions where we cannot avoid one another. We are forced to interface with each other every day, whether we like it

or not." This, he said was "nobody's fault" but the result of the country's history. No matter how we have tried to paper over the cracks over the years, it takes situations like this election and the result of this election to expose the cracks for what they really are. That kind of division and divisiveness in our society, have been, in my humble view, the singular most debilitating factor in this society. It has been the underlying cause of all our problems" (*Express,* December 4, 1995).

[5]Poet/artist LeRoi Clarke spoke for many aggrieved Afro-Trinidadians when he suggested that he would only be comfortable with a government that was composed of politicians of African descent because the latter tended to be "fair." Accused of being "racist." Clarke argued that he could not be "racist" since the African race was "dismantled." Clarke argued that Africans did not recognise themselves as Africans and were beaten into the role of being accommodationists who sought to please everyone but their own. Indians however demanded and got from a government perceived as Black more than they asked for. It was however possible, Clarke opined, that with an "Indian government in power, Indians would now find it uncomfortable to fancy their own race" (*Mirror,* December 8, 1995).

[6]The Jamaat was aware that a large segment of the population was hostile to it and that such hostility would make it difficult for the UNC to embrace it. One week following the election, the Jamaat, in a full page paid advertisement, sought to appease those elements. The statement was full of praise for Mr. ANR Robinson whose "cultured upbringing," "high level of statesmanship and nationalism" and whose international reputation they recognized and acknowledged. Bakr openly apologised to Mr. Robinson and his family:

> The time had come to shed the events of the past. We acknowledge the pain experienced over the past five years, and hope that we can work together, following the example of Mr. DeKlerk and President Nelson Mandela, between whom much more blood was shed.

The statement also appealed to the business community to be charitable to the poor. Businessmen were told that they had the Jamaat's support "in recognition of your role in the creation of jobs and wealth." Appeals for support for the new government also went out to the Christian leadership, civil servants and to the PNM as well. The latter were asked to join the UNC in creating a government of national unity. The Jamaat likewise took the opportunity to thank all those residents of the East West Corridor, San Fernando and Ortoire/Mayaro who listened to what they said during the campaign and whom they claim helped to determine the outcome of the election in the marginal seats. The African element in the community were also urged to "embrace their Asiatic brothers and sisters of India" and to resist the attempts of those who seek to promote disunity and conflict or frustrate the goal of creating national unity. (*Sunday Mirror,* November 12, 1995).

The statement also came close to making an apology for the events of June 1990. To quote Bakr, "to those whom we have offended, we simply ask you to understand the circumstances of the day, and to join with us in bringing into reality the words of our National Anthem, "every creed and race find our equal place." All of this was clearly done in the hope that the public would not hobble the UNC when it sought to deal with the compensation issue.

The "honeymoon" between the Jamaat and Robinson did not last long, however. In response to the latter's appeal to have July 27, 1990 recognized as an important day in the history of the country, Bakr replied that it was already so recognized. According to Bakr, "for people like Robinson, July 27, 1990 is a "nemesis." Anytime they plan to oppress poor people, they remember July 27." Bakr claims he was an "instrument of God" in 1990. "Whatever God use me for, he done use me.... One thing they will never do again is put the police and army on people's land again. They can't do [any] more wickedness to poor people again. I will rise up again. That's my nature." The Jamaat's Head of Security, Hassan Anyabile denied that Robinson was treated worse than another hostage. He was treated under the circumstances of war. For that's what it was. War! (*Sunday Mirror,* July 14, 1996).

One of the reasons why Bakr *et al* find it difficult to apologise for what they did had to do with the nature of the religious ideology which they espouse. As far as they were concerned in 1990, they had embarked a "jihad," a religious war against the "kuffir state" which, in their view, was determined to oppress and crush them. The aim of the oppression was genocidal; the target group was the African Muslim community. In their view, there was a "mortal threat" to their existence and they were thus forced to act in self defense, which their "law" and their religion enjoined them to do.

Bilaal Abdullah in fact argued that all major religions recognised the concept of "just war." The Bible, he says, recognizes that "there is a time for peace and a time for war." Muslims also recognize that one has to fight against evil. According to Bilaal, "Allah instructs us in the Quaran to neither oppress others, nor to allow ourselves to be oppressed. The fight of good against evil, which is waged perpetually on the spiritual plane, sometimes requires a physical manifestation." Hinduism too is clear on this point, argues Bilaal. "The Gita speaks of Krishna urging Arjun to do his moral duty at the Battle of Kuruksetra." (*Mirror,* August 11, 1991).

Given their belief in that what they did was justified, the Muslimee have found it difficult to apologise, even though they have expressed regret for whatever collateral damage their actions caused to innocents. To quote Bilaal, "unless I change my understanding of the mortal threat that I felt that I and others was under, it is difficult to talk about apologizing for what, in my mind, was self defence." The point being made here is that this group of Muslims believes that there is one law for true believers and one for "kuffirs." As Hasan Anyabile put it while commenting on the state's refusal to compensate them in spite of what the Court had enjoined, "we are following our laws. They are breaking their own again (*Mirror,* July 14, 1996).

Bakr, who described the Jamaat as "king makers" warned the UNC that problems could arise if compensation was not paid. As he said on the sixth anniversary of the attempted coup, "we have been victorious over all our enemies to date. The NAR lost all its seats in 1991 and the PNM lost in 1995. If the [UNC] kick up and become our enemy, they [will] lose too" (*Sunday Guardian,* July 28, 1996).

[7]The UNC assault on the black CEO's (many of whom headed profit making firms) was a major talking point during the June 24th local government election. The PNM and its supporters used the issue to heighten concerns that the Afro-Trinidadian was in mortal danger from a party which was bent on ethnic paramountcy. The UNC, for its part, claimed that the PNM stalwarts (fat cats) were using their office to enrich themselves. "There is proof that as poor people continued to "suck salt," the PNM big boys were living like lords off the "fat of the land" (*Express,* June 18, 1996).

[8]The Minister of Culture, Senator Daphne Phillips, accused the PNM of having built community centres mainly in areas in which it perceived it had political support (*Express,* January 26, 1995). The former Minister of Works, Mr. Colm Imbert was however critical of the UNC's shift of focus. He noted, *inter alia,* that the UNC had given the impression that the cancelled projects required an expenditure of $400m in 1996 when in fact construction was to be staggered over a 5-year period. Only $65m was to be spent in 1996. The UNC was accused of seeking to "systematically remove important projects in geographic areas represented by PNM members of Parliament" (*Sunday Express,* January 28, 1996).

The UNC Minister of Planning counter-claimed that the projects were being postponed in order to mobilise funds to repay a "large debt" early next year (*Express,* March 4, 1996). This was not what was said earlier, however.

[9]The PNM charged that the UNC government had decreased allocations to PNM controlled local government bodies and had increased transfers to UNC controlled bodies (*Guardian,* June 21, 1996). Mr. Kamaluddin Mohammed, a former PNM Minister, had no problem with the shift of resources. He noted that the PNM did the same. "Race was however not the criterion. Given the fact of scarcity, choices had to be made." The PNM allocated resources to areas where they got votes or hoped to obtain them" (*Express,* June 16, 1966).

[10]The editors reported that they were told to discontinue a column written by former MP for Chaguanas Hulsie Bhaggan who was a thorn in the flesh of Messrs Panday and Maharaj. They also claim that they were told to stop publishing material on the Jamaat al Muslimeen on the ground that the group was threatening the principal shareholder. They also were unhappy at being asked to submit copy and headlines to the Company's chairman for vetting.

The editors indicated that they were unaware that they were supposed to be operating within 1987 policy guidelines which required them to be cognisant of the fact that the *Guardian* was a member of a conglomerate group, and that the interests of the group were to be considered in determining editorial postures. This policy was said to have been superseded by one approved by the Board in 1992. The 1987 policy statement read as follows:

> The Guardian must maintain its independence without forgetting the fact that it was part of a conglomerate; that it should not be politically aligned; that its perspectives on issues should at all times be balanced and objective; and, that such tensions as might arise between a free press and the government in power should not result in adversarial postures by the paper. (cited in *Express,* April 3, 1996)

[11]Best's election night comment drew angry responses from Indians in general and the Attorney General in particular. It was said that he felt this way because he was "African" and the African party lost. Best's recommendation that the NAR should reconsider its arrangement with the UNC was one that did not sit well with most Indians. As one commented:

> In the autumn of his years, he chooses to put the entire country against the UNC and its supporters of all races. Doesn't Mr. Best see Caroni, Port of Spain, Enterprise, Princes Town as equal parts of Trinidad, and Indians Africans, Syrians, Chinese, Whites, French Creoles and people of mixed parentage as equally respectable citizens of Trinidad? Does he still look at the Indians of this country as aliens and people not deserving of political power in this country? Why must he, as a senior citizen, make such ludicrous and disparaging statements which insult the intelligence of more than half the population? (*Guardian,* July 3, 1996)

Best had welcomed the coming to power of the UNC, but had seemingly become disenchanted with that party (cf. "His Two Coalition Parties of Parties," *Sunday Express,* July 14, 1996).

Chapter 15

The Paths Ahead: Towards a *Dougla* Republic

This book, which, in a sense is a work still in progress, has sought to identify and analyse the various strategies which the Indian diaspora in Trinidad and Tobago employed over the past 150 years to come to terms with, as well as transform their economic, social and political environment. It was a struggle that had its parallels in Guyana, Suriname, Fiji, Mauritius, as well as in other sugar plantation economies in the Caribbean and South Asia. It was a struggle waged against great odds, given the fact that the immigrants were part of a culture which was not seen as valid or legitimate, either by the host societies, by those who preceded them as was the case in the Caribbean, or in the eyes of the Eurocentric colonizing powers which controlled those societies. The Indians were regarded as strangers and pariahs who were expected to remain behind the "walls" of the society, both visible and invisible, that were erected to segregate those who "belonged" from those who did not.

In the context of Trinidad and Tobago, the study used a broad brush to sketch the various pathways which the Indians trod in their efforts to broach the barricades of economic, social and political power, and the obstacles which they had to overcome in order to achieve the goal of full social incorporation, and the hurdles which remain to be forded as they now strive for hegemony and paramountcy. While the society has been forced to come to terms with the economic and political powershift that has taken place in the society, it is clear that the Indian presence is still not seen as being either natural or "national."

Indians are aware of this, and resent being characterized as being less than national. Resentment is usually forthcoming when expressions such as "Indian Cabinet," "Indian Power" or "Indian Government" are used to describe the new UNC-NAR regime. Anger is also expressed when commentators talk about "the Indianizing of the Government," an "Indian Grab for Power" or the "ethnicizing of the media." As far as Indians are concerned, they are as national as is any other group. They are merely Trinidadians who happen to be of Indian descent. In their view, it is no longer true to say that they are "outside the nation's behavioural mainstream." As one commentator asked plaintively, "who" and "what" constitutes "national" in the country? Must a Prime Minister who is Indo-Trinidadian always be called "Indian" and cannot be "national"? What makes the present regime Indian? (*Express,* June 20, 1996).

The new coalition regime insists on being called a "government of national unity." This characterization is not only meant to defuse hostility on the part of groups who believe they have been displaced, but also to reflect the fact that the government is a formal coalition between two parties, the UNC and the NAR, and that the Cabinet includes persons who are Hindus, Christians, Muslims, Afro-Trinidadians, Indo-Trinidadians, Euro-Trinidadians, Sino-Trinidadians and persons with other constructed identities. The constant repetition of this national unity *mantra* also reflects Basdeo Panday's belief that a purely Indian party cannot win or sustain power in Trinidad and Tobago today any more than could an Afro-Trinidadian party. In his view, that was the weakness of the DLP, and now the PNM. As Panday himself puts it:

> They are telling the people that this UNC government is only developing Caroni, that it moved all the money from Port of Spain and [is carrying] it to Caroni, and that they are only firing black people who are CEOs.... I want to tell you that the moment a leader decides to resort to race in

> politics, that is the day he has given up any hope of forming the Government. All he is doing is fighting for his political life. Because of the demographics, no political party could form the government unless it appealed to all races. (*Express,* June 6, 1996)[1]

It is for this reason that Panday has also sought to make highly publicized thrusts into Laventille, Sea Lots and the Beetham Estate, areas which are heavily peopled by the black underclass. Laventille is in fact a metaphor for the underprivileged areas of Afro-Trinidad. Gaining influence in Laventille is thus symbolically important to the UNC. Doing so not only humiliates the PNM whose alleged neglect of the area is highlighted; it also sends a signal to the national community that the Government is concerned not only with Caroni and the "plantation," but with Laventille and the "port" as well. In Panday's view, it is not a case of the "port" vs. the "plantation," but "port" and "plantation."

So far, much of the rhetoric about national unity is a "mere fig leaf" which belies the reality of what is being done by those in charge of the State apparatus. While Panday, populist par excellence, revels in rhetoric about the need for ethnic ecumenism, his parliamentary team and appointees on public sector boards etc., are quietly putting in place the scaffolding for the edifices of ethnic paramountcy that are being constructed. Nizam Mohammed, once a colleague of Panday in the ULF, was sensitive to this when he told the UNC that there was a gap between rhetoric and behaviour:

> We want true national unity, not mere political rhetoric; you talk about national unity on the one hand and do something else on the other and leave poor people wondering what the hell is going on in Trinidad and Tobago. We want true and meaningful unity. We want honesty [and] sincerity and a tangible demonstration of national unity by those who are in a position to demonstrate and lead the way. (*Express,* June 10, 1996)

The PNM too has accused the UNC of talking about national unity while pursuing policies which divide the nation. During the campaign for the June 24th Local Government election, the Leader of the Opposition in fact opined, perhaps with some exaggeration, that "race relations could never be worse that what it is in Trinidad and Tobago today." Manning called upon the population to stop it by their vote on June 24th (*Guardian,* June 21, 1996).

By way of reply, Indians argue that when Indians were being excluded from the corridors of political power, there were no anguished cries for power sharing, or talk about the need for a national unity government. No-one said that the pendulum had swung too far in the direction of the Afro-Trinidadian community. The PNM's response to this accusation is that it always sought to achieve the goal of racial unity and balance in everything it did, and that under PNM governments, Indians did as well or better than other groups. Indian achievement in education, and the fact that little poverty exists in Caroni, are cited as evidence of this, as is the fact that most of the towns along the East West Corridor and in South and Central Trinidad are dominated by businesses owned by Indians.[2] While the state might have been formally dominated by an Afro-Trinidadian élite, resource allocation did not favour that group. Indeed, the PNM believes that Whites, Chinese, Syrians and Indo-Trinidadians got more from the public trough in terms of contracts than did Afro-Trinidadians.

This view is not shared by Indians, especially where jobs in the public sector are concerned.[3] In the view of the PNM, however, it is pure myth that PNM power, when deconstructed, meant Afro-Trinidadian power. The symbolic capital which the latter possessed was not converted into significant economic capital (Ryan and Stewart 1994; Ryan and Barclay 1992; Ryan and La Guerre 1993).

The UNC's performance in other areas has had mixed reviews. During the local government campaign, the new Government made extravagant claims as to what it had achieved during the first 6 months of its existence. It in fact claimed it had done more in 6 months than the PNM had in 4 years. Chief among the achievements claimed was political and economic stability. According to the UNC:

> The Government, coming into office in the manner and against the background that it did, had as its first objective, the monumental task of holding the society together. It was the first time in the political history of Trinidad and Tobago that a labor leader had assumed the office of Prime Minister. It was not unreasonable, therefore, to expect that the business community would have apprehensions. It was also the first time that a citizen of Indian descent, an Indo-Trinidadian, had become Prime Minister, and it was understandable that there would be some degree of uncertainty about the future.
>
> It was in this context that the Government, and the Prime Minister in particular, had to spend a considerable amount of time and effort to dispel the fears and misgivings of those sectors of the society that were afraid of change. It was critical that whatever doubts and fears the business community may have had, would have to be dispelled as quickly as possible. Failure to deal with these doubts swiftly would have meant capital flight pressure on the value of the dollar and therefore, instability of the exchange rage and consequently, high inflation and a drop in the standard of living. The new UNC administration had to move swiftly to ensure stability.... We did! (*Unity Across T and T* 1996)

The pamphlet went on to list 36 achievements, many of which, like the "reconvening of Parliament by November 1995" were extremely trivial and routine. Many others were policies which were already in the pipeline; the UNC was simply seeing them through the policy making chain.

There were however a few initiatives which were policy products of the new regime. Among the more significant were the following:

- Lowering of personal income tax on individuals from 38% to 35%
- No Income tax for persons earning $20,000 or less
- Lowering of corporation tax from 38% to 35%
- Removal of VAT on a number of basic food items
- Raising the threshold for small business for the purpose of VAT registration to $150,000
- Reduction of the business levy from 0.5% to 0.4% and its complete removal for business with a turnover of $150,000 or less
- Allocation of $90 million to begin settlement of the debt owed to Public Servants
- Over 1,000 daily paid workers were made permanent in Boroughs and Regional Corporations
- Representatives of the Labor Movement were once more placed on State Boards
- The establishment of a National Tripartite Commission comprising Labor, Business and Government to find consensus on national economic issues
- Entering into 2 treaties and 1 legal assistance agreement with the United States covering extradition of persons charged with drug and other criminal offences, drug interdiction at sea, and legal co-operation in the apprehension of criminals.

The new regime sought to project itself as "people friendly," one that was concerned with the poor and the oppressed. The regime was however locked into a number of macro-economic policies and conditionalities dictated by international lending agencies which served to narrow its scope for manoeuverability. While it sought to nibble at the margins, it found it necessary to leave unchanged most of the basic policies which the PNM had put in place to get Trinidad and Tobago "NAFTA ready" and attractive to foreign investment. These included trade liberalization, divestment, and public sector downsizing, with all this meant in terms of the loss of jobs in the manufacturing and agricultural sectors, which now had to compete on a "level playing field" with imports from the North and elsewhere.

The new regime was strongly criticised by the trade union movement during the festivities held to mark Labour Day in June 1996 (at which the Prime Minister was present). It was also sharply criticised by the National Trade Union Congress (NATUC) which claimed that nothing of significance had really changed for the better in terms of workers since the new regime came to power. As NATUC complained, the UNC/NAR government had continued with all the privatisation arrangements put in place by its predecessor which it had savagely criticised during the November campaign, policies which had led to the casualisation of the work force, the loss of jobs and the hypothecation of the national patrimony. Continued NATUC:

> And how has the UNC Government dealt with various issues affecting workers (e.g. teachers), the unemployed (URP) and the self-employed (maxi-taxis)? Have they not demonstrated the same arrogance (and ignorance of the root causes of the problems) as previous regimes? We recall, for instance the statements by the Prime Minister himself and by the Minister of Public Administration to the effect that the (same wicked, anti-worker) IRA would be used by the Government as employer to discipline teachers. The URP, despite protestations by the government to the contrary, remains a political football. And the maxi-taxi drivers/owners problems were handled in the typical

bureaucratic style. (*Express,* June 8, 1996 and April 24 1996)

By way of defence, the regime claimed that it had only been in power for 6 months and needed more time to do the things which it wished to. One notes, however that it was the UNC leadership which had boasted in June that the country was now better governed than it had ever been, that there was nothing of which one could be critical, and that contrary to what happened with respect to the Robinson and Manning regimes, the country had since witnessed "real change" and not "mere exchange."

One issue which was being heatedly debated nationally following the November and June elections concerned the fate of the PNM. Was the PNM in temporary eclipse or was its decline terminal? If the decline was terminal, was it linked to the fact that it was led by Patrick Manning whom many regarded as an albatross around the party's neck? Manning was clearly politically disliked by the bulk of the Indian community. It was also evident that he was not respected by many of the gentrified élites in the Afro-Trinidadian community. A survey conducted by the author in January 1996 however indicated that Mr. Manning still had majority support among Afro-Trinidadians. The bulk of that support, such as it was, came from the grassroots of that community, especially from among older Afro-Trinidadian women (see Annexe 15). One however wonders whether the findings of that survey remained relevant following the local government elections given that that the PNM showed no encouraging signs of recovery. Indeed, the demand that the Political Leader of the PNM should give way to someone else became more insistent following the election.

The question that however needs to be seriously debated is whether the critical problem which the PNM faces is one of leadership or whether something more fundamental was amiss. By focussing on Mr. Manning, it may be that his critics were looking at the symptoms of the party's political morbidity rather than at the underlying causes of its present condition. While there is need to look at both symptom and etiology, the latter clearly deserves more attention. We ourselves have argued in this study that the tectonic plates which undergird politics in Trinidad and Tobago have shifted slowly but perceptibly over the years. The population is not as demographically segmented as it once was, and there has been a significant shift from rural areas to the suburbs along the East-West Corridor. The urban and sub-urban middle class has also grown, particularly from the seventies onwards, and is now very ethnically mixed. The children of the Afro-Trinidadian population are also not as wedded to the PNM as were their parents for whom voting PNM was once an act of faith. Their parents too seem to be overcome by political lassitude, perhaps because they no longer believe that there are any epic battles to be fought or won on behalf of the group through the conventional political process as they see it being manifest at the present time. They thus no longer respond with the same enthusiasm and automacity as they were wont to in the fifties and sixties. Their passion for politics seems to have become blunted by the experience of having triumphed so often, only to see the fruits of victory enjoyed mainly by others.

It has also become clear that the coalition which was built by Dr. Eric Williams between 1956 and 1961 has now been sundered, and that what remains of it does not appear to be broad enough to allow the PNM to win power again under normal circumstances. It is thus arguable that the failure of the PNM in November 1995 and again in June 1996 is due more to this abiding fact than with the political inadequacies of its current leader, whatever those might be. Lloyd Best has sought to conceptualize this development by arguing that the centre of gravity in the country has shifted from the "Port" to the "Plantation." To quote Best:

> The rapid changes of government in 1986, 1991 and 1995, culminating in the shift of the centre of gravity from the port to the plantation, have in no way resolved the underlying problem of a political system steeped in illegitimacy... The PNM defeat in 1995 was probably terminal. Its informal coalition, owed to Dr. Williams, has long since splintered at the top to the benefit of the "French

> Creole" ONR. Increasingly it is becoming vulnerable at the bottom as well. Garveyites and Butlerites, more than Afro-Saxons, are susceptible of being wooed into a coalition with the Hindus, especially when the latter are in charge of the patronage, the publicity, the police and the power of re-constituting the state. (*Express,* June 23, 1996)

Best claims that the Tobagonians left with ANR Robinson, the black intellectuals left with CLR James, the professionals with Hudson-Phillips, the Presbyterians with Winston Mahabir and the Muslims with Kamaluddin Mohammed. Continued Best:

> Mr. Panday understands. Notice the disproportionate number of Muslims he has sought to demobilize by astutely appointing them. He has clearly embarked on a fresh offensive not only among Baptists, steelbands and footballers. "Laventille" is merely a denotative expression for all of the vulnerable left behind after fully 40 years. Will the Opposition be saved by appealing to race? If not, with what other resources, what other devices? (Sunday Express, June 30, 1996)

Best's characterization is certainly overdrawn, and ignores the fact that the PNM still has significant support among most of the groups which he has identified. There is also little evidence that Afro-Trinidadians are decamping *en masse* to the UNC, though there is evidence that a few are doing so. One is talking about a trickle rather than a flood. But Best is right to claim that the PNM has lost support among many of the constituencies which were automatically attracted to it in the late fifties and early sixties, and that it is no longer seen by many, particularly those who are younger and ethnically mixed, as the natural party of government. One recalls George Chambers saying in 1986 that the psyche of the people of Trinidad and Tobago was integrated with the PNM. Clearly that is no longer true to any significant degree, (if it ever was so), particularly for those under 35.

Ironically, however, the PNM's voting support has shown no decline in terms of absolute numbers. In fact, that support has actually increased. What is critical to the future of the Grand Old Party, however, is the fact that electoral support for the UNC is increasing faster by a two to one margin. The UNC vote on June 24, 1996 was 178,800 while that of the PNM was 154,307, 60 percent of that which it won in the General Election. The UNC vote was 74 per cent of what it secured in November 1995. It is also worth noting that UNC candidates in the June 24th local government elections averaged 2,931 votes while PNM candidates averaged 1,268. Seven PNM candidates lost their deposits, something which has never happened before.

All the evidence thus indicates that the UNC is a party which is still growing in strength, while the PNM is showing signs of retarded growth and an inability to be genuinely competitive. Those who support the UNC, and they are still in the main Indo-Trinidadians, are keen to see the UNC consolidate and maintain its hold on the reins of power.[4] It is also becoming apparent that the UNC is not particularly scrupulous about how it uses the resources of incumbency to maintain political power.[5] The PNM, on the other hand, lacks élan, dynamic leadership and the economic resources to contain the aggressive thrusting of the UNC. It has also not succeeded in using the race factor to generate a stampede to the polls. One waits to see whether its fate is indeed sealed, or whether a combination of forced and unforced UNC "errors" and new PNM leadership would make a difference in the years to come.[6] Mr. Panday claims to have sensed a "wind of change" which will blow the PNM into the Gulf of Paria and into obscurity. Time will tell whether that wind will stall, whether it would turn into a tropical storm or a full fledged Caribbean hurricane that would, for the first time, not bear a Christian name.

The Case for Power Sharing

The issues raised before and after the November 1995 and June 1996 elections in Trinidad and Tobago on the question of national unity have served to bring into focus once more the question of power sharing. The Westminster paradigm emerged historically in a context where the dominant stratification pattern was informed primarily by considerations of class rather than by race, language, region, religion or some other "communal" cleavage. That paradigm provides that the party which wins a majority of the seats in parliament acquires a legal mandate to govern quite apart from whether it wins more than 50 per cent of the popular vote, an occurrence that is not unusual. The winning party invariably monopolises the fruits of the office and assumes the role of a trustee and exercises a political power of attorney on behalf of the nation as a whole. The role of the opposition is to oppose the government and in the process convince the electorate that its programme is better suited to address the problems at hand.

There are many who argue that the Westminster "winner take all" paradigm is monopolistic, legalistic and not suitable for ethnically plural societies such as those to be found in Trinidad, Guyana and many other "third world" countries. Sir Arthur Lewis (1965), for example, argued that in such societies, "consociational" rather than a "majoritarian" model is more appropriate. Basically, the consociational or "concurrent majority" model argues that what affects all must be approved by all. This is particularly important in multi-ethnic states where no group has an effective as opposed to a mere numerical majority and as such is unable to govern meaningfully and effectively on non-routine matters without the active involvement or concurrence of other critical interests without having to use coercion. This school of thought argues that one needs a multiple or over lapping mandate rather than a uni-layered mandate for such societies if effective government on a sustainable basis is to be achieved. In such societies, it is argued, ethnicity has to be formally recognized and even integrated into the electoral and in some contexts, the bureaucratic and constitutional system. In the majoritarian model, the state is formally de-ethnicised or, to put it another way, it is neutral, even if only formally.

One of the most articulate advocates of the consociational model, Aron Lijphart (1984), argues that "the real choice of plural societies is not between the British (majoritarian) model and the consociational model, but between consociational democracy and no democracy at all." Lijphart defines consociational democracy as government by an "élite cartel designed to turn a democracy with a fragmented culture into a stable democracy" (1959:216). The model calls for "government by a grand coalition of the political leaders of all significant segments of the plural society." It also involves a "concurrent majority" principle which allows minorities to veto policies which they consider unacceptable. It likewise involves some attempt at proportionality in the allocation of public resources.

Clearly, there are serious costs involved in the operation of such a model. One is that incumbent élites could collude in such a way as to suppress or make it difficult for other forces in the society to emerge. This in turn could give rise to the phenomenon of "extreme pluralism" or "irresponsible political outbidding," terms first used by Giovanni Sartori to describe the activities of political élites who assume extremist positions in order to draw attention to themselves and the causes which they espouse (Sartori 1966:137-176). The danger of "outbidding" in plural societies is that "ambitious politicians not included in the multi-ethnic coalition have incentives to generate demand for communal rather than national issues (Rabushka and Sheple, cited by Dew 1996: 202)." In so doing, they hope to defeat political rivals whose positions in the coalition force them to mute their extremism. Incumbents are often accused of having betrayed their communities, and of being guilty of "the apostasy suspicion," the feeling that they had sacrificed community goals in order to further their own political agendas and ambitions. The activities of such out elites could polarise the society and paralyse the political system.

According to Crawford Young, the challenge to consociational democracy is that "cultural politicians must compromise and bargain with other groups to obtain material advantage, yet in so doing must not appear to betray their own following" (Young 1976:138). The ability to bargain requires sensitivity to the subcultural concerns of the constituent groups in the system and a willingness to recognise and treat their claims as having validity. It also assumes the availability of material resources required to satisfy a modicum of the needs of constituent groups. Lijphart himself has argued that the success of the system depends, *inter alia,* on the balance of political forces in the coalition, the load that is imposed on the decision making system by ethnically sensitive policy issues, the volume of transactions which cross ethnic lines, the extent of the cohesion which exists within the groups, the level of public approval of the "elite cartel", and the existence or otherwise of a common external enemy (Lijphart 1977:12; cf. also Dew 1996:197-204).

Trinidad and Tobago's experience with formal coalitional politics well illustrates some of the costs and benefits of these arrangements. The most obvious benefit to the UNC is that its link to the NAR allows it to govern without constantly having to look over its shoulder as it would have had to if the NAR had merely agreed to give it "critical support" as Robinson claims was his original intention. This arrangement also allows the country to enjoy a stable political environment, at least for the time being. It likewise allows the UNC to make the claim that it is a "government of national unity" while striving to achieve hegemony.

The involvement of the two parties in the coalition has however made some elements in their respective memberships unhappy. Some UNC members have been critical of Mr. Panday, arguing that loyalists and old foot soldiers have been displaced to make room for "Johnny come latelys." Panday has been accused of allowing newcomers to the party to make decisions about who should or should not be allowed to contest elections on behalf of the UNC. Some dissidents have also charged that there is a Hindu-Muslim rift within the UNC and blame certain party élites for looking after one constituent element only. Some UNC stalwarts also claim that not enough URP jobs are being reserved for "UNC people." The issue is not whether the allegations are true or not. What is at work here is the "apostasy suspicion," the belief that in pursuing the goal of "national unity," the interests of the UNC's core following are being sacrificed.

This, incidentally, is a problem which Mr. Manning also faced in this attempt to widen the recruitment base of the PNM. Many blame the plight of PNM on his "looking for Indians" strategy. Some would say that by continuing to try to forge links with the Syrians, the Portuguese *et al.,* he is continuing to "betray and disrespect black people." Here again is the outbidding phenomenon at work.

Perhaps the best current example of the "outbidding" phenomenon is to be found in the NAR. Many NARites believe that Mr. Robinson has betrayed his followers in Trinidad, if not in Tobago. The NAR, they claim, is an "army without a general." They also believe that the NAR has not been properly rewarded for the support which it provides to the UNC. NAR ultras want a bigger share of URP and other jobs, and certainly expected a better deal in terms of the allocation of seats in the recently concluded local government elections. They feel that Robinson's political tongue has been much too still (One recalls that in 1971 and 1976, it was the DLP and the ULF which complained that the DAC had dealt unfairly with them in the run up to the elections which were held in those years).

One is not certain as to whether political outbidding would in time destabilise the UNC-NAR coalitiion. One simply wishes to advert to the possibility and to note that it is a central dynamic in the politics of all coalitions. Whether coalitions survive or not depends on their internal environment and how that environment is impacted upon by events, structures, and conjunctures which are external to it.

Given the ethnic heterogeneity of the population of Trinidad and Tobago, and given that communal consciousness is likely to become more highly politicised in the years immediately ahead, whatever might occur in the distant future, a strong case could be made that the political system ought to be restructured to take account of this abiding reality. Our historical analyses indicate that several attempts have been made to forge pre-electoral multi-ethnic fronts or coalitions, but that these failed because one group or another had come to feel that the balance of forces in the coalition did not accurately reflect their political strength, or that sufficient expression was not given to their desire to occupy more prominent positions.

The various coalitional efforts collapsed under challenge from constituent units for larger shares of the material resource pie that were available for distribution. The inability of the leadership elements to manage the ethnic tensions that inevitably arise in coalitional politics was also a contributing factor. Prior to 1995, the victims of coalitional failure were the Indians, and this holds true whether the party in question was in power, as was the case with the PNM and the NAR, or in opposition. In the latter instance, we had the experience of the first Democratic Labour Party (1958-1961), the Democratic Action Congress (DAC), the National Joint Action Committee (NJAC) and the United Labour Front (ULF). In the case of the DAC and NJAC, the Indian element was either marginalised or treated with insufficient regard. In the case of the DLP and the ULF, the "creole' elements within them were unwilling to cede primacy to Indians even though they constituted the electoral power base of the parties.

Similar assertions were of course made by Indian elements within the PNM and the NAR. Many of the Indians who supported the PNM believed that while Indians occupied positions of real political power within the party and the Government, the conventional wisdom was that an Indian would never be elected to the post of Prime Minister or Political Leader. It was always a case of an African leader and an Indian deputy.[7]

What form should the arrangements for our proposed "dougla republic" take? The political élites have so far shown no keen interest in any of the forms of proportional representation that have been attempted the world over.[8] They have for the most part only given consideration to pre- or post- election coalitions within the context of the first past the post system. Pre-election coalitional efforts have not been successful, and the experience of the NAR in 1986-1991 has rendered that formula suspect, at least for the time being. Lloyd Best has suggested that the pre-election coalition formula might work if the constituent units of the "party of parties" put their respective agendas on the policy table explicitly and bargain for their incorporation by the "Court of Policy." In this arrangement, no party would find itself ambushed by a sudden shift of policy. As Best puts it:

> We cannot continue to complain and protest in impotence and in futility about a political system which it is ours to make and, if necessary to remake in our graven image and likeness. We have to pass from the mere politics of parties and personalities to the politics of full participation. We need a politics of coalition and competition with many leaders. We need a politics of transparency with open and agreed procedures to devise the programme, to select the leaders, and to preserve the state of competition and of coalition alike. (*Express* August 13, 1995)

Following the June 24th bye-election Best elaborated further on the nature of the coalitional arrangement which he believed the existing conjuncture required. Best was of the view that the UNC had become "too rampant" since coming to power and that the pendulum had swung too far in the direction of the UNC. He also believed that the decline of the PNM seemed to be secular. To arrest these developments, new coalitional arrangements were called for. To quote Best:

> Our proposal is for a new party of parties. We have in mind a coalition party made up of the NAR-Trinidad (ONR) and the PNM as well as the movements and the parties which, in mid-1995, looked in anticipation to the party of

> the centre. This proposal has generated passions and jitters, the latter among the threatened, in opposition as much as government. Such a unit could come only from below; it would have to be welded together before the elections — not after them. It would be much like the party Tapia had in mind in 1977 and on which its leaders insisted in 1985 and 1986. (*Sunday Express,* July 14, 1996)

Best argues that the UNC itself is an "informal coalition" which only came into being in 1987 (cf. Chapter 8).

While agreeing that there is need for a politics of greater consensus, my own view is that in the present conjuncture, the parties in Trinidad and Tobago should retain their organisational integrity and campaign during elections as discrete units as parties do in Mauritius and as was done in Trinidad and Tobago in 1995 and 1996. This formula does not rule out arrangements to avoid multi-cornered contests nor does it rule out conflicts between coalition partners during or after elections. The outcome of elections would determine who leads the coalition formally. Post-election governing coalitions should be structured either by an agreement to consult and arrive at consensus on key policy issues or by a *concordat* that would bring representatives of significant parties or groupings formally into the cabinet. Both strategies should in fact be attempted. In essence, a case is being made here for a genuine government of national unity in which accredited standard bearers of all or most of the major ethnic groups and policy orientations would be visibly represented in the government of the day and allowed to have a say.

Given the absence of trust which currently obtains between the major parties and the political tradition of the PNM which frowns on coalitions of any kind. The arrangement might not work and there is the possibility that if the experiment fails, the fall out from the attempted "cure" might be worse than the disease. But given the tendency towards increased communal competitiveness that now prevails, and the poisonous rhetoric that has come to characterise public political discourse, the risk of experimenting with a new political paradigm seems to be well worth taking.

End Notes

[1]*Express* editor, Lennox Grant noted that the replacements for the fired CEOs were not Indian. He however admits that the perception in the East West Corridor that there was an agenda to these dismissals was real. In a comment on an article written by Reginald Dumas, "Raw Nerves in the Corridor" (*Express,* June 6, 1996), Grant wrote as follows:

> Examples of highly placed blacks coming to early grief under an Indian government are seen to signal a cancellation of the once-comforting "national unity" pledge. I think they are irrelevant to what Mr. Panday means by "national unity."
>
> In eight or nine months, the Panday government has done little to change the political, social or economic landscape. The discomfiture of a handful of people with names such as Brown, Jones, Gordon and Sealy is useful for PNM propaganda ("another [black] one bites the dust") but they remain a handful.
>
> Now into its ninth month, Indian power, advertised as "national unity", has been neither more nor less overtly damaging to this country than the black power represented by the Manning regime that went before.
>
> Mr. Dumas and others bear witness to a perception that is different. I don't doubt the existence of that perception in the East-West Corridor and elsewhere. That perception, so the teaching goes, is a political reality. But other perceptions, I am sure, attest to other realities, all of which co-exist, or compete, in today's Trinidad and Tobago.
>
> Black nerves, set on edge by the sight of Cabinet Ministers swearing themselves in with the Bhagvad Gita,

> is one reality of the East-West Corridor. But that says more about the black condition than about Indian power as we have known it so far. (*Sunday Express*, June 9, 1996)

At time of writing, one of the replacements was in fact Indian.

[2]According to a World Bank Report, (1995:5, 127-128)

> The incidence of poverty is highest in households headed by persons of mixed race (27.4%) followed by households headed by Afro-Trinidadians (24.8%) and Indo-Trinidadians (17.4%). Unemployment rates across ethnic groups also follow a similar pattern.

The study also indicates that the County of Caroni, in which Indians are in the majority, has the lowest incidence of poverty (5.9 per cent) of all the administrative districts in Trinidad and Tobago. In the county of St. George, the poverty index (poor but not extremely poor) was 25.0 per cent. County Caroni also had the lowest incidence of "extreme" poverty (0.8 per cent). In St. Andrew, 22.3 per cent were extremely poor while in St. George, 12.4 per cent were in this category.

[3]Indians argue that while some Indian business elements and professionals did well, there was still a great deal of poverty among Indians in many parts of the country. They also argue that the success which they achieved came inspite of, and not because of the PNM and the "French creole" establishment. The platforms for success were in fact established long before the PNM came to power. The economic boom of the seventies simply provided them with opportunities which, given their entrepreneurial drive, they took advantage of. PNM spokesmen however insist that in their zeal to appear "fair," Indians were intentionally given a significant share of public contracts. Former PNM Minister, Hugh Francis, argued that the PNM was driven to set up special institutions to help Afro-Trinidadians because they were being discriminated against by private sector institutions. To quote Francis:

> ...everytime you talk about black people, they say you are being racial. Trinidad and Tobago is a cosmopolitan society, but that doesn't mean blacks have to be invisible. My assertion of things black shouldn't be seen as being negative or interpreted as my not liking white people. Race and class cannot just be swept under the carpet. You can't just say that you are giving people equal opportunities because some people already have an advantage and you have to give the others a handicap in the race. So we have had to set up parallel institutions in this country. Why should we have had to set up a separate Small Business Programme? Why couldn't the banks have serviced small businesses in the normal way? And we all know the problems that people still have in getting loans from the banks. People of a particular complexion, a particular class are still very powerful. This business of interlocking directorates ... we tried to bring down ... the price of potatoes, onion and cheese, but they controlled everything, the distribution agencies, the outlets ... it took 1970 to get black faces in bank windows. (*Sunday Express,* August 3, 1986)

[4]As one Indian commentator, Siddharta Orie expressed it:

> In all spheres of human endeavour, the Indians in this country have just begun, like the morning sun, to rise and shine. What is important though, is that we ensure that Panday's moment in the spotlight is not a singular, cameo one, but that after him, there must be on the assembly line, ready and waiting to take over the reins of power, to shine as well, other rising sons and daughters of this diaspora.(*Independent,* July 5, 1996)

A similar point was made by another commentator:

> The tide is flowing in the direction of the UNC just as it flowed in the direction of the PNM for several years. Nothing can stop this flow. The PNM must play on the beach while the UNC rides the waves. (*Guardian,* July 3, 1996)

[5]As Lloyd Best accurately observes:

> Quite normal and wholly valid cultural differences between the two parties as incumbents and as managers have already surfaced as a factor bearing on occupancy. It was no longer a matter of Mr. Panday's acknowledged skill as a media person, which has long since set him apart from his rivals. What was now at issue was the capacity which the government was already showing to deploy the resources of the state to lubricate the UNCs expansion into hitherto inaccessible PNM areas.
>
> The PNM had played with the location of projects, with the distribution of jobs, of course, with the power of appointment in the public service and in the state enterprises. What it had never quite gained was that focus a party inevitably gets when forced to contemplate such prerogatives from the drought of 40 years in opposition. (*Sunday Express,* July 7,1996)

[6]Best has wondered aloud as follows:

> Mr. Panday will find incumbency too is costly. For every friend he makes, he will make enemies numberless. Do we have an architecture for wooing them across, not as individuals, but above all as triggers for splintering along the fault lines? (*Sunday Express,* July 7, 1996)

[7]This *cri de coeur* from Indians was well captured by Mr. Hardeo Hardath, PNM MP for Nariva in 1986 when he remarked that he "got the feeling of 'discrimination' — as if my leaders care not for me, my religion, my race and indeed my constituency. Does Mr. Chambers really want or care for Indians in the party, Parliament and Cabinet? I may be wrong, but that burning feeling is powerfully present" (*Express,* August 8, 1986). Hardath's view was echoed by another former PNM Minister, Sham Mohammed, in 1992. Mohammed was of the view that the time had come for an "Indian Prime Minister."

[8]A mixed form of proportional representation was recommended by the Wooding Constitutional Commission in 1974, but this did not find favour with the PNM and the other minority parties. No significant party seems to have an interest in using this devise to engineer coalitional arrangements. Given this, one has to consider other options (Wooding 1974).

Annexes

Annexe 1

Survivors of Another Crossing*

Marian Ramesar has written a delightful and well documented and reader friendly volume. *Survivors of Another Crossing* is a story of another traumatic Exodus, this time, the exodus of thousands of people who, driven mainly by crop failure, starvation and famine, defied taboo, and crossed the dreaded black water in search of the wherewithal to survive. Ramesar is quite unequivocal about the primary motivation for Indian emigration. As she writes:

> Emigration from India depended more on the threat of starvation than on the attraction of higher wages in the colonies. Contemporary observers repeatedly noted the stronger tendency to remain at home; that Indian peasants "will not quit their village so long as they have sufficiency in their own country" to bear the poverty and ills they know at home, than venture abroad under terms which made their return rather remote.
>
> In times of drought, poor harvests, and a succession of famines, there was intensified distress. It was these food shortages which were mainly responsible for pushing Indian migrants overseas during the period. Some of the areas most regularly affected by droughts [such as Fyzabad] were the ones which produced refugees and emigrants.

---

* *Sunday Express,* September 18, 1994.

The persons who migrated were in the main a sorry lot. An agent in Bengal described the recruits as

> ...paupers, whose garments were barely consistent with the requirements of decency; ornaments, save a few bangles of lead or glass of insignificant value, they have none. The average coolie's whole stock of goods would be dear at one rupee.

There were other reasons for migrating — political upheavals such as the Mutiny of 1857, inter caste or family quarrels, deceptive advertising by recruiters,or a search for adventure and fortune. But the key pre-disposing factor was economic deprivation.

Ramesar documents in great detail the economic crises which led individuals to leave their familiar environment, and the way in which they were dealt with by recruiters, agents and colonial authorities both in Trinidad and India. She also tells us a great deal about the types of persons who came to Trinidad, their castes and sub-castes, their craft vocations, their religious affiliation, their sex, the regions from which they came, their physical characteristics and much else.

Ramesar's account reminds us that the Middle Passage from Africa had its equivalent in the Passage from India. She quotes O.W. Warner about the "fear and trembling" that was evident on the faces of those who were about to leave India. As Warner wrote:

> If you see an emigrant ship leaving Calcutta, and if you watch the coolies' faces as they go on that ship, they are in fear and trembling the whole time. It is quite a mistaken idea that they are cheering on going off, and so, glad to go.

The journey of 11,000 miles took 100 days on the average. Many did not make the journey successfully. Beri-beri and various epidemics claimed many lives. One ship, the Moy, lost 46 out of its 520 passengers in 1904. Eighty others were hospitalized.

Ramesar's account also makes it clear that the indenture system, while not as harsh and psychologically brutal as slavery, was no bed of roses. The Indians were unfree and many were frequently harassed, jailed or fined for a variety of offenses. Under the terms of their contracts, they could not leave their estates without a pass; nor could they easily change their employers for whom they worked 45 to 50 hours per week depending on the season. The punishments for these and other offenses are well documented in the book. In 1907-1908 for example, 1,869 indentured immigrants were convicted for breaches of the Immigration Ordinance. In 1914-1915, the number convicted was 1,222.

Ramesar's book does not limit itself to exodus, arrival and settlement. It is also a documentary about transformation and about achievement. Particularly interesting was Chapter 4: *Activities of Time Expired Indians.* Ramesar tells us that by 1891, "free" Indians outnumbered indentured by nearly 6:1. Most of the Indians remained in the rural areas, but there were areas in Port of Spain where many were clustered. Peru (St. James) and Mucurapo village were two areas where some 4,000 were found. The capital city and San Fernando also had its share of beggars, cartermen, vendors, porters and inmates of various institutions such as gaols, hospitals, the House of Refuge etc.

Many of the Indians bought, rented or were given lands in lieu of return passages on which they cultivated sugar, rice, cocoa, vegetables, mangoes, citrus etc. In the process, as most agree, they made a tremendous contribution to the agricultural development of Trinidad.

Ramesar tells us that the land acquisition scheme was not designed to satisfy a desire on the part of the immigrants for cultivable land. It was designed by officialdom to avoid paying the costs of repatriation and also to maintain an available supply of labour on and around the plantation, especially in crop season. Indeed, only a small proportion of the immigrants accepted land in lieu of repatriation rights. Between 1845 and 1903, 119,887 immigrants came to Trinidad. Only 12,000 of these received land or other compensation in lieu of passage. Of the remainder, 22,642 were repatriated, 9,724 died or fled to Venezuela. Land grants were not always generous. Many in fact preferred lands which they bought themselves to the worthless pieces of swamp or lagoon land which they were often given. Sometimes they took the £5 which they were offered and left the land. Much of the land given was considered to be an unworthy substitute for a passage to India.

Not all Indians who remained worked on the land as their main occupation. Many saw and took advantage of the opportunities which were available on and around the plantation, and in the urban areas, to become a petty bourgeoisie. Ramesar draws on Rev. Morton (1891) to give us an idea of some of the occupations in which Indians were involved before the turn of the century:

> Usury at large interest; proprietorship of rum shops; proprietorship of cocoa estates, or provision shops, proprietorship of coconut estates, rice cultivation, milk selling, market gardening, gold and silver smithing, huckstering, peddling, grass selling, fishing, lodging, house keeping, charcoal burning, 5 year cacao contracting with a right to the crops grown, cane-farming on contract, skilled sugar factory labour as engine driver or estate headman or driver with opportunity to lend money to indentured labourers desiring to commute their indenture terms (at high rates of interest), skilled sugar estate labour jobs as grooms, cartermen, coachmen, laundresses, domestic servants, scavenging — "all Port of Spain roads were cleaned by Indians" — road making, railroad work, gardening at Botanic Garden etc.

According to the 1891 census, 43 per cent of the shopkeepers were Indians. Twenty four per cent were Chinese and 24 per cent were "Trinidadian" — more (likely Creoles and Portuguese). The Protector of the Immigrants, Charles Mitchell, is also quoted as follows:

> Nearly the whole of the retail shops in the island are in the hands of coolies except those in the town which are held by

> Portuguese and Chinese...if you go along the Eastern Main Road, with the exception perhaps of a Chinaman here and there, you will find nearly all the retail dealers except the shops in Arima which are branches of larger houses in town, all belong to coolies. In fact they form nearly the whole of the shopkeeping population of the island.

This was written in 1888.

Ramesar also provides evidence of the thriftiness of the Indians. Between 1897 and 1917, Indians constituted 42 per cent of the total depositors in the Government Savings Bank and their savings accounted for 32 per cent of all deposits. Much of their savings were also in land, jewelry or hidden away. Much was also remitted to India. In 1896, 1,253 Indians remitted £14,339 to India.

While most Indians were still poor by the turn of the century, some had become quite wealthy. Some of these were money lenders who acquired their wealth through usury. Many acquired substantial cocoa estates and were significant employers of labour. Ramesar in fact provides us with a fairly long list of those who were known to be rich.

The book also examines the old question of the opposition to Indian immigration which eventually led to its cessation in 1917, and the struggle of the Indians for full social and political empowerment between the first and second world wars.

The book is *must* reading for students of Trinidad history, both young and old, for political practitioners and analysts, and indeed for anyone interested in learning about the manner in which a people who left their villages 11,000 miles away in "fear and trembling," transformed themselves into a vibrant and economically resourceful community which believes that it is now on the verge of capturing political power from those to whom they were previously bonded. It is a story that is of course recapitulated elsewhere — in Fiji, Mauritius, Guyana and Suriname.

> Portuguese and Chinese — if you go along the Eastern Main Road, with the exception perhaps of a Chinaman here and there, you will find nearly all the retail dealers except the shops in Arima which are branches of larger houses in town, all belong to coolies. In fact they form nearly the whole of the shopkeeping population of the island.

This was written in 1888.

Ramesar also provides evidence of the thriftiness of the Indians. Between 1897 and 1917, Indians constituted 42 per cent of the total depositors in the Government Savings Bank and their savings accounted for 32 per cent of all deposits. Much of their savings were also in land, jewelry or hidden away. Much was also remitted to India. In 1895, 1,253 Indians remitted £14,330 to India.

While most Indians were still poor by the turn of the century, some had become quite wealthy. Some of these were money lenders who acquired their wealth through usury. Many acquired substantial cocoa estates and were significant employers of labour. Ramesar in fact provides us with a fairly long list of those who were known to be rich.

The book also examines the old question of the opposition to Indian immigration which eventually led to its cessation in 1917, and the struggle of the Indians for full social and political empowerment between the first and second world wars.

The book is *must* reading for students of Trinidad history both young and old, for political practitioners and analysts, and indeed for anyone interested in learning about the manner in which a people who left their villages 11,000 miles away in fear and trembling, transformed themselves into a vibrant and economically resourceful community which believes that it is now on the verge of capturing political power from those to whom they were previously bonded. It is a story that is of course recapitulated elsewhere — in Fiji, Mauritius, Guyana and Suriname.

[illegible] *Express*, August 1989 with amendments.

Annexe 2

Race and Ethnicity in Trinidad and Tobago*

The claims that "race" is the single most important variable which explains voting behaviour in the politics of Trinidad and Tobago has been challenged by a number of commentators over the years. Some argue that class and economic concerns are what motivate people to support one political party or the other. Others allege that whatever might have been true in the past, race is no longer relevant. PNM Political Leader, Patrick Manning, expressed the view during the 1995 election campaign that one of the most serious problems facing the country at the present time was the racial one. Some critics deny the continuing relevance of race and wondered whether Mr. Manning realized that the vast majority of the present electorate were children in the seventies and whether it had not occurred to him that the social realities of today, and race relations in particular, were quite different from those with which his political mentors had to deal. It was also noted that the thirty-year old voter of 1991 was only nine years old at the time of the "revolution" in 1970, and that there had been a social revolution in this country which gathered momentum in the late sixties, peaked in the seventies and was continuing even today. The result of this revolution was said to be visible not only in banks and business places, but also, especially, in the towns and villages, places where the politicians apparently hardly ever visit.

**Sunday Express*, August, 1989 with amendments.

It was argued further that harmony existed among the various racial groups in rural Trinidad and that the issues which were of concern to Indians and Africans alike were economic and not racial. As one critic, Dr. Geoffrey Frankson wrote, snapping his fingers at history in the process:

> The main concerns in the sugar belt these days have to do with the economic realities of being a sugar worker rather than being Indian; and who can best express these concerns will find a ready audience regardless of his race. So, too, the urban poor are mainly African. But there are few Trinidadians so idiotic as to see the race of the vagrants as being of any explanatory significance. The main problems that now concern us are unemployment, social deviance, inappropriate education, inadequate health care and insufficient housing. Any attempt to correlate these problems with race of to find solutions that will favour one race over another is doomed to failure, and by and large the people recognize this. Even if a politician were foolish enough to seek a mandate on the basis of his race, what purpose would that serve when he went to Parliament? Even if a political party were to win enough seats on the basis of race to form a government, what would it say to the International Monetary Fund (IMF)? (*Express,* August 15, 1989)

Clearly, Frankson was confusing what politicians did in order to get elected with what they do after winning power. He was also guilty of the bourgeois error of universalizing his own "common sense" perceptions as to what ranking ought to be given to the problems facing the society and of making the assumption that they were indeed the perceptions of a majority of the other principal groups in the society.

In order to defuse the criticism that he was unaware of what was said and done by members of the various racial groups as they interact in their "inner circles," Frankson agreed that the society was still socially segmented:

> We will continue to use racial epithets when we are angry or frustrated; we will continue to lime in groups which

> reflect the racial preponderance in our homes and neighborhoods, and we will inevitably compare and contrast the appearances, performances, successes and failures of various, groups, racial and otherwise. Furthermore, there will always be instances of racial discrimination to complain about, for there will always be racists among us and some of them will acquire power. But, in spite of all this, we can state with confidence that we do not have a racial problem in this country, and there is no reason for politicians to suggest otherwise. (ibid.)

Whether or not we have a "racial" problem depends on the context, the "season", and the time and place. But there is indeed a tendency to confuse "race" and "ethnicity" and to ascribe genetic considerations to what is in fact socially or culturally conditioned. Frankson asserted that while race was not a genuine social problem in Trinidad and Tobago ethnicity was of increasing significance. As he wrote:

> There is a fine distinction between race and ethnicity which is of increasing significance in local politics. Whereas one's race is a purely genetic inheritance, one's ethnicity is a reflection of the social, cultural and, most important these days, the economic experiences through which one is socialized. Where racists believe in the genetic superiority of one set of people over another, ethnocentrists - which incidentally is what most white South Africans claim to be - seek to preserve the social and economic characteristics with which they identify themselves. Certainly there are racists in Trinidad and Tobago, loads of them. But their racism is a personal problem rather than a social one. It is not a problem of communities of one race squaring off against communities of another race. That is not a real problem in Trinidad and Tobago, and there is no reason to believe that it is going to become one. (ibid.)

Members of the Tapia Group have also argued that "ethnicity" provides a more relevant explanation of voting behaviour in Trinidad and Tobago than race, and has accused

SARA pollsters of over-emphasizing the "race" factor in their polls. As one wrote, "it is this over-emphasis on the factor of race, to the virtual exclusion of others, which has fuelled much of the criticism of [SARA] polls." The Tapia group prefer to talk of ethnic groups or "tribes" rather than race, and they advance the view that "there are nine such tribes or nations in our midst, with the Africans of the North and the Hindus of Caroni-Naparima constituency being the dominant two, the "super-powers" around which the others normally orbit by changing their affiliation or the terms of their affiliation as the situation evolves." The other "tribes" listed are the Tobagonians, the Butlerites of the Oil Belt, the Black Power "Garveyites" of the North, the Muslims, the Presbyterians and the mis-named "French Creoles." These minor "tribes" ally with one or the other two dominant groups as the situation suggests they should:

> The two constant poles of contradiction and conflict have been, first the black wage earning mainstream in the capital region, and secondly, the farmer/worker merchant mainstream from the sugar belt. We do now have the makings of a theory which explains most of the facts and confirms that Trinidadians behave as rationally as everybody else.

Burton Sankeralli has recently "discovered" a "third tribe" which he claims is a transformation of the Eurocentric elite, once termed "French Creoles" into a full blown ethnic group, the neo-Europeans. This group, he defines as follows:

> The core of this grouping has been the local whites or so-called French Creoles and the elite class of light browns. However, it has expanded to include such elements as the Portuguese, Chinese, Syrians, the racially mixed and even some elite Africans and Indians. Some of these have indeed remained distinct ethnic enclaves yet they function in the society out of a Euro-centric centre. (*Sunday Express,* May 12, 1996)

The key to the self-definition of this group is said to be the "ideology of the rainbow." "The rainbow ideology well illustrates the distinction between "race" and "ethnicity." The Euro-rainbow people are multi-racial, but mono-ethnic. Yet there is implied in this, a "white shift"" (ibid.).

Benedict Anderson prefers to use the term "imagined communities" instead of ethnic group to define the fictitious phenomenon being analysed. As Anderson observed, "[ethnic or communal community] is imagined because the members of even the smallest nation will never know most of their fellow members, meet them, or even hear of them, yet in the lives of each lives the image of their communion" (cited in Premdas 1995: 2). Ethnic groups are however not always imagined. Some are while others are not. Some ethnic markers are invented while others are indelible and not easily erased though they may be back burnered. One however agrees fully with Sankeralli, Frankson, *Tapia* and others that a distinction must be made between "race" *per se* and "ethnicity." The terms are often used interchangeably even by those who know better when in fact, technically speaking they are quite different. It is now generally agreed that "race" is not a scientific term and that the taxonomic classifications used to locate persons in one racial group or another are subjective and are usually effected by the dominant groups, and that politics defines things in accordance with its own needs and practices and not in accordance with the alleged characteristics of the things defined. Race has often been used to exclude or isolate groups from citizenship and juridical power.

Gunnar Myrdal noted in his *An American Dilemma,* that the "negro race" is defined in America by the white people, but that this definition is at variance with that held in the rest of the American continent where the criterion of racial status is cultural rather than phenotypical. One recalls that in South Africa, the Japanese were classified as white while the Chinese were classified as non-white. The question of who is a Jew and who is not is also a subject of great controversy, even among Jews.

Colette Guillanmin has also argued in an important essay ("The Idea of Race and its Elevation to Autonomous, Scientific and Legal Status," UNESCO 1980) that "race" is not a scientific concept but an ideology of the bourgeois ruling classes. She dismisses the argument that groups have a *natural* origin, and that their characteristics are somatically endogenous rather than being socially created as a fiction designed to justify the claims to preeminence of the rising classes of the mid-nineteenth century and colonial expansion. "Dominance, she notes, seeks to conceal itself behind the idea of difference":

> It is virtually important for us to know how and upon what grounds the idea arose that certain social relationships are natural, irrespective, in the last resort, of politics or economics, and reflecting only Nature itself together with its constraints and its inevitability. For let there be no mistake: what is urged upon us in the form of racial (or natural) symbols is the great law of obedience to order and necessity, the law enjoined in so many different ways by oppressors upon the oppressed. Whether in its triumphal or in its apocalyptic form, the notion that the power of instinct is the driving force of history is drummed into us over and over again. For the last hundred years, dominant groups have brought forward one version or the other according as to whether they themselves are going through a period of expansion or of anxiety. If they are winning, that is because, according to the Darwinian interpretation linked to the rise of the middle classes, they are stronger, more capable and more persevering than others and because the predominance of their group is guaranteed by the natural order; those they dominate are subjects by nature, or in short, inferior. If the dominant groups are, or look alike, losing, that is because, according to the de Gobineau version, linked to the decline of the aristocracy, they are fewer and of finer quality than the rest, and have been 'overwhelmed' by the once subjected masses whose very numbers prove their coarseness or, in short, their inferiority. (ibid., 38)

Guillaumin challenges the view that race plays a causative or determining role in social processes or that groups are "frozen" into some intrinsic form of being with qualities that are external.

Rejecting "somatic, genetic or endo determinism of social behaviour," she argues that politics, history and environment have more explanatory power than "race" as variables which affect social behaviour. As she complains, "wherever there is a power relationship, a somatic trait is found or invented."

Guillaumin also questions the counter view that a specific culture and not genetics is what differentiates one group from another, and that this culture is transmitted primarily through language. In her view, the notion of cultural specificity is not very different from the traditionalist belief in the existence of somatic barriers radically differentiating human groups:

> In practical terms, the refusal to see that history and social relationships are constituent elements of so-called 'cultural' forms may be dangerous. It may for example, lead to the defence of social traits which are merely an expression of dependence and domination, and thus tend to perpetuate certain consecrations of inferiority. The inability to speak the (or a) dominant language, the inability to acquire techniques, and so on, tend to prolong helplessness and oppression, or at least to leave people still exposed to manipulation, defenseless against the very weapons of domination they reject. In fact, the famous "specific cultural characteristics" are often, perhaps usually, mere crystallization of domination, setting oral against written culture, 'natural' knowledge against 'scientific', traditional language against the language of mass communications and technology. It is interesting to note that a group which finds itself in a dominating position in a given relationship shows little concern if a dominated group refuses to acquire some of its own cultural traits, whereas the dominating group is usually extremely favourable to any action on the part of the dominated which lessens their opportunities for contracts, decreases their potentiality for struggle, or in general reduces them to the level of folklore. When the children of the bourgeois classes are taught several languages, we do not hear them (multilingual as they are) complain or talk about the psychological evils of bilingualism, though the latter is supposed to do irreparable damage to dominated groups. (ibid., 64)

If we can agree that the concept of race is a pseudo scientific one which is of relatively recent vintage, what then is a ethnic group. Is that concept any more scientific? One sociologis H.S. Morris, defines ethnic group as a "distinct category of th population in a larger society whose culture is usually differen from its own. The members of such a group are, or feel themselve or are thought to be bound together by commonalities of race c nationality or culture." The argument here is that it is minorit recent immigrant, or pariah groups which are "ethnic" groups an not the larger dominant group. In the United States, for exampl it was the later and not the earlier immigrants who were describe as "ethnics."

Another sociologist, Andre Beteille (1967) argues that

> The concept of ethnic group is somewhat broader in its scope than that of race. Ethnic differences might be based at least partly on race as in the case of Malays, Chinese and Indians in Malaysia or of Negroes, Indians and whites in the Caribbean. They might also exist in a society which is racially more or less homogenous as in the case of the Pathans in West Pakistan and Afghanistan or of some of the multi-tribal systems in East Africa.

Beteille notes that Hindus and Muslims do not belong t separate races and that in fact both are racially very mixed. Thi he notes, is only to be expected since the majority of Indian Muslim are the descendants of converts from Hinduism. Moreover, whil there has been a great deal of linguistic and religious conflict i India, there has been little "racial" conflict:

> Hindus and Moslems have co-existed as communities in different parts of India for a millennium. Religious difference have been associated with a host of other differences in ways of life. These differences have not always been the same, but the fact of difference has remained, heightened at times and subdued at others. Hindus and Moslems might not differ in physical type but religious ideology has provided each community with a basis for consciously organizing its identity in opposition to the

> other. Over the centuries, the two communities have borrowed much from each other and during the last few decades they have been exposed to similar forces of change. But this has not erased the boundaries between them. In fact, the pattern of Hindu-Moslem relations in recent Indian history would seem to show that groups might become more conscious of their opposed identities precisely at a time when external differences between them are being reduced.

rish Catholics and Protestants also belong to the same "race," ut differ fundamentally on a number of non-racial attributes which eads one to characterize them as different ethnic groups.

The late Jamaican sociologist, M.G. Smith (1994: 31) has owever been critical of some of the attempts which have been nade to differentiate between the concepts of race and ethnicity. mith is of the view that in the era after the Holocaust, there was concerted movement afoot to discredit once and for all the heories of race that had become entrenched in European social cience, and that UNESCO was viewed as the authoritative vehicle or this ideological movement. The aim of most biologists, nthropologists, sociologists et. al. was to "exorcise the pernicious ffects of racial concepts of psychology and culture, perhaps first pplied systematically to mankind by Linnaeus (1758-1759)."

In Smith's view, however, in seeking to rid mankind of the orrendous evil of racism, Western scholars of race proceeded to hrow out the baby with the bath water. He argues that most of nankind still belong to one or other of a very few racial stocks, ven if there are groups whose identity remains uncertain (Smith 994: 35). He also laments the fact that although most of the hysical features used to classify races are polygenic, biologists educed from monogenic clines that "there are no human races." mith was at a loss to explain how social scientists made such a najor illogical leap. The basic reason, in his view, was ideological. t was an attempt to create an "illusory defense" against racism or acialism (ibid.,43).

Smith was however at pains to point out that there is nc ground for attributing differences of psychological aptitude anc cultural potential to the varying phenotypically different stocks Nor do groups remain fixed for all times. To quote Smith:

> Racial stocks are continuously in process of change or evolution due to a multiplicity of factors. They are neither closed, fixed nor uniform, since each undergoes continuous change. Second,there is no valid evidence that racial stocks differ in their psychological aptitudes and predispositions or in their cultural potentials. Third, while the few widely recognised and easily distinguished races together include most of mankind, there are many people who cannot be reliably placed in either of these categories. Fourth, there is no valid biological basis for the idea that the races of mankind form a hierarchy of any kind. Fifth, there is no valid evidence that racial miscegenation is biologically harmful in any way. (ibid., 36)

What then is Smith's view of an "ethnic" as opposed to a "racial" group? Ethnic groups are generally defined as population which are distinguished by real or putative common ancestry, o distinctive cultural characteristics such as language, religion, art music, games, kinship and family practices, either separately o together. Race is determined by phenotype while ethnicity i determined by culture.

Smith's basic conclusion is that ethnic prejudice, or wha he calls ethnocentrism, has existed in almost all parts of the worl and at all times, and predated capitalism and imperialism. It wa merely given "scientific" justification by Victorian biology Presumably, it always will exist in one form or another Ethnocentrism may however be virulent and comprehensive or i might be neutral and benign. To quote Smith:

> We are confronted, then, by the contrast between such genuinely benign ethnocentrism and the more familiar variety common in developed societies that involves prejudice and negative stereotypes of other peoples. When ethnocentric beliefs and ideas denigrate and stereotype other

> peoples and their cultures, they become racist if they assume that the negatively valued traits are hereditary, ineradicable and transmitted by descent. (ibid., 57)

The existence of ethnic differences or consciousness does not necessarily mean that conflict is inevitable or that ethnic groups would organize politically on the basis of their perceptions of differences. Whether they do or not depends on a host of other circumstances which change over time and place. As Beteille (1967) notes:

> People might be highly conscious of their difference, whether physical or cultural, without their consciousness acquiring a political form. In traditional Indian society, there were not only differences between castes; but people were universally aware of those differences. Yet castes were not always organized into mutually antagonistic groups. They began to organize themselves into associations at a time when people were beginning to feel that caste consciousness would fade away. The course of political conflict remains unpredictable. There is no general theory which can enable us to delineate in exact terms the relationship between cultural differences and their organization into mutually antagonistic groups.

It was once assumed that ethnic groups in the Caribbean would be socialized into the mainstream in due course and that the differences between them would in time disappear. We now know that while in many cultural contexts, the differences are of little significance, in many others they continue to be very important, and show no sign of disappearing.[1]

End Note

[1]For a recent and useful discussion of race and ethnicity in the Caribbean and elsewhere cf. Ralph Premdas, *The Enigma of Ethnicity: An Analysis of Race in the Caribbean and the World* 1993, School of Continuing Education, University of the Wes Indies, St. Augustine, Trinidad. See also Premdas, *Ethnic Identity in the Caribbean: Decentering a Myth,* University of Toronto November 1995.

Annexe 3

Panday and the Politics of Alienation*

Are Indians in Trinidad and Tobago "alienated"? Yes!, says Basdeo Panday. No!, exclaimed Speaker of the House, Occah Seapaul also an Indian. Who is right and who is wrong? Are both right for the wrong reasons? In the absence of quantitative data, it is difficult to say. Even with quantitative data it might be difficult to establish the truth of the matter since not everyone is clear as to what is meant by "alienation." One is not sure whether Panday himself is clear as to what he means. At times he uses the term polemically rather than analytically.

The term "alienation" is defined in one dictionary as "deprivation, entire or partial of mental power," "the legal transfer of property or title to another," "the state of being alienated". The 19th century German philosophical school however used the term in a different way. The concept is popularly associated with Karl Marx. Marx did not however invent the concept but gave it a certain twist. For purposes of this column, we deal only with the concept as defined by Marx from whom one can safely assume Panday borrowed it.

**Sunday Express,* June 14, 21, 1992.

Marx himself used the term in many different ways. He

distinguishes between religious, philosophical, political and economic alienation. Religious alienation, he tells us is "a matter of consciousness." Economic alienation is however the basis of "real life." Work in a capitalist society leads inevitably to alienation, Marx tells us. Under capitalism, the worker is forced to "alienate" or sell his labour power to the capitalist who is an "alien power" confronting and exploiting him. In selling his labour, the worker is not merely securing his own survival. He is "alienating" himself in a process of production that is spiritually and physically dehumanizing, a process which robs him of all creativity. Under capitalist production systems, men do not own their tools or the materials of their product and have no control over production or investment decisions. Only the capitalist can be creative. Marx would however have us believe that the capitalist too is alienated in a fundamental sense though he may enjoy "a semblance of human existence." Both are however victims of the same inhumane system. "The laws of capitalism rule the capitalist as much as the proletarian." The worker becomes a mindless cog in an impersonal productive process. In one sense then, alienation and robotization mean much the same thing to Marxists.

We see here that the term alienation is being used in various ways depending on context. Similarly, in applying the term to Trinidad and Tobago; Panday employs the term to mean many things. At times he uses the term to refer to all "have nots" in the system, who are, in his view, victims of the exploiting "French Creole parasitic oligarchy" and the black salaried and managerial élite which it co-opts and corrupts to do its bidding. In using the term in this way, Panday comes close to Marx who used the term alienation as synonym for *class exploitation*.

Panday however more frequently uses the term to refer to the political and cultural condition in which he claims Indians find themselves in the "mainstream" of the society. What they find there, argues Panday, is racism or pseudo racism. The PNM, he says uses racist tactics to mollify its restive supporters in order to stay in power. Racism in his view, is used as an opiate, a fig leaf to conceal the party's fundamental nakedness.

Panday however sees racism as going beyond the imperatives of party politics. He clearly believes that the wider society discriminates in many ways against Indians, making the latter feel "alienated" in the process. Like the worker in Marx's capitalist society, they feel a sense of "alienness", hostility even, in the wider society. They likewise feel a sense of utter powerlessness, at least politically, since they are not represented in critical areas of the political structure in proportion to their numerical and economic significance in the society. Panday said he felt "ashamed" when he went to the Inauguration of the President in 1992 and found "not one Indian in the parade." Things like that generate "alienation", he complained.

Panday's complaints resonate widely among Indians. Some, seemingly a minority, however disagree with his thesis. Among them is Occah Seapaul, who in a powerful speech on Indian Arrival day in 1992, told her audience that she felt very saddened "whenever she listened to people trying to convince her brothers and sisters that they are an alienated lot." As Seapaul continued:

> How can we be aliens when an ancestral effort went into giving birth to the soul of this nation? How can we be aliens when this is the land that has nourished and nurtured us? From what are we alienated and by whom? Is it from economic development? I trust not, because Indians as a race have done remarkably well through their thrift and industry in achieving economic progress. As a race we certainly cannot feel alienated on the educational front because the records of both the past and present are replete with scholastic achievement of men and women of our race. Indians might once have lagged behind politically. This was no longer so. Whatever the conditions and circumstances of the past which resulted in such lagging, it certainly is not true to say that our men and women are not making their contributions on the political front.

Seapaul hinted that Indians were themselves in danger of becoming racist and felt driven to warn them against letting the "seeds of the term alienation" take root in their consciousness. Indian leaders, she warned, had a responsibility as did others to ensure that narrow nationalism did not prevail. "Consciousness of Indianess must not degenerate into racism since infiltration of racial poison into the consciousness can only spell disaster. The war we have to fight is not a racial way against our brothers and sisters but a war against the economic crisis of the country."

Seapaul's remarks provoked an angry response from Panday who promptly described her as a "pseudo racist" who had used race to elevate herself in a racist political party. Panday also insisted that he had a duty to speak out against alienation since if it was not dealt with, it would fester and burst out as it did in June 1990 and more recently in Los Angeles. "It only takes a match to ignite the fire."

What does one make of all of this? Let me first say that I do not believe that Panday and his talk about alienation is the *cause* of escalating racial consciousness in the country. Nor do I see Panday as a voice blowing in the wind, so to speak. Panday is in fact giving form to feelings that are deeply felt, feelings which have long been latent and which will not be stifled, no matter what attempts are made to induce him to button his lips.

Marx used the word utopian to describe the wish for a socialist society before the objective conditions were ripe for the realization of that society. I'm sufficiently marxist to argue that the non-racial society which Seapaul and all of us wish to see is utopian and will be awhile in coming, if it does come at all. The sense of being alienated and marginalized is in fact likely to *increase* rather than *decrease* in the short run. Why do I say this?

Indians in Trinidad and Tobago are feeling alienated not because there is *more discrimination* against them, but because there is now less of it. The less of it there is, the more impatient they become to remove the last frustrating vestiges. Revolutions or rebellions, whether physical or cultural, never take place when social problems are at their worst. They come when things have begun to improve and social groups become intolerant of the slow pace of change. The perception of "alienation" is in fact a by-product of increasing Indian embourgeoisement. The problem also has to be viewed in a wider sociological and international context.

Indians of all denominations, but particularly Hindus and Muslims, are no longer deferential to "creole" and western society as they once were. They appreciate that they have vital alternatives that are in some respects superior to what the West has to offer. What we are witnessing can in fact be likened to what has been called the "Hansen effect." Marcus Hansen, an American historian, talked about a process of ethnic identification encountered by various immigrant generations. The first generation is generally pre-occupied with the problem of economic survival in the host society. The second generation seeks to gain greater social acceptance by trying to shed its social past. The third generation, more economically secure and established, becomes anguished and alienated by the bastardization of its identity and feverishly seeks to "fight cultural fire with cultural fire." As Hansen put it pithily, "what the child wants to forget the grandchild wants to remember." In contemporary America and in Britain, many second generation immigrants of Caribbean parentage are to be found among the rebellious and socially irredentist element. In a curious way, all groups in the New World are transplants and therefore alienated in varying degrees. All are "hyphenated."

This desire to recapture one's identity, even if symbolically, has been observed among all immigrant groups in the Americas — the Irish, the Italians, the Cajuns of New Orleans, the French in Quebec ad the Afro-Americans, who in the seventies said no to the alienation which they were experiencing in the New World. The Chinese, the Indians, the Syrians and the blacks in the Caribbean diaspora are also part of this near universal phenomenon. The symbolic ethnicity which they seek to recapture is characterized by a nostalgic allegiance to the culture of the immigrant generation, or that of the old country. It is also evidenced by love for and pride in old traditions that are felt though not incorporated into everyday behaviour. The need for symbolic or ornamental identity is situational. The context determines the desire to access the alternatives.

There was a time when it was assumed that given economic growth and cultural assimilation, ethnic groups would all disappear in the crucible of what Israel Zangwill as far back as 1908 termed the "melting pot." The "melting pot" theory was however part utopian dream and part political ideology. It was ideology in the sense that some individuals wished to see all the constituent groups of the Americas lose their uniqueness and become a new and distinctive American or Caribbean product through genetic and cultural "pureeing." Others, including many immigrants, were opposed to the cultural homogenization concept since they wanted to retain their cultural distinctiveness and the integrity of their family.

The "melting pot" theory is no longer fashionable since it is clear that ethnic groups the world over are not disappearing and are in fact re-asserting themselves. As one recent UN publication put it: "... although the notion of race has been called into question by science, it still retains such significance in people's minds that it permits them to define physically and psychologically the separation between *"us"* and *"them"*, despite the illusory nature of that separation ("Races and Ethnic Groups: Are They Psychologically Necessary!" UNIC, March 14, 1996). Proclaim-ing that race does not exist does not terminate the debate about somatic or cultural distinctions and which ones are superior or otherwise and useable as a criterion for ethnic cleansing. Alternative concepts of cultural and structural pluralism have now become more fashionable as public policy.

The term "cultural pluralism" was coined by the psychologist Horace Kallen in 1924 in a essay entitled *Group Psychologies of the American People* to define a society in which ethnic groups would all retain their distinctiveness but co-exist in harmony and respect. Some pluralists have taken Kallen's concept further arguing that ethnic groups can become culturally assimilated while yet retaining an element of distinctiveness. Milton Gordon, for example, argued that most ethnic groups in America have adopted many of the cultural norms of the dominant culture — food, dress, language etc., and in many respects have become culturally homogenized and indistinguishable. Yet they retain elements of their own uniqueness. There remain overlapping identities and loyalty systems that are either latent or active. "The groups have their own social life, practice endogamy, move into compact ethnic neighbourhoods or ghettoes." Gordon argued that "*structural pluralism* is the major key to the understanding of the ethnic make up of American society while cultural pluralism is the minor one."

This concept of "structural pluralism" may well serve to explain what is now taking place in Trinidad and Tobago. It is clear that there is creole culture which all groups buy into in *varying degrees and at various times.* In that sense, "all ah we is one." We all eat the same roti, pelau and chow mein, play mas, fete etc., though not with the same zest, rhythm, élan and completeness. Some groups, or elements thereof, however, wish to partake of two worlds, the world of the ethnic in which certain primary esteem needs are satisfied and the everyday creole world in which they are viewed as an "inferior" subculture.

Writing about contemporary Latin America, in a UNESCO volume on *The Future of Cultures* (1991,1992), Dennis Goulet observes that a process of cultural resistance is also very much at work among Amerindians and Blacks. History records that cultural communities can preserve their identity over long periods of time even under conditions of extreme duress, thanks to "secondary adaptation." Secondary adaptation occurs when an oppressed community or culture exhibits subservience in its surface behaviour, an apparent servility which lulls the dominant cultural group into complacency and lessened repressive vigilance. "At a "secondary" or covert level, however, the oppressed group engages in cultural resistance; in code language it affirms its sense of identity and pride, mounts educational campaigns against domination, at times even organizes open revolts." Goulet notes that these groups have also become aware that it is only by reasserting their differentiated cultural identity that they can press their collective claims upon society.

What does all of this have to do with alienation? My thesis is that significant elements of all groups in the society feel a sense of alienation in differing degrees, the difference being a function of the extent to which the larger society recognizes as valid and legitimate the core elements of their cultural inheritance and conceded them the right to celebrate it. With respect to the Hindus, official endorsement for the teaching of Hindi in the schools system, or the making of Indian Arrival Day a Public Holiday will probably meet some of these esteem needs and may help to defuse the sense of alienation which they feel, but once this is done, the focus will inevitable be directed to other values that are disparaged by the wider society. Indeed, the problem will never be "solved" though it might be "dissolved" when an Indian becomes Prime Minister in his own right rather than by courtesy of the political leader of the party to which he belongs. That however will merely serve to shift the problem elsewhere. Other groups will then begin to complain more openly about *their* alienation, as Afro-Trinidadians have in fact begun doing in 1987 and 1992 when they feared, mistakenly,that an ethnic power shift had already taken place.

It is concerns such as these which informed the statement which I made in a quiet classroom in Toronto, Canada, and which was megaphoned by the media, that an "intensive struggle" was developing in Trinidad and Tobago between the two major racial groups. I make no apologies for adverting to that pessimistic scenario, though I would wish to be proven wrong. My comment was however not "wild" or lacking in objectivity as some have alleged. It was informed by what occurs in multi-ethnic societies when competition for scarce resources increases or when adventitious events serve to vitalize latent ethnic fears and anxieties. I however agree that once the process of polarization begins, it is often difficult to reverse it since group leaders and spokesmen feel the need to demonstrate publicly which side they are on. Moderates who seek to calm emotions and mediate differences are invariably swept aside once the forces of polarization pass a certain point.

One hopes that the society finds a formula to satisfy the basic minimal physical and physic needs of all the constituent groups, since if it does not, the scenario outlined may well come to pass. The problem however needs to be openly ventilated, all be it with moderation, since it will not go away by itself. The facts need to be exposed, though facts in themselves are open to interpretation or misinterpretation. But we would never take the false view that our festive calendar leaves us no time to be violent and that "it" could never happen here. I seem to recall that "it" was never supposed to happen in Sri Lanka, Fiji or Sarajevo in Yugoslavia. But it did. Let us remember that those who do not learn from history are condemned to repeat it. Even so, as Goulet reminds us, "History is full of surprises and many events which occur were not predictable at an earlier time." These unexpected outcomes may not necessarily be "irrational," but their rationality was often not manifest before the fact.

Annexe 4

The Jamaat, the NAR and the Caroni East By-Election*

Mr. Panday has denied that there is any political link between the UNC and the Jamaat al Muslimeen; Mr. Wilson has resigned as Political Leader of the NAR and the NAR executive has repudiated Mr. Wilson's decision, and has gone back to bed with the UNC. What are we to make of these developments? With respect to the Jamaat, I believe that Mr. Panday is not telling all he knows about what is brewing there. Abdullah Omowale gave a hint of this when he openly indicated that "there could be no true political unity in Trinidad and Tobago without the involvement of the Jamaat al Muslimeen." While he admitted that "there was no official or backroom alliance between the Jamaat and the UNC," he was sanguine in his "hope that there will be an alliance." He also indicated that the current NAR-UNC formula for unity was "defective," and that unity without the involvement of the Jamaat would be flawed, given the "fact" that the Jamaat represents the people at the grass roots level of the East West Corridor, a view that is clearly a fiction of Mr. Omowale's imagination.

Clearly however, there must have been some discussion of the Jamaat's offer to provide help to the UNC in marginal constituencies and those along the Corridor. My own view is that

**Sunday Express,* August 7, 14, 1994.

the UNC will be hurt rather than helped by any link with the Jamaat, but it remains to be seen whether the UNC "oligarchas" would so conclude. But we know that politics, like marriage, makes very strange bed fellows.

The other issue which invites comment is the "divorce" which has now taken place between the Political Leader of the NAR and the NAR Executive. It is not immediately clear why Mr. Selby Wilson made a unilateral decision to withdraw from the common platform agreement, even assuming he was in fact deeply concerned by what he feared was an undeclared UNC-Jamaat link. One recalls A.N.R. Robinson's unilateral decision to have the DAC boycott the 1971 General Election. Do our political leaders ever learn or is it that they have short memories? It may of course be that Mr. Wilson was the hapless victim of cross pressure from the two ethnic segments of the suburban fringe which constitute the core élite of the NAR, the one which wants to strengthen and gentrify the UNC, and the other which considers the UNC an anathema to be shunned like the proverbial plague, and that he resolved this agonizing dilemma by surrendering his tinselled crown, perhaps to make room for Mr. Dookeran on his return. Whatever the outcome of his opera bouffe, I remain convinced that the UNC has already gobbled up much of the NAR's mass support outside the Corridor and that the NAR (with or without Mr. Wilson) has little by way of dowry to bring to any marriage that might be brokered between now and 1996. Such a brokered marriage would be politically hypergamic with the UNC being the dominant partner who will determine the conditionalities of the union and who will occupy the master bedroom and who the maid's quarters.

NAR: DANCING WITH THE WOLVES*

In his interesting account of his relations with Mr. Basdeo Panday, Mr. Selby Wilson, Political Leader of the NAR, revealed that it was the UNC leader who approached him about an accommodation for the Caroni East by-election and not the other way around as many previously believed. This columnist was among those who were not aware that it was Mr. Panday, who finding himself in a bit of political heat, decided to take the political virgins of the NAR for a romp in the proverbial haystack. The question to be determined is why was the seduction now deemed opportune?

One recalls that in the Laventille by-election of May 1994, Mr. Panday spurned Mr. Wilson's advances. What then was different in Caroni East, a constituency that everyone assumed the UNC would win easily? My guess is that Panday was seeking to divert attention from Hulsie Bhaggan's spirited challenge by seeking to recreate the euphoria of 1986. If what I am told about the growing grass roots support for Bhaggan around the country is only half correct, I can understand why Panday might have considered such a diversionary tactic to be worth a try. Why not sleep with the devil again to gain a kingdom? Mr. Wilson, it would appear, was suspicious of Panday's motives — he characterizes the latter as being "fluid", a euphemism for wily or devious — but allowed himself to be persuaded by an element within the NAR whom he again euphemistically described as UNC-NAR "floaters", that a bed sharing accommodation with the UNC should be engineered.

**Sunday Express,* August 7, 1994

Mr. Wilson's analysis of the motives of the latter is instructive. As he notes:

> Because of the structure of the NAR and because the UNC, as it were, splintered off from the NAR,both parties have a significant number of people whom I call "floating voters" between the UNC and the NAR,people who are sympathetic towards the NAR and sympathetic towards the UNC as demonstrated in the Pointe-a Pierre elections where we saw the UNC's majority come by the movement of persons who voted for the NAR in the 1986 elections switching their allegiance to the UNC. And there are floating sympathizers of both parties. Indeed, some of the pressure for the movement toward joining up with the UNC came from these supporters in that they are always advocating that the parties must get together again and try to recreate 1986. (*Sunday Express,* August 7, 1994)

The real aim of such re-engineering was, as Wilson admits, to "capture electoral success." The talk about national unity was really little more than window dressing, smoke and mirrors.

Mr. Wilson should of course have added that just as there are "floaters" between the NAR and the UNC, there are also "floaters" between the NAR and the PNM, and that the attempt on the part of the former to gravitate towards the UNC would be accompanied by a corresponding move by the latter to the PNM. The question then was whether this was a zero sum game or whether there would be any net gain when the political dust settled, and if so, who would be the beneficiary?

My own judgement is that both the UNC and the PNM would in fact gain, but that the NAR as an organization would be totally consumed in the process though its spirit might serve to change the ethos of both major parties. This would however be at variance with what Mr. Wilson hoped the NAR would become. In his view, "unity" should not be the by-product of "superficial and ephemeral relationships. Unity should not be forged by two leaders getting together and saying "we win." It had to be something more substantial coming from the base of the community expressing this desire and virtually pushing the leaders in that direction."

Wilson's further hope was that the NAR would [once more] become a "strong entity on its own in order to bring to bear its political philosophy in amalgamating with any other party, whether it is the UNC or any other party."

Assuming that this goal was realizable, and I have strong doubts that it is, my own view is that the NAR executives did the wrong thing by becoming part of the UNC platform since, in doing so, they compromised their Party's organizational integrity. They were simply being used as a political sex object by the UNC which would discard them, as Panday and others were [in 1987], when the political wicket starts to play badly, as it inevitably will if the UNC is given a turn at the crease and the economy continues to contract.

The UNC however calculates that there were some meaningful short-term gains to be achieved. The one to which I have already alluded, was the neutralization of Hulsie Bhaggan. Then there is the tantalizing prospect of making a deal with the erstwhile enemy, ANR Robinson, who it is assumed still controls the two Tobago seats. Would it not be ironic if those two seats were required by the UNC to gain office and Mr. Robinson was again to become kingmaker or even Prime Minister, assuming he still hankers after ministerial office or that he would ever agree to work with Panday who continues to flagellate him on political platforms? Would it not be equally ironic if as a result of the accommodation, Trinidad becomes a political "ward" of Tobago? Would Tobago in fact agree to be yoked to the UNC? Would the St. Vincent model work in Trinidad and Tobago?

Panday is aware that for all kinds of structural reasons, the UNC on its own would find governance more difficult than the PNM now finds it, and may be hoping that the NAR might provide the cross ethnic legitimacy and the implementation capability which a UNC government will lack. As Mr. Wilson indicates, Mr. Panday (borrowing from Lloyd Best) made the point that he was "not only interested in winning, but needed to win an election in such a manner that he would be able to govern. In other words, he was signalling that in order to be an effective government you had to have a united people." In sum, an NAR link might give a UNC victory the sustainability which it might not be able to engineer on its own. This is particularly critical since the investing community, both local and foreign, is happy with the PNM and could well go on "strike" if a new hegemon emerges following the election of 1996 with whom it does not feel comfortable.

All of this suggests that the run up to the election will be very highly charged and that ethnic war drums will be warmed and beaten by those who calculate that only by such means would power be secured or maintained. Some are even predicting that the level of ethnic polarization would approximate or even exceed that seen in 1961.

Annexe 5

The Unity Platform and the Caroni East By Election*

he results of the by-election in Caroni East held on August 27, 1994 has raised more questions than it provided answers for the shape of politics in Trinidad and Tobago on the "road to 1996." The only thing that is certain is that Miss Sagewan won the election on behalf of the UNC, defeating Mr. Persad of the PNM in the process, and that the former got 62.5 per cent of the votes cast while the latter received 34.5 per cent. The results in fact closely mirrored almost exactly the demographic characteristics of the constituency in ethnic terms which suggests that neither the PNM nor the NAR/UNC "Accommodation" was able to vault the ethnic divide.

Several contested views have been advanced as to what was responsible for the outcome of Monday's election. One view, attributed to Chaguanas MP. Hulsie Bhaggan, is that most UNC activists and supporters boycotted the poll and that the machinery used and the support which Miss Sagewan received represented the NAR's addition. It would seem that Miss Bhaggan is so anxious to de-legitimize Mr. Panday and the UNC leadership that she is

---

**Sunday Express*, September 25, 1994.

prepared to make more extreme claims about their irrelevance than is justified. I however share her view that the manner in which the UNC dealt with her and her spirited response to their challenge did turn off many prospective voters. The "Hulsie Factor" was however only one of many that served to deny Mr. Panday the big victory which he had hoped to receive and which he hoped would have allowed him to claim that he was within sight of receiving the "mandate of heaven."

The low keyed nature of the PNM campaign also had something to do with the turn out. Mr. Rowley has denied (disingenously) that the PNM deliberately under stimulated the constituency. I rather suspect that the policy of avoiding open meetings and the decision to opt instead for cottage meetings was done as an experiment. It was felt that open meetings would serve to sharpen ethnic tension which in turn might serve to increase voter turn out, which in this case, would favour the UNC as it did in Pointe a Pierre. It was a clever strategy which seems to have worked to give the UNC victory a pyrrhic dimension.

The cynical nature of the unity arrangements (between the UNC and the NAR) and the confusion which it generated might also have served to turn off elements in the electorate who remember that just months ago, some of the same persons who were being embraced were classified as political, if not personal enemies. Miss Bhaggan in fact may have a point when she claimed that Mr. Panday's "disrespect of the people" led them to abstain. As he put it:

> Mr. Panday was disrespectful to the people. Only in gutter politics can one feel that you can tell people just anything and they will still turn around and vote for you.

In the absence of an empirical opinion survey, one cannot be certain as to why people did not turn out to vote in large numbers and why those who did, voted in the manner in which they did. One therefore has to speculate. But it seems clear that factors other than weather must be adduced to explain what happened.

The other issue that was brought to a head as a result of Monday's election was the role of Tobago in the UNC-NAR *entente.* The question was (earlier) raised as to whether Tobago would allow itself to be yoked to the UNC or whether it would use its two votes to give it negotiating leverage as did "Son" Mitchell in St. Vincent. It would seem that the latter option is being considered by opinion leaders in the NAR.

Mr. Panday's chicken counting exercise forced Tobago Narites to warn him that he should not assume that Tobago was in his bag. Miss Nicholson was in fact quoted in the *Trinidad Express* as saying that there was "no ground level support for the unity platform in Tobago." There was also resentment that the NAR executive members in Trinidad and Tobago did not consult those in Tobago before they agreed to associate with the UNC platform. As Mr. Benedict Armstrong put it:

> The NAR is a National party and the executive should have communicated with us before embarking on a decision as far reaching as this was. We do not think that this is the way Tobago wants to go. We support Selby Wilsons' position. We were very disturbed when he got involved in the first place and we were relieved when he pulled out. We were very distressed when the executive decided they wanted to go in.

Tobagonians also have the option of returning to the PNM camp and one waits to see what will be offered Tobago by the respective camps in return for its support. Mr. Panday has said that the UNC will fight in Tobago if the Tobago NAR does not endorse the unity platform. As a national party, the UNC should or course contest all seats. One is however not aware that the party has any meaningful presence in Tobago.

There are some who believe or fear that Mr. Panday might in fact surprise everyone and get enough seats to give him more bargaining leverage than he has now. We have however already indicated that the 2 Tobago seats cannot be assumed to be part of the UNC-NAR Accommodation arrangement. Even assuming that they were, it is not clear where the other 3 seats would be won. Some claim that Tunapuna, which is 42 per cent Indian, St. Joseph, which is 40 per cent Indian and Ortoire-Mayaro, which is 47 per cent Indian, are possibilities. The argument is that disenchantment with Mr. Manning and with the Government's economic policies could lead to a withdrawal of enthusiasm on the part of traditional supporters of the PNM. If this is coupled with a high turn out for the UNC, the demographic dimensions which have conduced to PNM majorities or pluralities in the past could conceivably be neutralised to produce a UNC victory.

This scenario is unlikely to play out for two reasons. In the first place, it does not take account of Miss Bhaggan's insertion into the political thicket, and one does not yet know where that "loose cannon" would eventually land. It also does not take into account the phenomenon which was witnessed along the Corridor in 1976 when PNM supporters who were inclined to either vote Tapia, the DAC or stay home found themselves re-assuming their fundamentalist political posture out of concern for a possible ULF victory. My own feeling is that the PNM will again prevail in 1996 and that Mr. Panday will be denied the "mandate of heaven" one more time, assuming of course that he does in fact want it.

Annexe 6

The Arithmetic of Indian Demographic Power*

Basdeo Panday is reported as having said that Indians are the single largest ethnic group in the country. In one sense, he is correct in this assertion. According to the 1990 census, people of Indian descent constitute 40.3 per cent of the total population, those of African descent 39.6 per cent while Whites and Chinese were recorded as being 0.6 per cent and 0.4 per cent respectively. It is however worth noting that the mixed population has grown from 16.3 per cent of the population to 18.4 per cent. One is not entirely certain whether this 2.1 per cent increase is due to miscegenation (including douglarization) or reclassification. It may in fact represent a bit of both, and it may well be that the two major "ethnic" groups are in fact equal in size.

Panday however made a number of interesting observations with respect to size of the Indian population and their attitude, viz., that even though Indians are no longer a minority, they still behave as though they are. As he lamented, "when in 1945, Indo-Trinbagonians celebrated the 100 Anniversary of Indian Arrival Day, Indians constituted 27 per cent of the total population. They accepted the fact that against a background of racial voting, they could not and would not participate in any meaningful way in the

---

**Sunday Express,* January 8, 1994.

governance of the country. Today, Indians constitute the largest single ethnic group in the country, yet many of them are of the same view still." According to Panday, the minority syndrome has sunk so deeply into the psyche of the Indians that even when the minority becomes the majority,they refuse to accept that fact, and continue to behave as though they were still a minority.

In commenting on Panday's remarks, we need to draw attention to the fact that the "minority syndrome" has had a positive impact on the attitudes and behaviour of the Indian population. The fact that they were a distinct minority, both numerically and culturally, led many Indians to strive harder to obtain whatever was considered necessary for achieving success and status mobility in Caribbean society, primarily education and moneyed wealth. The struggle to overcome the obstacles which prevented them from being regarded as "full" citizens in Trinidad and the Caribbean has paid off to the extent that in terms of both education and money and what these buy, the Indian community is no longer subordinate, and in many areas is clearly in a position of dominance or imminent dominance.

Panday is however correct when he notes that many Indians (including himself, I might add) still behave as though this is not so, and as such continue to complain about comprehensive marginalization, alienation and victimization by elements within the "parasitic oligarchy." Members of the latter element are also accused of seeking to destroy the leadership of the UNC to ensure that the growing socio-economic power of the Indian community is not translated into political power following the elections of 1996.

What is said above is not meant to deny that there are still many who, acting either as individuals or in institutional contexts, still regard Indians as less than full citizens in Trinidad and Tobago society, 150 years after the arrival here of their ancestors. By the same token, there are many Indians who, for cultural and other reasons, regard non-Indians as inferiors and discriminate against them in a variety of contexts, both private and public. *The Report on Employment Practices in the Private Sector* prepared by the Centre for Ethnic Studies in 1992 provides ample evidence of this.

Panday is right when he argues that "if Indians want to be treated with equality, then they must struggle for a just and equitable society; it is only when all peoples are treated equally, that by definition, Indians will be afforded equality." "Indians", he further warned, "cannot be equal in isolation; they will succeed in obtaining equal treatment in a just and equitable society in which all peoples are treated equally and with equity."

My own considered view is that the Indian community has made an extremely valuable contribution to Trinidad society, as have other groups, and that, to use Panday's words, "Trinidad and Tobago is a much richer society economically, socially, culturally and politically, because of that fateful arrival." Interestingly, Panday has argued that Trinidad and Tobago as a nation should "thank God for the day the Indians first come to this country." He argues further that like the American pilgrims, Indians should also do so "when they recall the circumstances in the land of their birth which brought them here. I am sure they would want to remember and celebrate that day with prayers and thanksgiving, with joy and merriment in a heart overflowing with appreciation and gratitude." This is a novel argument which reminds me of those who thank the slavers for "rescuing" them from Africa and transporting them to the Americas.

While it may make more sense (in the view of some) to celebrate the ending of indenture rather than the arrival of the first Indians, if Indians share Panday's view that their arrival in Trinidad and Tobago constituted a "kind of emancipation" and wish to celebrate it, the society would agree to give up one of the existing holidays, perhaps Republic Day, and celebrate Indian Arrival Day as a national holiday instead....

One of the fears which I have about the forthcoming celebrations marking the 150th year of the arrival of the Indians in Trinidad and Tobago is that the celebrations would be milked for political advantage. Was Mr. Panday in fact sending a message to the Indian community when he told Indians that they should no longer think of political power as something which is beyond their reach now that they are in fact the largest single ethnic group? There is of course every reason why Indians as a group should wish to play a more prominent role in the political life of the community via the UNC or any other party. One however hopes that the anniversary celebrations will not be blatantly used as a political platform to advance the political ambitions of incumbent or aspiring élites. Should this happen, other groups in the society may be tempted to use the occasion to beat their own rival drums. If so, what is billed as a national celebration, may turn out to be something quite different. It may well be that 1995 would not be a good year to call general elections. The costs to the country may well exceed such benefits as might accrue to any political party.

Annexe 7

Indians: Their Worst Enemy*

Basdeo Panday is arguably one of the most quixotic political figures in contemporary Caribbean politics. While he is perfectly predictable and politically correct in terms of what he says, at least publicly, on the issue of the share of the national product that labour should enjoy, he is a bundle of contradiction on the question of the relationship between ethnicity and social and political incorporation in Trinidad and Tobago. On this issue he is all over the place. At one time he is a "national" leader who seeks to mobilize the oppressed of all ethnicities whether from Laventille or Tableland, while at others he is the ethnic leader *par excellence*. At times one wonders what views he really holds on the ethnic question in Trinidad and Tobago, and what he says about "others" when in private.

Panday has always boasted that he sees politics in terms of class rather than race, and he can in fact point to his record of involvement with parties such as the Workers and Farmers Party, the United Labour Front, and the National Alliance For Reconstruction, all of which represented genuine attempts to ford the ethnic divide, but had their centre of gravity in the non-Indian element in the society at the leadership level. To his credit, Panday, who by 1976 had emerged as the undisputed maximum political

**Sunday Express,* March 12, 1995

leader of the Hindu community, was always willing to stand down in favour of a non-Indian leader.

It is however clear that Panday did not give way because he felt that Indians were not "fit" to hold Prime Ministerial office. He did so because he was aware that if Indians were to escape the "sugar cane jail" to which the conjunctures of "History" had sentenced them, he had to forge coalitions of convenience with others who felt oppressed by the PNM hegemony and who needed a mass base outside the urban and con-urban strongholds of the PNM if they were to wrest power from that Afro-Trinidadian dominated organization.

Panday, it would seem, is now convinced that the age of PNM dominance is over, and that with the demise of the NAR, the rights of succession belong to the UNC. As such, he seems to have decided that after 150 years of being in the wilderness and of genuflecting to others in the arena of national political leadership, the time had come to mobilize the Indian population to make a bid for political power. Those who opt not to be so mobilized thus have to be demonised and called *nemakahrams,* people who are prepared to sell their souls and betray their ancestors for a mess of pottage from the new oligarchy. Panday will of course deny that this is his strategy, and has sought to mask his game plan by saying things about those whom he calls pseudo racists in the Afro-Trinidadian community who pretend that they are ruling in the interest of the Africans, when in fact they are governing in the interest of the parasitic clique. It however seems clear to me that while the main text of Panday's pre-election message articulates a cross racial appeal against the parasitic oligarchy and their spokespersons, the sub-text represents a naked communal appeal.

In saying that Indians "were their worst enemy," willing to sell their birthright for a jacket and tie, a wig and a gown, a seat in the Senate, or a little contract here and there, Panday was attacking elements within the Indian bourgeoisie who were forging links with the wider community in various ways and in the spaces that are being opened up as the state becomes more ethnically neutral. He is telling them that they have a higher responsibility to support their *jhat* in its quest for a turn at the crease. This of course is not the first time that Panday has attacked Indians whom he considered guilty of *neemakharamism.* Winston Dookeran and those who remained with the NAR in 1987 were also tarred with that dreadful and unbearable brush. So too was Hulsie Bhaggan when she broke ranks with the UNC.

Panday is of course not alone in arguing that Indians who break ranks with their base community and join non-communal organizations and political parties are somehow less "Indian" than those who remain within the fold. Indians who managed to rise out of the squalor and servitude of the sugar cane plantation and who chose the "door of cosmopolitanism" to use Ismith Khan's phrase, have often been accused of turning their backs on their poorer kin in their anxiety to become accepted by the so called "national" society. Khan in fact reminded this element that "democracy deals with numbers and not with small affluent intelligentsia and aristocrats in small clubs." In sum, if power was to be won, political mobilization had to regard ethnicity as a prime resource.

Panday has often accused the "creole" community in general and the PNM in particular of discriminating against Indians in certain critical areas of public life. Few would seriously deny that there is merit to this allegation just as no one could deny that Indians also discriminate against non-Indians. And Panday is politically correct when he warns Indians that "they could not achieve equality for themselves in isolation or to the exclusion of other groups in the society since Indians do not have a wall around them and are inextricably bound up in and form part of the society."

The problem, however, is that one cannot logically demand that Indians be given equal access to the opportunities and resources of the society and then condemn them as traitors when they embrace them. Individuals in plural societies identify themselves in many ways. Nation, religion, sect, region of origin, caste, colour, class, occupation, gender, age and family are only some of the markers of identity. Collective memories are also important markers. People emphasize one marker or the other depending on the context. Some markers "stain" more than others and are thus more visible, i.e., they are more emotionally significant and capable of displacing other less primary loyalties and obligations.

Indians in the Caribbean are faced with the perennial dilemma of all marginalized ethnics, viz., whether to function as an ethnic or seek to become mainstream, whatever that might mean at any given time or place. Invariably, the individual ends up being cross pressured between his many worlds.

In the context of Trinidad and Tobago, Indians are not ethnically homogenous even though they belong to the same fictional or imagined "race." Some 60 per cent of them are Hindu. Approximately 25 per cent of them are Christian with the remaining 15 per cent being Muslim. Some are urban while others are rural. Some are very rich while some are very poor. Some are community oriented while others are more cosmopolitan. The cross combinations are myriad. If India is a country of a "million mutinies" and differences, why should Panday assume that the descendants of those who came across the "kali pani" would be any different? Thus, when he talks about Indians being their "worst enemy," his remarks will be positively received by some and savagely rejected by others. One is thus not surprised that some Indians who are every whit as proud of their "Indianess" as is Panday, deny that they are for sale simply because they have either joined the PNM, accepted a senatorship, a speakership, a national or civic office of one kind or another, or an appointment to the board or the top management of one of the conglomerates owned and managed by those whom Panday demonises in the parasitic oligarchy.

Indians are of course not the only ones who have had this charge of being their own worst enemy thrown at them. The black bourgeoisie have also been so attacked and described variously as "Black Britishers," "Afro Saxons" or persons with "black skins and white masks." Whereas it is more the custom for blacks to accuse each other of lacking in community spirit or refusing to bond together for economic and community upliftment as do Indians, Syrians and the Chinese, it is now the Indian community that is being openly accused by persons like Panday and Pandita Indrani Rampersad of destructive divisiveness.

Panday however has to be warned of the consequences of the mobilization strategy that he seems to have decided to adopt in his desperate last ditch quest for political power. He needs to be reminded that while it is easy to summon the proverbial ethnic genie, it is difficult to get it to go back into the bottle. This is particularly so at a time when societies such as ours no longer have the economic resources to mop up discontent. Panday might be right in his view that this is not the time for platitudes and pretty speeches. Pretty speeches would however be equally useless if the dogs of war are unleashed by those who feel that the time had come to play the ethnic card openly in the contest for political office.

Annexe 8

Bearing the Trinity Cross*

The controversy over the naming of the nation's highest award, the Trinity Cross, once again raised the question as to whether Trinidad and Tobago is essentially a homogeneous country in ethnic terms or whether it is "plural." If we look at what the 1990 Census tells us about the religious composition of the society, we find that Christians are in the majority. They account for some seventy per cent of the population while Hindus and Muslims together account for 29.6 per cent. In racial terms, the 1960 Census data tells us that the Indian population was 37 per cent while in 1980 it was 40 per cent. In 1990, it was 40.3 per cent.

It is also worth noting that while Indians constitute the largest single "racial" grouping in the society, accounting for 40.3 per cent of the population, non-Indians account for 59.7 per cent. We note further that in 1990, 122,477 persons or 27.2 per cent of the Indian population were Christian. The data likewise indicate that the largest single denominational group among the Christian Indians is Catholic and not Presbyterian as commonly believed. Catholicism is the denominational affiliation claimed by 34,077 of the Indians. The figures for other groups are Presbyterians 33,733, Pentecostals 29,205, Sanatanists 108,759, Other Hindus 154,767, Muslims (Asja) 23,193, and Muslims (other) 37,759.

**Sunday Express*, September 10, 1995.

If one were to compare this data with what were available in 1930, one would see the extent to which the Christian Indian population has grown in the past 60 years. In 1930, the total Indian population was 354,503. Of these, 22,750 or approximately 6.5 per cent were Christian. There were 8,469 Catholics, 3,946 Anglicans and 10,335 Presbyterians. In sum, the Christian population had increased by over 400 per cent in the years after 1930. The denominational groups and their percentages of the Indian population in 1990 are shown in Table 1.

Table 1. Religious Affiliations of Indians - 1990 Census

Religion	Frequency	
	Total	Percent
Hindu-Other	154,767	34.2
Hindu-Sanatanist	108,759	24.0
Presbyterian	33,773	7.5
Roman Catholic	34,077	7.5
Islam-Other	37,759	8.3
Islam-Asja	23,193	5.1
Pentecostal	29,205	6.4
Other Christian	13,492	3.0
Anglican	4,073	0.9
Seventh Day Adventist	4,079	0.9
None	3,075	0.6
Baptist-Orthodox	908	0.2
Jehovah-Witness	2,568	0.1
Methodist	302	0.7
Not Stated	2,943	0.6

What the figures indicate is that the majority of the population of Trinidad is Christian and non-Indian. If the matter were to be decided purely on the basis of numbers, then the Trinity Cross should remain as the country's highest national honour. But we need to ask questions about what the numbers mean on this particular issue. How intensely does the non-Christian minority as a whole, as opposed to some of its assumed spokespersons, feel about the matter? We note, for example, that those who claim to speak for Baptists do not in fact represent the views of the majority. Are Indians who are Christian unequivocally so, or do they have split allegiances which make them take a different view on the matter from say Catholics who are not Indian? We would also need to know how many Indians who are Hindus or Muslims in fact object to the use of the appellation, Trinity Cross. One suspects that there is no unanimity of view within either the Indian Christian community or the Indian non-Christian community.

One however has to see the contestation over the naming of the honour in terms other than the purely arithmetic. What we are in fact witnessing is a renewed assertiveness on the part of elements in the Indian community who are demanding a greater share of power in the society. This assertiveness, which achieved momentum in 1970 as a result of the "Black Power" movement, and which gained added force following the victory of the NAR in 1986, is being waged on many fronts. The recent controversy over the allocation and naming of public holidays is one case in point. The hijab issue provided another occasion for some elements in the Muslim community to flex a bit of social and cultural muscle. Some Muslims insisted that their daughters be allowed to wear this form of head dress to Catholic schools where the uniform does not permit its use. One also recalls the hullabaloo over the Government's declaration that the steel band was the national instrument, and the issue as to whether Hindi should be taught in the Secondary Schools. Complaints have also been heard from time to time about the lack of "real ecumenism" in inter-faith services such as those which mark the opening of the Law Courts.

One lawyer complained that "inter-faith" meant a Hindi pundit would say some mantras, an Imam would give a blessing or message, but that the sermon would always be based on Christian scripture and be delivered in a Christian Church. (I was amused to be present at a PNM political meeting which was being addressed by an Imam who referred to the new UNC government as a "cross" which the nation has to bear).

The inclusion of the term "Cross" in the label given to the country's highest honour is also said to contribute to the sense of "alienation" and lack of patriotism felt by many. The Secretary of the Caribbean Hindu Centre claimed that it was an "affront to the dignity of the non-Christian population." As he asked further, "how can such a large part of our population feel a sense of belonging and patriotism when the highest award to which they can aspire evades their very presence by acknowledging the Christian "Cross" and failing to recognise the Muslim "Crescent" or the Hindu "Om"?

Non-Christian reaction to the demands of Indian cultural activists vary. Some take up extreme positions. As far as they are concerned, Indians have gone "culturally mad" and are bent on group aggrandisement at the expense of the rest of the community. Some even say that "they" should be given two or perhaps three counties in central and south Trinidad in which to do their "thing" or that a "line" has to be drawn somewhere lest they succeed in "grabbing" everything that is of material and symbolic value to the "mainstream" of the society.

Others take a more dispassionate view of the matter and regard what is taking place as being quite normal and expected. Older generations of Indians were, with a few exceptions, prepared to defer and genuflect to the dominant Eurocentric and Christian value system of the society, preferring to concentrate instead on economic, cultural and educational self-help and improvement. They saw themselves as being marginals in the society who had to petition the establishment for opportunity and political protection.

Now that a certain platform of achievement has been reached in several critical areas of the society, group confidence is high. As such, challenges to the social and political system that would not have been forthcoming forty or fifty years ago are now undertaken with truculence and impatience. The closer Indians get to the promised land of cultural parity, the more frustrating and irritating perceived slights become. One can thus expect more barricades to be stormed. Excess will certainly attend some of these challenges as has been the case when other minorities, whether based on gender, religion, race or some other variable, stake claims for equality. In order to end up where one wishes to settle, one often has to make exaggerated demands which frighten the other party into accepting a compromise with which all can live.

As galling as it might be to fundamentalist Christians, the use of the term "Cross", (some Hindus insist that the Swastika is a Hindu Cross and Hinduism has a trinity concept of the religious figures of Brahama, Shiva and Khrisna), a religious symbol with religious significance for only one section of the population, should be discontinued, and a more culturally neutral term found to denote the country's highest national honour. It should be done quickly and with grace. Those who chose the label did so without giving much thought to the implications of their decision, simply because it was epistemologically difficult for them to do so. The world today is however quite a different place from what obtained in the forties, and fifties and sixties. Then, societies were unthinkingly rushing along the path of Westernization without asking questions about the validity and universality of Western cultural assumptions. Multi-culturalism is however now a widely cherished goal in many societies. Inspite of all our differences and the antics of our fanatics, we may yet prove that it can be made to work in Trinidad and Tobago.

Annexe 9

Ethnic Ticket Balancing in Trinidad and Tobago: 1995*

Modern political parties have always attempted to present balanced tickets to the electorate. Ticket balancing in Trinidad and Tobago, to be effective, however cannot be a mere matter of creating genotypically balanced slates. There is also the question of the extent to which Indo-Trinidadians who carry PNM standards or Afro-Trinidadians who do the same for the UNC are seen to be legitimate spokesmen for their groups. Indians who join the PNM are often seen as "deviants" or opportunists by those who consider themselves to be more "authentic." Those who are Christian, whether Presbyterian, Catholic, Anglican or Pentecostal, are not seen by traditional Indians as being genuine representatives of Indian interests. They are seen to belong to a distinctive confessional sub-group with a consciousness, status, and style that sets them apart from the more Hinduized or Islamicized Indians. They are even said to be readily recognizable by Indian insiders.

Hindus and Muslims who join the PNM are also seen as *nemakharams,* (that unbearable blemish) persons who have betrayed their ancestors for a mess of pottage, "their own worst enemy." If this is indeed so, then the Indian candidates chosen by the PNM to contest the election might not prove to be the political

**Sunday Express,* October 22, 1995.

call card Manning assumes them to be. The same however holds for Afro-Trinidadians who "shack up" with the UNC. They too are seen as "deviants," betrayers of their ancestral obligations.

The view that Christian Indians are still a group apart is however not universally accepted. In their study of religion and culture in Trinidad and Tobago, Drs. Ralph Premdas and Harold Sitahal (in Ryan: 1991) note that while it is true that Presbyterians were generally wealthier and more westernized in the pre-Independence era, class distinctions between them and the Hindus and Muslims have now largely disappeared, thanks to the economic boom of the seventies. The other markers which once separated the groups are no longer as readily recognizable as they once were. This is particularly so of those who have become embourgeoisified.

The two authors argue that political competition has also helped to generate a sense of solidarity within the Indian community:

> The capture of power by the PNM and its perceived discriminatory policies against Indians released a powerful motivation for Indian unity. After thirty years of such a regime, Presbyterians found solace and security not with their Christian Creole and Mixed Race confessional compatriots, but with other Indians. One result has been the almost complete erasure of any cultural and social distinction of consequence between Presbyterians and Hindus and Moslems in the same economic class category. The more westernized Presbyterian vis-a-vis the Hindu middle class person has become something of a myth. The Presbyterian has been re-Hinduized. Many seek their roots within their ancient Indian culture in reaction to Creole assertions of a rediscovered African identity and the subsidies and biases of the state for Calypso. (ibid., 348)

This is probably more true of Christian Indians who live in rural communities surrounded by Hindus than it is of their urban counterparts. In sum, community involvement may be more important than religion.

Be that as it may, both the PNM and the UNC have made it clear that they have no interest in any "one love" formula that would involve a diminution of the hegemony of their respective parties. In the case of the PNM, that position has always been asserted. Dr. Williams was congenitally allergic to any political formula that would require the PNM to share political power with any group. So was Mr. Chambers and now Mr. Manning. It was for this reason that Dr. Williams was as savage as he was in his criticism of the Wooding Constitution Commission. In his view, the agenda of the Commission, which he deemed "illogical," was "to create confusion and break the centralisation of Parliament, Cabinet and the [PNM] political party."

Mr. Panday, vociferously encouraged by the militants and ethnic revivalists within his camp, also declared himself unwilling to bend his back yet another time to accommodate office seekers. Panday also believes that the time had come for Indians to stop capitulating to others who feel that the Prime Ministership is not safe in the hands of Trinidadians who happen to be Indians. As he told the conference marking the 150th anniversary of the arrival of Indians in Trinidad and Tobago:

> ... the base from which the Indian politician (more correctly the politician of Indian descent) emerged in Trinidad and Tobago was itself a constraint upon his further development as a national leader. In a society in which African political dominance has held sway for some forty years, the Indian politician is often seen as a threat to this domination. This fear is encouraged by the African political elite and the unseen hand of the business conglomerates who see their continued strangle-hold on the economy as being inextricably bound up with the political fortunes of the PNM or its equivalent. The propaganda used is that the Indians have land and business, and all the African has is the patronage of the state. Should the Indian seize political power, the Africans would have nothing. This appeal to primordial instincts has been difficult to resist. So powerful has been this propaganda that even Indians with nothing believe it. Hence the success of the campaign that should there be an Indian Prime Minister, he would take away all

the jobs which were given as patronage to Africans and give them to Indians.

Like Jagan in Guyana, Panday is clearly anxious to retain the dominant position of the UNC, though he was prepared to "dress up his slate" with a few persons (Assam, McClean, Raphael, McSween etc.) on a "Civic List." One however hopes that this "Civic List" is not comprehensively marginalised as has been the case in Guyana. One also waits to see whether if or when the citadels of power are in fact captured by the UNC, "one love" would in fact prevail, or whether one hegemony would seek to replace the other, with all this could mean for the stability of the state. We recall for the sake of the record that Mr. Panday has on more than one occasion promised to form a government of national unity if the UNC were to win the election.

Annexe 10

Ethnicity and Electoral Boundary Making in Trinidad and Tobago*

I have been asked by a reader of this column to respond to a number of questions that have arisen in his mind following upon remarks made by me during what he refers to as a "race" forum hosted by the U.W.I. At the risk of causing some of my critics, to have an apoplectic fit, let me repeat very briefly what I said. My first comment was that an "Indo-Trinidadian dominated" party will come to power in the next 10 or 15 years." Now one does not need to be reminded that one cannot predict with any accuracy what will happen 10 or 15 years from now. One cannot even predict with accuracy what will happen 1 week from now. Yet we all make projections based on what we think or believe we know to be true. In my case, I was simply looking at demographic trends as I understand them and made projections as to what they are likely to yield down the road. No hidden political agendas informed my remarks. I was not seeking to comfort or scare anyone though it is clear that many people were scared or comforted, or affected to be.

I agree that my remarks invited one to conclude that political power is not now in the hands of Indo-Trinidadians. Most people would agree with me that that is indeed the case, though

---

**Sunday Express*, April 10, 1994.

some argue that appearances to the contrary notwithstanding, the power shift of which I speak has already taken place. Real power i.e., social and economic power they would say, is not where it appears to be on the surface. My own judgement is that we are now in a transition stage, and that the dialectically driven transfer of power to the new hegemon has not yet taken place.

My remarks on the subject of gerrymandering were not of recent vintage. In my *Race and Nationalism in Trinidad and Tobago* which was written in 1970 and published in 1972, the following statements were made about a debate which took place in the Legislature in 1961. We reprint those remarks in the hope that they help to explain to the individual concerned what was meant by my comments on boundary drawing:

> The debate on the report of the [Boundaries] commission provides extremely rich evidence in support of our fundamental thesis, that *ethnicity is the dominant variable in the political life of Trinidad and Tobago.* Whatever the issue, sooner or later the trails lead to the ethnic configuration of the community. The PNM insisted that the redrafting of the boundaries had nothing to do with race. It was a logical and scientific attempt to correct the cartographical indiscretions of the old regime. The DLP were, however, convinced that the PNM had counter-gerrymandered the community in an even more shameful way. The opposition member on the commission, who submitted a minority report, saw the majority report as a 'death blow to democracy.'
>
> The DLP complained that the commission had violated its terms of reference, which stated that constituencies should represent approximately 12,000 voters, and that any substantial departure from that figure was to be applicable only in the case of sparsely populated areas 'which, on account of size, isolation or inadequacy of communications', could not adequately be represented by a single member. The DLP member of the commission maintained that while he agreed that Tobago should be given two seats on this basis, even though the total voting population of the island was around 13,500, the PNM

delegation refused to do the same in other sparsely populated areas in Trinidad. Instead of overloading the urban areas, they did just the reverse. Most of the urban seats were 300 voters under the 12,000 pilot figure, while most of the rural areas — 3 — exceeded it by 300, a discrepancy of some 600 voters. One seat in the capital city carried as few as 11,492 voters, while seats in the rural Indian belt carried as many as 12,735, 12,467, and 12,589, to give differences of over 1,000 voters.

During the debate, the PNM did more to point up the indiscretion of the former regime than to correct the impression that it had used the returns of previous elections to create majorities for itself. Six additional seats were given to the county of St. George, which, admittedly, was the fastest growing in terms of population. But it was precisely in this area that the PNM had shown itself strong. The county, if Port of Spain were to be included, now had thirteen of the thirty seats, all of which were expected to, and did in fact, go to the PNM.

The PNM took no chances even in Port of Spain, where the boundaries were redrafted to make sure that all potential DLP areas, i.e., the upper-class and upper-middle-class residential areas, were attached to heavily working-class areas where the PNM had been consistently strong. The DLP was not given an outside chance to gain a seat in the capital city as they had done in the 1958 and 1959 municipal elections. The PNM refused to accept the suggestion that they should have gone beyond the Port of Spain city limits, as they had done in San Fernando, to include part of the suburbs of St. George, which might then have been given eight seats, all of which would have had a potential electorate closer to the 12,000 mark. In the countryside there was strong evidence to substantiate the DLP's claim that the PNM had herded as many Indian voters as was possible into constituencies which they could not possibly win, and had extracted from such areas large blocks of Negro voters who were then recombined into new constituencies.

Ten of the thirty constituencies contained populations which were more than 50 percent Indian. The DLP won them all. Whether or not there was any truth in the claim that one minister had boasted, that the constituencies were 'scientifically gerrymandered is difficult to say. But the evidence certainly suggests that the cartography was undertaken with the electoral returns of the previous elections in mind. The Government's delegation on the commission had been advised by a PNM constituency delimitation committee, which included some of the best surveyors in the country. As the report of the general secretary to the Special Party Convention, held in September 1961, declared, 'The committee carried out its assignment wonderfully, and advised the PNM members on the commission accordingly, the result of which is well known to all party members'. The DLP, it was noted, had no comparable backroom boys.

The DLP was extremely incensed at what they considered to be political immorality on the part of a supposedly honest government. They claimed that it was now possible for the PNM to get a majority of seats with a minority of the popular vote. What is more, they could win the election without the support of the rural south and south-east. As the Honourable Stephen Maharaj warned, 'Importance must not only be attached to one portion or section of Trinidad. The people in the cities, the people in places like St. George, are dependent on the people of the rural areas for their very life, and their very existence ... and so are the people of the rural areas dependent on the North. We cannot separate Trinidad.... the action of this Government has certainly given a different status to different citizens. (Ryan 1972:243-246)

Annexe 11

The *Leela* of Occah Seapaul*

Political decision making is invariably a messy business. Very rarely are the choices to be made unequivocally between the forces of "good" and the forces of "evil," or ones in which all parties win. Inevitably, there are winners and losers, a balance of good and evil. All this is by way of an attempt to re-examine the question of who "won" or "lost" in the continuing "leela" (saga) of Occah Seapaul vs. the PNM. I am already on record as saying that in this unfortunate affair, everybody has lost—Seapaul, Maraj, the UNC, the PNM, the Prime Minister, and the country at large, and I have no reason to revise that view.

There are however some new dimensions to the issue. One has to do with Ralph Maraj's pumped up tirade against the PNM leader in which the actor clearly got the better of the politician. I do not for one minute agree with Mr. Maraj's charge that the PNM has been guilty of hooliganism and constitutional thuggery in this particular matter. At most, the Party was guilty of making a "forced error," if I might borrow a term from tennis. As I see it, having forced Mr. Gift (who incidentally was both male and Afro-Trinidadian) to resign, the Government had little option but to suggest to the Speaker that she too should resign having regard to the facts that emerged during the Court matter against Mr. Jattan. The Prime Minister also claimed to have discovered a

---

**Sunday Express,* August 13, 1996.

number of things about Miss Seapaul's business activities which, in his view, served to make her unfit to occupy the office of Speaker, an office which is "two heart beats" away from the Presidency, so to speak. Mr. Manning claims that he felt sufficiently concerned about the information in his possession to bring it to Miss Seapaul's attention. Miss Seapaul however flatly denied that anything was amiss.

We are all aware that the Speaker refused to resign as most clear thinking people believe she ought to have done in the circumstances, her gender notwithstanding. The Speaker of course did not agree that her private activities blemished her official role, and instead argued that she had done nothing which, in the context of Trinidad and Tobago's political culture, warranted resignation. What is more, she now claims that in "standing firm" she was "standing up for the constitution," a claim which the UNC, for its own expediential purposes, has chosen to sustain. Mr Panday has covered his flank by saying that while he disagreed with Miss Seapaul politically, he was not prepared to stand by and see her "humiliated."

Miss Seapaul has now adopted an even holier than thou posture, feeling perhaps that none of this has "happened by accident," and that "synchronicity" is at work. Having burnt many of her professional bridges, she is now of the view that some soul force has opened up a wonderful road ahead for her, and that henceforth, she would serve as a "light to all people in this country" as they lock horns in a fight to the finish with the "forces of intellectual darkness". Her brother was apparently to be part of this moral and leadership offensive, perhaps to insert himself in the UNC and ride (or capture it) as others had before.

It would seem that Mr. Manning and the PNM leadership had in fact been eavesdropping on the Speaker and had come to the view that this was precisely what informed the latter's quixotic behaviour in Parliament once she had decided that she would not resign. In refusing to do so, the Speaker clearly set upon a course of action which was designed to frustrate the Government at every turn. The Speaker's Chair was transformed into a bully pulpit from which to hector errant parliamentarians and judges just as lawyers had been when they appeared before her in the Courts. Seapaul also skillfully used the procedural power which the Speaker enjoys in the parliamentary process to her advantage. She also cleverly invoked gender as a resource in this epic battle. Others, quite cynically and in some cases understandably, invoked race on her behalf, perhaps seeing her struggle as an extension of the conflict which the Prime Minister had with her brother, which many saw in ethnic terms. The Opposition, for its part, had a vested interest in embarrassing the Government politically, and was a willing instrument in this political confrontation.

Even though the Acting President claims that the Government had "reliable information" as to what Miss Seapaul planned to do, it is of course difficult to prove that she would have done any of the things which it is alleged she was about to do. She has in fact deemed them to have been "legally impossible." A besieged government may however have felt that she might have tried to do them anyway in order to either hold on to an office which she valued dearly or to punish the government for daring to humiliate and shame her publicly.

It is also possible that the events of 1990 informed behaviour in 1995. In 1990, the NAR leadership had information about what the Jamaat al Muslimeen intended, but chose to dismiss such reports as "old talk." The PNM leadership may thus have been determined to prevent such a *reprise,* especially since they were being bitterly accused of weakness and a failure to anticipate and counter the "wiles" of Miss Seapaul. Interestingly, former President of the Senate, Michael Williams has observed that both the Jamaat al Muslimeen and the Speaker used "unauthorized strategies" to disenfranchise the electorate. The difference between them, in his view, was choice of instrument and not of aim.

Clearly, a harried Government was faced with a situation where they could not dismiss the possibility that Miss Seapaul would be crazy enough to seek to disable the government by refusing to recognize the Court's order to reseat the leader of the House, Mr. Valley, and by suspending two additional PNM members which could have eroded the Government's parliamentary majority if Mr. Maraj had voted with the UNC and the NAR, and Miss Bhaggan had chosen to vote against the Government. In politics, anything is possible. There was also fear that the Speaker might have gone even further and use the cover of Standing Order 43, Section 12 to suspend or adjourn (not prorogue) Parliament. That item of the Standing Order provides that "...in the case of grave disorder arising in the House, the Speaker may, if he thinks it necessary to adjourn the House without question, put or suspend the sitting for a time to be named by him."

One also has to factor into the analysis the fact that the Government not only had a major strike on its hands in the oil belt, but that Carifesta VI was imminent as was the important meeting of the Association of Caribbean States on Trade, Tourism and Transportation. All of these matters required time and attention since governments do not have the luxury of having to deal with one issue at a time. One could thus understand why the government sought to use the emergency provisions of the Constitution to bring closure to this matter. In this context one recalls Harry Truman's seizure in 1952 of the strike threatened steel mills whose output was required for military purposes, an action that was taken without explicit statutory authority and which later found disfavour with the American Supreme Court. Truman had to make a painful decision, and he did, leaving the jurists, the pundits, and posterity to argue as to whether he was right or wrong.

Having sought to divine what might have been in Seapaul's mind and that of the Prime Minister and his close colleagues, I still hold to the view that the government should have given the Speaker a bit more rope to hang herself, which is what she would have done had she sought to execute the alleged plot. The public would then be less divided in its view as to whether the action was justified or not. The question might however be asked as to what options would the government have had if the Speaker had done the things which the government feared she would do? There were two possibilities open. One was to seek the help of the Court as Mr. Valley did. The other was to call an election. One understands why the government did not wish to call an election now. The country does not want it, as SARA surveys indicated, and it would have been bad for the economy. It is always unwise to rely on the Courts to settle issues that are political. That, however, is precisely what has happened. The state of emergency has in fact settled nothing and has merely opened up a new can of political, legal and constitutional worms that will wiggle within and gnaw away at the body politic for a long time to come.

Moreover, Seapaul is still formally Speaker, and continues to enjoy all the perks of the office. All that has happened is that she has lost a great deal of social status and legitimacy now that her colourful personal and business life are the subject of discussion on every street corner, cocktail party, bar and hairdresser salon. She has been able to mobilize a measure of gender support, and not surprisingly, a considerable amount of ethnic support which she is now seeking to convert to her political project. My own feeling, however, is that Miss Seapaul's attempt to use the bleach of politics to launder and re-engineer herself will not prove sustainable, and that her political career would get no further than Ms. Bhaggan's has, if that far. I cannot see her being of much electoral value to the UNC either. Nor can I see her returning to either the bar or the bench. That leaves business. But that too has its difficulties as time will make clear.

And what of her brother's political future? Mr. Maraj has said a great deal about the PNM and Mr. Manning's leadership style. Some of what he has said might well be true, and the party and analysts would certainly need to debate those issues in the near future. It is however unfortunate that these things were said on a UNC platform by someone who still claims membership in the PNM. This is *nemakharam* behaviour, and one wonders whether any serious political party would want someone in its ranks who is as unprincipled as Maraj, unless race is to function as an override to all else. One notes that the UNC now insists on PNM like discipline within its own ranks, leading some of its members to accuse it of seeking to create a party oligarchy and dictatorship of its own.

One well understands Mr. Maraj's bitterness and his desire to destroy Mr. Manning politically. Mr. Maraj is however clearly a political babe in the woods if he does not understand that such attacks, coming from him in the given circumstances, would strengthen rather than weaken Mr. Manning in much the same way as Miss Bhaggan's attacks on Mr. Panday seems to have strengthened, rather than weakened him. The rules that govern politics in plural societies differ somewhat from those in homogenous societies, particularly those that are small. In plural societies, it is not always prudent or "politically correct" for someone from a rival group to attack an icon from another competing group without running the risk that the attack, however justified, might be de-legitimized simply because of the source from which it came.

Some comment is also warranted about Mr. Maraj's claim that he is still legitimate because the victory in San Fernando West was his and not that of the PNM. One wonders just who is hallucinating. It is true that the electorate of San Fernando West is 42 percent Indian. But is Mr. Maraj assuming that the fact that he is Indian led all of these people to vote for him, and that had the PNM put up someone else, say a non-Indian, the UNC would have won the seat? Mr. Maraj is clearly signalling his intention to join the UNC which he expects would win the next election. If this occurs, as he believes, he would expect to become part of a UNC Government in which, as he says, Mr. Panday would be a "good" Prime Minister, Mr. Maharaj a "good" Attorney General and Mr. Wade Mark a "good" Minister of Labour. All that I can do for the time being is to wish Mr. Maraj and Miss Seapaul luck in their new political reincarnations.

Annexe 12

Statement to Parliament by the Honourable Attorney General on the Seapaul Issue

The government last evening advised the Acting President of the Republic to proclaim a State of Emergency limited to the City of Port of Spain. Subsequently an order of detention was served on the Speaker of the House of Representatives Madame Occah Seapaul. Madame Seapaul will remain in detention at her residence #9 Mary Street St. Clair until further order.

For the past few weeks the Parliament of the Republic of Trinidad and Tobago has been subjected to action by the Speaker which is unprecedented and which now threatens to usurp the rights of the elected representatives in Parliament, and in particular that of the representatives of the majority. Indeed these actions were aimed at destroying the very parliamentary democracy to which we all subscribe.

The government has, throughout this unfolding drama, sought to act with restraint and within the bounds of proper legal, parliamentary and Constitutional procedures. We saw it as our duty to uphold the dignity of Parliament and that of the Office of Speaker, as we endeavoured to protect the interest of the citizens of Trinidad and Tobago.

Whilst as a Government we had several options, it was our hope that we would not have had to apply the ultimate constitutional powers of the State. At every stage we hoped that good sense would prevail; that at most, moral suasion and established Parliamentary procedures and conventions would prevail. Regrettably this was not to be.

In keeping with this approach the Government did pursue the following courses of action:

(1) It initiated private and confidential discussions with the Speaker. This failed.

(2) The Government then was forced to file a motion of no confidence in the Speaker.

(3) Common decency and established conventions dictated that the Speaker not be a Judge in her own cause. The application of this convention was dismissed by the Speaker.

(4) The Government then introduced a constitutional amendment which was passed in the Senate with overwhelming majority support.

These measured and procedurally correct approaches have been met at every turn by arbitrary and capricious action by the Speaker. In short, the Speaker effectively sought to frustrate the will of the elected members of Parliament, the representatives of the people.

The final act of usurpation was the suspension by the Speaker of the Honourable Member for Diego Martin Central in clear breach of the Standing Orders and procedures of Parliament. Even then, recourse was first had to the courts of this country. It was only when there were clear indications that the order of the court would not be accepted by the Speaker, and that the reckless suspension of other government members was to follow, that the final option had to be exercised. Make no mistake the constitutional option of declaring a state of emergency was always available, but the Government chose to exercise it only to prevent the systematic overthrow of the duly elected Government and the dangerous instability which would have followed such an action.

A state of emergency under our Constitution is a vital instrument to be utilized in order to preserve our democracy. The Government is concerned however that we as a country shall return to a normal state in the shortest possible time. The Government recognizes that a state of emergency such as this would occasion some inconvenience to some members of the national community. We however believe that this is much more palatable than the state of constitutional crisis into which the Speaker was leading this Parliament and this country.

It should be noted that while the regulations will restrict without permission, the holding of public meetings in the City of Port of Spain, no curfew will be in effect either in Port of Spain or any other part of the country. The normal day to day activities of citizens will, for all practical purposes, remain unaffected by the proclamation of last evening.

The Government is committed to maintaining our democracy which is founded on the principle that the elected members of Parliament must uphold the Constitution and the Law. It is no part of our tradition that any persons or group of persons whether elected or not should seek to control or overturn our Parliament and our other democratic institutions. Any such action must be firmly resisted by right thinking citizens and met with the appropriate legal and constitutional response.

This Government in carrying out its mandate which was obtained in free and fair elections will govern with sensitivity, caring and resolute commitment to defend the interest of all the people of Trinidad and Tobago. In so doing, the Government will not be intimidated by, nor succumb to threats and subversion in whatever form they may choose to express themselves.

Annexe 13

Age, Class, Gender, Race and Voting Disposition in the 1995 Election

Age, class, gender and ethnicity were clearly at work in the 1995 general election. These variables clearly influenced the turn out rate as well as the parties to which support was given. Let us first look at the way age correlated with disposition to vote. Looking at Table 1, we find a clear relationship between age and voting intention. Older persons were more determined to vote. Only 53 per cent of those who were 18-21 said that they would definitely vote, compared to 75 per cent for the 41-50 and 80 per cent for the 50 plus age groups. When the vote intentions for the 18-21 were aggregated, we found 66 per cent of them saying that they would either definitely or probably vote, 12 per cent saying that they would definitely not vote, and 21 per cent saying they were uncertain.

Table 1. Age and Disposition to Vote

	18-21	22-30	31-40	41-50	50+
Definitely Vote	53	63	67	75	80
Probably Vote	13	14	17	16	12
Definitely not Vote	12	10	7	4	1
Uncertain	21	11	7	4	6
Non Response	1	2	2	2	2

Table 2. Importance of Election

	18-21	22-30	31-40	41-50	50+
Very Important	47	48	51	56	63
Important	25	22	24	22	23
Not Very Important	13	17	15	14	3
Uncertain	13	9	5	5	5
Refuse to Say	2	3	5	3	6

Disposition to vote is always related to the issues involved in an election or the context of the election. How important did the various age cohorts consider the election? The older one was the more inclined one was to deem the election "very important" or "important." Sixty-three per cent of those 50 years and over saw the election as being "very important" while another 23 per cent deemed it "important" for a combined total of 86. At the other end of the age spectrum, we find 47 per cent of the 18-21 deeming it "very important," for an aggregate of 72 per cent, a difference of 14 per cent.

When the data were looked at in terms of ethnicity and gender, there were interesting differences in the way in which the cohorts responded. Afro-Trinidadians aged 18-30 revealed a weaker disposition to vote than their Indo-Trinidadian counterparts. Only 50 per cent of the former of both genders said they would definitely vote, while 18 and 19 per cent said they would probably vote. The aggregated figures for males 18-30 was 68 per cent while that for females was 69 per cent. The remaining Afro-Trinidadian males were either not planning to vote — 10 per cent — or were uncertain — 21 per cent. One quarter of the Afro-Trinidadian females said they were definitely not voting while 7 per cent were uncertain. When we look at Indo-Trinidadians we found that 75 per cent of the males and 69 per cent of the females saying they would definitely vote, and 9 and 14 per cent saying they would probably vote. The aggregate for Indo-Trinidadian males was 84 per cent and for Indo-Trinidadian females 83 per cent.

Table 3. Ethnicity and Disposition to Work

	Age 18 - 30 Years			
	Afro-Trinidadian		Indo-Trinidadian	
	Male %	Female %	Male %	Female %
Will Definitely Vote	50	50	75	69
Will Probably Vote	18	19	9	14
Will Definitely Not Vote	10	25	5	3
Uncertain	21	7	10	13

Social class was also an important factor which was assumed to be related to disposition to vote. We were curious as to whether lower class Afro-Trinidadians would show a lower disposition to vote than their Indo-Trinidadians counterparts. We found that the differences were not as significant as assumed. Seventy-five per cent of the Afro-Trinidadians belonging to the lower strata said that they were definitely voting while 7 per cent said they would probably vote. Five per cent said they would definitely not vote while 13 per cent said they were uncertain. In terms of the Indo-Trinidadians, 83 per cent were definitely voting while 2 per cent said they would probably vote while 8 per cent said they were unsure. When the figures are aggregated we find that 82 per cent of the Afro-Trinidadians in the lower strata were disposed to vote while 18 per cent were not. For the Indians 85 per cent were positively disposed while 15 per cent were not. The differences were thus not statistically significant.

Turning next to the middle strata, we found that the aggregated figures for the African middle class were 81 per cent positive and 19 per cent negative while for Indo-Trinidadians it was 92 per cent positive and 8 per cent negative. At the upper/ upper middle level, the comparable figures were 95 per cent positive for the Afro-Trinidadians and 98 per cent positive for the Indo-Trinidadians.

When we look at whom the male youth of both ethnic communities said they preferred to win, we find more equivocation among Afro-Trinidadians than Indo-Trinidadians. Fifty-two per cent of the Afro-Trinidadians aged 18-21 said that the party which they preferred to see win was the PNM. Thirteen per cent chose the NAR and 17 per cent had no particular party preference. Nine per cent were uncertain. Their Indo-Trinidadian counterparts were less equivocal. Seventy-nine per cent preferred to see the UNC form the next government.

The pattern was a bit different when we considered data on the preferences of those aged 21-30. Both the Afro-Trinidadians and the Indo-Trinidadians said they preferred the PNM and the UNC in roughly similar proportions — 65 per cent and 67 per cent respectively. When we compared the younger cohorts with their elders, we found that pro-UNC sympathies increased dramatically among Indo-Trinidadians over 50 while the same did not happen with PNM elders. Sixty-six per cent of the Afro-Trinidadians over 50 chose the PNM while 13 per cent chose the UNC. Eighty-one per cent of the Indo-Trinidadians over 50 chose the UNC while 9 per cent chose the PNM.

Table 4
Party Preferred to Form Next Government (Males)

	18-21		21-30	
	African	Indian	African	Indian
PNM	52	3	65	7
UNC	0	79	6	67
NAR	13	10	16	10
Uncertain	9	0	3	5
Refuse to Say	9	3	2	3
Other				

It has been argued that the voting pattern in the 1995 election reflected the racial divisions in the society perhaps more than was the case in the last 3 or 4 elections when there was an element of cross ethnic voting on the part of Indo- Trinidadians. Polling data however suggest that there was some cross voting despite the intense pressure put on both major ethnic groups by platform speakers and communities to vote for co-ethnics. The data indicate that more Indo-Trinidadians — 18 per cent — were disposed to prefer the PNM than Afro-Trinidadians were disposed to prefer the UNC. Only five per cent of the latter said that they would vote for the UNC. Eleven per cent of the mixed element said they preferred the UNC. Six per cent of the Afro-Trinidadians opted for the NAR as did 4 per cent of the Indians.

One is not certain that voters actually carried through with the dispositions indicated in the poll which was conducted in mid-October, 1995. Fewer Indians seem to have actually voted for the PNM. Election data suggests too that the turn out rate among all groups but particularly among Afro-Trinidadians was generally lower than the poll indicated. There is also the question as to whether the electoral register was inflated. My belief is that it was inflated, perhaps by as much as 20 per cent. The Elections and Boundaries Commission is understandably reluctant to remove names of persons on the list (though there have been some curious omissions, more likely than not in error rather than in an attempt to disenfranchise).

Annexe 14

PNM's Evaluation of its Performance in the 1995 General Election

Regional Supervisors

* Limited financial resources
* Lack of commitment and motivation on the part of several members of the campaign teams which included members of the constituency executive
* Absence of strong, effective leadership to plan and execute the campaign
* Campaign managers lacked the authority, and the co-operation of other members of the Executive to manage the campaign
* Many non-functional party groups
* Weak candidate
* Replacement of campaign manager two weeks before the election
* Fighting among Executive members

* Insufficient spot meetings

* Smear campaign by party members

* Neglect of the constituency by the incumbent

* There was hardly a visit by the Political leadership or a member of Government to 80 per cent of the electoral districts (under review) during the four years preceding this election

* The system of caretaker representatives in "opposition" constituencies yielded a high level of frustration and disappointment

* The theme of "Leadership that's working" or performance being emphasized did not resonate sufficiently with the voters, more so in the face of evidence of rising crime, high unemployment and a sense of alienation among many members

* The Party was not seen to have "offered" the electorate anything to attract its vote. The Public Service debt remained unresolved; the Labour movement seemed alienated or not being courted; the prospect of unemployment remained; the URP programme continued to be woefully inadequate and was an irritant and a source of discontent for many members. The highly successful "caring" theme of 1991 was all but lost or abandoned

* There was insufficient enthusiasm and empowerment among members

* The other party projected a racial relationship with its supporters, stating it is time for the Indian to

govern, in order to gain more support from the East Indian community

* Supporters failed to vote for the PNM because of insufficient/no employment on URP

* Absence of party groups in various sections of the constituency

* Insufficient emphasis paid to the number of voters and the area of the polling stations in respect of transporting voters to and from Polling Stations on election day

* Constituency was not properly serviced over the last term.

* Canvassing was not done thoroughly in certain areas

* No proper registration/re-registration exercise was done

* Lack of managerial skills and cohesion among the leaders in the community

* Poor communication with sporting, cultural and other groups in the area

* Late selection of candidate and the controversy associated with same created a "less enthusiastic environment in which to work"

* The absence of assets, like public address systems, tables, chairs, offices etc.

* The Campaign Office was the former URP Office

* Ineffective communication on Election Day, particularly with Area Managers

* A constituency executive designed only to operate within the URP framework

* Animosity between party groups and constituency executives

* Accuracy of canvass data and insufficient time to re-enter localities and review information obtained from canvass.

DIFFICULTIES ENCOUNTERED

* The feeling by constituents that at election time the Party Executive "must run the money"; constant demand for material things — jerseys, cups, food etc.

* No financial support from central fund for the Implementation Committee.

RECOMMENDATIONS (REGIONAL SUPERVISORS)

* A real effort will have to be made to ensure that even in the weak constituencies and certainly in the marginal ones, that all concerned focus on ensuring that PNM's election machinery works effectively

* As a general policy, all constituencies should embark on building a reservoir of funds so that they could effectively respond any time elections are called

* That the immediate and main focus shall be the proper registration of all individuals eligible to vote and the education of the electorate on the importance of their exercise of that right

* That a "mentor" programme shall be instituted were marginal and other disadvantaged constituencies could be adopted, and technology (eg., information, skills) transferred to upgrade those constituencies to an advantageous position

* Proceed immediately to deal with the problem of in-house fighting with the affected constituencies. The best approach will be to disband the existing Executives and replace them with members who are loyal and willing to work for the Party

* Change of Constituency Executive so as to reflect the composition of the Constituency

* The leadership of the Party must take immediate steps to allay the concerns of some constituencies that they are being taken for granted and not treated with the same consideration and respect afforded to others.

RECOMMENDATIONS (CAMPAIGN MANAGERS)

* The need for a massive re-education programme utilizing the technology and resources available to the party in general, and on the island in particular, would act as a catalyst to motivate the electorate especially the younger generation.

Annexe 15

Attitudes Towards the Post-Election Leadership Crisis Within the PNM

There has been a great deal of controversy as to whether given the PNM's loss of office following the November 6th General Elections, former Prime Minister Patrick Manning should resign as Political Leader of the PNM. Mr. Manning has stubbornly refused to do so arguing that his continued leadership was twice endorsed by the Party's General Council. Demands that he resign however continued to be made by PNM supporters. Given the welter of opinions expressed on the issue, it was difficult to determine how extensive or otherwise was the support for such a demand. Mr. Manning himself seemed to believe that he [had] more party support than press reports indicate, and that the criticisms [were] geographically concentrated and not indicative of how party members, supporters, and well wishers from all parts of the country and all strata of the society [felt].

In an attempt to obtain empirical information as to the balance of opinions held by party supporters and others on this issue, SARA conducted a survey during the period January 12-15. One thousand and two persons (1,002) were interviewed in ten constituencies, three of which were in the South, two in Central and five along the East West Corridor.

I

Respondents were first asked which party they voted for on November 6th. Fifty-five per cent of the Afro-Trinidadians said that they voted PNM, 7 per cent said they voted UNC, 6 per cent reported that they voted NAR, while 31 per cent refused to say. Eighty nine per cent of the Indo-Trinidadian population reported that they voted UNC, 7 per cent said they voted PNM, while 2 per cent claimed they voted NAR. Three per cent refused to answer. Among the mixed population, 42 per cent voted PNM, 19 per cent claimed to have voted UNC and 12 per cent NAR. Twenty six per cent refused to say (Table 1).

TABLE 1. Voting, by Ethnicity - 1995

	Ethnicity		
Party	Afro-Trinidadian	Indo-Trinidadian	Mixed
PNM	56	7	42
UNC	7	89	19
NAR	6	2	13
Refuse to Say	31	3	26

What are we to make of these figures? Why did so many Afro-Trinidadians refuse to reveal how they voted while Indo-Trinidadians were less reticent? Were some of these individuals, persons who did not vote PNM but who are unwilling to admit that they did not do so? Then too, did 7 per cent of the Afro-Trinidadian population vote for the UNC? It is a well known fact that more people usually claim to have voted for a winning party and less for the losing party than actually voted for those parties. We are not certain whether this was the case in this exercise. It is however possible that more Afro-Trinidadians and persons of mixed ancestry voted for the UNC in November than was previously the case. We note that in SARA's pre-election poll, 5 per cent of the Afro-Trinidadians sampled and 11 per cent of the mixed group said that they would vote for the UNC. It seems that there might indeed have been a last minute swing to the UNC following its endorsement by former members of the NAR which served to "wrong foot" the predictions of the polls.

II

When asked what action Manning should take in terms of the leadership of the PNM, 54 per cent of those who claimed to be members of the PNM said he should remain as Political Leader until 1997 when elections for the party leadership were due to be held. Twenty-eight per cent felt he should call a Special Convention of the Party to allow the matter to be determined by party delegates. Only 16 per cent felt he should resign immediately. Two per cent did not know.

Of those who were not party members, 27 per cent felt he should wait until 1997, 31 per cent said he should resign immediately while 29 per cent felt a Special Convention should be called. In sum, PNM members were twice as likely to advise Manning to remain as Political Leader than were non-PNM members (Table 2).

Table 2. Attitudes to Manning's Continued Leadership

Options	PNM Members	Non-PNM
Remain until 1997	54	27
Resign immediately	16	31
Call Special Convention	28	29
Do Not Know	2	9
Refuse to Say	0	3

Afro-Trinidadian females were more inclined to want Manning to remain as Political leader than Afro-Trinidadian males. Thirty-seven per cent of the males wanted him to stay until 1997. Twenty per cent wanted him to resign and 34 per cent wanted him to go the convention route. The figures for women were 45 per cent, 13 per cent and 29 per cent respectively. The figures for females of mixed extraction were closer to those for males — 38, 21 and 28 per cent respectively.

When we considered the data in terms of which party respondents voted for in the last election, we found a plurality of PNM voters - 48 per cent- expressing the view that Manning should remain as leader. Thirty-three per cent wanted a Special Convention, while 16 per cent wanted his resignation. Thirty per cent of those who voted NAR believe he should stay until 1997, 23 per cent wanted a Special Convention and 16 per cent wanted him to resign, the same as was the case in respect of PNM voters. Two thirds of those who voted UNC (65 per cent) believed Manning should resign, 9 per cent believed he should stay until 1997, while 14 per cent indicated support for the calling of a Special Convention (Table 3).

Table 3. Attitudes to Manning's Leadership, by Party Voted For

Options	PNM	NAR	UNC
Remain until 1997	48	30	9
Resign immediately	16	16	65
Call Special Convention	33	23	14
Do Not Know	2	27	10
Refuse to Say	1	6	23

More Afro-Trinidadians — 41 per cent — wanted Manning to remain as Political Leader of the PNM than wanted him to resign immediately — 16 per cent. Just under a third of them — 31 per cent — wanted him to let the party decide in a Special Convention. The mixed population was more evenly divided among the three options. Thirty-two per cent wanted him to remain until 1997, 29 per cent wanted him to resign, while 28 per cent wanted him to let the Convention decide. Indians were more unequivocal. Eighty-one per cent wanted him to resign immediately, 6 per cent felt he should remain until 1997, while 11 per cent endorsed the idea of a Special Convention. This finding indicated that the effort which Manning expended to bring the Indian community into the PNM between 1986 and 1996 was neither acknowledged nor reciprocated (Table 4).

The data suggest that the calling of a Special Convention should hold no terrors for Mr. Manning since one has to assume that some proportion of those who wanted the matter determined by such a Convention would in fact vote to revalidate his leadership. In sum, the Special Convention might well have proven to be the mechanism to heal or plaster the wounds in the party, especially if it was linked to a plan for organizational restructuring, and new arrangements for the election of leaders, deputy leaders and party chairmen.

Table 4. Attitudes to Manning's Leadership, by Ethnicity

Options	Ethnicity		
	Afro-Trinidadian	Indo-Trinidadian	Mixed
Remain until 1997	41	6	32
Resign immediately	16	81	29
Call Special Convention	31	11	28
Do Not Know	9	1	9
Refuse to Say	3	1	2

Annexe 16

King Creole is Dead! Long Live What?*

Some months ago, I expressed the view that given the demographic and other trends that were manifest in the society, the Indian community would capture political power sometime in the first decade of the 21st century ("Balance of Power Up For Grabs," *Sunday Express,* March 13, 1994). I was severely criticized for making such a statement. Some Afro-Trinidadians felt that my prophecy could become self-fulfilling. Their concern was that social science could enter into reality and transform it. Indo-Trinidadians, for their part, felt that in making the comment, I was bell ringing for the PNM. I was even asked how much the PNM had paid me to make such a comment. That important historical event has materialized earlier than predicted, albeit in a tentative form. What occurred may in fact be the overture to the political "big bang" of which I spoke. One suspects that we have now come to the end of the era of Afro-Creole political hegemony and are on the cusp of a new one, *mantras* about national unity notwithstanding.

History does not always flow along clearly channelled paths. Individuals or events often intervene in ways that create the illusion that flows are being dammed, detoured or reversed. In the end, however, the social forces at work surge with seeming impatience, dragging along in their wake those who would seek

**Sunday Express,* November 26, 1995.

to paddle upstream. The process by which Mr. Panday became Prime Minister of Trinidad and Tobago, seemingly against his better judgement, is instructive. Mr. Panday has often been heard to say that he considered the job of Prime Minister to be a "stupid" one to which he did not aspire. He has also confessed that it is not only power that intoxicates, but that even the smell of power has that hallucinatory effect! "History" has however "spited" (his word) Panday for being imprudent enough to be around when it determined that the time had come for a descendant of the survivors of the second crossing to take over the reins of power from those to whom it had passed in the first and second republics that followed upon Independence. His is now the task of being the beast of burden, the one fated to bear upon his back the hopes of those who came to this crisis ridden land 150 years ago. One wishes him well in his odyssey. One likewise hopes that he will prove equal to the responsibilities imposed upon him as well as those which he has imposed upon himself — solving the complex problems of crime, unemployment, alienation and marginality. He has started with surefootedness, and one can only hope that at the end of the day we would have had meaningful change rather than a mutation of élites, or to use Mr. Panday's pet phrase, "mere exchange."

In an interesting paper presented to a Conference held in August this year as part of the celebrations marking the 150th Anniversary of the arrival of Indians in Trinidad and Tobago ("Trade Unionism, Politics and Indo-Caribbean Leadership"), Panday volunteered his views as to why it took as long as it did for an Indian to become Prime Minister of Trinidad and Tobago. The problem, he tells us in reference to the elections of 1976, was that "while working class Indians were prepared to vote across the racial line, the majority of the African electorate of the working class were not ready to take the plunge." Panday also made reference to the events of 1981 when Indians were told to abandon the ULF and vote for the ONR, since "only the ONR, as an African party, could beat the other African party, the PNM." Panday alluded to these events to "demonstrate the difficulties that confront the Indian politician, or rather the politician who happens to be born of Indian descent in plural societies such as Trinidad and Tobago, Guyana, Suriname and Fiji."

Panday was also sternly critical of Indian political élites who, out of a sense of hopelessness, felt that they could only obtain political office by hopping aboard an African driven political chariot. Such individuals not only "accept their own inferiority" but actually "participate in their own denigration." The tendency to self-denigration "produced the political window dressing and tokenism of the Kamaludin Mohammeds and the Hardeo Hardatts of the PNM, and the Winston Dookerans, the Bhoendradatt Tewaries and the Sahadeo Basdeos in what was left of the National Alliance for Reconstruction (NAR) government following the expulsion of the ULF element from the Party in 1988. They [felt that they] would only be accepted in the party if they were prepared to settle for office without power." But was it not possible that the persons named were pursuing the cherished goal of national unity using other political vehicles?

By 1995, Panday was beginning to see light at the end of the darkened tunnel. In his view, the PNM no longer had the resources which were available to it in the petro-boom era to bribe the electorate. As such, peoples of African descent were beginning to view politics in terms of policies and programmes rather than in terms of race. As Panday exulted: "Issues [are] now being looked at instead of the blind appeal to race. If this trend continues, the question will no longer be who we go put, but what we go put. The politics seems to be moving in the direction of issues as race is put on the back burner. Soon this topic will be of historical and academic significance only, and there will be no such thing as the Indian, African or Chinese politician. Politicians will be judged by their works and not by their race."

The results of the election seems to have convinced Panday, that the much hoped for breakthrough to non-racial voting did in fact occur. The evidence for this claim is said to be the fact that the UNC received a great deal of support along the East West Corridor — 2,506 votes in Diego Martin Central, 1,536 votes in Diego Martin East, 1,737 votes in Diego Martin West, 1,916 votes (6,000 in some accounts) in Port of Spain South, 2,371 votes in St. Anns East, 1,650 votes in Laventille\Morvant and 827 votes in Laventille West. The assumption is that these voters were Afro-Trinidadian. While it is of course difficult to determine with absolute certainty that they were not in fact Afro-Trinidadians, we think it is relevant to point out that there are hundreds of Indians on the voting lists in all of these constituencies, and that there is a close correspondence between the numbers of votes received by the UNC and the Indian names on the voter list. The comparable figures are 2,269 in Diego Martin Central, 2,206 in Diego Martin East, 1,735 votes in Diego Martin West, 2,765 in Port of Spain South, 2,945 in St. Anns East, 1,979 in Laventille East\Morvant, and 870 in Laventille West. Many of these votes went to the NAR in 1986 and 1991 while a few went to the UNC in 1991.

One wishes that the breakthrough had in fact occurred since the only way that the society can avoid complete polarization, with all that follows therefrom, is to have two parties with genuine and broad-based multi-ethnic support competing for those votes which are not cemented to one Party or another. The evidence however suggests that very little of this happened on November 6th. While one can "style" or "shape" "history," one cannot easily force its movement too far beyond the radius within which the experience of the people permits it to range.

My own view is that many underclass blacks stayed at home or on the blocks on election day. They were "pushed" away from the PNM and not "pulled" towards the UNC as is being alleged. While there were of course some exceptions, voters, like masqueraders in a big band, got into their respective ethnic sections once they began approaching the "political grandstand." But as happens during Carnival, once the "stage" is crossed, voters shed their political costumes and proceed to mix, mingle, make love and in other ways make believe that Trinidad and Tobago is one "nation" rather than two or perhaps three "nations" or "jati" (if we treat Tobago as the third) that have different value systems which lay beneath the veneer which seems to unite us and which informs the life choices which they make.

The society now stands on a critical threshold. Everyone is trying to be polite and civically responsible, at least in public. The power retentionists and the irredentists are however girding their loins, and only time will tell whether we will go the way of other plural societies or whether we will be the exception. The social scientist and historian in me cautions against a Pollyanish optimism. I am however sustained by the story of the determined reformer "who fights on, though he has already lost — and occasionally goes on to win. Since he acts, he learns from his mistakes and from the resistance he encounters, and frequently ends up as a wily individual from whom [the society] may learn a trick or two." Over to you Bas!

Annexe 17

All Yuh Look for That!*

Political upheavals invariably mirror themselves in cultural upheavals. The opposite is also usually the case. Some might argue that "true" political change only comes about after changes in culture and the economy predispose the society to countenance certain kinds of political realignments. Whatever the truth of the matter (and the reality is much more complex), there is no question that the 1996 season generated a substantial number of calypsoes which chronicled and analyzed the revolutionary political events of 1995 in much the same way as calypsoes of the late sixties and seventies mirrored the revolutionary political events of those years.

Among the most outstanding songs in this genre were those produced by Luta, Kurt Allen, De Lamo, Chalkdust, Rudder, Sugar Aloes, Cro Cro and Brother Marvin. While the compositions noted above were all of a high order (I particularly liked the deft way in which Rudder treated the battle between the PNM leadership and Occah Seapaul), the songs that resonated most with their audiences and created the most controversy were those sung by Cro Cro (see Text below), Sugar Aloes and Brother Marvin. Clearly, these men echoed the views of many.

These calypsoes captured the varying currents of fear and hope that were swirling about madly in the society before, during

---

**Sunday Express,* February 25, 1996.

and following the 1995 elections — fears on the part of Afro-Trinidadians that they were losing political hegemony, the hopes of Indo-Trinidadians that 1995 would witness their eventual Indian political arrival, and the dialectical responses to these two concerns which took the form of prescriptions for "national unity." The reactions to the calypsoes also make clear that Trinidad and Tobago is not a seamless society when it comes to matters of race, and that, as it did on Carnival day, the society moves to the right, to the left, to the North, to Central, and to South on the issue. In short, we are all over the place. The idealist in public is invariably ethnocentric or a racist in private.

I have argued elsewhere that one of the features of that election was that the turnout rate among the black underclass was considerably lower than it was in 1991, while the reverse was the case among Indo-Trinidadians of all classes. The burden of Cro Cro's song was to endorse that analysis. Cro Cro however went further and told his co-ethnics that they should not now cry tears of blood, and that they have only themselves to blame for what happened *(They Look For Dat).* Sugar Aloes hewed to the same line. He told PNM supporters that they must "now eat the bread the devil knead" and "Who Did Not Vote Sorry". In doing so, they angered those who seem to take the view that quite apart from what others (i.e., Indians) might have done on November 6, Afro-Trinidadians must support and vote for parties on the basis of principles and policies and not on the basis of race. Cro Cro does not agree. Using "Sat Maharaj" as a metaphor, he looks around the society and observes what other groups are doing, and urges his co-ethnics to do the same.

One might argue that the calypsonian should use his medium to make normative appeals to the society rather than merely reflect what he sees. But most calypsonians are street poets and not preachers. To expect them to be other than what they are would be asking too much. Indeed, if they were to seek to be preachers, calypso would be boring and everybody but the evangelists would boycott the tents.

While it is possible to argue that Cro Cro's song appeals to tribal instincts and that it makes certain assumptions about how political power is won, used and retained, my own feeling is that the label "racist" is abused when applied to his song. One has to make the distinction between ethnocentrism, racial consciousness, racial pride and racism. One can be ethnocentric, racially conscious or racially proud without assuming that one's group is superior to others, or that society should be organized in such a way as to allow one chosen group to denigrate or oppress another less privileged group forcibly. Ethnocentrism, as the late M.G. Smith, the Jamaican sociologist, reminds us, can be benign and value neutral. "'Racism' means something more. When ethnocentric beliefs and ideas denigrate and stereotype the peoples and their cultures, they become racist if they assume that the negatively valued traits are hereditary, ineradicable and transmitted by descent." If Cro Cro is deemed racist, then there are few people in the society, the Prime Minister included, who are exempt from that charge. Many who accuse Cro Cro of being racist are in fact being hypocritical, and do not pause to examine the beam in their own eyes.

What is the message of Cro Cro's song, bearing in mind that the message of a song is much more than what its lyrics actually say. Africans, he said, should "open their eyes" and seek to "rise." Instead, they continue their preoccupation with unnecessary partying, activities which drain their collective energy and resources. While many do not like Cro Cro's style or his lyrics, (Keith Smith calls him, quite unfairly in my view, the "baron of bile"), I regard him as a secular evangelist who has chosen to take on the unrewarding task (in the context of Trinidad society) of using the medium of the calypso to speak specifically to people of African descent, to give them the "kick start" they need (empowerment) to "go out front" and join the highways leading to educational and economic advancement.

When one deconstructs Cro Cro's lyrics, he is merely saying in song what NJAC said in 1970 and what other ethnically conscious black intellectuals who recognize the plight of blacks, especially black males, continue to say 25 years later. In this regard, one is not clear what the Women Working For Social Progress (WWSP) mean when they talked about the complacency of the Afro-Trinidadian being a myth, when all the analyses being done about the construction of Caribbean masculinity and black performance in the schools point in this direction. (Incidentally, Ella Andall's lament about *Lost Generation* makes the same point). To say, as the WWSP does, that Cro Cro's song does not recognize that Africans and Indians are not homogenous, and that there is in reality a great deal of differentiation, is to ask the calypsonian to do much more than his medium permits.

Cro Cro also savagely chastises Afro-Trinidadians for being *nemakharams,* ingrates who continue to put pressure on other blacks and who allow themselves to be used. He likewise accuses them of not recognizing their collective strengths — and in so doing, makes the same point that Panday did when he accused Indians of being their "worst enemy." To quote Panday:

> We are too easily prepared to sell our birthright and that of our fellow men for a mess of pottage from the tables of the new oligarchy. Some will sell for a jacket and tie and a ministry, some for a wig and gown, some for a seat in the Senate, some for a little contract here and there. Our detractors say we are the victims of a curse, which like a virulent plague threatens to engulf the entire community.

Incidentally, Cro Cro was not the first to comment on the apathy of the blacks and their attitudes towards voting. As Gordon Rohlehr has reminded us in his book, *Calypso and Society in Pre-Independence Trinidad,* Lord Melody did the same in the calypso, *Apan Jhaat* which was a commentary on the Guyanese elections of 1957. To quote Melody:

> Mr. B should a come first
> But black people too conniving and pompous
> They should have done like the Indian
> Walk down to the polling station But no!

They want a aeroplane
Because the weather report say it will rain
And with that they sign their destiny
My people too stupid, believe me.

Like Overand Padmore (*Sunday Guardian,* February 18, 1996), I exonerate Cro Cro on the charge of being a racist or a racialist, though ethnocentric he might be. (Is he an 'anti racial racialist', to borrow a term used by the poets of négritude to defend their stance on the racial question?) I however disagree with him in terms of how he dealt with the charges of sexual harassment brought against the Prime Minster. My own view is that if the matter had to be dealt with at all, it should have been handled with greater "spin," subtlety, and taste. His lyrics clearly went beyond the pale.

I would however disagree with the suggestion that the National Carnival Commission (NCC) or some such body should seek to censor calypsoes, or that the judges should use political correctness as a criterion for choosing a winning calypso. Once that is done, I agree with Cro Cro that calypso and much else that we value is "gone." One is indeed relieved that the Government has chosen to ignore the advice of those who urged Panday to sue Cro Cro for defamation. Having regard to the amount of goodwill which Mr. Panday lost as a result of his battle with *The Guardian,* it would have been politically suicidal for him to do so.

And what can we say, albeit in brief, about Brother Marvin. *Jahaaji Bhai* [Brotherhood of the Boat] was a beautifully crafted calypso and was certainly one of my favourites. Its plaintiveness was haunting. Many Afro-Trinidadians have however been critical of the calypso (some characterized it as an "insult to Africans") for its alleged historical inaccuracy and its pointed charge that Afrocentrics "play ignorant" and talk about "true African descent" when, if they took a trip back to their roots, they would see "a man in a *dhoti,* saying his prayers in front of a *jhandi* (prayer flag). While it is not clear whether Marvin intended to do so (he may have only been rhyming), it seems that he was suggesting that Africans borrowed much from India rather than the other way around, as Molly Ahye suggested in her reply (*Guardian,* February 17, 1996). My own view, however, is that a calypso is not a history dissertation or social science, and should not be judged by the canons of academia. In passing, we note that while it is true that Marvin seems to have downplayed the experiences of the first survivors of the first crossing, Stalin made much the same error in "Caribbean Man" when he ignored the presence in the Caribbean of the descendants of the survivors of the second crossing.

The calypsoes have however provoked a great deal of useful debate about who and what we are as a society. It has also served once again to pull the mask off our individual and collective faces, and confirms my view that ignoring the race question as some privileged groups advise will not lead to its disappearance. Indeed, the responses to the two calypsoes remind me very much of the reaction to the verdict of the O.J. Simpson trial. Forty per cent of the population applauded Cro Cro with both hands while another forty per cent applauded Brother Marvin with equal enthusiasm. The remainder either gave Cro Cro and Marvin a "one hand clap" or made less dissonant choices.

And what can one say about the Sonny Mann case except to express profound shame that the incident ever happened. Mann, an Indian, was stoned by angry black youths and prevented from performing at the Soca Monarch Finals in the week before Carnival. It is not clear whether Mann was abused because he had threatened to get the Courts to stop the show from taking place; because he had initially been debarred from performing because his popular chutney soca "Lotay La" was over two years old and did not therefore qualify for inclusion, or because some people felt that calypso, soca and carnival were Afro-Trinidadian preserves and that Indians were moving too swiftly to penetrate that space. We note, however that several Indian calypsonians (Syrians and Whites as well) have performed in the calypso tents and in national contexts without incident and that in the one case where there was incident, the performer, Denyse Plummer was "white" or "off white."

November 7th I see Blackman cry
Look blood still running from Black people's eye
But I remember when I sing "Rise Africans Rise"
And I beg Black man to open his eyes
While I was singing and busting my liver string
Black man asking me where Atlantik playing
Then they put they voting finger on the shelf
So today Blackman you must blame yourself
Cause when I sing they don't listen to what Cro Cro say
Blackman telling black man how black man come out to party
I remember when I sing "Sham We Don't Want it"
Them same brothers say Cro Cro singing s.....
So today is not my fault that you lose your heart
Black man all you look for that
I wonder why black man always want a kick start
Black man all you look for that

A man on a charge for interfering
Black man all you still go and vote for him
Black man how on earth you could condone this
Your daughter might have to work in this man's office
Then imagine this sex silver-headed pest
Quail fingers under your daughter's dress
Me eh saying that Patrick shoulda win
But even Jim baker woulda be better
All them woman who went Beijing the other day
About this mister what all you have to say
Concerning this thing all you silent and talking peace
So the office girls must be at the mercy of this beast
He was charged so whether it is false or true
I'm concerned because I have a daughter too
I talking from my heart I telling you flat
Blackman all you look for that
I wonder why black man always want a kick start
Black man all you look for that

Tobago I am really surprised about you
All you take part in that jackassness too
So why all you always against Trinidad so.....
But all you smile when Robbie marry to Panday
I hope all you understand what Sat Maharaj say
If he daughter marry a black man he chop she flat
Tobago all you look for that

Remember slavery on the plantation
Massa used to use black man to beat black man
So when I hear 17-17 I got a pain
Black man give black man soup but black man want ham
Black man intention is to pressure he own black man
He give them soup they say he treat them like outcast
So now black man take smoke herring in your ....
"Sat" and them could always say what they want
Black man always have a fear of going in front
Black man does tell this man
Boy why you don't shut up
Crocs I sure this year they go lock you up
But the truth does offend these people eh soft
They might just pay a man to bump you off
But I go sing until I grow or until I fall
And if I dead then is my funeral
Arthur Robbie on behalf of the Africans
With two seats breds you have the sword in your hand
I spoke to Leroy Clarke and Khafra Kambon
Up to now they can't understand what going on
You went and was up in Africa
When Abu Bakr reach and the shooting start ...
all you look for that
And if your daughter should pass in the prime minister's path
All you look for that.

Annexe 18

Basdeo Panday: History's Beast of Burden*

Basdeo Panday has been named "Individual of the Year" by the *Trinidad Express.* It is an award that was justly deserved. In essence, Panday's achievement was to do what few people assumed he, or any other person of Indian ancestry would ever do, viz., become Prime Minister of Trinidad and Tobago in the 20th century. In the context of the Caribbean, Panday thus has to be seen as a "history maker."

Panday has accepted the award with characteristic but calculated modesty, insisting that he has done nothing so far to deserve it and that the award should in fact be re-named in honour of persons with whom he intends working to achieve the goal of changing the society — reducing poverty, destitution, homelessness and unemployment in Trinidad and Tobago. He blamed former Prime Minister Patrick Manning for making the "awful error" of abdicating the responsibility of the government to deal with unemployment, concentrating instead on the imperatives of globalization. One waits with bated breath to see how the UNC-NAR regime would fulfill the awesome responsibility of achieving the twin goals of growth and job creation while responding to those very imperatives which Panday admits his own government cannot escape.

**Sunday Express,* January 7, 1996.

In a real sense though, Panday's achievement is both an individual and a collective one. It is a collective achievement in that it constitutes the media's celebration of the political coming of age of a community which had spent 150 humilitating years in the cane pieces and barrack yards of colonial and post-colonial Trinidad. It is an individual achievement in the sense that Panday, unlike many who entered the political arena during the years of PNM hegemony, not only stayed the course, but was able to retain the loyalty and support of a substantial communal following. Lloyd Best too has stayed the course and has enriched our political discourse in the process; unfortunately for Lloyd, and unlike Panday, he remains a shepherd without a flock. Most, if not all of the others who were part of the political class of the sixties, have since become mere footnotes in our political history, persons whom few now remember.

But Panday did more than survive the many political and personal crises which he has had to confront. Over the past 30 years, he has made many political errors, or what seemed to many to be errors. Many of these would have proved fatal to the careers of less resourceful political actors. Panday however managed to re-emerge from these crises, phoenix like, with increased political strength. Part of this strength of course lay with the nature of his ethnic base which, for reasons that are both cultural and situational, is far more tolerant and forgiving of errant behaviour on the part of its political leadership than obtains in respect of other communities. Some of Panday's indiscretions would have caused instant political death to leaders of other ethnic fragments. The parameters within which leadership flourishes and dies are not the same for all ethnic players, as Manning is painfully discovering.

Panday has also over time become a master of the art of speaking with a forked and serrated tongue, an art which politicians must master if they are to function as national leaders in the quicksand of plural societies. To succeed, such leaders have to operate on two tracks, one that is ethnic and one that is national and cosmopolitan. Panday speaks the language of class politics, but he is also adept at pushing ethnic buttons when needed to maintain the loyalty of his flock.

Panday's strength is that he understands better than Robinson and Manning how to be rhetorically promiscuous, how to mix ethnic, class and national signals so that on balance he appears to be a national rather than a communal leader. As he himself observed:

> Trinidad and Tobago is a most difficult land to govern because of its highly plural nature. What is more, unlike some other plural societies, people are forced to live in conditions where they cannot avoid one another. We are forced to interface with each other every day whether we like it or not. No matter how we have tried to paper over the cracks over the years, it takes situations like this election and the result of this election to expose the paper cracks for what they really are. That kind of division and divisiveness in our society have been, in my humble view, the singular most debilitating factor in this society. It has been the underlying cause of all our problems.

The challenge now facing Panday is to show that he can use the resources which the office of the Prime Minister now puts at his disposal to do that which he has accused Williams, Chambers and Manning of being unable or perhaps unwilling to do.

Since November 6th, Panday has tried to mute or perhaps even silence his ethnic voice, at least in public. He has correspondingly raised the decibel level of his national voice, insisting in the process that the society cannot move forward unless it finds a formula to give effect to the widely desired but highly controversial goal of "national unity," whatever that might mean in practice. Knowing that some of his followers were beginning to behave in a vengeful and truculent manner, he openly warned about the costs and consequences of racial arrogance. He has also sought to project the message of humility and ethnic ecumenism in his own demeanour and, in a real sense, the messenger has become the message.

What is also interesting is that the national community and the media seem willing, at least for the time being, to forget Panday the ethnic leader and to acclaim him in his epiphany as a consensus leader. The reaction to his post-election speeches as well as his initial statements as Prime Minister were well received. The outpouring of concern over his health also seemed genuine, though it was clearly informed by strategic considerations. Several groups have a vested interest in the state of his health. Co-ethnics are aware that there are many who do not share their ethnic agendas and who therefore wish and indeed expect Panday and his team to fail. They thus have an interest in his success and that of the UNC-NAR co-partnership. Panday is thus their ethnic beast of burden, their buffalo.

Many non-Indians also want Panday to manage his health problems since they see him as the only person in that coalition whom they could accept as Prime Minister. The thought of having him replaced by either [Lawrence] Maharaj, [Ralph] Maraj, Humphrey or Sudama literally fills them with fear and trembling. Some PNM supporters also believe that if Robinson were to succeed Panday, it might serve to "resurrect" the NAR, a miracle that would be achieved at the expense of the PNM. They thus want the coalition to survive for a period that is long enough to give their party time to sort out its thorny and potentially destructive leadership problems and rebuild for the next encounter.

There is likewise a seeming determination on the part of many to *behave* in a manner that is ethnically correct in spite of what they might think about recent events. No one wants to be held responsible for shattering the current ethnic and social peace. Everyone wants the prevailing "era of good feeling" to be sustained. Panday is a beneficiary of that unarticulated consensus; his illness also conduces to the generation of an eerie sense of calm. No one wants to attack him too frontally, or question his sincerity; but everyone knows that it is only a matter of time before some accident or blunder on the part of some minister, functionary or interest grouping triggers the mechanism that would restart the elbow bashing and mud wrestling process.

Panday's problem is to find a formula that would allow him to reconcile the expectations of those who see him as a class hero, an ethnic hero or a national hero. If, for example, he sets out to do what he has signalled he intends to do to deserve the "Individual of the Year" award, he would no doubt make many friends. He might however also wreck the fragile economy and the foreign exchange regime in the process, and in so doing bring down the wrath of the "parasitic oligarchy" (both domestic and international) on his greying head. If he does nothing to disturb the *status quo,* he would also upset many who expect him to re-distribute material and symbolic resources along ethnic, social and geographical lines in order to address the problem of alienation about which he spoke so much. Having been the protean man of all seasons while in Opposition, Panday is now forced to make the difficult choices that all leaders who wish to leave their mark must make. One waits to see whether he will indeed tame the roaring lion or whether the lion would in fact devour him as it did Chambers, Robinson and now Manning.

Annexe 19

Polling and Elections in Trinidad and Tobago: 1981-1995*

The polls that SARA conducts have been around for some 19 years. Much of the bashing which they attract comes from groups who believe that the analyses which they provide are inimical to their political agendas and electoral prospects. There is also the problem that many who comment do so without knowing what pollsters do. Part of the problem is that commentators mistakenly assume that the views expressed in my weekly column inform the methodologies used in the survey and that I cook the books to achieve a preferred result. Polls are really nothing more than snapshots of the opinions which people in a group or the larger society have at a particular point in time. As opinions change in relation to changing events, the findings of polls change.

In 1981, for example, ONR spokesmen were systematically hostile when SARA predicted a PNM victory. ONR spokesmen were also critical of the polls for laying bare the fact that ONR support came mainly from the gentrified French Creole and Indian élites while the PNM's support came largely from the Afro-Trinidadian community of all classes. Given this, the ONR was bound to lose. I recall one stalwart ONR supporter, telling me

---

**Sunday Express,* November 19, 1995.

that the acronym ONR meant "Oh No, Ryan," as if I was responsible for creating the reality that was reflected in the poll data.

In 1986, the attacks came from the PNM, and SARA was accused of all manner of heinous things. The major finding of the SARA poll in that year was that a "political earthquake of major proportions [was] shaking the political structure of Trinidad and Tobago" and that constituencies which normally voted strongly in support of the PNM were going to go to the NAR. The results of the election followed quite closely the projections indicated by the poll.

Following the crisis in the NAR which led to the expulsion of the ULF element in the coalition and the formation of the UNC, the polls recorded the continuous haemorrhaging of support from the NAR to the PNM and the UNC. Pro NAR critics accused SARA of deliberately seeking to engineer the death of that party and its replacement by the UNC and the PNM when in fact its only function was to serve as the messenger who reported the demise of the NAR in Trinidad, if not in Tobago. In those years, the polls and my column were the darling of the UNC and there was no talk then of the author being anti-Indian. Indeed, the accusation was that the column was too lenient with Messrs. Panday *et al.,* who were then being demonized by the gentrified élites who then supported the NAR.

The polls which preceded the 1991 elections provoked even more controversy. The poll that was conducted in November had the NAR ahead of the PNM and the UNC. The percentages were, 33, 24 and 12 per cent respectively. The NAR, which had been saying that the economy was turning around, concluded that this had indeed begun to happen, and that it was the right time to go to the polls. Many accused SARA of deliberately "setting up" Mr. Robinson so as to induce him to go to the polls. I have consistently denied this, and still do. The accusation simply made no sense. Why risk one's reputation or integrity for a mere political party, great as it may be? Mr. Robinson and some of his advisers were looking for a wind with which to set sail and chose one which was not sustained.

It is true that a poll conducted one month later indicated that the pro-NAR wind had become becalmed and that the positions had been reversed. The PNM was now ahead with 34 points, with the NAR and the UNC following with 24 and 20 percentage points respectively. What explained the differences in the report published in December of 1991 from that of November? In our report on the poll, we observed that many of those who in November were uncertain as to how they had planned to vote, who had refused to say, or who said they would not vote for any party — 28 per cent altogether — were now more disposed to say what they would do. I can only assume in retrospect that many who were previously reticent came out on the side of the PNM once the bell had been rung.

Another problem with the interpretation of polls is that many people who read what they say more often than not concentrate on the headlines which newspapers use to market the survey and ignore the fine print of what the investigator himself says. Authors of newspaper columns never write headlines and are at times surprised or embarrassed by them.

Mr. Panday, for example, has said that the 1991 survey was wrong in that it gave the UNC only 3 seats. Nothing could in fact be further from the truth. What the report actually said was as follows: "The UNC, for its part, has clearly gained support over the past two weeks and seems to have more or less vaulted the hurdle which Kelvin Ramnath and Rampersad Parasram sought to put in its way. Responses to all the questions suggest that the UNC is still the party which is preferred by a majority of Indians. Despite what seems like a tense cliff hanger in terms of the proportion of the electorate's support which the three major parties are likely to obtain, my own projections, based on *non-polling* data relating to the social composition of all 36 constituencies, suggests that the PNM is currently ahead in 16 constituencies by margins that range from 7 to 18 points. In none of these constituencies does the PNM's percentage exceed 50 per cent. In the case of the UNC, it leads in 3 seats by margins ranging from 6 to 16 points and is ahead in 2 others by 4 points. *The NAR is not convincingly ahead in any seat in Trinidad* but has a fair chance to win 9 of those seats and the two in Tobago. These conclusions are however still tentative since the percentages used to compute the probable outcomes include the "don't knows" and the "refuse to say."

This cautious statement is now taken by all and sundry to arrive at the gospel like conclusion that SARA gave the UNC 3 seats when it in fact won 13. The fact is that poll findings often galvanize political actors to take actions which may falsify the findings of the poll. In 1991, the poll stimulated the UNC into making a last minute drive which led to an eclipse of the NAR which was forced into third place. The latter party however still received 24.50 per cent of the popular vote compared to the UNC's 29.06 per cent. The UNC got 13 seats for its effort and the NAR a mere 2 seats, both in Tobago.

The 1995 election was the most difficult one to predict of all the post-Independence elections, particularly in the marginal PNM seats, and one was always aware that calling seats could prove fatal to any pollster's reputation, particularly if the poll was done early in the campaign. The decision to return to the field to do an update was informed by a perception that the disposition of the electorate seemed to be changing all the time in response to the smoke and mirror games played by the political élites. Given the time and resources available, however, it was only possible to sample 4 constituencies using small samples.

In my report on the findings of that mini-survey, I warned that the samples taken in each of the constituencies were small and that the margins of error could be as high as 8 percentage points plus or minus. "As such," continued the report, "we hesitate to say unequivocally that the PNM would win the four seats." What we did say was that "given the known ethnic balances in the four areas, the PNM [was] favored to hold all four seats [but that] outcomes in these and other constituencies would depend very heavily on which party is better mobilized to motivate its supporters to actually come out and vote."

Clearly, the UNC was better mobilized to do so in St. Joseph and Barataria\San Juan both physically and in terms of goals to be achieved. Many traditional PNM supporters on the other hand had become "gone against," and stayed away from the polling booth while the same was not true for the UNC. Supporters of the latter had a critical motive to turn out, and so they did! Our calculations indicate that the turn out of the Indian population (both Muslim and Hindu) in Barataria/San Juan was of the order of 78 per cent while that of the non-Indian population was of the order of 58 per cent. In the case of St. Joseph, the comparative figures were 84 and 50 per cent respectively.

Disenchantment with the PNM, the PNM Government and its leader were clearly operative factors, particularly among the black under class. Structural adjustment policies which generated increased joblessness led to the belief among this group that the PNM did not really care for its baseline supporters and was catering too much to other communities which deserted it when the chips were down. The "apathy" which was evident in the Laventille by-election had become pervasive. The 3.2 per cent increase in support which the party received nationally came mainly from the gentry which felt it had to stop the march of the UNC at all costs.

While the poll was correct in many fundamental things, it was in error in some of its conclusions with respect to the PNM marginal seats because it failed to factor in a sufficiently high disaffection rate on the part of sections of the Afro-Trinidadian population. We factored in a 10 per cent differential in turn out while the actual rate was 20 to 30 per cent! The failure was one of judgement rather than ONE OF either method or integrity. Note however that the difference between victory and defeat in the two constituencies which SARA erroneously put in the PNM camp — Barataria San Juan and St Joseph was 945 votes in one case and 604 in the other out of a total electorate of well over 22,000 voters. Interesting too is the fact that using a different method, another election eve poll [conducted by Market Facts and Opinion for the *Sunday Guardian*] made similar projections and suffered similarly.

Criticisms have been forthcoming from some persons about the sampling strategy used in the SARA polls. The claim that SARA uses quota sampling rather than a probability strategy is correct. I however know of no major polling firm anywhere in the world which uses probability sampling to predict elections. Unless they are using the telephone as the medium for conducting the interviews, all use variations of quota sampling techniques which are cheaper and faster to execute. The formulae for determining the quotas chosen are defined by the assumptions which the pollsters make about the critical characteristics of the population which need to be factored into the analysis being undertaken. There are of course many well known problems involved in using this strategy, but all sampling strategies have problems associated with them.

Miss Bhaggan and Messrs. Assam and others have also criticized SARA for presenting polling day by racial category and Miss Bhaggan seems to be arguing that by doing so I caused her to lose her seat or her deposit. I would willingly pay for Miss Bhaggan's deposit if I believed that pollsters had the kind of power which she claims we have. The claim is of course a nonsense.

The view that by disaggregating the data in terms of ethnicity, SARA aggravates the problem is however an arguable one. My own belief, however, is that the disaggregated survey data only put numbers on a phenomenon about which most people in the society are instinctively and experientially aware. The television cameras also did a good job of telling us very clearly who was supporting which party by holding up a mirror before the crowds that attended meetings. All that SARA did was to put some numerical estimates on what was being brought into living rooms via the electronic media.

Unlike Jamaica, which is a homogeneous society with a stable two party history, polling in Trinidad and Tobago, a perversely plural society, is an extremely tricky affair and constitutes a nightmare for pollsters. This is especially the case where more than two parties are in the race. I often told the late Carl Stone that calling seats accurately in Jamaica was a "piece of cake" compared to what was required in Trinidad. Here, the pollster is always holding "Jack" or "King" at best and is always aware that the voter could trump him by playing "Ace."

Annexe 20

Towards National Unity: The Aranguez Declaration

Basdeo Panday

Speech to Mark the Inauguration of the United National Congress October 16, 1988

Now that we have embarked upon the second phase of our struggle for a society that is fair and equitable, a society which is free from discrimination, corruption, nepotism and favouritism, a society in which there is equitable distribution of the resources of the state, we must do so with the greatest humility.

As we approach our task of nation building we do so with hatred and malice towards none; without spite, envy, greed, malevolence or bitterness of any kind. Rather, our approach must be one filled with love and compassion, joyous in the knowledge that the mission upon which we have embarked is a noble one, and as surely as day follows night, we are bound to succeed.

The task of nation building is not, and has never been, an easy one. The road is long and narrow, turning and twisting with many ups and downs and with many bridges to cross. This race is not for the swiftest, but for those who endureth to the end.

Some twenty-three years ago when I joined this great struggle, which began with our ancestors long before some of us were born, the objective was the creation of a new society in which all our peoples would feel that they are being treated as equals, in which there is fairness and justice, and in which all our citizens, regardless of race, colour, creed, regardless of sex or class or accident of birth would feel that they truly belong. Throughout the years that objective has remained as constant as the northern star — immovable, unshakable and resolute.

I have taken this position not only because it is a morally just and correct one, but also because I am convinced that in a country like Trinidad and Tobago, with its peculiar demographic distribution, the smallness of our size and our unique historical antecedents, it is impossible to solve our economic problems unless we first resolve our social and political problems. It is for that reason, and that reason only, that in 1965, when, like the proverbial fool that rushes in where angels fear to tread, at the tender age of thirty two, I plunged headlong into politics, I did not join the existing PNM or the DLP. I felt that their political strategies, if not their stated objectives, were to divide the society along racial lines in order to gain and sustain political support.

Instead I joined with C.L.R. James and Jack Kelshall and Stephen Maharaj, and Clive Phil and Max Ifil and Dr. Makan Dube, George Bowrin and George Weekes to form the Workers and Farmers Party to contest the General Elections of 1966 — needless to say with disastrous results for all of us who dared to challenge the politics of race. Thirty-six of us lost our deposits. Those were the days when Patrick Solomon and Robinson were in the PNM and Alloy Lequay and Sahadeo Basdeo were in the DLP. The country was not yet ready for the politics of national unity.

In 1971 we were part of the no-vote campaign for the removal of the voting machines. In 1976, despite our devastating defeat in 1966, we did not succumb to the PNM/DLP politics of race but formed the United Labour Front, with George Weekes and Raffique Shah, and Joe Young and Clive Nunez, and Francis Beddoe and John Humphrey to do electoral battle with those who were still steeped in the politics of divide and rule. It would seem that the leopards do not easily change its spots.

In 1981, the ULF joined with the DAC and the Tapia House Movement under Lloyd Best to form the National Alliance in yet another effort to unite our people and end once and for all the divisive tendency towards racial politics. In 1983 the National Alliance embraced the ONR in a loose accommodation, eventually to become the NAR of 1985 — the most valiant effort yet to forge genuine national unity in this historically plural society of ours. Never before in the political history of this country has there been so persistent a struggle to end racism and forge genuine national unity by so committed a group of men such as you see on this platform here today.

And yet, there are those who now shamelessly try to label us as racial, merely because we persist in our quest for equality without which there can be no national unity; and because we have refused to allow the trappings of office to lure us from our chosen path of nation-building. But when they make this allegation, as they are going to do in a new propaganda offensive, all you have to do is to ask them to point to one single word or one single act that I have said or done over my 23 years of politics which indicates that I, or anyone of us here, are racial. And you will find that that will be the end of the argument, since there is not a single act, word or deed that they can point to as evidence of their spurious allegations. But they persist because, having failed to roll back the recession and turn the economy around, their only hope of hanging on to political power is to divide our people. It is the only way they know how the leopards of the sixties have not changed their spots. Truly it has been said that those who have not learnt from the mistakes of the past are condemned to repeating them. What they do not understand is that our peoples, having tasted of the nectar of unity in 1986, will never return to the politics of race.

Why has this nation so over-generously endowed with natural resources, failed to transform these two beautiful islands of ours into a paradise? Was it the lack or absence of political power? Surely not! The PNM has unshakable power for thirty (30) years, twenty four of which were as an independent nation. And yet they failed to transform us into an economically prosperous nation. Power, therefore, is not the critical variable in the formula for economic advancement.

Was it financial resources? Well, between the years 1972 and 1984 the powerful PNM had collected over 60 billion dollars in revenues. And at the end of it all, they could not provide so basic a necessity as a regular supply of drinking water for a mere 1.2 million people. It is logical to conclude therefore, that an abundance of financial resources is also not the critical variable.

If neither money nor power is the critical variable, then what is? What is that secret ingredient in the recipe for economic well-being that has eluded us for so long? I humbly submit that the major reason for our economic backwardness has been our failure to mobilize our most valuable resource, and that is — our human resource. You can have all the political power and all the financial resources you want; unless you mobilize your human resources there can be no hope for economic development.

The most valuable resource in any society is its human resource; but this is more so in Trinidad and Tobago because of the smallness of our population — now a mere 1.3 million souls. The importance of our human resource may not have been so critical had we been an India or a China with millions of people.

What is even more significant is the fact that ours is a highly multi-racial society in which our citizens of Africans and Indians descent form the bulk of population. In almost equal numbers they stand equi-posed against an historical background of suspicion and antagonism, of envy and jealousy, real and imagined. It is trite knowledge that if half your population is going to the right and the other half is going to the left, there is no way such a nation can move forward. A nation's intellectual manpower is always a proportion of its population. You cannot divide the intellectual, technical and technological manpower of so small a society into two racial blocks, pitted one against the other and still hope to achieve economic well-being for the whole society or indeed any part thereof. The politics of divide and rule is the surest way to economic disaster as our history has shown. It was the reason for the failure of the old PNM as it is the reason for the failures of Robinson and what is left of the NAR.

The mission of the NAR, its *raison d'etre,* its reason for being born, was to fill this void; to unite all our peoples of whatever race, colour, creed, or whatever class or gender, the Indian the African, the white, the mixed; the Hindu the Muslim, the Christian, under one banner with one song in their hearts; one people whose only battle cry was — ONE LOVE.

On the 15th December 1986, after decades of trials and tribulations, after many alliances and compromises, after much sacrifice and tears, I thought — at last, at long last, we have reached the promised land, where all shall be treated as equals, where none shall feel discriminated against, where no longer shall a single citizen of this blessed land languish under the debilitating feeling of alienation, and where all can confidently say they truly belong. On the 15th we stood on the threshold of such a dream.

And on the 16th December,1986, 360,000 of us handed to Robinson a nation that was united as Trinidad and Tobago had never before been united in its entire social and political history. And we told him: "Here you are, great leader. We have laboured long and hard to garner the grain from fields and the fruits from the vineyard. Your soldiers are united and stand ready to do battle against the greatest odds. Now lead us to the land of plenty and happiness."

And amid much rejoicing and pomp and splendour, he was smiling as he accepted the mantle of leadership. But deep in his heart was a hidden agenda. Within a period of less than one year, Robinson did what no Trinidadian thought was possible. He completely destroyed all our hopes, all our aspirations and all our dreams of ever ushering in the new society. In one fell swoop he smashed up the NAR, abandoned the Manifesto, and sought to polarize the nation along racial lines in the hope of creating a political base for himself in Trinidad by re-creating the old PNM/DLP syndrome.

If twenty months after the most stunning electoral victory in Trinidad and Tobago the vast majority of our citizens are disenchanted and disillusioned, it is not because the Robinson regime failed to provide all the jobs and all the water and all the electricity; nor is it because he failed to fix all the potholes or clean all the drains. It is because he so callously smashed our hopes and he destroyed our dreams of building that new society. It is because he so shamelessly robbed us of the best chance we have ever had of ending our historical tendency to divisiveness and discrimination, of ending the alienation of so many of our people. He squandered the best opportunity we had of establishing a society in which we can all live in love and happiness, with peace, bread and justice for all.

Having destroyed the NAR, it was only a matter of time before he was forced to abandon its Manifesto and eschew the mission of national unity. But having abandoned the Manifesto, Robinson is now a man without a plan. With no sense of direction, it is inevitable that he would fall back on the old strategy and tactics of the former regime of which he was a founding member together with the ancient Patrick Solomon.

Be that as it may, there is really no reason for despondency. Indeed, there is no room for the loss of faith and courage and the will to fight for what we believe in. Whatever we do, we must always remember that this country is ours. It is yours and mine.

And no one is going to come from Mars or from Russia or Cuba or from the United States of America to transform this country into the kind of place we want it to be for ourselves and our children yet unborn.

We and we alone will have to do that. We should not want it otherwise. If by some miraculous wave of the wand this land could suddenly be transformed into Paradise, we would not wish it so, for we shall then have lost the joy, the ecstacy, the nobility of building and shaping with our own hands, our own blood and sweat and tears, so great an object of our love — this blessed land, our blessed home.

To be discouraged now is to negate the desire for noble sacrifice in this sacred task of nation building. In any event, why should you be sad when in fact you are winning the struggle? Have you not succeeded in removing the crippling weight of PNM stagnation that has frustrated every effort for change over the past twenty years? If we did nothing else on December 15, 1986, we at least achieved one thing. By exploding the myth of PNM invincibility and peacefully removing the monolith from office, we have not only demonstrated to the people the power they possess, but we have also created a state of political flux and political dynamism. And it is only in a state of political flux and dynamism can there be change — whether for better or worse. The people will decide now in which direction we go.

But the fact is that even though you have won a tremendous battle, you have only crossed the first bridge. The road of nation-building is long and arduous. There are many twists and turns and ups and downs and many bridges to cross. You cannot cross the second bridge before you have crossed the first. At long last we have had the strength to cross the first bridge. Now we must summon up our energies to cross the second bridge. We know where we have come from, we know where we are, and we know where we want to go.

Our first task is to ensure that this nation is never again divided along racial lines. Despite the desperate efforts of Robinson, Tewarie, Jennifer Johnson, Alloy Lequay and Pamela Nicholson, we must resist any and every move to fracture the society. That is of the utmost importance. My brothers and sisters, do you remember the argument I pursued in the 1986 Elections campaign? If for some that was an election gimmick, for me it was a matter of life and death. I said then PNM would never lead us out of the economic mess because the strategy they used to win the elections was to divide the country into racial blocks. But having won the elections, they are faced with a divided population. They could never then mobilize our human resource; and without such mobilization there could be no economic progress. How they made their beds so they would have to sleep. How they won so they would have to rule. If you win by dividing the population you can only rule by perpetuating the policy of divide and rule.

I also argued that it was for that very reason that the NAR alone could succeed in rolling back the recession. If we united the people in order to win, then having won, we would have a united people with all our human resources already mobilized and ready for the kind of action that is required for economic progress. You will recall that, that is exactly what happened. On December 16, 1986, we had for the first time a population that was willing to sacrifice, to change their work ethic, to put their shoulders to the wheel free of charge, a people willing to pay the price of change, the kind of change they had so overwhelmingly voted for. Remember the fantastic response to the national clean up campaign? What a glorious sight that was! Love and cooperation and goodwill exuded from every corner of the country.

What a tragedy that such goodwill should be dissipated in so short a time by one man merely to satisfy his greed for absolute power. It is enough to make you cry. But this is not the time for crying. We must not despair. If we united our people once, we can do it again. We can and we must return to the spirit of December 16, 1986. We must re-kindle the fires of hope and the faith and self-confidence that we can unite this nation yet again to achieve meaningful change. That was the mission for which the NAR was born. And even though the NAR is now dead, that mission must live on. We must never abandon the dream of a moral and just society.

The mandate you have just given us to form a new political party is the first step in ensuring the re-incarnation of the original NAR — a new vehicle by which we shall continue the struggle for economic prosperity through national unity and national mobilization, ensuring the widest and deepest participation of the people in the decision making processes. When the NAR begin to disintegrate about a year ago, many of our activists urged us to form a new political party. We resisted that pressure, because we believed that the formation of a political party does not consist merely of the publication of a constitution and a manifesto. It should not be the decision of a few, but the result of an overwhelming desire of at least thousands of our citizens. So we waited for this historic day.

Now that thousands of our citizens have given us that mandate, we must proceed by practicing what we preach. We must not rush out to publish a constitution, print application forms, and declare ourselves a political party. We must spend the next couple of months holding discussions with the widest cross section of the population — with the workers and farmers, the employers and manufacturers, the businessmen and the religious organization, the youths and the women, the self-employed and the unemployed — in order to find out from them the kind of political party they want to see, the kind of policy and programmes they want implemented. All must be given an opportunity to participate in the formation of the party and the formulation of its policies. Even the party name and symbol should be the result of the widest public participation. We must consider a national competition to find a party name and symbol and a party song.

In the economic crisis that seem to be enveloping us, and out of which Government seems unable to extricate us, their are several burning questions crying out for the intervention of the collective wisdom of the people. The most critical issue facing the nation today is unemployment. Is the answer retrenching 25,000 public servants, 2,000 teachers and 7,000 sugar workers? Does the answer lie in a policy of deliberate unemployment creation so as to lower the wages in order to attract foreign investment? Is devaluation the answer? Will the present Government's contractionary economic policy get us out of the mess? How do we deal with the problem of foreign exchange? What do we do to halt the collapse of once very prosperous businesses? Assuming that oil prices remain depressed, what kind of energy policies are appropriate to the present circumstances? These are not problems that defy solution as the present Government would have us believe. The answers, however, do not lie in hiring the finest minds or the most renowned economist to produce a blue-print for balancing the budget or increasing the GDP and the GNP. Any first year student in economics can tell you that in order to balance the national budget you must spend less than you earn. What they do not tell you is the extent of human suffering involved, and how many human souls would be destroyed in the process. What is even more significant is the fact that they do not tell you the degree of sacrifice that is required for implementation of their Macro Plan, or whether the population is willing or able to endure such sacrifice at this particular juncture. Only the people can tell you that.

But what are the most appropriate mechanisms for consulting the people? All developmental plans must have as their objective the well being of all our citizens. It is the people who will be called upon to implement the programmes. They must, therefore, know before hand what is in it for them. They must see a light at the end of the tunnel. Without their fullest cooperation the most grandiose economic plans are doomed to failure. That is why we lay so much emphasis on mobilization of our human resource and participation in the decision-making process. It follows, therefore that the success of any plan for economic development depends not only on the technical feasibility of the plan but to a much greater extent on the irrevocable commitment of the people to its implementation. How are you going to get that commitment unless the people's input is such that they feel confident that the plan is of the people, by the people, and for the people. You must take the people into your confidence and tell them the truth.

A development plan does not have to be the ultimate in technological accuracy. Its psychological acceptance by the people is much more important. That and that alone will give them the patience and the will to build a new society. Therein is the failure of Robinson's NAR. Having shattered the unity for which we fought so hard to build — a unity that is vital for progress, Robinson can get all the money from the IMF. At the end of it all we shall be no better off. And the people know it. We are seeing that feeling of hopelessness expressing itself in the thousands of our citizens who are fleeing this country every month to brave the cold uncertainty of the unknown rather than tolerate the Robinson regime for so much as a day. They can no longer stand the empty promises and downright lies that have become the only weapons of the Government in its desperate but futile attempts at survival.

Even the most sycophantic supporter of the Robinson regime (an endangered species if ever there was one) admits that there is a crisis of confidence in the Government. No one believes a word they say anymore. Not the local people; not the foreign investors. Not the public servants, not the teachers, not the workers, not the employers, not the businessman,not the farmers, not the unemployed. Not even the children. How do you expect a nation to move forward when there is such a total lack of confidence in the Government? The new Party will have to move swiftly to restore confidence both nationally and internationally. There are many devices we can propose to achieve this end.

We believe that there are vast resources to be found among citizens of Trinidad and Tobago both at home and abroad that can go a long way to resolve some of our foreign exchange problems. All they need is the confidence to bring it back home or put it into circulation. Why not allow them to open foreign currency accounts in our local commercial banks? A proposal I have been trying to get the Minister of Finance to agree to since our return from North America a year ago. That would eliminate the fear of loss through devaluation, while giving them access to foreign exchange without having to go through the Central Bank, should they wish to invest or carry on other business activities. It is done in most Western countries.

If we want to attract foreign investors the strategy must be not to depress wages, but to build up a reliable infrastructure of water, electricity, roads and communications, financial institutions and the control of crime. The wages in Guyana and Haiti are much lower than that of Trinidad and Tobago. Yet they do not attract foreign investment.

There must be a clear and unambiguous policy on the repatriation of profits. Equally important is the need to remove the dead hand of the bureaucracy that has strangled so many business ventures. After almost two years of the Robinson regime, corruption and favouritism, nepotism and backwardness continue to be the order of the day — particularly in the Ministry of Industry and Enterprise. The Aliens Landholding Act which continues to scare away potential investors is being retained in its present form to provide yet another opportunity for discrimination and corruption.

We promised in the Manifesto to do something about the Aliens Landholding Act. Two years later it is still on the Statute Books. Even though foreign investment is important, this must not be at the expense of our local businessmen. I find it extremely difficult to understand why concessions are being granted to foreign businessmen which are being denied local businessmen. How will the latter be able to compete with their foreign counterparts. If the EPZ is so good, then why not grant the same concessions to our local businessmen and so convert the entire country into an Export Processing Zone?

I think the time has come for us seriously to consider the removal of foreign exchange controls and to transform Trinidad and Tobago into an intentional financial centre. The Singaporean experience is worthy of study. Trinidad and Tobago's geo-physical and geo-political attributes make us admirably suited to become the international communication centre of the Western Hemisphere. But that, of course, would entail the opening up and freeing up the society and the economy - something Robinson will never do. He is too obsessed with power and control of anything and everything around him. Ask the "yes-men" who are now posing as Ministers, and they will tell you so provided of course that Robinson is not within hearing distance.

We feel that we can make a serious dent in the unemployment situation by fulfilling some of the promises made in the Manifesto. In that much publicized document, we indicated that the two main pillars of our plan to roll back the recession were to re-activate the construction sector and the agricultural sector.

Before he was removed as Minister of Works, Settlements and Infrastructure, John Humphrey had already put in place plans for putting to work the billions of dollars worth of idle machinery by the development of some one hundred sites for housing and agricultural development spread throughout the country. Not only has the Government abandoned these plans, but they have allowed a great deal of this machinery to be bought up for little of nothing from companies in receivership and re-exported with huge profits, most of it remaining in foreign banks. This is machinery we had bought with scarce foreign exchange. This senseless policy obviously makes reconstruction so much harder when Robinson retires to Tobago after the next General Elections.

From the Ministry of Agriculture, renamed the Ministry of Food Production, Forestry, Marine Exploitation and the Environment, all we have had after almost two years is talk and more talk. The only change has been the change of name and a Minister who speaks as if he is permanently constipated. It must be obvious to all that what is needed in this area is the allocation of adequate resources for the provision of access roads, irrigation and flood control, the provision of adequate markets, refrigeration and down-stream agro-processing facilities, and the honest distribution of State lands for agriculture. I dare the Minister of Agriculture to reveal to the nation how much State lands have been distributed and to whom it was given.

The industrial relations climate in the country today is the worst it has been for the past twenty years, and the Government's answer to the problem is to close down and/or give away to certain conglomerates as many State Enterprises for as little as possible in the shortest time possible.

For decades we have argued that the viability of an enterprise, whether public or private, depends on productivity and proper management. The problem has always been how to improve productivity and proper management. The problem has always been how to improve productivity. The records of the National Consultation on productivity held in 1982 will confirm our stand on this issue. We maintain that productivity has to do with worker motivation. You cannot motivate the worker by meek exhortation, by simply telling him to produce more when such production redounds not to his own benefit but to the benefit of others. A worker is no different from others in the society who are motivated by self-interest. We therefore, advocate the tri-sector concept of economic organization, starting with the public sector - the State Enterprises. Under the Tri-Sector arrangement, the Enterprise is owned by the State, the workers and the private sector as equal partners and the profits are shared equally. In this way the worker becomes part owner and so you remove the worker's feeling of alienation and he is motivated to produce. Which worker would want to strike against his own business? Which worker will slack on the job when he knows that the more he produces the better off he will be?

It was John Humphrey, Kelvin Ramnath, Trevor Sudama and I who argued the case for the inclusion of this concept in the NAR Manifesto. Robinson pretends that he never heard of the idea. Gordon I can forgive. He unashamedly admits he never read the Manifesto — even before they abandoned it. I was amazed to hear and see on the TV on the night of Thursday last Robinson telling foreign investors that the reason Government took so long to get the country moving is because when we took over the Government they had ideas but no plans.

Our detractors condemn us for criticizing the Government but not putting forward proposals. They seem to have forgotten that we spent three years working out those proposals and that they are contained in the Manifesto. The tragedy is that even if the Robinson regime now decided to implement the Manifesto, they cannot. The instrument for implementing the Manifesto was a united NAR as originally conceived. And it is precisely because he has destroyed that instrument that we must now set about the task of forging another political instrument to fulfil the mission which we began twenty three years ago and for which the advent of the NAR was but a stage in the process for meaningful change.

Nations are not built in a day or a year or even a decade. The United States had to have a civil war before it became a nation. France had a bloody revolution, while the British cut off one King's head and banished another. We are but twenty six years old and we are not doing too badly. We have removed a stagnant regime that had held unassailable power for thirty years without shedding one drop of human blood. We must now move on to fulfil the historic mission of the original NAR by giving birth to a new political instrument. That is the solution you have decided upon today.

The new party must be founded upon principles for which we must stand irrevocably committed. There must be no compromise on the issue of:-

1. Racial and regional equality and the establishment of permanent institutions and mechanisms which will ensure that all our citizens regardless of colour, class or religious beliefs will have an equal opportunity for social and economic advancement based on merit and not on political patronage.

2. We must commit ourselves to the mobilization of all our peoples regardless of political affiliation for the creation of job opportunities so as to provide at least basic necessities for the poor and powerless, the aged and the helpless.

3. We must make it clear that in the new dispensation, private enterprise has a vital role to play, subject to the provision of legislation to prevent the creation of monopolies and cartels.

4. We must guarantee the freedom of trade unions and the strengthening of the collective bargaining process. In this regard there is urgent need for legislative reforms after consultation with the labour movement and employers.

5. Since the Westminster model has proved inadequate to meet the hopes and aspirations of our people as a developing nation, we must strive for genuine constitutional reform. We must create a political system that is more relevant to the nature of the society at this given juncture.

There is a lot of work to be done. Indeed, we are living in exciting times when we can be the makers of our own history. It is a rare phenomenon that one generation is called upon twice in two decades to influence the course of history. It is even rarer to be blessed with that opportunity three times in less than thirteen years.

On the 18th March 1975 — Bloody Tuesday — we united thousands of Africans and Indians workers which led to the formation of the ULF and the beginning of the end of racial politics of the PNM/DLP era. On the 15th December 1986 we united the nation to remove the monolithic PNM after 30 years of stagnation and so set the stage for freeing the nation from the cancer of corruption and nepotism. Today, the 16th October 1988 Almighty God has once more blessed us with the opportunity of making history yet again.

This day will remain in your memory for as long as you shall live. You shall recall this day as you tell stories to your children and grand children of how on this momentous occasion you had the courage to stand up and be counted among those who changed the course of our history.

Annexe 21

Trinidad and Tobago Election Results, 1991-1995

	Year	PNM	UNC	NAR	Other	Rejects	Voted	Elec-tors	% Voted	Winner
Arima	1991	8,819	1,158	4,091	168	108	14,344	22,448	63.9	PNM
	1995	8,752	3,893	1,478	0	205	14,328	24,120	59.4	PNM
	Variance	(67)	2,735	(2,613)	(168)	97	(16)	1,672	4.5	
Arouca North	1991	8,132	1,965	3,537	141	49	13,824	21,779	63.5	PNM
	1995	9,508	4,281	626	0	71	14,486	22,978	63.0	PNM
	Variance	1,376	2,316	(2,911)	(141)	22	662	1,199	0.4	
Arouca South	1991	10,204	1,233	2,975	182	43	14,637	24,349	60.1	PNM
	1995	11,47	23,350	962	68	110	15,962	26,998	59.1	PNM
	Variance	1,268	2,117	(2,013)	(114)	67	1,325	2,649	(1.0)	
Barataria/ San Juan	1991	6,052	4,689	2,626	188	64	13,619	21,981	62.0	PNM
	1995	6,666	7,611	0	105	89	14,471	22,603	64.0	UNC
	Variance	614	2,922	(2,626)	(83)	25	852	622	2.1	
Caroni Central	1991	4,511	7,628	2,434	240	66	14,869	21,662	68.7	UNC
	1995	5,494	10,547	0	0	43	16,084	23,835	67.5	UNC
	Variance	983	2,919	(2,434)	(240)	(23)	1,205	2,173	(1.2)	

Source: Compiled from records of the Elections and Boundaries Commission.

Trinidad and Tobago Election Results, 1991-1995 - Cont'd

	Year	PNM	UNC	NAR	Other	Rejects	Voted	Electors	% Voted	Winner
Caroni East	1991	4,250	8,177	2,537	0	71	15,035	21,028	71.5	UNC
	1995	4,524	10,264	0	0	198	14,986	22,607	66.3	UNC
	Variance	274	2,087	(2,537)	0	127	(49)	1,579	(5.2)	
Chaguanas	1991	2,837	9,259	3,206	226	114	15,642	22,407	69.8	UNC
	1995	3,274	11,936	0	1,279	132	16,621	24,505	67.8	UNC
	Variance	437	2,677	(3,206)	1,053	18	979	2,098	(2.0)	
Couva North	1991	3,197	9,210	2,292	266	112	15,077	21,424	70.4	UNC
	1995	3,648	11,847	0	114	116	15,725	23,154	67.9	UNC
	Variance	451	2,637	(2,292)	(152)	4	648	1,730	2.5	
Couva South	1991	5,020	8,277	1,958	234	100	15,589	22,155	70.4	UNC
	1995	5,302	10,922	0	113	83	16,420	23,926	68.6	UNC
	Variance	282	2,645	(1,958)	(121)	(17)	831	1,771	(1.7)	
D/Martin Central	1991	8,840	416	5,266	144	38	14,704	23,368	62.9	PNM
	1995	10,091	2,608	0	364	117	13,180	23,687	55.6	PNM
	Variance	1,251	2,192	(5,266)	220	79	(1,524)	319	(7.3)	

Source: Compiled from records of the Elections and Boundaries Commission.

Trinidad and Tobago Election Results, 1991-1995 - Cont'd

	Year	PNM	UNC	NAR	Other	Rejects	Voted	Electors	% Voted	Winner
D/Martin East	1991	7,111	375	5,280	119	49	12,934	20,863	62.0	PNM
	1995	8,613	1,797	1,578	129	127	12,244	21,558	56.8	PNM
	Variance	1,502	1,422	(3,702)	10	78	(690)	695	(5.2)	
D/ Martin West	1991	9,051	299	5,348	156	55	14,909	22,732	65.6	PNM
	1995	10,112	1,536	1,698	76	82	13,504	24,345	55.5	PNM
	Variance	1,061	1,237	(3,650)	(80)	27	(1,405)	1,613	(10.1)	
Fyzabad	1991	5,867	6,044	2,556	1,480	611	6,008	23,446	68.3	UNC
	1995	6,886	10,077	0	298	98	17,359	24,811	70.0	UNC
	Variance	1,019	4,033	(2,556)	(1,182)	37	1,351	1,365	1.7	
La Brea	1991	8,492	3,174	2,558	0	79	14,303	21,352	67.0	PNM
	1995	9,152	5,266	512	0	168	15,098	22,801	66.2	PNM
	Variance	660	2,092	(2,046)	0	89	795	1,449	(0.8)	
Laventille East/ Morvant	1991	10,485	629	2,757	179	75	14,125	23,939	59.0	PNM
	1995	11,059	1,650	865	40	154	13,768	26,079	52.8	PNM
	Variance	574	1,021	(1,892)	(139)	79	(357)	2,140	(6.2)	

Source: Compiled from records of the Elections and Boundaries Commission.

Trinidad and Tobago Election Results, 1991-1995 - Cont'd

	Year	PNM	UNC	NAR	Other	Rejects	Voted	Elec-tors	% Voted	Winner
Laventille West	1991	10,947	211	2,034	232	77	13,501	23,524	57.4	PNM
	1995	10,487	827	856	60	126	12,356	25,652	48.2	PNM
	Variance	(460)	616	(1,178)	(172)	49	(1,145)	2,128	9.2	
Naparima	1991	3,216	8,478	2,906	321	57	14,978	21,664	69.1	UNC
	1995	3,404	12,342	0	0	193	15,939	22,703	70.2	UNC
	Variance	188	3,864	(2,906)	(321)	136	961	1,039	1.1	
Nariva	1991	5,965	7,554	2,560	268	118	16,465	22,983	71.6	UNC
	1995	6,199	10,453	269	0	113	17,034	24,726	68.9	UNC
	Variance	234	2,899	(2,291)	(268)	(5)	569	(1,743)	2.7	
Oropouche	1991	2,480	9,689	3,222	0	84	15,475	21,818	70.9	UNC
	1995	2,720	12,499	0	0	168	15,387	23,006	66.9	UNC
	Variance	240	2,810	(3,222)	0	84	(88)	1,188	(4.0)	
Ortoire/ Mayaro	1991	7,578	6,013	2,563	0	86	16,240	23,375	69.5	PNM
	1995	8,201	8,944	0	0	274	17,419	25,092	69.4	UNC
	Variance	623	2,931	(2,563)	0	188	1,179	1,717	(0.1)	

Source: Compiled from records of the Elections and Boundaries Commission.

Trinidad and Tobago Election Results, 1991-1995 - Cont'd

	Year	PNM	UNC	NAR	Other	Rejects	Voted	Electors	% Voted	Winner
Point Fortin	1991	8,625	1,797	4,561	210	86	15,279	22,153	69.0	PNM
	1995	9,404	5,640	0	0	74	15,118	23,514	64.3	PNM
	Variance	779	3,843	(4,561)	(210)	(12)	(161)	(1,361)	4.7	
Pointe-a-Pierre	1991	5,580	5,388	4,131	245	46	15,390	22,821	67.4	PNM
	1995	7,055	9,367	0	83	156	16,661	23,914	69.7	UNC
	Variance	1,475	3,979	(4,131)	(162)	110	1,271	1,093	2.2	
Port-of-Spain/ St.Ann's West	1991	8,487	241	4,242	324	81	13,375	22,780	58.7	PNM
	1995	9,517	1,270	1,252	152	36	12,227	22,042	55.5	PNM
	Variance	1,030	1,029	(2,990)	(172)	(45)	(1,148)	738	3.2	
P.O.S South	1991	7,141	472	4,119	175	60	11,967	21,499	55.7	PNM
	1995	7,568	1,916	1,123	137	101	10,845	19,929	54.4	PNM
	Variance	427	1,444	(2,996)	(38)	41	(1,122)	(1,570)	1.2	
Princess Town	1991	6,202	7,404	2,489	333	125	16,553	23,610	70.1	UNC
	1995	6,837	10,821	0	0	181	17,839	25,023	71.3	UNC
	Variance	635	3,417	(2,489)	(333)	56	1,286	1,413	1.2	

Source: Compiled from records of the Elections and Boundaries Commission.

Trinidad and Tobago Election Results, 1991-1995 - Cont'd

	Year	PNM	UNC	NAR	Other	Rejects	Voted	Elec-tors	% Voted	Winner
S/Fernando East	1991	9,399	1,808	3,749	0	57	15,013	22,579	66.5	PNM
	1995	9,806	4,621	481	0	96	15,004	23,045	65.1	PNM
	Variance	407	2,813	(3,268)	0	39	(9)	466	1.4	
S/Fernando West	1991	6,934	2,073	5,087	88	50	14,232	21,506	66.2	PNM
	1995	7,748	6,460	616	0	130	14,954	22,253	67.2	PNM
	Variance	814	4,387	(4,471)	(88)	80	722	747	1.0	
Siparia	1991	2,957	10,426	2,143	289	81	15,896	22,962	69.2	UNC
	1995	3,149	13,136	0	0	214	16,499	24,177	68.2	UNC
	Variance	192	2,710	(2,143)	(289)	133		603	1,215	1.0
St. Ann's East	1991	9,661	761	3,106	144	97	13,769	22,479	61.3	PNM
	1995	9,768	2,371	947	205	158	13,449	23,775	56.6	PNM
	Variance	107	1,610	(2,159)	61	61	(320)	1,296	4.7	
St. Augustine	1991	4,375	6,846	3,401	217	88	14,927	22,368	66.7	UNC
	1995	5,121	9,701	493	62	190	15,567	22,383	69.5	UNC
	Variance	746	2,855	(2,908)	(155)	102	640	15	2.8	

Source: Compiled from records of the Elections and Boundaries Commission.

Trinidad and Tobago Election Results, 1991-1995 - Cont'd

	Year	PNM	UNC	NAR	Other	Rejects	Voted	Elec-tors	% Voted	Winner
St.Joseph	1991	5,927	4,615	3,497	185	128	14,352	22,267	64.5	PNM
	1995	6,960	7,564	0	396	130	15,050	22,948	65.6	UNC
	Variance	1,033	2,949	(3,497)	211	2	698	681	1.1	
Tabaquite	1991	4,017	6,982	4,496	0	87	15,582	22,242	70.1	UNC
	1995	4,407	10,870	0	0	241	15,518	23,343	66.5	UNC
	Variance	390	3,888	(4,496)	0	154	(64)	1,101	3.6	
Tobago East	1991	2,551	29	6,730	50	49	9,409	15,092	62.3	NAR
	1995	2,432	0	5,254	0	89	7,775	16,299	47.7	NAR
	Variance	(119)	(29)	(1,476)	(50)	40	(1,634)	1,207	14.6	
Tobago West	1991	3,071	0	6,152	50	22	9,295	15,560	59.7	NAR
	1995	3,517	0	4,873	0	67	8,457	17,001	49.7	NAR
	Variance	446	0	(1,279)	(50)	45	(838)	1,441	(10.0)	
Toco/ Manzanilla	1991	9,097	3,553	3,460	255	98	16,463	23,795	69.2	PNM
	1995	9,565	6,206	687	61	157	16,676	26,226	63.6	PNM
	Variance	468	2,653	(2,773)	(194)	59	213	2,431	(5.6)	

Source: Compiled from records of the Elections and Boundaries Commission.

Trinidad and Tobago Election Results, 1991-1995 - Concluded

	Year	PNM	UNC	NAR	Other	Rejects	Voted	Elec-tors	% Voted	Winner
Tunapuna	1991	6,872	4,173	3,266	257	114	14,682	22,476	65.3	PNM
	1995	7,467	7,223	368	58	103	15,219	22,683	67.1	PNM
	Variance	595	3,050	(2,898)	(199)	(11)	537	207	1.8	
TOTAL	**1991**	**233,950**	**151,046**	**127,335**	**7,366**	**2,775**	**522,472**	**794,486**	**65.8**	
	1995	**255,885**	**239,816**	**24,938**	**3,800**	**4,790**	**529,229**	**837,741**	**63.2**	
	Variance	**21,935**	**88,770**	**(102,397)**	**(3,566)**	**2,015)**	**6,757**	**43,255**	**(2.6)**	
TOTAL (% of Votes)	**1991**	**44.8%**	**28.9%**	**24.4%**	**1.4%**	**0.5%**	**100.0**			
	1995	**48.4%**	**45.3%**	**4.7%**	**0.7%**	**0.9%**	**100.0**			
	Variance	**3.6%**	**16.4%**	**(19.7%)**	**(0.7%)**	**0.4%**				
TOTAL (% of Electors	**1991**	**29.4%**	**19.0%**	**16.0%**	**0.9%**	**0.3%**	**65.8**			
	1995	**30.5%**	**28.6%**	**3.0%**	**0.5%**	**0.6%**	**63.2**			
	Variance	**1.1%**	**9.6%**	**(13.1%)**	**(0.5%)**	**0.2%**	**(2.6)**			

Source: Compiled from records of the Elections and Boundaries Commission.

Bibliography

Bahadursingh, I.J., ed. 1987. *Indians in the Caribbean.* New Delhi:Sterling Publishers Private Limited.

Baptiste, Owen, ed. 1976. *Crisis.* Port of Spain: Inprint.

Béteille, André. 1967. "Race, Caste and Ethnic Identity." In *Race, Science and Society.* New York: Columbia University Press.

Birbalsingh, Frank, ed. 1993. *Indo-Caribbean Resistance.* Toronto: TSAR.

Blanshard, Paul. 1947. *Democracy and Empire in the Caribbean: A Contemporary Review.* New York. N.p.

Blumer, Herbert, and Troy Duster, eds. 1980. *Theories of Race and Social Action.* Paris: UNESCO.

Braithwaite, Lloyd. 1953. "Social Stratification in Trinidad and Tobago." *Social and Economic Studies* 2 (2&3).

Capildeo, Surendath. 1961. Tape recording of DLP political meeting, 16 October, Queen's Park Savannah, Port of Spain, Trinidad.

CSHAA. 1995. *The Harassment of the Honourable Basdeo Panday.* Washington: Centre for the Study of Harassment of African Americans.

Central Statistical Office. 1993. 1990 Population and Housing Census: Institutional Report. Port of Spain: Central Statistical Office.

Central Statistical Office. 1994. Report on Education Statistics, 1990-1991. Port of Spain: Central Statistical Office.

————————. 1995. 1990 Population and Housing Census. Vol. VIII, Income Report. Port of Spain: Central Statistical Office.

Cudjoe, Selwyn R. 1985. Foreword to *The Still Cry: Personal Accounts of East Indians in Trinidad and Tobago during Indentureship (1845-1917),* by Noor Kumar Mahabir. USA: Calaloux Publications: USA.

Dabydeen, David, and Brinsley Samaroo, eds. 1996. *Across the Dark Waters. Ethnicity and Indian Identity in the Caribbean.* London: MacMillan Caribbean.

Democratic Action Congress. The ULF-DAC Alliance: The Truth about Why the Talks Failed. N.p., n.d.

————————. 1976. DAC Manifesto. N.p.

Dew, Edward. 1996. *The Difficult Flowering of Suriname: Ethnicity and Politics in a Plural Society.* Uitgeversm-aatschappij Paramaribo, Suriname: Vaco N.V.

Dookeran, Winston. 1995. "Business Presence and Civic Identity." In *Celebration of 150 Years of the Indian Contribution to Trinidad and Tobago,* edited by Brinsley Samaroo et al. Trinidad and Tobago:Cariflex Ltd.

Draper, Theodore. 1965. *Castroism: Theory and Practice.* New York: Praeger.

Dubois, W.E.B. 1965. *The Souls of Black Folk.* New York: Fawcett.

Elections and Boundaries Commission. 1977. Report on the Parliamentary Elections 1976. Port of Spain: EBC.

Elections and Boundaries Commission. 1982. Report on the Parliamentary Elections 1981. Port of Spain: EBC.

—————— . 1987. Report on the Parliamentary Elections 1986. Port of Spain: EBC.

—————— . 1992. Report on the Parliamentary Elections 1991. Port of Spain: EBC.

—————— . 1996. Report on the Parliamentary Elections 1995. Port of Spain: EBC.

Gosine, Mahin. 1986. *East Indians and Black Power in the Caribbean: The Case of Trinidad.* New York: Africana Research Publications.

Government of Trinidad and Tobago. Civil Lists, 1957-1977. N.d.

——————. Register of Applications. Service Commission Department. N.d.

—————— . Examinations and Testing Section. Service Commission Department. N.d.

Green, William. 1976. *British Slave Emancipation: The Sugar Colonies and the Great Experiment, 1830-1865.* England: Oxford University Press.

Guillanmin, Collette. 1980. "The Idea of Race and its Elevation to Autonomous Scientific and Legal Status." In *Sociological Theories:Race and Colonialism.* United Kingdom: UNESCO:

Haraksingh, Kusha. 1995. "Western Law and Indians in Trinidad: Social Engineering in the Diaspora." Paper presented at ISER/ NIC Conference, Challenge and Change: The Indian Diaspora in Its Historical and Contemporary Contexts, UWI, Trinidad, August.

Harewood, Jack, and Ralph Henry. 1985. *Inequality in a Post-Colonial Society: Trinidad and Tobago, 1956-1981.* UWI, Trinidad: ISER.

Harvey, Franklyn. 1974. *The Rise and Fall of Party Politics in Trinidad and Tobago.* Toronto: New Beginning Movement.

Humphrey, John. 1990. Speech given at political meeting, Princes Town, Trinidad, May 14.

Jules, Vena. 1994. *A Study of the Secondary School Population in Trinidad and Tobago: Placement Patterns and Practices.* UWI, Trinidad: Centre for Ethnic Studies.

Kanhai, Rosanne. 1995. "The Masala Stone Sings: Indo-Caribbean Women Coming into Voice." Paper presented at ISER/NIC Conference, Challenge and Change: The Indian Diaspora in Its Historical and Contemporary Contexts, UWI, Trinidad, August.

Khan, Ismith. 1987. "Image and Self-Image." In *Indians in the Caribbean,* edited by I.J. Bahadur Singh. New Delhi: Sterling Publishers Ltd.

Klass, Morton. 1961. *East Indians in Trinidad: A Study in Cultural Persistence.* Columbus University: New York.

La Guerre, John. 1974. "Afro-Indian Relations in Trinidad and Tobago." *Caribbean Issues* 1 (1) (April).

——————, ed. 1974. *From Calcutta to Caroni. The East Indians of Trinidad.* Trinidad: Longman Caribbean.

——————. 1994. "Three Graduates of Lion House, Chaguanas." In *The Lotus and the Dagger: The Capildeo Speeches, 1957-1994,* edited by Siewah Samaroo. Trinidad: Chakra Publishing House.

Lewis, Arthur. 1965. *Politics in West Africa.* London: Allen and Unwin.

Lijphart, Arend. 1959. "Consociational Democracy." *World Politics* 21 (2) (January).

————. 1977. *Democracy in Plural Societies: A Comparative Exploration.* New Haven : Yale University Press.

————. 1984. *Democracies: Patterns of Majoritarian and Consensus Government in Twenty One Countries.* New Haven: Yale University Press.

Lovelace, Earl. 1988. "The On-going Value of our Indigenous Traditions." In *Trinidad and Tobago: The Independence Experience 1962-1987,* edited by Selwyn Ryan. UWI, Trinidad:ISER

Mahabir, Winston. 1978. *In and Out of Politics.* Trinidad: Inprint Caribbean Ltd.

————. 1987. "Our Diasporas: Sowers and Seed." In *Indians in the Caribbean,* edited by I.J. Bahadur Singh. New Delhi: Sterling Publishers Ltd.

Mahabir, Noor Kumar. 1985. *The Still Cry: Personal Accounts of East Indians in Trinidad and Tobago during Indentureship (1845-1917).* USA: Calaloux Publications.

Maharaj, Ramesh. 1993. "Challenges to East Indians in Trinidad and Tobago." In *Indo-Caribbean Resistance,* edited by Frank Birbalsingh. Toronto: Tsar Book.

Malik, Yogendra K. 1971. *East Indians in Trinidad: A Study in Minority Politics.* London: Oxford University Press.

Marshall, Calder. 1939. *Glory Dead.* London. N.p.

Marsini, E. 1992. *"The Futures of Culture, Volume 11: The Prospects for Africa and Latin America."* Future-Oriented Studies Programme, March. N.p.

Millette, David. 1995. "Guerilla War in Trinidad, 1970-1974." In *The Black Power Revolution of 1970: A Retrospective,* edited by Selwyn Ryan and Taimoon Stewart. UWI, Trinidad: ISER.

Mohammed, Carl. 1995. "Indian Education in Trinidad." In *Celebration of 150 Years of the Indian Contribution to Trinidad and Tobago,* edited by Brinsley Samaroo et al. Trinidad and Tobago: Cariflex Ltd.

Moore, Dennison. 1995. *Origins and Development of Racial Ideology in Trinidad: The Black View of the East Indian.* Trinidad: Chakra Publishing House.

Morris, H.S. 1967. "Some Aspects of the Concept of Plural Society." *Man.*

Myrdal, Gunnar et al. 1994. *An American Dilemma: The Negro Problem and Modern Democracy.* New York: Harper.

NAR. 1996. NAR Conference Agreement Documents, April.

Neehall, Roy. 1993. "The Creation of Caribbean History." In *Indo-Caribbean Resistance,* edited by Frank Birbalsingh, 1-12. Toronto: Tsar.

Panday, Basdeo. 1988. Towards National Unity: The Aranguez Declaration. Speech to Mark the Inauguration of the UNC, October 16, Aranguez, Trinidad.

___________. 1995. "Trade Unionism, Politics and Indo-Caribbean Leadership." In *Celebration of 150 Years of the Indian Contribution to Trinidad and Tobago,* edited by Brinsley Samaroo et al. Trinidad and Tobago: Cariflex Ltd.

Patasar, Mungal. 1995. "Modern Trends in Indo-Trinidad Music." In *Celebration of 150 Years of the Indian Contribution to Trinidad and Tobago,* edited by Brinsley Samaroo et al. Trinidad and Tobago: Cariflex Ltd.

Persad, Kamal. 1988. "Racism Against the Indians in the Eastern Caribbean." *The Indian Caribbean Review Committee* (January).

—————. 1993. Series of Articles in *The Indian Struggle for Justice and Equality against Black Racism in Trinidad and Tobago (1956-1962)* by Indian Review Press. Trinidad and Tobago:Indian Review Press.

Phillips-Lewis, Kathleen. 1988. "The Trinidad Cocoa Peasants and their Struggle for Acceptance, 1890-1930." Paper presented at UNESCO/UWI Conference, Slavery, Emancipation and the Shaping of Society, UWI, Trinidad, December 8-10.

PNM. 1966. The People's Charter: A Statement of Fundamental Principles. Major Party Documents. Vol. 1. Port of Spain: PNM.

Premdas, Ralph, ed. 1993. *The Enigma of Ethnicity: An Analysis of Race in the Caribbean and the World.* UWI, Trinidad: School of Continuing Studies.

—————. 1995. *Ethnic Identity in the Caribbean: Decentering a Myth.* University of Toronto.

Rabushka, Alvin, and Kenneth Shepsle. 1972. *Politics in Plural Societies: A Theory of Democratic Instability.* Columbus: Charles E. Merrill.

Ragoonath, Bishnu. 1996. "The 1995 Elections: How the Votes were Really Shared." Mimeograph. UWI, Trinidad: Department of Government.

Ramesar, Marianne P. 1994. *Survivors of Another Crossing: A History of East Indians in Trinidad, 1880-1946.* UWI, Trinidad: School of Continuing Studies.

Ramsaran, Dave. 1993. *Breaking the Bonds of Indentureship: Indo-Trinidadians in Business.* UWI, Trinidad: ISER.

Report of the Franchise Committee of Trinidad and Tobago. Council Paper No. 35. Port of Spain, 1944.

Rohlehr, Gordon. 1990. *Calypso and Society in Pre-Independence Trinidad.* Port of Spain: Rohlehr.

Ryan, Selwyn. 1972. *Race and Nationalism in Trinidad and Tobago.* University of Toronto Press.

___________, ed. 1988. *Trinidad and Tobago: The Independence Experience, 1962-1987.* UWI, Trinidad: ISER.

Ryan, Selwyn. 1989a. *Revolution and Reaction: Parties and Politics in Trinidad and Tobago, 1970-1981.* UWI, Trinidad: Multimedia Production Centre.

___________. 1989b. *The Disillusioned Electorate: The Politics of Succession in Trinidad and Tobago.* Trinidad: Inprint Caribbean Ltd.

___________. 1990. *The Pursuit of Honour: The Life and Times of H.O.B. Wooding.* UWI, Trinidad:ISER.

___________, ed. 1991. *Social and Occupational Stratification in Contemporary Trinidad and Tobago.* UWI, Trinidad, ISER.

___________. 1991. *The Muslimeen Grab for Power: Race, Religion and Revolution in Trinidad and Tobago.* Trinidad: Inprint Caribbean Ltd.

Ryan, Selwyn, and Lou Anne Barclay. 1992. *Sharks and Sardines: Blacks in Business in Trinidad and Tobago.* UWI, Trinidad, ISER.

Ryan, Selwyn. 1992. "Guyana: Beyond Ethnic Paramountcy." In *Guyana at the Cross Roads,* edited by Dennis Watson and Christine Craig. University of Miami.

Ryan, Selwyn, and John La Guerre. 1994. *Report on Ethnicity and Employment Practices in the Public and Private Sector in Trinidad and Tobago. Vol. 1. The Public Sector.* UWI, Trinidad: Centre for Ethnic Studies.

Ryan, Selwyn, and Taimoon Stewart, eds. 1994. *Entrepreneurship in the Caribbean: Culture, Structure, Conjuncture.* UWI, Trinidad:ISER.

———, eds. 1995. *The Black Power Revolution of 1970: A Retrospective.* UWI, Trinidad: ISER.

Ryan, Selwyn. 1995. *Ethnicity and the Media in Trinidad and Tobago.* UWI, Trinidad: Centre for Ethnic Studies.

———. 1996. "Democratic Governance and the Social Condition in the Anglophone Caribbean." New York: UNDP.

Ryan, Selwyn, Roy McCree, and Godfrey St. Bernard, eds. *Politics, Patronage and Community in Laventille.* Forthcoming.

Samaroo, Brinsley. 1995. "The First Ship - the Fath Al Razack." In *Celebration of 150 Years of the Indian Contribution to Trinidad and Tobago,* edited by Brinsley Samaroo et al. Trinidad and Tobago: Cariflex Ltd.

Samaroo, Brinsley et al. 1995. *Celebration of 150 Years of the Indian Contribution to Trinidad and Tobago.* Trinidad and Tobago: Cariflex Ltd.

Sartoni, Giovanni. 1966. "European Political Parties: The Case of Polarized Pluralism." *In Political Parties and Political Developments,* edited by Joseph La Palombara and Myran Weiner. NewJersey: Princeton University Press.

SBDC. 1996. *Sector Assessment Study for the Small Business Development Programme in Trinidad and Tobago.* Forthcoming.

Selvon, Samuel. 1987. "Three Into One Can't Go." In *Indians in the Caribbean,* edited by I.J. Bahadur Singh. New Delhi: Sterling Publishers Ltd.

Siewah, Samaroo, ed. 1994. *Lotus and the Dagger: The Capildeo Speeches, 1957-1994.* Trinidad: Chakra Publishing House.

Singh, H.P. 1993. *The Indian Struggle for Justice and Equality against Black Racism in Trinidad and Tobago (1956-1962).* Trinidad:Indian Review Press.

Smith, M.G. 1993. "Race and Ethnicity." In *The Enigma of Ethnicity: An Analysis of Race in the Caribbean and the World,* edited by Ralph Premdas. UWI, Trinidad: School of Continuing Studies.

Tothill, Vincent. 1939. *Doctor's Office.* Blackie and Son: London and Glasgow.

United Labour Front. 1976. ULF Manifesto. N.p.

——————. 1976. First Statements of the Policy and Programme of the ULF. N.p.

Wood, E.F.L. 1922. *Report on Visit to the West Indies and British Guyana.* London: HMSO.

Wooding, Hugh. 1974. *Report of the Constitution Commission.* Port of Spain: Government Printery.

World Bank. 1995. *Trinidad and Tobago: Poverty and Unemployment in an Oil Based Economy.* Washington: World Bank.

Young, Crawford. 1976. *The Politics of Cultural Pluralism.* Madison: The University of Wisconsin Press.